A TIME FOR WAR

A TIME FOR WAR

· ROBERT SMITH THOMPSON ·

A TIME FOR WAR

FRANKLIN DELANO ROOSEVELT
AND THE PATH TO PEARL HARBOR

PRENTICE
HALL
PRESS

New York   London   Toronto   Sydney   Tokyo   Singapore

Prentice Hall Press
15 Columbus Circle
New York, New York 10023

Library of Congress Cataloging-in-Publication Data

Thompson, Robert Smith.
    A time for war:Franklin D. Roosevelt and the path
to Pearl Harbor/Robert Smith Thompson.
    Includes bibliographical references and index.
    ISBN 0-13-653338-8
    1. United States—Foreign relations—1933–1945.   2. World War,
1939–1945—Causes.   3. Roosevelt, Franklin D. (Franklin Delano),
1882–1945.   I. Title.
E806.T54   1991
973.9—dc20   90-23704
                                                            CIP

Manufactured in the United States of America

10 9 8 7 6 5 4 3 2 1

First Edition

For Judy

CONTENTS

PROLOGUE

All morning long the crowds had been converging on the White House. People were shivering; they had their collars turned up and their hands stuck in their pockets, but nobody was leaving. Men and women were packed together in rows, many of them on tiptoe as they tried to peer past the posts of the tall iron fence. Just after noon, the throng stirred. The glass front doors under the north portico of the executive mansion slid open and President Franklin D. Roosevelt, a cape hung over his shoulders and his hand on the arm of James, his son, came into view.

Hobbling across the pavement, the president looked grim. Mrs. Roosevelt walked just behind him. She was wearing a stole and a hat with a veil. Flanked by two Secret Service agents, each with a tommy gun under his arm, the Roosevelts clambered into the back seat of a waiting limousine; the agents got in too. Then, preceded by one armored car and followed by seven more, all of them with their lights flashing and their sirens blaring, the presidential automobile snapped forward. Passing the onlookers by the White House fence, it swung around the corner of the Treasury Building and raced through the intersections along Pennsylvania Avenue, heading east toward Capitol Hill.

The slopes around the Capitol were aswarm with marines, bayonets mounted and guns at the ready. Above them, every window of the House of Representatives was packed with detectives and, along the driveway that led to the House, hundreds of policemen kept crowds penned up behind wooden barricades. Soon the crowds were cheering anyway. Racing up the hillside, the president's car approached the barricades, turned in toward the House entrance, and stopped. Franklin D. Roosevelt entered the Capitol of the United States.

Inside the House chamber, the members of Congress had already taken their seats. Down at the edge of the well sat the justices of the Supreme Court, cloaked in their robes of black silk. Justice Hugo Black, the civil libertarian from Alabama, was dabbing his eyes with a handkerchief. Just behind him and in full uniform were General George C. Marshall of the army, Admiral Harold R. Stark of the navy, and General Thomas Holcomb of the Marine Corps. The cabinet was nearby: Secretary of State Cordell Hull looked worn, stricken with grief. Mrs. Roosevelt had gone to the Executive Gallery, and behind her sat Harry Hopkins, the president's closest aide; just beside her was Mrs. Woodrow Wilson. The gallery and the floor grew hushed. Vice-president Henry Wallace had taken his place on the podium and Sam Rayburn, Speaker of the House, had walked to the lectern. Rayburn's bald head was glistening. He lowered his gavel.

The time was 12:23 P.M. The date was December 8, 1941.

"Senators and representatives," Rayburn cried out. "I have the distinguished honor of presenting the president of the United States."

The place went wild.

Still leaning on his son's arm, President Roosevelt reached the lectern. He was dressed formally, in striped trousers and a black morning coat, and his hands gripped hard at the sides of the desk. His expression was solemn. Waiting for the applause to subside, he leaned toward the microphones and began his address:

"Yesterday, December 7, 1941—a date which will live in infamy—the United States of America was suddenly and deliberately attacked by naval and air forces of the empire of Japan. The United States was at peace with that nation and, at the solicitation of Japan, was still in conversation with its government and its emperor looking toward the maintenance of peace in the Pacific. Indeed, one hour after the Japanese air squadrons had commenced bombing in the

American island of Oahu, the Japanese ambassador to the United States and his colleague delivered to our secretary of state a formal reply to a recent American message. And while this reply stated that it seemed useless to continue the existing diplomatic negotiations, it contained no threat or hint of war or of an armed attack."

The House chamber was still. The president continued:

"It will be recorded that the distance of Hawaii from Japan makes it obvious that the attack was deliberately planned many days or weeks ago. During the intervening time the Japanese government had deliberately sought to deceive the United States by false statements and expressions of hope for a continued peace. The attack yesterday on the Hawaiian Islands has caused severe damage to American naval and military forces. I regret to tell you that very many American lives have been lost. In addition American ships have been reported torpedoed in the high seas between San Francisco and Honolulu.

"Yesterday the Japanese government also launched an attack against Malaya.

"Last night Japanese forces attacked Hong Kong.

"Last night Japanese forces attacked Guam.

"Last night Japanese forces attacked the Philippine Islands.

"Last night Japanese forces attacked Wake Island.

"And this morning the Japanese attacked Midway Island."

Roosevelt continued, his jaw jutting forth.

"Japan has therefore undertaken a surprise offensive extending throughout the Pacific area. The facts of yesterday and today speak for themselves. The people of the United States have already formed their opinions and will understand the implications to the very life and safety of our nation. As commander in chief of the army and navy I have directed that all measures be taken for our defense. But always will our nation remember the character of the onslaught against us."

Applause erupted and then faded away. Roosevelt's voice ranged forth across the chamber: "No matter how long it may take us to overcome this premeditated invasion, the American people in their righteous might will win through to absolute victory."

The ovation was thunderous. President Roosevelt concluded:

"I believe that I interpret the will of the Congress and of the people when I assert that we will not only defend ourselves to the uttermost but we will make it very certain that this form of treachery shall never again endanger us. Hostilities exist. There is no blinking the fact that our people, our territory, and our interests are in grave danger. With confidence in our armed forces—with the unbounding determination of our people—we will gain the inevitable triumph—so help us God.

"I ask that the Congress declare that since the unprovoked and dastardly attack by Japan on Sunday, December 7, 1941, a state of war has existed between the United States and the Japanese Empire."

The president's speech had lasted six minutes. An hour later and with only one dissenting vote, the Congress complied with his wish: It declared war on the empire of Japan. Four days later, Hitler's Germany declared war on the United States of America. America had officially entered World War II.

■ ■ ■

Why did we do it? In the traditional view, America after World War I had turned to isolation, remaining neutral toward the conflicts that, by the 1930s, were engulfing the countries of Europe and Asia. Being neutral, we failed at first to realize that Germany and Japan were the world's primary aggressors, inexorably on the march and with eventual designs on the United States. When we did recognize the threat, furthermore, we sought only to appease those aggressors. We did start to rearm but we did so too late. Catching us by surprise at Pearl Harbor, the Japanese launched what President Roosevelt termed an "unprovoked" attack. We entered World War II because the Japanese bombed Pearl Harbor.

So, at least, goes a theory widely held to this very day. But more questions arise. *Why* did the Japanese bomb Pearl Harbor? Why did Germany, only days after the Pearl Harbor attack, declare war on the United States? The United States, after all, had the mightiest economy and thus potentially the mightiest military in the history of the world. Were the leaders of Germany and Japan stupid? Were they crazy? Were they, perhaps, scared?

Answers to these questions have emerged only in fragments, like an archeologist's shards. In the Douglas MacArthur papers, housed in what amounts to the general's shrine in Norfolk, Virginia, documents from mid-1941 reveal American plans for the bombing of Japanese ships and factories. In the National Archives a copy of the MAGIC intercepts, U.S. decodings of Japanese diplomatic messages in 1941, show Japanese fears that America was going to start bombing them early in 1942. In the Franklin D. Roosevelt Library, adjacent to the president's mansion that overlooks the Hudson River, papers reveal that late in 1940—more than a year before Pearl Harbor—an American aviator, a Chinese lobbyist, and two cabinet-level secretaries were laying plans for the firebombing of Tokyo; the meeting took place with the president's approval. In the historical library at York University, close by the minster, the diary of Lord Halifax, Britain's ambassador to America in 1941, shows that on May 2, 1941, Halifax lunched with Roosevelt and that F. D. R. expressed the hope at that time that U.S. patrols in the Atlantic would provoke Germany into war. The British Public Record Office, near Kew Gardens in London, has evidence that in both July and August, 1941, Roosevelt told the British that he intended to provoke a war. In a book published in New York in the early 1980s, an author revealed that William Donovan, Roosevelt's coordinator of information (and later director of the wartime Office of Strategic Services) had received a warning from the British that the Japanese were about to attack Pearl Harbor.

■ ■ ■

The traditional view of why America entered World War II is a myth. Neither isolationist nor truly neutral, President Franklin D. Roosevelt and his administration forced Germany and Japan to go to war with us. *Why* Roosevelt did so is another—and an enthralling—question. The answer to this question goes back at least to the start of the twentieth century.

PART I

.

1900-1937

CHAPTER

1

THE CHINA INCIDENT

Lunching in the slopes west of Peking, in a lodge high in the Fragrant Hills, two American women, along with their Chinese servants, were peering back down the mountainside. The date was May 28, 1900. The women were worried. Through the boughs round their balcony, they could see, far in the distance, the checkerboard of farmyards that led to Peking. They could also see smoke, a column of smoke rising against the blue of the sky. The two women, Mrs. Herbert Squiers, the wife of an American diplomat posted to China, and Miss Polly Condit Smith, a young visitor from the States, would soon learn the significance of the smoke: On the outskirts of the capital, members of a Chinese secret society called the *I-Ho-Ch'üan,* translated by westerners as the "Righteous and Harmonious Fists" or just "Boxers," had set fire to the train station at Feng Tai. The Boxer Rebellion had reached the outskirts of Peking; soon it would reach the edge of the legation quarter.

To its residents, the foreign diplomatic corps, the legation quarter in Peking had long been a haven. Wedged against the walls of the Forbidden City, the quarter was open only toward the east, where it faced a Methodist mission headquarters and a broad and busy thoroughfare. Of Chinese doings beyond that thoroughfare, the diplomatic community knew virtually nothing. Life in the Peking compound, like life in the similar compounds of Tientsin, Shanghai, Amoy, and Canton, meant manicured lawns, champagne at dinner, cards in the evening, late rising in the morning, and, despite China's decades of decline, turmoil, and terror, no trouble. Trouble came.

3

"The Boxers . . . ," the guests kept repeating, "the Boxers." On
May 24, 1900, the diplomatic community of Peking assembled for
a party at the British legation. Clustering around underneath the
trees and the paper lanterns, people were exchanging agitated whis-
pers. The occasion for the party, which was the gala event of the
season, was the eighty-first birthday of Queen Victoria. The guests
had little to say about the queen. They were too busy talking about
the Boxers. The Boxers, people had heard, were seen to enter the
city and then to attack the legation quarter. One Britisher, Sir Robert Hart, was strolling around from group to group, giving reassurance. Tall, bald, and proud, Sir Robert headed the Chinese Imperial
Maritime Customs Service (the device by which the British collected China's tariffs, making certain that China repaid its debts)
and had done so for nearly forty years. So he was the resident
expert on things Chinese. The Boxers. . . . They intended no harm,
he averred. They were merely letting off steam.

Four days later, the Boxers were burning the Feng Tai train
station and snipping telegraph lines to Tientsin by the coast. Then,
on June 13, hordes of Boxers exploded into the streets just east of
the legation quarter, smashing windows and setting fire to shops.
Darkness fell. Flames licked around to the north of the city and,
in the middle of the night, the Peking cathedral went up with a
roar. The siege of Peking was under way.

At last, Sir Robert Hart took alarm. On June 29, 1900, a note he
had had smuggled out of Peking reached Tientsin. It read: "Foreign
community besieged. . . . Situation desperate. MAKE HASTE!"

Out in the world beyond, telegrams began flurrying from capital
to capital. Governments flustered over whether they should create
a rescue mission (yes), who should command the expedition (a German, eventually, a Count Alfred von Waldersee), and whether the
Japanese should take part (finally, at the insistence of the British,
yes). Then the countries took action. Tientsin received a host of
foreign soldiers, Sikhs in their turbans, Italians with plumes, Zou-
aves in their uniforms of red and blue, Russians, Germans, Japanese
(with the largest contingent), and, in their Sam Browne belts and
cavalry hats, Americans. (Without consulting Congress, President
William McKinley had ordered 5,000 U.S. troops from Manila to

China.) At the end of the first week of August 1900, the international expedition set off for Peking.

At dusk on August 13, 1900, shells poured into the legation quarter, reaching a crescendo by nightfall. Trumpets were blaring in the darkness and, from inside the legation quarter, foreigners could make out cries of "*Sha! Sha!*" ("Kill!" "Kill!"). Just about everybody, even missionaries who had fled from the countryside, took up guns; people secured themselves behind overturned desks or unemptied vats of nightsoil. Boxers were pouring into the quarter.

Then, over the din and from outside the legation quarter, the diplomats and their families, and the missionaries, began to hear the boom of guns, big guns, foreign guns, their guns. The international relief force had reached Peking.

■ ■ ■

The siege was over but its significance lingered on. The Chinese dynasty, forced to pay an indemnity to the foreigners, lost face; in 1911 it would collapse altogether. Great Britain, once ruler of the waves as well as of the coast of China, had to rely on others to help lift the siege; Britain's days as a Far Eastern power were numbered. The United States, the newest of the Pacific powers, proclaimed the Open Door policy (a statement of America's right to trade in China *and* of China's right to safety and peace) and used its share of the Boxer indemnity for the education of young Chinese; America, hoping to guide the Chinese through the shoals of anarchy, was associating itself with China's educational and economic development. Russia, after the siege of Peking, withdrew its force from China but kept it in Manchuria; Russia saw Manchuria as a potential colony. And Japan grew concerned.

Roughly half a century earlier, in 1853, Commodore Matthew C. Perry, sent on his mission by President Millard Fillmore, had steered into Tokyo Bay with a flotilla of four black-painted ships, two of them warships under sail and two sidewheelers powered by steam. The moment had marked the "opening" of Japan. To an extent, Japan had been open already; Dutch merchants and scholars, allowed to base themselves in Nagasaki, had informed the Japanese of Western depredations along the China coast. So Perry's presence had been alarming. It had seemed to presage the extension of Western imperialism from China to Japan. Indeed, even while Perry was negotiating—as Mount Fuji rose in the background, he had presented Fillmore's letter (although by this time Franklin Pierce was president) to Japanese emissaries, asking for comity and commerce—powerful elements in Japan had started to prepare the Meiji Restoration, hurtling the country into modernization, economic and military. Military modernization meant becoming imperialist, like the European great powers, and after winning a war against China in the 1890s, Japan had seized Taiwan and Korea as colonies. During the Boxer Rebellion, to be sure, Japan had shown the West a cooperative face. But Japan's expansion had coincided with Russia's and America's expansion. The leaders of Japan, therefore, had begun to look to Manchuria as a buffer.

Manchuria lay next door to Korea; Korea was a Japanese colony. Japan reckoned that if Russia colonized Manchuria, it might also try to colonize Korea. In 1904 Japan went to war with Russia.

■   ■   ■

On the night of February 8, 1904, Russia's Pacific fleet lay snug at its anchors where Manchuria's Liaoning Peninsula crooked down into the sea like a finger, at Port Arthur. Tucked in behind the mouth of the harbor, cruisers and battleships stood in long rows. The lamps by the piers were extinguished; nonetheless the ships stood out in silhouette, for café windows behind the waterfront were ablaze with light and, up on the slopes that ringed the port city, a party was taking place at Admiralty House: Imbibing champagne, Russian naval officers were relaxed and merry, confident that their two destroyers, patrolling the waters outside the port, could ward off any danger.

Just before midnight a Japanese flotilla, its lights turned off, was slipping around these two destroyers and closing in on Port Arthur. On the bridge of the lead vessel, Admiral Toge Heihachire was watching the coastline closely. As the promontories that formed the two sides of the harbor's mouth arose before him, he could make out the outlines of the Russian ships. He gave an order. A Japanese destroyer slid in through the opening of the harbor—and a three-funneled Russian battleship exploded in fire. The Russo-Japanese War had begun.

The Japanese triumphed. They captured Port Arthur; they occupied Kwantung, the peninsular region above Port Arthur; and they sank most of Russia's Baltic fleet, sent halfway around the world to join the fray. The Russian ships, antiquated and ill-prepared, had tried to make the run to Vladivostok up through the Tsushima strait. Formed by two islands about twenty-five miles apart, the Tsushima strait lay roughly halfway between Japan and Korea. The Russian ships had steamed through the strait in single file and Japanese ships, slipping out from behind the islands, had opened fire. Yamamoto Isoroku, then a Japanese ensign, described the battle in a letter to his parents:

> When the shells began to fly above me I found I was not afraid. The ship was damaged by shells and many were killed. At 6:15 in the evening a shell hit the *Nisshin* [Yamamoto's cruiser] and knocked me unconscious. [Actually one of the *Nisshin's* own guns had burst.] When I recovered I found I was wounded in the right leg and two fingers of my left hand were missing. But the Russian ships were completely destroyed and the dead were floating on the sea. When victory was announced at 2:00 P.M., even the wounded cheered.

Inviting Japanese and Russian delegates to Portsmouth, New Hampshire, President Theodore Roosevelt mediated the end of the war. Japan got a controlling interest in Korea, the rail line in southern Manchuria, and several Chinese ports that had belonged to the Russian Empire; Russia got out of having to pay a huge indemnity to Japan; and America got both countries to honor the Open Door policy in China. Theodore Roosevelt's interest was that of East Asian stability. With Russia crushed in battle, however, Japan had emerged as East Asia's most potent military power. To warn Japan against aggression, therefore, Roosevelt sent a flotilla of sixteen U.S. battleships, the Great White Fleet, all the way around the world in 1907; pointedly, they put in at Tokyo Bay.

■   ■   ■

A great shift was taking place. Roosevelt had complained that "no human being . . . could be as untruthful, as insincere, as arrogant—in short, as untrustworthy in every way—as the Russians." But now, to Americans, Japan was becoming the villain—out in Port Arthur the Japanese were harassing Americans. A case in point: Nearly all the mail to Willard Straight, a young American consul in Mukden, the Manchurian capital, had to pass through the Japanese post office in Port Arthur, and Japanese mail was always given precedence. Official correspondence from Washington came in sealed pouches, but other mail was repeatedly opened in transit. His consular code was stolen, American freight frequently arrived in bad shape, and it was difficult to obtain redress for damages. Trademarks were borrowed, altered, and appropriated. Straight was disgusted. "The Japanese," he wrote, "want everything for nothing. [They] are absolutely lacking the sense of gratitude. . . . Suck the blood and give naught in return. Such are the Japanese. . . ." The Japanese, Straight added, "all hate us, all of them, officers and men." The Americans were beginning to hate them back.

■ ■ ■

JAPAN SOUNDS OUR COASTS
Brown Men Have
Maps and
Could Land Easily!

Blaring forth this headline on December 20, 1906, the *San Francisco Examiner*, William Randolph Hearst's principal newspaper, inaugurated one of Mr. Hearst's principal projects, a war scare. "Japanese in companies of 40 are having infantry drill after dark [in Hawaii] two or three nights a week [and are] armed with rifles," the article explained. Wrote the *Examiner*: "The Japanese of Hawaii have secreted enough rice to feed the entire population for seven months. [There have been] recent arrivals of Japanese troops in the guise of coolies [who are] secretly preparing for hostilities."

Hearst as always was in tune with the times. San Francisco was witnessing anti-Japanese riots and, in October 1906, the city's board of education created a special "Oriental public school," a segregated establishment for all children whose parents were Korean, Chinese, and Japanese. Protests from Tokyo only whipped up more riots and left Californians lusting after still more bad news.

Hearst delivered. In 1907, under the headline JAPAN MAY SEIZE THE PACIFIC SLOPE! Hearst ran a two-piece article by Richmond Pearson Hobson, a congressman. Declared Hobson: "The Yellow Peril is here. Absolute control of the Pacific Ocean is our only safety. . . ." Landing an army of "1,207,700 men," Hobson went on, Japan would soon be able to "conquer the Pacific coast"—besides taking over China. The "Japanese," the congressman insisted, "are the most secretive people in the world . . . , rushing forward with feverish haste stupendous preparations for war. . . . The war is to be with America."

Yet the Japanese had their own jingoism. "Stand up, Japanese nation," cried the *Mainichi Shimbun*. "Our countrymen have been humiliated on the other side of the Pacific . . . by the rascals of the United States, cruel and merciless like demons. At this time we should be ready to give a blow to the United States. Yes, we should be ready to strike the devil's head with the iron hammer."

Warmongers on both sides of the ocean were looking for blood—and governments tried to pull back. In the Root–Takahira agreement of late 1908, America acquiesced in Japanese control of Port Arthur and Japan pledged to keep its hands off the Philippines, Alaska, and Hawaii. But Japan and America had no real meeting of the minds. The Americans swore by the Open Door policy and the Japanese wanted commercial control.

CHAPTER

2

CRISIS IN THE OLD ORDER

"I am baptized, sworn in, vaccinated—and somewhat at sea. . . ." So wrote Franklin D. Roosevelt to his mother on March 17, 1913; he had just taken the oath of office as assistant secretary of the navy. He "would have to work like a turbine to master this job," he confessed, but master it he would "even if it takes all summer." Roosevelt was true to his word. Nearly every morning in that summer of 1913, Roosevelt would emerge from the front door of 1733 N Street, his Washington row house, stride down the walkways to the State and Navy Building, now the Old Executive Office Building, go to his desk, and learn. He learned fast. He learned that if he was ambitious, and he was, he had to build a solid base of political support; he learned that he could have such a base if he became chief representative of the views of the navy. He also learned that these views were implacably hostile toward Japan.

■ ■ ■

The hostility ran deep on both sides, and had for a decade. The spring of 1913 brought renewed conflict with Japan. In California the legislature had passed a law forbidding land purchases by Japanese immigrants; outraged, the government in Tokyo had pressed President Woodrow Wilson to veto the act. Wilson had no authority under the Constitution to do so and, accordingly, did nothing. Ever suspicious of Japan, the navy began agitating for the transfer of ships to the Philippines; Assistant Secretary Franklin D. Roosevelt took the cause to the public. In September 1914, he wrote an article advocating a naval buildup in the Pacific; and in December 1915, he hinted to a Cincinnati audience that Germany might be seeking an alliance with Japan. The audience was receptive: In early 1915, Japan had pressed China to accept the Twenty-one Demands, a document that insisted on Japanese control of central China.

But young Roosevelt had to abandon his mission. On the night of April 2, 1917, Franklin and his wife Eleanor rode in a carriage in a rain shower to the Capitol of the United States. They were going to hear President Woodrow Wilson ask the Congress to declare war on Germany.

■ ■ ■

Ensconced in his corner office in the old State Department Building, Secretary William Jennings Bryan was beside himself with outrage. This was the great, or near-great, Bryan, the populist, the anti-imperialist, the three-time Democratic nominee for president, once the boy orator from the River Platte in Nebraska. Bryan was a boy no more: With his wide girth and nearly bald skull, he looked the part of a diplomat. His appointment as secretary of state had been a political payoff; but he still possessed his oft-touted principles—and he resented the fact that President Wilson regarded him as a clown. What was going on in U.S. foreign policy left him aghast.

Practically from the outbreak of World War I in August 1914, on, the Wilson administration had abandoned America's traditional neutrality and sided, in effect, with the British. With President Wilson's approval, State Department counselor Robert Lansing (grandfather of John Foster Dulles) acknowledged Great Britain's right to search neutral (i.e., U.S.) ships for contraband; since Britain had blockaded Germany, Lansing's view redounded to Great Britain's advantage.

In early 1915, Germany turned to submarine warfare; and on May 7, 1915, a German U-boat sank the British liner *Lusitania*;

more than 120 Americans aboard the vessel lost their lives. But even though the *Lusitania* had been carrying munitions purchased in America and destined for Great Britain—Woodrow Wilson was shown the true bill of lading—the president sent a harsh note of protest to Germany. Going over to the White House, Secretary Bryan demanded that the president protest Britain's blockade of Germany just as harshly. Wilson refused—and Bryan resigned. Lansing became secretary of state.

The tilt toward Britain continued. Wilson allowed U.S. banks to lend the Allies a sum that rose to $2.5 billion, the president retreating from "the true spirit of neutrality" to a position based on "strict neutrality." By late 1915, a historian has commented, President Wilson had become a partner, and not always a silent partner, in the Allied "economic campaign to strangle Germany." On February 26, 1917, while protesting Britain's interception of U.S. mail and blackballing of U.S. firms that traded with Germany, Wilson also asked Congress for authority to arm American freighters; thus, by force, he challenged Germany's counterblockade of Great Britain.

∎ ∎ ∎

Soon after America's entry into the war, President Wilson spoke to the Congress again, this time to enunciate his famous Fourteen Points. After a brief prologue, the president spelled out his program, which included "open covenants . . . openly arrived at"; freedom of shipping; freedom of trade; the adjustment of colonial claims; autonomy for the various nationalities under Turkish rule; guarantees of the "territorial integrity" of the Balkan states that had been under the rule of the Austro-Hungarian Empire; and guarantees of the "independence and territorial integrity of Poland." These principles became known as Wilsonianism.

We remember Wilsonianism and its fate as a series of faded old photographs. Here we see Woodrow Wilson in Paris 1919, smiling, doffing his tall silk hat, walking through confetti and surrounded by placards that proclaimed him the savior of the world. There we see Wilson, haggard and gray, back in America, forcing himself to speak over and over from the platform at the rear of his train, straining in desperation to rally the people to his sacred cause, America's entry into the League of Nations. And over there we see him on a stretcher, being carried back into the White House after his paralytic stroke, his League treaty rejected by the Senate. We remember Wilsonianism as dead. And we remember wrongly. The Wilson dream of free trade, national self-determination, and world peace remained—and it was given support by the fact that during the war America had become the world's largest economy.

At every point in the Fourteen Points, Wilson's political aptitude shined through. Open covenants meant rule by law, a notion dear to the hearts of Americans. Freedom of shipping and freedom of trade—both were good for the port of New York and the cotton-exporting South. Adjustment of colonial claims had anti-British undertones, ever popular with a major Democratic party constituency, the Irish. In autonomy for "nationalities under Turkish rule" lay the genesis of America's support for Israel. As for the "territorial integrity" of the Balkan states, America's smokestack cities were full of immigrants from Hungary, Yugoslavia, and Czechoslovakia. And Poland—Wilson's support for Polish freedom won hearts and minds in great industrial cities from Pittsburg to Milwaukee. Good politics domestically, Wilsonianism was an enduring force internationally.

■   ■   ■

Washington was all abuzz. Bundled up against the rawness of the autumnal morning, on November 12, 1921, spectators on 17th Street, around the corner from the White House and facing Constitution Hall, were craning their necks. They were watching a procession. Car after car would whisk down the pavement, park, and let out one or two elderly gentlemen. Dressed in dark overcoats and silk top hats, these men passed between the Grecian columns at the front of Constitution Hall, entered the great front door, and disappeared. The gentlemen, statesmen from Europe, Japan, and America, had come to attend the Washington Conference. President Warren G. Harding had convened the conference. And even though he was a Republican, the conference would be the very embodiment of Wilsonianism—it was supposed to preserve the peace of the world.

Inside the hall, by ten in the morning, the dignitaries had gone to their boxes; Mrs. Harding sat beside the vice-president, Calvin Coolidge; Mrs. Charles Evans Hughes, wife of the secretary of state, sat nearby. Chief Justice and Mrs. William Howard Taft were in a special section. William Jennings Bryan arrived late, wearing a silk hat and a flowing black cape. Moments after his arrival, the crowd inside started shouting, and mispronouncing, "Briand," the name of the French premier. Bryan stood up to take a bow but the people ignored him. He sat down in a huff.

Around a huge U-shaped walnut table down on the floor, the various representatives were taking their seats. French, Italian, and Japanese figures were present. Tall, white-haired, and elegant, Arthur James Balfour headed the British delegation. Elihu Root, former secretary of state, and Henry Cabot Lodge, chairman of the Senate's committee on foreign relations, had places just by the head of the table. And at the very bottom of the U, Secretary of State Hughes, erect and bearded, and with a scowl so grand that people likened him to Jove, presided. After the president entered, sitting directly beside Hughes, a minister offered a prayer. President Harding spoke briefly.

Then Hughes took the floor, and for his listeners he had a considerable surprise. "I am happy to say," he declared after he finished his preamble, "that I am at liberty . . . to submit to you a concrete proposition for an agreement for the limitation of naval armament. As Hughes spelled out the sacrifices America might make, his biographer tells us, the delegates "caught their breath and moistened hot lips. . . ." The "United States," Hughes proclaimed, "is willing to scrap all [its battleships and cruisers]." He then challenged the other great powers to do the same.

The Britishers present were stunned. Lord Balfour, scribbling some notes, did manage not to change his expression. Admiral Alfred Chatfield, however, "turned red and then white. . . ." Arthur Hamilton Lee, first lord of the admiralty, "half rose and whispered to Balfour." First Sea Lord of the Admiralty David Beatty looked like a bulldog that had been "poked in the stomach." Japan, Hughes continued, would have to scrap prized battleships and give up plans to build even more.

"With the acceptance of this plan," Hughes concluded, "the burden of meeting the demands of competition in naval armament will be lifted. . . . Preparations for offensive war will stop now." As Hughes uttered these last words, Constitution Hall erupted in cheers. People hugged each other and waved their hats. William Jennings Bryan fluttered a large handkerchief as he wiped huge tears from his cheeks. Commented William Allen White, the newspaperman from Kansas, "Of all the human conclaves I have ever witnessed, the gathering of the disarmament conference in Washington furnished the most intensely dramatic moment."

By no means did America, or anybody else, scrap all the great ships—Hughes's dramatic speech was little more than a bargaining ploy. But his address—along with the fact that a State Department cryptologist, Herbert O. Yardley, had cracked the Japanese code and could tell Hughes just when the Japanese would accept his terms—did help him to get what he wanted: limitations on the power of Japan.

Dominated by Charles Evans Hughes, the Washington Conference agreed on three principal pledges. Japan promised to keep its Pacific islands, once territories of Germany but mandated to Japan by the League of Nations, free of fortifications. (In return, Britain and America promised no new fortifications in Hong Kong or the Philippines.) Japan promised to limit its capital ships at the ratio of five for Great Britain, five for the United States, and three for Japan. And Japan promised to abide by the Nine-Power Treaty, an agreement guaranteeing the Open Door policy plus the independence of China. Signed on February 6, 1922, by the United States, the British Empire, France, the Netherlands, Portugal, Italy, Belgium, China, and Japan, the Nine-Power Treaty, in the first paragraph of the first article, read: "The Contracting Powers, other than China, agree . . . to respect the sovereignty, the independence, and the territorial and administrative integrity of China."

America's gains were even greater. America had persuaded Britain to renounce its own 1901 treaty with Japan. America had required Japan to evacuate the Shantung Peninsula, occupied during World War I, and to return customs control and sovereignty to China. America had demanded, and gotten, cable rights on Yap in the Pacific. America had forced Japan to leave Siberia, which the Japanese had invaded in 1919, and to give the Soviets the northern half of Sakhalin Island.

Japan also got access to vast loans from Thomas Lamont, the New York banker. And Japan "behaved" just as long as the loans kept flowing.

■ ■ ■

Situated a score of miles above the Ohio River and wedged close to the West Virginia border, Noble County, Ohio, was an extension of Appalachia: Its hills were rolling, its farms were poor, and its people were without education. When they spoke they said things like, "over to yen side of the hill," or "I done it unbeknownst to ye"; they sounded quaint. On September 3, 1925, however, Noble County, Ohio, blazed to the center of worldwide attention.

During the night the huge dirigible *Shenandoah*, en route from New Jersey to Minnesota, was caught in a thunderstorm that was pummeling the upper Ohio Valley. The commander hoped to ride out the storm, but the winds were too powerful and the *Shenandoah* began to spin as if in a twister. There was a crashing sound, the ship's nose broke off, there was another crashing sound, the control compartment with the commander and thirteen others snapped loose and hurtled to the earth, and then a massive blast scattered the rest of the *Shenandoah* for miles around the rolling hills and poor farmyards of Noble County, Ohio.

Such a disaster normally would have no effect on America's foreign relations. On this occasion, however, a firebrand army air corps brigadier general named Billy Mitchell got into the act, accusing the War and Navy departments in Washington of "incompetency, criminal negligence, and almost treasonable administration of national defense." Infuriated, the government court-martialed Mitchell and convicted him of insubordination. Mitchell's trial made him famous—and brought things he had been saying to the direct attention of Japan.

"On the coast of Asia," said Mitchell, "we find the island empire of Japan, owning or aspiring to own all the islands from Kamchatka to the Strait of Malacca"; once in control of the island chain off the

Asian mainland, Mitchell insisted, the Japanese inexorably would push on across the Pacific, toward the Antipodes, toward Hawaii, toward Alaska. And how should this Japanese expansion be stopped? "[W]hat will have to be done," Mitchell proclaimed, "is to push an [American] offensive from island to island through the north by way of Canada, Alaska, the Kuriles, to the coast of Japan, making direct attacks on the centers of strength of the Japanese empire."

■　■　■

Underneath the chandeliers and the big brass fans of the Majestic Hotel in Shanghai, on December 1, 1927, a wedding was about to take place. This wedding was to be anything but ordinary. In many ways, it marked the start of China's war with Japan.

Fully "1,300 persons were present in the ballroom," gushed *The Shanghai Times*. "All chairs at tables were filled. . . . Outside the ballroom, a crowd of approximately 1,000 Chinese had gathered and were standing by quietly hoping to glimpse the [bride and groom]. Before the ceremony began, the foreign orchestra played foreign music. There was an expectant hush, a craning of necks. . . ." Then, accompanied by his best man, Chiang Kai-shek, leader of China's new Nationalist government, entered the ballroom; the cameras began to grind. Another hush, another craning of necks, and to the time-honored tune of "Here Comes the Bride," the bride, Soong Mei-ling, one of three daughters of Shanghai's late but wealthiest banker, accompanied by her brother, T. V. Soong, also entered. If ever a marriage was one of convenience, this was it.

After the collapse of the Manchu dynasty in 1911, China had sunk into anarchy. Warlords, who were sometimes bandits, sometimes soldiers, sometimes gangsters, and sometimes blends of all three, established their power in this region or that; expanded domains or lost them; and sometimes claimed, and soon forfeited, the right to reign in Peking. The Japanese had seen how to gain from the chaos: a bribe here, a threat there, and Japan's commercial concerns found their way into one Chinese province after another. By the middle of the 1920s, however, Chinese patriots wanting to end such Japanese penetration were rallying to Chiang Kai-shek. To many (albeit not to the Communists) he seemed almost a savior.

Yet even saviors need money. The Soongs had money—and their enterprises needed protection—and so a Soong–Chiang political alliance was strengthened by this marriage.

As Soong Mei-ling entered the ballroom of the Majestic Hotel, reported *The Shanghai Times*, the cameras began to grind

> furiously. Miss Soong carried a huge bouquet of white and pink roses. Both she and the bridegroom posed for the cameraman before the ceremony. Then came three bows to the portrait of Dr. Sun Yat-sen [the late founder of the Kuomintang, now Chiang Kai-shek's party]. . . . A calm Chinese voice was then heard reading the certificate of marriage. . . . A final bow was made to the guests. The orchestra was playing and hand-clapping was heard as the new Madame Chiang walked from the platform with her husband and the two posed under a huge bell of roses while pictures were taken.

Added *The North China Herald*: "After many photographs had been taken, the bride retired with the bridesmaids and tables were set. . . . However, while this was being arranged, the bride escaped from the retiring room and neither she nor the bridegroom was seen again by the guests."

Small wonder: Generalissimo and Madame Chiang Kai-shek had slipped away to the new capital, Nanking. There, fortified with new funds, Chiang soon launched the northern expedition. He already controlled the south—at least nominally—and now he looked forward to controlling the north. The Japanese saw him as a threat to their interests in Manchuria.

The United States was not an ally of China in any way in the late 1920s: The Chinese revolution was a threat to American as well as Japanese interests. Furthermore, in the view of one U.S. diplomat, China was not yet "a full-fledged member of the family of nations." Soon, however, China would be useful—to help contain Japan.

■　■　■

The Japanese saw still more. And they believed proofs of American hostility were piling up.

Senator Henry Cabot Lodge, Republican from Massachusetts and chairman of the Foreign Relations Committee, was a small man with a trimmed and pointed beard, a scholarly demeanor, and well-bred manners. He was also a racist. In 1924, he had steered the Immigration Act through Congress; the measure banned further Japanese immigration into the United States. Japanese citizens proclaimed boycotts against American goods; and an American magazine awarded each member of Congress who had voted in favor of the law a certificate for service "in furthering the cause of war."

On the evening of May 19, 1927, a young man named Charles A. Lindbergh checked the weather reports, climbed into his airplane, the *Spirit of St. Louis*, on Roosevelt Field on Long Island, and just before eight o'clock in the morning took off for Paris. Americans, succumbing to the ballyhoo surrounding the flight, saw his accomplishment as a miracle. Japanese, realizing that aviation now was the long arm of foreign policy, saw it as a threat.

After 1922, Japan and Britain had engaged in a race to see who could build more cruisers. For several years the United States abstained from the competition. Then, early in 1929, the Congress appropriated funds for an aircraft carrier and fifteen heavy cruisers. The Washington Conference system was all but dead.

Early in September 1929, the American stock market broke. It did recover, and on September 19, the average index quoted in *The New York Times* was at an all-time high. Then the index slipped again, falling down, ever downward, and the Great Depression began. The Depression proved disruptive not only at home, but also abroad, for early in 1931 Congress passed the Smoot-Hawley Act, putting into law the highest tariff in the history of the American republic. The consequences of Smoot-Hawley were bad enough in places like Cuba, where unemployment shot up and mobs took to the streets. But the effects in Japan were disastrous: America had been Japan's largest market and now Japan was desperate for funds and outlets elsewhere. The elsewhere lay on the mainland of Asia in Manchuria and China.

■　■　■

Weihaiwei, meaning the "oceanic guard station at Wei," lay near the northern tip of China's Shantung Peninsula; Port Arthur, on the southern tip of the Liaoning Peninsula, was only eighty-nine miles away from Weihaiwei. Facing each other across the Gulf of Chihli, therefore, the two ports formed a gateway to Peking. To guard that gateway from the Russians, the British late in the nineteenth century leased the land that ringed the harbor. Britishers found the place delightful. With "its exquisite climate, russet mountains, blue sea, and lovely bay," wrote *The New York Times*,

> Wei-hai-wei as a summer resort could not be surpassed, and every year hundreds of foreigners journey from the fierce heat of Shanghai and Tientsin. There are boating, fishing, golf, lawn tennis, riding, the best swimming in the world, snipe, hares, and woodcock to shoot in season, and enchanting walks. It is possible to dance, play bridge, and talk scandal every night, or live the life of a hermit with equal ease. And there are no telephones.

The good times ended. Citing costs, the British relinquished their lease to Weihaiwei. After a brief ceremony on September 28, 1930, Reginald Fleming Johnston, the Weihaiwei governor and tutor to the last Chinese emperor, signed a piece of paper and boarded a ship for England. Newspapers around the world played up his departure. The British, after all, were abandoning a part of their empire—and the Japanese took notice.

Japan had bet its fortune on the dollar. Now, with Wall Street in collapse and the British scaling back, the Tokyo government saw a kind of salvation. It saw an opportunity to extend its influence in the northeastern reaches of China.

■ ■ ■

Barely visible in the darkness, a Japanese soldier was hunched over a railroad track. The track belonged to the South Manchurian Railroad, the night was that of September 18, 1931, and the soldier was wiring some sticks of dynamite. He was careful, burying the sticks so they would throw up dirt but leave the rails themselves unharmed. The job done, the soldier and his companions lingered about in the gloom, waiting for a Chinese patrol to come by. The Chinese appeared. A Japanese pushed the plunger, the powder exploding and the Japanese opening fire on the Chinese. The Manchurian incident was under way. Using the explosion as pretext, Japanese forces quickly seized Mukden, the capital of Manchuria, then soon the entire province. The Japanese renamed the province Manchukuo, meaning "Manchu country"; they gave the place a new ruler, Henry, or Aisin-Gioro P'u-yi, the last Chinese emperor; and they actually got a few countries, such as El Salvador, to recognize the region as a sovereign state.

But Japan had seized Manchuria in violation of the Nine-Power Treaty, Manchukuo was no more than a puppet state, and Americans were appalled. Secretary of State Henry L. Stimson announced, on January 7, 1932, that the United States refused to "admit the legality of any situation de facto [or] to recognize any treaty or agreement . . . which may impair the treaty rights of the United States or its citizens in China, including those which relate to the sovereignty, the independence, or the territorial and administrative integrity of the Republic of China, commonly know as the open-door policy. . . ." This was the Stimson Doctrine, or foreign policy by nonrecognition. Stimson remarked that he felt armed with "spears of straw and swords of ice."

∎ ∎ ∎

For Japan was closing the open door. As "you take off from Tokyo's Hanada Airport," W. B. Courtney, an American journalist, wrote for *Collier's* in the mid-1930s, "Fuji, the world's most perfect mountain, fills your window for half an hour; then you are over the cracked green leather of the Inland Sea. Japan offers nothing familiar to the American eye; neither does Korea when you slide across the red and warty nose it sticks into the riffles of the Yellow Sea. But when you cross the Yalu River and come over Manchukuo, there is a quick and bewildering change. . . ." After he was on the ground and rolling along in a train, Courtney thought the terrain looked like America. "Southward you stepped through a region of reddish soil, thinly studded . . . with pines that might have been the . . . Carolinas. . . . On the Mongol plains to the westward, you might be in Nebraska, while east . . . you . . . come upon wild gorges [and] mountains . . . which remind you of the Appalachians. . . ."

The landscape was about all that resembled America. In Manchuria, Courtney continued, the Japanese were "transforming an entire country—nearly half a million square miles—one sixth the size of the whole United States . . . into a single unified fortress. A nation where every railway, every road, every town and village, is designed first of all for its military effectiveness; where a population of nearly 40 million lives [is] always under martial law . . . ; and where there is no free commerce, except under military passes."
"Manchukuo" was an armed camp. Step by step, American businesses in the region were experiencing the squeeze. As Japanese forces took over the "various public utilities, railways, electric plants, and so on," Carl Crow, another reporter explained, "each was supplied with a 'Japanese adviser.' This was a serious blow to American business. . . . One of the first things the 'Japanese advisers' did was to advise the discharge of American engineers and their replacement by Japanese. The next step was to replace Chinese purchasing agents by Japanese, who, as they spoke nothing but their own language, were literally as well as figuratively deaf to the sales arguments of everybody except their own nationals. The American salesmen thought the worst had happened when they were compelled to deal with a purchasing agent who could not speak English. But a little later they ran into an even more noxious obstacle; for the specifications asking for . . . supplies were written in Japanese instead of English, as had been the custom in the past. . . ." The Japanese also set up an oil monopoly, banishing Texaco, Socony-Vacuum, and the British-owned Asiatic Petroleum Company. "British and American protests that this [is] a direct violation of the open-door policy [have produced] no results."

Almost unanimously, the American press was portraying Japan as a bad guy. Edgar Snow followed suit.

Born in Missouri, Snow had gone out to the Far East as a reporter, learned Chinese, interviewed Mao Tse-tung (Snow would go on to write the best-selling *Red Star Over China*) and wrote a series of articles for the old *Saturday Evening Post* in which he prophesied that Japan and America would go to war.

One is "unprepared for the . . . Japanese success in claiming the cities [Manchuria] as their own," Snow wrote in the first of his pieces. "Where formerly you rarely saw a spangled kimono or heard the drag of the wooden geta, today in many places the streets . . . seem imported bodily from Japan, with the drably clad natives a mere background for the costumes and homes of Japanese." In Dairen, near Port Arthur, Snow reported, every "shop bursts with neatly packaged goods—Japanese predominating, of course—every street is the scene of brisk building activity. . . . [F]uturistic . . . office buildings, numerous playgrounds, public gardens [abound] in circles from which the wide streets radiate spoke like. . . . On its spacious macadam roads that spread for miles beyond the town, out toward old Port Arthur, thousands of substantial new buildings and suburban homes are being erected, served by luxurious busses, by clean Japanese-made trams and trains, by the cheap taxis that have driven the rickshaws almost out of existence." Japan was remaking Manchuria in its own image.

Japan did not stop with Manchuria. In China's Jehol Province, just below the Great Wall, the Japanese were duplicating the Manchurian model. Snow described how: "The South Manchurian Railway, . . . spearhead of Japanese conquest above the Wall, . . . moves into China proper, with the cooperation of the Chinese bureaucracy. It opens branches in Tientsin, Peking, Tsingtao, Taiyuanfu . . . and Shanghai. . . . It is establishing numerous dependent companies to monopolize—by special agreement with . . . northern puppets . . . the exploitation of North China's . . . coal, her remaining resources of iron and other valuable minerals, her annual cotton crop, and her airways and railways development. Meanwhile, the Japanese are . . . detaching the northern salt, land, opium, railways, telegraphs and surtax revenues, as well as the maritime customs from Nanking's control, to convert the region [north China] into an exclusive Japanese market."

Snow went even further. "We may be sure of one more thing. Japan's secret agents have contacts with leading rebels in every subject country. Through them, when war comes, Japan will instigate rebellions against white imperialism in India, Burma, Malaya, the Dutch Indies, Borneo, Indo-China, the Philippines, and elsewhere." Where was it all going to end? The "answer," Snow wrote, "is that the Japanese advance is not going to end—until it meets determined opposition."

And the Japanese were starting to live in fear of the terrorism of China's secret societies. The origins of these societies, also known as triads or tongs, were lost in the mists of the past, although they had begun to surface in the records of the seventeenth century. Secret societies were peasant societies, often with religious overtones, often made up of outlaws, bandits, desperadoes. Convening in caves and forests, or in remote wayside hostels, they had long perfected clandestine modes of communication. Blue and white willow pattern plates, familiar and reproduced countless times in the West, actually contained codes: Peach trees symbolized renewal, or rebellion, and gates were clues for routes of escape. Agents of the dynasty often smashed the plates. They could not, however, smash the tongs, which flourished especially in the delta of the Pearl River. Indeed, as nineteenth-century Cantonese-speaking Chinese fanned out from their native country, they took their tongs with them; from Saigon, Manila, Singapore, Rangoon, and Batavia to Honolulu, Los Angeles, San Francisco, Chicago, and New York, the tongs offered jobs, ran protection rackets, dealt in drugs, and, in time, offered help to China.

The Japanese learned all this the hard way. During and after World War I, as they began to infiltrate China, they found themselves confronted with anti-Japanese boycotts—organized by secret societies. Then, in 1932, as they invaded Manchuria, they also attacked Shanghai. So fierce was the city's resistance—organized by the secret societies—that they had to withdraw. They never forgot.

■ ■ ■

Hidden by its acres of horse paths and oak trees from traffic on Connecticut Avenue and situated on a hilltop that overlooked Rock Creek Park, Woodley, an old mansion, was long an unofficial residence for Washington's highest and mightiest. Built by an uncle of Francis Scott Key, it had been home to a commodore, a senator, a cabinet secretary, and, in the summertime, four presidents; and in

1929, to the tune of $800,000, it became the residence of Secretary of State Henry L. Stimson.

Stimson was about as close to being an aristocrat as an American could get. After attending Andover, Yale, and Harvard Law, he made a fortune on Wall Street; then he served as governor of the Philippines, secretary of war, and, under President Herbert Hoover, secretary of state. Stimson was establishment personified. Cool and controlled, Stimson had represented the ideals of fair play, stiff upper lip, and all that. "All that" had marked him an Anglophile; and along with the rest of his equally Anglophilic lawyer-banker-diplomat caste, he had inherited from Britain the conviction that if countries were allowed wantonly to violate the treaties they had signed, the world would be unstable and the democracies would be in danger. To Stimson, therefore, Japan's invasion of Manchuria—and the subsequent closing of the open door—ultimately meant a threat to America. As secretary of state, Stimson had refused to recognize Manchukuo.

Later he wished he had gone further, hitting Japan with a boycott. As he was going out of office, in fact, Stimson became a behind-the-scenes anti-Japanese activist. Such activism, he was pleased to learn, had a friend in court—the new president of the United States, Franklin D. Roosevelt.

On January 9, 1933, Stimson, lame-duck secretary of state, met with the president-elect in the Roosevelt estate in Hyde Park, New York. Met by the president's car at the old brick Poughkeepsie train station, Stimson rode up along the Hudson River for about three miles, then turned off the highway on a lane that went through an orchard. As the trees parted, the car parked right in front of the porch of a rambling two-story house. The house, Stimson commented in his diary, "is an old house which has gradually been built upon in addition. . . . There were a good many things of historical interest in it [Stimson would have been referring to the dozens of old naval prints and the huge Chinese vases, brought back in the century before by Roosevelt's Delano grandfather, a merchant in the China trade] but the general furnishings . . . gave the impression of confusion, and this was even so of a large room which they had built on and which they were evidently very proud of. It was a

beautiful room in shape and size and had his library of books."
Roosevelt conferred with Stimson in that library.

The conversation covered the world but honed in on Japan. Stimson wrote, "I found that Roosevelt had a personal hereditary interest in the Far East. He told me that one of his ancestors, I think a grandfather, had held a position there and that his grandmother had gone out to the Far East on a sailing vessel. . . . He took a lively interest in the history as I told it. He said that it was his belief that Japan would ultimately fall through economic pressure. . . ." Roosevelt already was thinking of economic warfare.

On May 17, 1934, Stimson met with Roosevelt again, this time over lunch in the White House, and Stimson came away elated. Roosevelt had told him about a conversation, back in 1902 at Harvard, with a young Japanese. The Japanese, Stimson recorded, had told young Roosevelt of a "100 year Japanese plan . . . which involved the following steps . . . : (1) an official war with China to show that they could fight and beat China; (2) the absorption of Korea; (3) a defensive war against Russia; (4) the taking of Manchuria; (5) taking of Jehol; (6) the establishment of a virtual protectorate over northern China from the Wall to the Yangtze; (7) encircling movement in Mongolia and the establishment of the Japanese influence as far as Tibet . . . ; (8) the acquisition of all the islands of the Pacific including Hawaii; (9) eventually the acquisition of Australia and New Zealand. . . ." President Roosevelt believed, Stimson wrote, that events were bearing out the prophesy.

Stimson agreed. By 1936 and 1937, he was huddling with Chinese spokesmen such as Hu Shih, the intellectual, and H. H. K'ung, the finance minister, exploring ways to stop Japan.

▪ ▪ ▪

Perched on a hilltop near the palace in Tokyo stood the embassy of the United States and there, on the snowy night of February 25, 1936, Ambassador Joseph C. Grew was hosting a diplomatic dinner. With his ramrod posture, Back Bay Bostonian accent, majestic eyebrows, and reserved charm, Grew could have been an ambassador straight out of central casting. He was, in fact, America's top career diplomat and, as such, he had dedicated himself to the task, difficult at best, of building America's friendship with Japan. So he often hosted dinners, inviting especially prominent Japanese whom he considered to be moderates.

One such moderate, his guest of honor that night, was the admiral and former prime minister Viscount Saito Makoto. During the dinner Grew learned that Saito had never seen a talking movie. For after-dinner entertainment, therefore, Grew arranged for a showing of *Naughty Marietta*. Saito was kindly, but old, and Grew feared that his guest would fall asleep. But Saito loved the show. Swept along by the singing of Nelson Eddy and Jeanette MacDonald, he applauded and laughed and wept, staying at the embassy until well after midnight. Grew walked him to the embassy door. Five hours later, Saito was dead, shot more than thirty times in his bed.

The incident of February 25, 1936, had erupted. Emerging from their Tokyo barracks, two dozen officers and some 1,500 troops occupied government offices, attacked members of the imperial household, and murdered several ministers of the cabinet. The rebels soon made their intentions known: They hoped to purify the government, increase spending on the military, and make Japan more aggressive—in China.

The U.S. embassy afforded Ambassador Grew a perfect post for observation. With a pair of binoculars, he wrote in his diary, he could "pick out rebel soldiers in the prime minister's residence, while in the street below stood loyalist barricades." Two days passed. The rebels and the loyalists were still in a face-off. The government then made a special appeal to the rebels. From a balloon floating high over the prime minister's residence, a banner proclaimed the emperor's offer of pardon. Then, at the residence, the rebel banner, a white tablecloth, came sliding down the flagpole. The incident was at an end.

But Japan was on the march. Back in 1935, at the London Naval Conference, Yamamoto Isoroku, by then an admiral, refused to renew the Washington Conference's ratio of 5-5-3 for capital ships; a naval arms race was starting up. Now, in 1936, Tota Ishimaru, a lieutenant commander, published a book entitled *Japan Must Fight Britain*. Did Tota speak for the navy? Late in 1936, an Australian shipper with ties to the British admiralty took some Japanese officers out for drinks. They became talkative. "It is their intention," the shipper wrote in an intelligence report, "to dominate the whole of the coast of Eastern Asia. . . . If England were sending a fleet east, Japan would know at once, and . . . would sink half the ships before they reached Singapore. . . . The Netherlands Indies would be occupied within a week. . . . They would not tackle Australia until they had command of the sea. . . . In general the Japanese are convinced that they have a 'mission' to improve the world."

• • •

Circling the mountains of north China early in December 1936, a passenger plane aligned itself with the runway near Sian and began its descent. Snow lay over the hillsides and only the runway was clear. The airplane landed, and out stepped Chiang Kai-shek. Waddling along in their down-filled jackets and caps with earmuffs, a row of Chinese officers came up to greet him; their leader was Chang Hsueh-liang, the local warlord. Chiang spoke briefly with Chang, then repaired to a hotel at the foot of the mountains. There, accompanied by a score of bodyguards, he set up headquarters. The headquarters, Chiang hoped, would mark the end of a long campaign.

For nearly a decade, Chiang had been trying to exterminate the Communists—doing so had been integral to his unification of China. The core of the Communist party, however, had eluded him and after the Long March out of southern China, had holed up close to Sian, in the caves of Yenan. But now Chiang thought he had them: In return for favors, Chang Hsüeh-liang was going to use personal troops to go up to the caves and flush the Communists out. That at least was the idea.

Up before dawn on December 12, 1936, Chiang performed martial exercises, splashed cold water on his face, and then stood stark still. From somewhere outside the hotel, he could hear the sounds of gunshots. A runner came to his room: Mutineers, soldiers of Chang, the local warlord, were forcing their way into the hotel; Chiang Kai-shek should leave at once. Still in his nightshirt, barefooted, and minus his false teeth, which were resting on a ledge in the bathroom, the generalissimo fled. Outside all was dark. Climbing a wall, Chiang fell straight into a moat, spraining his ankle. He managed to whisper for help. Aides heard him, hauling him out and dragging him over the snow to a cave.

Chiang said later that as "the day gradually dawned, I could see from the cave that the Li Mountain was surrounded by a large number of troops. Then I heard the detonation of machine guns and hand grenades near my headquarters. I knew that my . . . bodyguards . . . continued their resistance and that the rebels were using artillery to attack them. It was about nine o'clock, after which time no more firing could be heard. The rebels were looking for me. Twice they passed the cave in which I took cover but failed to discover me. . . . Then the rebels made a more thorough search. I heard one of the mutineers above the cave saying, 'Here is a man in civilian dress; probably he is the generalissimo.' . . . I then raised my voice and said, 'I am your generalissimo. Don't be disrespectful. If you regard me as your prisoner, kill me, but don't subject me to indignities.' The mutineers . . . fired three shots in the air and shouted, 'The generalissimo is here!'"

Limping out of the cave, Chiang stormed, "Shoot me and finish it all!" The leader of the rebels replied: "We will not shoot you. We only ask you to lead our country against Japan."

That was the point. In his drive against the communists, Chiang had largely ignored the Japanese menace. Now he was going to have to change his ways. Back at the hotel, but this time in captivity, Chiang Kai-shek had a stream of powerful visitors: his wife; T. V. Soong, her brother; and, since Chang Hsüeh-liang had arranged the kidnapping with the help of the Communists, Chou En-lai.

Who said what and to whom in the hotel we shall never know. This much, however, is clear. Chiang Kai-shek signed a pledge to "admit all parties to share the joint responsibility of national salvation," to "end all civil war immediately," and to "adopt the policy of armed resistance against Japan." Then Chiang left the hotel, free again. And almost immediately, throughout China from Peking and Tientsin in the north to Canton in the south, but especially in Shanghai in the middle, Chinese terrorists began to strike at the Japanese.

■ ■ ■

Willard Price, an American author, lived in Japan and, in the summer of 1937, happened to be vacationing in a fishing village some thirty miles from Tokyo; his next-door neighbor happened to be the emperor of Japan. Full of curiosity and taking notes, for he knew a good book topic when he saw one, Price kept his eyes open. Hirohito's seaside house, he recorded, was unpainted and "weathered a dull gray. The plainness of the place was a surprise."

Awakening often at dawn, Price would see the emperor outside, wearing a "three dollar chrome Japanese watch" and chopping wood in the garden. Later Hirohito would row out into the surf, looking for marine specimens and handling the net and spear himself; "fully-clothed attendants and courtiers in morning coats [would] march hip-deep into the water, on either side of his fishing boat, to bow and then pull it in."

On the beach one day, Price came across a book the emperor had left behind in the sand. Picking it up, he saw that it was Aesop's *Fables* in Japanese. Price hoped to keep the book, "but a guard snatched it up and conveyed it reverently away." Out here on the seashore, Price concluded, Hirohito was living an idyllic life. The emperor, however, soon went back to Tokyo. There he learned of the incident at the Marco Polo Bridge.

Just southwest of Peking stood the Lukuoch'iao, or the Marco Polo Bridge. The bridge itself was of little import, for in many places it was broken and the little stone lions that marched along its railings were crumbling. The incident that took place near the bridge, on the night of July 7, 1937, also was of little import in itself. And the facts of what happened are murky. At some point during the night the commander of a Japanese regiment, on maneuvers out of Tientsin, seemed to have discovered that one of his soldiers was missing. He also seemed to have approached a Chinese fort, standing at one end of the bridge, and demanded entry—he may have wanted to search for the missing soldier. The Chinese seemed to have refused his request. But one fact is clear. The Japanese regiment and the Chinese fort exchanged gunfire in the middle of the night.

In the morning, the Chinese and Japanese commanders in Peking met, agreeing to end the fighting then and there. In Tokyo and Nanking, however, the governments of the two countries decided to go to war. The Chinese government did so because of Chiang's deal in Sian—and because Chinese of almost all political persuasions had had all they would take of Japanese bullying; the Japanese government did so because it wished to put a stop to Chinese terrorism—and because Japanese of nearly all political persuasions wanted to end their China problem.

Thus began what the Japanese called the "China incident." Japanese troops spread into north China; Chinese troops moved up to meet them; Chinese troops also reinforced Shanghai; and in the water of the Whangpoo River, the Japanese cruiser *Izumo* dropped anchor. Late in the afternoon of August 14, 1937, its guns began to fire. They were firing in the direction of the Palace Hotel at teatime.

■ ■ ■

High over the Shanghai harbor and standing right at the heart of Shanghai's international settlement, the roof garden of the Palace Hotel was crowded with foreigners. An awning, rust-brown like the sail of a Chinese junk, shaded about half the terrace. Out in the other half, potted plants spread their leaves, and umbrellas shaded the tables. Water spraying from a fountain cooled the air. The tiles along the floor were gleaming, for Chinese servants sprinkled them hourly to temper the heat. Other Chinese servants glided and bowed, carrying silver trays. Some of the customers were drinking tea, others whiskey, wine, or vodka. Under the awning a Russian string quartet was playing Vivaldi, the pizzicati barely audible over the burble of talk. The talk was taking place in many languages: German, Russian, French, some Chinese, and English. Then, suddenly, the talking ceased. People on the rooftop had heard a distant thudding.

A few of the foreigners walked over to the railing. On the Bund below them (bund, an embankment, was a Hindi word that the British, back in the glory days of their empire, had shipped into Shanghai, along with opium and Bibles), the streets were in turmoil, crammed from the waterfront to the facades of the bank buildings

with beggars, old women, children, coolies, coolies pulling rickshaws, coolies abandoning rickshaws, coolies running with poles on
their shoulders and squeezing past limousines, and all of them frantic to race as fast as they could away from the pier area. Beyond
the piers, the guns of the *Izumo* were blazing away. The Sino-
Japanese war had started.

■ ■ ■

About a month later, William Verbage, a professor from Minnesota
State Teachers College, told reporters what happened next. On tour
with a group of fellow academics, he had just reached the Palace
Hotel late that fateful afternoon. The tour leader was Dr. Robert
K. Reischauer, the elder son of an American missionary family and
an instructor in Japanese at Princeton. After the group reached
Japan, Reischauer had hoped to proceed to Peking. War had broken
out in North China, however, so he booked the group straight to
Shanghai. It checked into the Palace Hotel. While the tour members went to their rooms, Reischauer stayed downstairs, filling out
forms. He was standing next to a plate glass window.

Up in his room, Professor Verbage felt "comparatively safe," he
said. He and his roommates were "rather joking about the whole
situation. There was a lot to be tended to. Our baggage hadn't come
up. The laundry hadn't appeared. There were meals to be arranged
for. . . . We were sitting in our room on the 5th floor when we heard
firing start from the Japanese warship. We looked out the window.
The crowd on the Bund was running for Nanking Road. . . . [They]
were running right into Nanking Road [which was perpendicular to
the Bund]." Verbage and his companions walked across the fifth-
floor lobby. "We were out on a little balcony," he went on. "We
could see the ship's shots exploding overhead."

Soon Verbage saw three airplanes come in, just below the cloud
cover; the airplanes were Chinese. "We saw the ship's shots exploding close to them. . . . Then we saw three bombs released from the
planes. They came down almost together, one a little lower than
the other two. We ducked back into the hotel just as fast as we
could go."

The airplanes, out of Nanking, were supposed to bomb the *Izumo*. They missed.

Huddled behind an overstuffed chair just inside the balcony, Verbage felt a series of shocks. "It was all over in a few minutes," he recalled. "We heard a woman scream. . . . We couldn't see anything. Dust and plaster filled the air. It was like walking in a fog. [People] were coming down from the roof garden. Their faces were white with plaster, and blood was coming out through the white."

Verbage went downstairs. In the main lobby people were lying all over the floor. "The front window was blown in," Verbage said. "There must have been 12 to 20 injured and dying people lying about. We didn't see Bob [Reischauer]." Normally Reischauer would have been easy to spot, for he was dark-haired, wore horn-rimmed glasses, and was taller than just about anybody else in the lobby. At last, indeed, Verbage did see him. Reischauer "was standing with one arm on the counter and the other over the shoulder of a wounded Chinese. Bob couldn't have stood alone. One leg was absolutely no good." A slice of plate glass window had sheared off one of his heels.

Commandeering a motorcycle, an ex-marine in the tour group got Reischauer into the sidecar and, threading his way through the rubble and the bodies, found the way to the Shanghai General Hospital. Reischauer, however, was bleeding profusely. By the time he reached the hospital, he was dead.

The Reischauer death made front page news in America. He was, after all, the citizen of an obstensibly neutral country.

■ ■ ■

Three events, each out of the spring of 1937, cast doubt on America's true neutrality. The Chinese government had begun to send presents to American officials, especially to President Roosevelt. The U.S. Treasury had begun to buy Chinese silver, granting China a kind of foreign aid. And the Chinese government had begun to pay money to an American pilot, Claire Chennault. His job was to reorganize the Chinese air force; and although he was retired from the U.S. Army Air Corps, he had plenty of contacts in Washington. In time, he would make full use of those contacts.

CHAPTER
3

SHANGHAI 1937

A s the *President McKinley*, a liner that had steamed down from Japan, reached the coast of China and turned in at the mouth of the Yangtze, a "brilliant sunlight suffused the . . . estuary," wrote U.S. Marine Captain Evans F. Carlson. Carlson had gone from Washington to Japan, then secured a berth aboard the *McKinley*—for Carlson, sent personally by President Franklin D. Roosevelt, was going to China on an undercover mission.

The sunlight, Carlson wrote Roosevelt, in one of the books he later wrote about China, "brought into sharp relief the green of the fields off to the west, a welcome contrast to the foul yellow of the intervening water. And it played about the decks and superstructures of the [Japanese] vessels of war which flanked our course, now and then finding a polished surface on which its rays seemed to bounce. . . . The war vessels rose at anchor, and each flew at its stern the flag of the Rising Sun of Japan. Squat destroyers bobbed . . . behind light cruisers, and up ahead the bulky superstructures of heavy cruisers lurched . . . back and forth. . . . Decks were clear for action and guns pointed . . . toward the western shore. As the *McKinley* turned into the Whangpoo [the Whangpoo, a tributary of the Yangtze, flowed southwest and, at its great bend, formed the harbor at Shanghai], . . . two divisions of light bombing planes rumbled overhead, their lower wings also bearing the red emblems of the Rising Sun. Presently they strung out into single file and the leader dived swiftly towards the dome of the administration building of the new Chinese Civic Center of Greater Shanghai, followed in column by his five companions. Small puffs of smoke drifted up from the dome, showing that the bombs had hit their mark. It seemed unreal, but we were witnessing war—the opening stage of Japan's effort to dominate the Chinese people."

Carlson, a lanky, hawk-nosed fellow, the son of a Congregationalist minister, had been to China before: He had served two tours there as an intelligence officer, spoke some Chinese, and had become a bit of an expert on Far Eastern affairs. Then, in the middle of the 1930s, Carlson won a plum assignment. He had gone to Warm Springs, Georgia, there to command the marine unit present to guard the president. Carlson became a frequent visitor in the Little White House.

The Little White House, purchased by Roosevelt back in the 1920s after he was stricken with polio, was no more than a cottage. Inside the front door, a hallway paneled with pine led past a bedroom, then straight on into the living-dining room. That room was usually cluttered with ashtrays, papers, books, telephones, yellowed etchings of ships on the walls, a hooked rug tossed across the pinewood floor, a sofa, and, close by the fireplace, an overstuffed chair, its leather cover cracking.

The chair was Roosevelt's favorite; and with Carlson on the sofa opposite and Margarite LeHand, a White House secretary, sitting nearby on a straight-backed chair, during the evenings when the president was in Warm Springs, he would chat, tell stories, and listen to Carlson. Carlson felt at home there—in a letter to Miss LeHand dated March 17, 1937, he expressed thanks for having been "in the bosom of the family." The president also put his trust in Carlson; at some point early in March 1937, Roosevelt made a special request.

He asked Carlson to go to China again, to serve as the president's own ears and eyes to determine if China, with U.S. aid, could survive. Carlson would leave the United States in July 1937. Once in China, he would send letters directly to the White House. The letters, although intended for Roosevelt, would be addressed to Miss LeHand. Roosevelt that way would have no outward tie to the gathering of intelligence.

. . .

As Japanese bombers crossed the face of the moon over Shanghai, crowds of foreigners were gathering on the Bund. One of these foreigners had parked his car near the river to watch the destruction. A stringer for *The New York Times* later wrote that this young man was "of the third generation of a firm established in China nearly 100 years ago . . . of immense properties, which had made his family known along Asia's coast from Vladivostok to Singapore. Then he abandoned his automobile, joining the others at the pier."

This was the night of August 18, 1937; and the young man was Evans Carlson. The international settlement had disgorged more than 1,000 persons, clutching their children and their luggage, who hoped to get safely aboard the *President McKinley*. They crammed their way onto a pier and, clamboring into a series of small boats, set off on the three-mile journey down the Whangpoo, right into the midst of the firing. Chinese gunners were shooting from both sides of the river at the Japanese ships and the Japanese ships were shooting right back. Flashes of fire arched through the darkness and, wherever the shells hit, smoke billowed upward, reddened by the glow of the flames below. The American refugees reached the *McKinley* unharmed. Seamen aboard the USS *Augusta*, a cruiser that had come down from the north China coast, were less fortunate. Landing on the deck, a shell exploded, injuring eighteen sailors and killing one, a young Louisianan named Freddie John Faigout.

Enraged, Admiral Harry E. Yarnell, a tall, slender Iowan who now commanded the *Augusta*, prepared a cable:

THE POLICY OF CINCAF [Commander in Chief Asiatic Forces, meaning Yarnell] . . . IS TO . . . OFFER ALL POSSIBLE PROTECTION AND ASSISTANCE TO OUR NATIONALS. . . . NAVAL VESSELS WILL BE STATIONED IN PORTS WHERE AMERICAN CITIZENS ARE CONCEN-TRATED AND WILL REMAIN THERE UNTIL IT IS NO LONGER POSSI-BLE OR NECESSARY TO PROTECT THEM. . . . THIS POLICY [is] BASED ON OUR DUTIES AND OBLIGATIONS. . . . OUR NAVAL FORCES CAN-NOT BE WITHDRAWN WITHOUT OUR FAILURE TO OUR DUTY AND WITHOUT BRINGING GREAT DISCREDIT ON THE UNITED STATES NAVY.

President Roosevelt read this cable—and registered no objection. The administration was going to maintain an American presence in China, even in the face of Japanese pressure.

That pressure was mounting. On "the night of the 18th [of August 1937]," Evans Carlson wrote to President Roosevelt two nights later,

> a Japanese destroyer anchored 300 yards ahead of the *Augusta*, which is tied up in midstream opposite the center of the Bund. Another anchored opposite Soochow Creek [which flowed into the Whangpoo just north of the Palace Hotel, thus separating the British-American international settlement and Hongkew, the Japanese district], and headed down the Whangpoo. At 10:20 P.M., these destroyers opened fire on Pootung, which is on the right bank of the river. The cannonading continued for 20 minutes. We were all amazed at the cheek of the Japanese. They were so anchored that any counter fire from the Chinese would . . . drop in the international settlement.

By August 23, Carlson wrote in a subsequent letter, there had been

> a great deal of shelling, mostly by Japanese gunboats in the Whangpoo, considerable bombing, and a lot of machine-gunning. . . . The wanton destruction of foreign property . . . was bringing no military gains [for the Japanese], and had the appearance of a deliberate attempt to cripple foreign interests.

Another letter from Carlson was a shocker. Late in August 1937, Japanese airplanes had swooped down upon the limousine of Sir Hughe Knatchbull-Hugessen, the British ambassador to China, and machine-gunned him in the back; Carlson had talked with Lovet-Fraser, a British diplomat who had been in a car just behind the ambassador's. The diplomat said, Carlson wrote, that "there was no question" about the Japanese intent. The ambassador's car had been marked out plainly with British flags. The Japanese, furthermore, had dropped a bomb between the two cars, "evidently with the intention of wiping out the party so that there would be no eyewitnesses." Carlson concluded: "This is . . . a turning point in our relations with the Far East. It appears that Japan intends to . . . eliminate foreign commercial competition."

Other grim news was reaching the desk of the president. Bodies of Chinese, foreigners in Shanghai had noticed, had been floating down the Whangpoo; A. R. McGinnis, an American oil executive, found out why. His job, he told *The New York Times*, took him daily on launch trips up the Whangpoo and back. Upriver, he noticed, Japanese troops were lining Chinese snipers along wharves, knotting their wrists behind their backs, shoving them in the water, and peppering them with bullets. The Japanese were also beginning to harass foreign reporters. By August 19, 1937, Japanese soldiers had broken into the office-apartment of Hallett Abend, the *New York Times* stringer in Shanghai, five times. They had scanned his telegrams, rifled through his files, and accused his Chinese assistant of being a spy for the Americans.

Elsewhere in China, too, Americans were having their troubles. Venturing outside the U.S. embassy in Peking (America was maintaining two embassies, one in Nanking and one in Peking), Otto Geissberger, a young marine from North Bergen, New Jersey, had the bright idea of photographing a column of Japanese marching. To his surprise, he found himself surrounded by Japanese soldiers who, grabbing and smacking at him, were trying to haul him away. He got away only by yanking his film out of his camera. U.S. Marines in China thereafter were under standing orders to take no pictures—no pictures of the Japanese conquest of north China.

The Japanese celebrated that conquest by floating balloons. Streamers hung from the balloons, announcing: "The Japanese Army Preserves the Peace of East Asia."

■ ■ ■

Meanwhile, under a muggy Washington sky, a cavalcade of cars passed through the gates of the White House and pulled up under the portico. The day was a Monday, August 16, 1937. President Roosevelt had tried to take a relaxing weekend, going out on the river aboard the presidential yacht *Potomac* and catching some sunshine from the deck in the rear. Late on that Sunday afternoon, unfortunately, a navy seaplane had taxied up to the yacht. The plane bore the latest intelligence reports from Shanghai: Dr. Robert Reischauer was dead; the warship *Izumo* was shelling the city; and Japanese troop ships were on their way to mount a full-scale invasion.

Roosevelt went straight back to the White House. From there his secretaries summoned top officials to meet him in the morning. So, fanning themselves in the August heat, they arrived: Rear Admiral James O. Richardson; Secretary of War Harry Woodring; the State Department's Far Eastern expert, Stanley K. Hornbeck; and, wearing a hat and a dark suit despite the humidity, Secretary of State Cordell Hull. They all disappeared into the White House.

Taking the elevator, the men filed into a large yellow oval-shaped room, the president's office; they took seats around the desk. The desk, originally that of President Hoover, was a jumble of ashtrays, books, carvings of Democratic donkeys, letter openers, paperweights, and a pen stand adorned with nautical instruments. A cradle telephone sat by the left hand of the president. Bulking huge in his wheelchair, Roosevelt let out a cheery greeting. Then he got down to work. He was worried.

Closeting himself with his advisers, he considered his choices. In the mid-1930s, Congress had passed a series of neutrality acts, requiring belligerent countries to pay cash for whatever they bought in the States and to ship such goods in their own vessels (the cash-and-carry principle)—*and* requiring the president, when two foreign countries were in a state of war, to declare an arms embargo. Since Japan could produce its own weapons, however, and China could not, having to make purchases overseas, an embargo would hurt China more than it would hurt Japan. So Roosevelt made a move that was not a move. He decided that he would "find" no war. He would wink at the sale of arms to China.

He also sent 1,200 marines to guard Americans and their property in Shanghai. Secretary of State Cordell Hull announced this step to the press.

■　■　■

Outside the granite-faced center of Shanghai, cut in the Chapei and Nantaie, the Chinese slums, the streets were piling high with stones and mud and the bodies of human beings; the Chinese seemed determined to resist Japan at any cost. Writing to Roosevelt, Evans Carlson documented the resistance.

Driving out to Chapei on the evening of August 29, 1937, Carlson and two American journalists spotted a flight of Japanese observation planes overhead; they steered "under a tree," Carlson wrote, "and took the precaution of concealing ourselves . . . until they had departed for their base." Carlson moved onto a highway. As "columns formed moved out I noted that their [the Chinese] road discipline was excellent. They kept to the left of the road, allowing motor vehicles to pass on the right. No lights were visible and no smoking was permitted. All motor vehicles were camouflaged with brush and branches of trees. These people have become thoroughly air-minded." They had also become defense-minded. The Chinese, Carlson informed Roosevelt, "are prepared to go to any extreme rather than submit further to Japanese impudence and domination."

Watching the Chinese, Carlson was becoming a believer. Late in September 1937, he convoyed to Nanking with three Chinese, one of whom was a Blue Shirt, or a member of Chiang Kai-shek's secret police. About thirty miles outside Shanghai, Carlson wrote to the White House, their auto became mired in a mud hole. A "dozen other motor vehicles, mostly trucks, were also mired there, and as dawn approached everyone became extremely nervous, for we made a beautiful target for an air attack. A shovel was needed and I endeavored to find one, to no avail. . . . In the meantime the soldier in charge of our guide truck came back to inspect the situation. He was a short wiry individual. . . . Presently he disappeared, and I saw him walking on a narrow path between rice paddies towards a small village. . . . In twenty minutes he returned, followed by at least fifty of the villagers, each carrying two bundles of straw. The straw was then placed in the ruts. . . . Then the men took hold of the car and practically lifted it on the straw-filled ruts, and we went on our way." Carlson was impressed: "All the initiative and resourcefulness had been provided by that soldier, who came from a class low in the social strata." Such persons, the peasants, Carlson was convinced, would form the heart of the Chinese resistance.

But could China sustain its resistance? Only, Carlson thought, if America helped. And time was running short.

■ ■ ■

As Carlson's convoy reached Wushi, up along the Yangtze River, a "flight of 22 Japanese planes passed overhead in the direction of Nanking. They were flying at between 12,000 and 15,000 feet, so we had no need to fear an attack on us. At Che Yung, 30 miles east of Nanking, a second flight of 12 planes passed over, also flying high. We were held up by . . . gendarmes until after the raid was over. We could hear the bombing very distinctly." Once in Nanking, then, Carlson noticed that buildings were painted a "grayish black to reduce their visibility. Everywhere you look there are holes in the ground—bombproof. I estimated that there are 50,000 of them. The population has . . . become ground moles burrowing in the earth whenever the Japanese planes come over." And Japanese planes were coming over daily. By the end of September, the Japanese had won control of the air in the lower Yangtze Valley. They were using that control, Carlson concluded, to "conduct unrestricted bombing in Nanking."

■ ■ ■

In Secret Service jargon, Roosevelt's train was POTUS, standing for President of the United States; it was the 1930s equivalent of Air Force One. The presidential car itself, painted kelly green, was a comfortable affair, its rear compartment furnished with sofas, a desk, wing-backed chairs for visitors, and, for the president himself, a special low-backed chair. The windows, of course, were of bulletproof glass; Roosevelt never tired of watching the scenery, even at night. Many times he had made the trip from Washington to Hyde Park; many times he had watched as the illuminated Capitol dome and the tiny lights along the Potomac receded and then gave way to the darkness.

In September 1937, Roosevelt made one of these many trips home. This time, however, instead of returning directly to the capital, he set off for the west.

■ ■ ■

Pulling out of the Poughkeepsie station and soon rolling across the cornfields of the Midwest late in September 1937, the presidential train reached Wyoming, Montana, Idaho, Washington, and even Oregon, then started back east. President Roosevelt had wanted new scenery and a rest, but, as always, he politicked. Seated on the back platform of the train, he "gave his chatty little homilies . . . , grasped the hands of local politicians, confabbed with governors and senators." The crowds were large and Roosevelt was happy—he was talking cheerily of expanding the programs of the New deal even further. Then, on October 5, 1937, in Chicago, he changed the subject.

Press reports had been alarming. In mid-September 1937, U.S. insurance underwriters, *The New York Times* reported, had estimated that private American citizens around Shanghai had lost $25 million in property. One such American was J. H. McKinnon of Houston, manager of the Poplar Groves Dairy Farm just outside Shanghai. For the fourth time in ten days, he had told the American consulate, Japanese airplanes had bombarded his land. During the last attack, sixteen Japanese bombers flew over the farm for two and a half hours, killing 250 of the dairy's pedigreed cattle and destroying the physical plant. The barns had been flying large American flags.

Reacting strongly to news reports, Roosevelt in a meeting of the cabinet referred to Italy, Germany, and Japan as "bandit nations." By the time he reached Chicago, he was seething.

A motorcade swept Roosevelt through the Loop and up to the Outer Link Bridge, just finished by the Works Progress Administration; Roosevelt was scheduled to give a speech of dedication. Holding himself at a lectern and nodding toward the nearby office building of the *Chicago Tribune*, that bastion of American isolationism, Roosevelt announced that he had chosen Chicago for a speech of "definite national importance."

Under an ashen sky laden with storm clouds, Roosevelt began his speech. Alluding to the Japanese assault on China—an assault Roosevelt said was without "justification of any kind"—the president declared that if international lawlessness became much worse, the Western Hemisphere itself could come under attack. But what steps to take? The "peace-loving nations," Roosevelt stated, "must make a concerted effort in opposition to those violations of treaties and those ignorings of humane instincts which today are creating a state of international anarchy and instability from which there is no escape through mere isolation or neutrality." The anarchy and instability, the president feared, were likely to spread: "The peace, the freedom, and the security of 90 percent of the world is being threatened by the remaining 10 percent who are threatening a breakdown of all international order and law."

Roosevelt was reaching the climax. "When an epidemic of physical disease starts to spread," he asserted, "the community approves and joins a quarantine of the patients in order to protect the health of the community against the spread of the disease." The administration, Roosevelt promised, would try to stay out of war. He was, however, frank. "War is a contagion," he said. "It can engulf states and peoples remote from the original scene of hostilities. We are adapting such measures as will minimize our risk of involvement, but we cannot have complete protection in a world of disorder in which confidence and security have broken down."

Back in his car in the presidential train, Roosevelt asked. "How did it go, Grace?" He was speaking to Grace Tully, one of his White House secretaries. The crowd, she responded, had been enthusiastic.

"Well," Roosevelt allowed, "it's said now. It was something that needed saying."

Upon his return to Hyde Park the next day, Roosevelt sat on his front porch, chatting with the reporters. They besieged him with questions. What had he actually meant to say back there in Chicago? What did he mean by "quarantine"? Whatever he meant, how did he intend to enforce it?

"I can't tell you what the methods will be," Roosevelt answered. "We are looking for some way to peace; and by no means is it necessary that that way will be contrary to the exercise of neutrality."

But what *did* Roosevelt intend? What *had* he meant by "quarantine"? Was the word a threat against Japan? Was it a trial balloon? Was it merely a device to hide his own doubts? We can only guess.

Two points, nonetheless, are clear. In Roosevelt's judgment, Japan was an international outlaw—an outlaw that, unless stopped, would menace America. And in his roundabout politician's talk—

"by no means is it necessary that that way will be contrary to the exercise of neutrality"—Roosevelt had implied that he might very well cease to be neutral.

■ ■ ■

Responding swiftly to the quarantine speech, the Japanese sent Roosevelt a warning. In the U.S. embassy in Tokyo, Eugene H. Dorman, Ambassador Grew's Japanese-speaking lieutenant, received a representative of the government, Matsukata Kojiro. They discussed the Japanese reaction to Roosevelt's speech. The people, Matsukata said, were bitter. Dorman relayed these words to Washington in a cable dated October 12, 1937: Once they

> had believed that the attitude of the United States was so fair that a final solution of the "Pacific problem" was at hand, and the people in control were prepared, as a token of their appreciation, to throw the "Open Door in China wide open to the United States" and to any other country taking a similar impartial position. "But that is all finished," said Mr. Matsukata, "and the same people are saying that, if the United States continues along the policy which was recently announced, Japan will have to get ready."

■ ■ ■

On one day late in September 1937, eighty Japanese airplanes bombed Nanking for seven hours straight. Two days later, Japanese submarines in the Hong Kong harbor sank seventeen Chinese junks, killing at least 300 persons aboard. Twenty-two nations in the League of Nations condemned the attack.

On October 8, 1937, the Chinese government charged that the Japanese, in violation of a Geneva convention, had begun using poison gas. On October 10, 1937, foreign visitors inspecting the Red Cross hospital in Nanking interviewed four Chinese soldiers, men who displayed telltale blisters and burns. The soldiers, the visitors concluded, had been exposed to mustard gas.

On October 13, 1937, the Japanese government apologized formally for the machine-gunning of the British ambassador. That same

day, three Japanese airplanes swooped down toward the Shanghai–
Nanking highway, machine-gunning another column of British cars.
Like the ambassador's, these automobiles were flying conspicuous
British flags.

On October 23, 1937, U.S. Marines in Shanghai's international sector saw a Japanese airplane drop an incendiary bomb. Painted silvery
white, it seemed to be floating rather than falling; yet it landed with
enough force to dent the pavement. Then it exploded, spewing flame.
One American was injured: Marine Sergeant R. Coleman from Atkins,
Arkansas, burned his hands as he tried to stifle the clothing, all ablaze,
of a Chinese women who was burning to death.

On October 25, 1937, two dozen foreigners, mostly British and
American, dressed in sporting clothes, were riding horseback on
Keswick Road, close to the edge of the international settlement. A
Japanese airplane dived upon them five times, belching machine-
gun bullets, scattering horses and riders, and killing one British
soldier, Royal Ulsterman W. MacGowan. An American businessman
in the party, C. H. Sprague, a Standard Vacuum executive from
Cleveland, said that the riders' clothing had been plainly civilian. Sir
Charles Little, the presiding British admiral at Shanghai, called the
attack "impudent, savage, and ruthless." The Japanese apologized.

On October 27, 1937, a Japanese airplane attacked a British military outpost in a western section of the international settlement.
The airplane dived five times and, on its last dive, British antiaircraft guns fired back, making a strike. Out on the USS *Augusta*,
Admiral Harry E. Yarnell announced that his own gunners would
open fire on any attacking plane immediately.

Early in November 1937, a foreign journalist saw Japanese airplanes drop roughly 350 bombs on one village up the Yangtze.
"Japanese pilots went through moves they would have performed
in a public expedition," he wrote. "Squadrons of three or four planes
would power-dive from high altitudes, dropping missiles of great
weight and explosive character upon Chinese farmhouses made of
bamboo and mud plaster with tile roofs." In another Yangtze village,
a missionary doctor saw the Japanese drop "conservatively" 160
bombs. People "brought to our hospital were horribly mutilated,"
including "a man with his left ear torn to shreds, his left biceps

almost severed, his right foot almost torn in half, . . . and his genitals badly mutilated."

Because of such incidents, feelings between Japanese and foreigners, not to mention Chinese, were bitter. The "Japanese," Captain Carlson reported to the White House, "have a blind hatred for all those [foreigners] who have opposed them. The list includes Admiral Yarnell. . . . By 'opposing' I mean . . . that these officials have refused to lend the assistance to the Japanese which they have suggested or requested, in the course of their operations against the Chinese."

■ ■ ■

From a darkened room high in a hotel over the Bund, an American reporter wrote from Shanghai, midway through November 1937: "[Y]ou look out across the curve of the Whangpoo toward black, silent Pootung Point. The point is inside [the] great U of the river. Once it was crowded with life, jammed with warehouses, mills, shipyards, its shores lined with junks, tugs, lighters, and sampans. Tonight it is a place of death. The gaunt blackened ruins of factories are etched against the sky. The shore is lined with sunken craft. . . . On your right, her lights blazing and her foremasthead flag streaming in a searchlight's beam, lies the great gray *Augusta*, symbol of America's power in the Oriental war zone. Her rails are draped with shrapnel mats and her guns are bared and ready. . . . Over to the northeast a solitary light marks the Japanese landing field, whence come the droning bombers to drop their loads of death. . . . Closer in, on your left, are Hongkew and Chapei and Yangtzepoo— great muddled blocks of tiled houses, concrete factories, warehouses, and stores. Whole blocks have been blasted into heaps of rubble. Streets are choked with debris. . . . So here you are, in a balcony seat, looking at a modern war—and if a chunk of shrapnel doesn't crash through the window or a tracer bullet sing by your ear, you'll be all right."

■ ■ ■

The Chinese were not all right.

Executing a great flanking movement, the Japanese had landed new forces at Hankow, close by the coast and just south of Shanghai, and with those reinforcements had pushed in behind the main Chinese positions. The Japanese now had Shanghai in a vise. Yard by yard, the Japanese were squashing the city's resistance.

A "row of Chinese houses, with balconies protruding from second stories, faces the Ziccawei Creek [in the Chinese sector of Shanghai]," Evans Carlson noted on November 13, 1937. "I give you this detail," Carlson informed the president, "in order to . . . picture to you one of the most dramatic scenes I have ever witnessed." When the Japanese tried to cross Ziccawei Creek, Carlson had calculated, a sharp engagement would take place. Early in the morning of November 10, 1937, consequently, he and a Commander Overesch had proceeded to the area, renting a room with a balcony. At eleven the next morning, the

> show started. Two Japanese tanks . . . rolled up the road to the west . . . , not 75 yards from us. The Chinese opened with a terrific machine gun barrage, the Japanese replying. . . . [Japanese planes] zoomed overhead, dropping their bombs after powerdiving. From the alleyways . . . we could see squads of Japanese soldiers moving stealthily towards the road bordering Ziccawei Creek. . . . The soldiers tossed smoke candles out into the road. 75 yards from us two armies were fighting to the death, employing most of the implements of war known to modern science. I kept my camera glued to my eye, snapping pictures whenever the smoke thinned out. . . . After an hour the Japanese scored several direct hits. . . . Presently we observed a Chinese soldier carrying a wounded comrade through the muddy waters of Ziccawei, which was waist deep. Inch by inch he dragged along. Our hearts were in our mouths, for fear that he would stumble, or that the Japanese fire would reach him before he gained the northern bank. But he made it, and willing French hands drew the two up to the French post.

Then, down along the Route de Ziccawei, other Chinese troops began to cross the creek. They had just given up. Save for the western zones, Shanghai now was in Japanese hands. The war, and China's resistance, simply shifted, moving inland.

CHAPTER
4

THE YANGTZE RIVER
WAR

As you steamed into the mouth of the Yangtze River, you might have seen the north shoreline, or the south, but you could not see both at the same time; the Yangtze River at its delta is less a river than an ocean. Indeed, whole fleets of ships, those of Jardine, Matheson, and Company, Butterfield and Swire, the Dollar Line of America, the Japanese Nisshin Kisen Kaisha, and the China Merchants' Steamship Navigation Company, plied the Yangtze, setting out from the Shanghai docks. From Shanghai alone more than 14,000 steamers each year chugged inland; and nearly half the population of China lived along those inland reaches of the Yangtze Valley. For all those millions of persons the Yangtze was the only route to the the outside world that was China's only source of material.

Once it controlled Shanghai, Japan's next task was obvious. It had to sever the Yangtze River valley from the world outside. Otherwise the Yangtze could be a conduit of supplies to China. So the Japanese did what they had to do. They severed away.

On November 18, 1937, Japanese authorities announced their intention to seize control of the Shanghai customs service—descendant of the old imperial customs service. Under the new arrangement, a reporter asked, would customs revenues still go toward the repayment of debts to the West? The Japanese government, a spokesman announced, asserted its "right to act independently."

On November 29, 1937, Japanese marines, in search of vessels they could use for troop transport, boarded an American-owned launch, anchored off the French concession at Shanghai. Ripping off the American flag, they threw it into the Whangpoo. After a protest from Clarence E. Gauss, the U.S. consul-general in Shanghai, the Japanese returned the launch to its owners.

On December 3, 1937, Japanese troops at Shanghai marched into the international settlement. Stringing out barbed wire barricades, they closed down major avenues (at one intersection, Japanese machine guns were pointing in all four directions) and took command of several foreign establishments: the Shanghai Race Club; the Grand Theater; the foreigners' Y.M.C.A.; the China United Departments; and, up on Bubbling Springs Road, the Park Hotel, described in a guidebook of the time as the "tallest building in the Far East [with] 205 luxuriously furnished rooms and apartments." At each of these sites, Japanese troops refused to let anyone other than their own nationals enter or leave. Only upon a vigorous protest from U.S. Marine Colonel Charles F. B. Price did the Japanese withdraw.

On December 5, 1937, at Suhu, a Yangtze River city above Nanking, Japanese airplanes bombed a British gunboat and two British merchant vessels. All three ships had been displaying the Union Jack.

Also on December 5, 1937, in his Nanking headquarters, guarded by a dragon-roofed gate and overlooking willows and a lake, Chiang Kai-shek sat with his leading generals to make a decision. The Japanese were demanding nothing less than the surrender of Chiang Kai-shek. Should he surrender? In the end, Chiang and his advisers calculated that they could sustain the war. Two days later they flew upriver to Hankow. Hankow would be the new capital. From there Chiang's government would continue its efforts to find foreign help.

The Japanese wanted to seal off that help. Back in November 1937, the Japanese had filed a protest with the French: A number of countries, Britain, Sweden, America, and France itself, the Japanese had complained, had been using the Haiphong harbor, in French Indochina, as a conduit for supplies into China. If these supplies continued to flow, the Japanese stated, their naval forces would seize Hainan Island, off the southern coast of China, and blockade Haiphong. As if to confirm the threat, Japanese forces on December 1, 1937, seized Chikkai Island, some forty miles below the mouth of the Pearl River. Fleeing from Chikkai to Hong Kong, Dr. Harry Blaber, a Maryknoll missionary, told reporters that Chikkai was sure to be a base for Japanese operations to the south.

Then, on December 10, 1937, near Hong Kong another crisis erupted. Putting out from Hong Kong Island, a British customs vessel reached a point just west of the colony's territorial waters. A Japanese destroyer closed in, intent on giving chase. The British captain dashed back into his own waters, but the Japanese kept coming, and under fire he had to beach his vessel. The next day, December 11, 1937, a Hong Kong police launch went out to inspect the scene—and found nothing. The Japanese had refloated the customs ship and hauled it away.

The Japanese action, of course, was piratical. But like Indochina, Hong Kong was a pipeline into China. As *Time* reported, "arms poured into China through Hong Kong, where stevedores worked overtime unloading . . . British-made planes, tons of munitions, and other war materials." So Japan would have to close even the Hong Kong pipeline—and China would need a new avenue of supplies.

■ ■ ■

Standing at the edge of a cliff, Tan Pei-ying peered down. Below him was a gorge of the Salween River, in the northern Burma, and over that gorge, somehow, Tan was going to have to build a bridge. Tan was an engineer in the employ of the Chinese government; and China, fearing that Japan would shut down the coastline and knowing that the supplies coming in from the Soviet Union (and they *were* coming in) were few and far between, had been casting about for a new overland route. But where?

Centuries before, the Chinese knew, traders with India had used a trail down through the mountains of Yunnan Province, in southwestern China, a trail that had wound down through Burma and along the Saluppin River as far as Rangoon. Marco Polo, in fact, had used that trail; and as late as the early twentieth century, according to missionary accounts, elderly Chinese in Yunnan remembered elephants out of Burma bearing tribute to Peking. By

1937, of course, the elephants were gone, and most of the trail itself was overgrown. Parts of a road, nonetheless, did exist: The British had constructed a rail line from Rangoon up through colonial Burma; and an American firm in about 1900 had built a steel bridge over the Gokteik Gorge near Lashio, a Burmese town just inside the border of China; and just outside Kunming, a walled Yunnanese city, a governor called One-Eyed Lung had laid down about 200 miles of a pathway. The distance between the end of that pathway and the start of the Gokteik bridge, furthermore, was only 300 miles—by air. But on the ground. . . .

On the ground, because of the mountains and gorges and valleys, the distance was more like 600 miles. As Tan Pei-ying looked down the cliffs that arose straight from the jungle floor that was the Salween Valley, he made some calculations. It was late November 1937, and if he was to carry out his assignment, digging a road down to Burma, time would be short: By May at the latest, the monsoons would pour in and all work would stop. So Tan had little time. He also had few resources, no steam shovels, no graders, no great trucks—only a few compressed air drills and hundreds of thousands of people. Tan would have to build his road with people—people who would have to bring their own woks and their own rice, people who would bring their own baskets, people who would have to scratch out the road with their fingernails.

This was to be the Burma Road. Those who would survive— and thousands upon thousands of Chinese peasants would perish in building the Burma Road—were going to have to endure landslides, dysentery, malaria, thirst, hunger, and the ever-looming threat of Japanese bombers.

Yet the Burma Road itself was only the end of a longer road, and that longer road was a road made of money, money with which China could pay for supplies. That longer road traced back to the Treasury Department in Washington.

■   ■   ■

Son of a financier and ambassador, owner of a Hudson Valley estate, neighbor, and probably closest friend of Franklin D. Roosevelt, Henry Morgenthau, Jr., was secretary of the treasury. He was not much to look at: Morgenthau, two correspondents wrote late in the 1930s, was "the least imposing of the great officers of government. A tall, heavy, ungainly man, he has a nervous smile, small, nervous eyes, and a high, nervous voice. He is slow thinking and slow speaking. He has an exasperating habit of repeating statements which he thinks important, occasionally stutters, and is always forgetting names. When his memory fails him, he snaps his fingers and utters a sort of low cry, intended as an appeal to his companions to supply his deficiency. He is self-conscious without self-confidence, a born worrier, and inclined to be suspicious. Indeed, at first acquaintance, a doglike devotion to the President seems to be his only affirmative trait."

Morgenthau also was a Roosevelt liberal: "For Elinor," Franklin D. Roosevelt once had scribbled on a photograph of the two men, sent to Morgenthau's wife, "from one of two of a kind." Like Roosevelt, Morgenthau found events in China morally outrageous.

Morgenthau, at least from a distance, knew a great deal about China. Upon becoming secretary in 1934, he had organized what he called the Treasury Foreign Service, and he had fanned agents around the world. Thus he had been able to keep up with global finance. Dr. J. Lossing Buck, economist, Treasury Department official, and former husband of Pearl Buck, the novelist, was a Morgenthau agent: For months in 1937 he lived in the Palace Hotel, almost next door to Sir Frederick Leigh-Ross, an international troubleshooter from the British Exchequer, and never once had Sir Frederick cottoned to what Buck was up to. Buck was a deal maker, and having sidled up to Generalissimo and Madame Chiang Kai-shek, had funneled intelligence back to Morgenthau.

Morgenthau in turn—with Roosevelt's full support—had chosen to back "Chiang Kai-shek to the limit of his ability. His [Morgenthau's] first move had been to help the Chinese Treasury to reestablish itself on a new basis," meaning that the United States would start to buy Chinese silver.

More precisely, in the spring of 1937, the Chinese government asked Morgenthau to buy 50 million ounces of their silver—on deposit in New York vaults. On July 8, 1937, Morgenthau met in his office with H. H. Kung—China's finance minister, a brother-in-law of Chiang Kai-shek, and a graduate of Oberlin College, K'ung looked equally at home in Confucian gowns and Western, wing-tipped collars—and relayed good news. President Roosevelt, Morgenthau informed K'ung, had instructed the Treasury Department to "do everything it could to keep China strong."

Pleased and sycophantic, K'ung broke out in praises of the Roosevelt administration. Morgenthau in particular was a "farsighted statesman."

The flattery may have worked. In July 1937, Morgenthau purchased 62 million ounces of Chinese silver at $.45 an ounce and in November 1937, at the same price, Morgenthau picked up an additional 50 million ounces.

Then Morgenthau and the State Department went head to head. Early in December 1937, Morgenthau wired Roosevelt (the president was off on vacation):

AM DINING WITH THE CHINESE AMBASSADOR [C. T. WANG] TONIGHT AND WOULD LIKE TO HAVE YOUR ADVICE BEFORE SEEING HIM ON THE FOLLOWING PROPOSITION. . . . AM INCLINED TO TELL THE CHINESE THAT WE WILL BUY ANOTHER FIFTY MILLION OUNCES OF SILVER FROM THEM OVER A PERIOD OF THE NEXT TEN WEEKS.

On December 2, Roosevelt wired back his approval—adding only that Morgenthau ought to run the idea past the State Department. State thought the idea was questionable, even provocative; Japan, after all, might object. Knowing that Roosevelt was on Morgenthau's side, however, the State Department used ambivalent wording to phrase its objection. Future extensions of funds to China, State said in a memorandum to Treasury, might be contingent "on any possible questions of neutrality that may arise." Morgenthau read the memorandum and reread it twice. Was State saying yes, no, or maybe?

On December 8, 1937, memorandum in hand, Morgenthau trotted next door to the White House. Scanning the document, Roosevelt was scornful: The State Department's language, he said to Morgenthau, was "the most stupid . . . I have ever read. When they recommend that we add to the agreement to give China a foreign exchange loan a statement, 'This may be canceled in case of a Neutrality Proclamation,' this would be playing into the hands of somebody like Senator Nye [the North Dakota Republican and isolationist]."

"Or the Japanese," Morgenthau said.

"Fix up an agreement with them [State] right away in writing," Roosevelt instructed.

Armed now with presidential authority, Morgenthau did so. And the Japanese could only draw an obvious conclusion. In the Sino-Japanese war, the United States was neutral in name alone.

■ ■ ■

With the engine of his Hawk fighter plane fueled and idling, Claire Chennault, the pilot, was in his cockpit, waiting at the end of the Nanking runway. The hour was just before daybreak, on December 11, 1937; the American embassy had left Nanking already and Chiang Kai-shek himself had ordered Chennault to fly up to Han-kow. Although a stubborn man, Chennault was willing to comply.

If he delayed, he might be in danger. He was, after all, a foreign agent, an American in the pay of the Chinese government.

A leather-faced loudmouth from the swamps of Louisiana, he had flown with the old Army Air Corps but by 1936 had been grounded. He had grown deaf; he suffered from chronic bronchitis; and in his insistence on the importance of pursuit planes, he had offended superior officers. So they had retired him. Back home in Louisiana and hospitalized, Chennault probably had been close to a clinical depression.

Then Chennault had a reprieve. Early in 1937, he learned that Madame Chiang Kai-shek wanted him to come to China; would he examine the state of the Chinese Air Force? Practically bounding from his bed, Chennault accepted the job—and by June 1937, he was in a Chinese government building in Shanghai, waiting to meet the Madame. She won him over immediately. Pretty, vivacious, and totally in control, she flashed through so many emotions that Chennault was unable to do much else than gape. "I reckon you and I will get along right good in building up your air force," Chennault had drawled at last. "I reckon so," she had drawled right back, speaking in a Georgia accent. Chennault later wrote in his diary: "She will always be a princess to me."

After the outbreak of war, Chennault stayed on in China, trying in Nanking to organize an air raid warning net—bells, sirens, bugles, gongs, anything loud enough to tell people when the bombers were coming. The net did little good. Early in November 1937, Chennault and a few journalists climbed atop the Metropolitan Hotel; they wanted a clear view of an air raid. Nanking stretched out below them as a "homogeneous pattern of gray structures. . . . It was a hot stale day with thin clouds hanging over the city . . . ," one of the journalists wrote. "Presently . . . 18 Japanese bombers approached. . . . The drone . . . grew louder and louder. . . . The bombers broke formation and in single file descended to an altitude below 2,000 feet and machine-gunned and strafed the defenseless city below. . . . The bombers passed so close to [the hotel roof] that [we] could plainly see the bloodred meatballs painted on the wings."

Such bombers had been flying in at will. "We are down to 5 Hawks and two Boeing P-26's" Chennault wrote in his diary in mid-November 1937. Most of his pilots, Chinese, were dead.

So now, in the predawn of December 11, 1937, Claire Chennault was waiting to continue the war from farther into the interior of China; and he was waiting for the first glimpse of light. A ray of sunshine broke over the walls of Nanking. Chennault touched at his goggles. His plane lunged and raced, and away he went and up, bobbing against a rising current of air and turning westward from the smoldering city of Nanking.

In the yellowing curve of the Yangtze below lay the still dark form of a gunboat. It was the USS *Panay*.

CHAPTER
5

THE *PANAY*

I n the wardroom of the USS *Panay* hung a bronzed plaque:

USS *Panay*
Mission
For the protection of American life and property
in the Yangtze River Valley and its
tributaries, and the furtherance of American
good will in China.

Allowed by a 1903 treaty to ply the main rivers of China, the *Panay* was one of half a dozen American gunboats that made up the Yangtze patrol; and as the plaque in the *Panay's* wardroom implied, the mission of the Yangtze patrol was to protect the interests of Americans in China, their firms, their churches, and their ships.

The mission also was to uphold a way of life. In U.S. Navy circles during the 1920s and 1930s Yangtze patrol duty was a cherished assignment. As a participant put it, "elaborately furnished apartments, with battalions of houseboys, cooks, and amahs for the children, could frequently be leased from the local European residents [in Shanghai] going on leave to their homelands. Rentals were phenomenally low, as were all other expenses. Curio and silk shops bulged with the choicest products of Chinese artistry at irresistible prices. Attractive clubs [provided] special recreational facilities. . . . Fairly early in the afternoon, the tennis courts would begin to fill

56

at the Country Club on Bubbling Springs Road, at the Cercle Sportif Français in the French Concession, and out at the more distant Columbia Country Club. . . . By evening, ladies and gentlemen in evening clothes sat on the terraces for the aperitif, or cocktails, as American customs began to take hold. These sessions, following the tennis, golf, or riding of the later afternoon, culminated in sumptuous, many-course dinners."

At times, to be sure, the Yangtze patrol had to face danger. In the middle of the 1920s, as China's revolution raged up and down the Yangtze River valley, the U.S. gunboats and their personnel did come under fire.

On the whole, however, the officers and the families of the Yangtze patrol, especially in Shanghai, lived like royalty. Open-to-the-sky dinner-dance rooms at the Park Hotel were open all night every night. At "Ciro's even small parties customarily ordered magnums of champagne. The Alhambra, St. George's, and numerous other night spots, as well as the restaurants, served the choicest foods of every clime. . . . [Shanghai's] skyline blazed with noon lights at night."

But then the lights went out. After the *Panay* crisis of December 12, 1937, the Japanese were in command of the valley. The life of the Yangtze patrol soon came to an end.

■ ■ ■

Early in the afternoon of December 12, 1937, six Japanese naval bombers lined up on the runway at Chang-chou, a town below Nanking, awaited orders, took off, and started to follow the great curve of the Yangtze River. One of the pilots, Okumiya Masatake, later wrote an account of the flight. He had flown up from Shanghai just that morning and, putting down at Chang-chou, had received an intelligence briefing. "We were informed," Okumiya stated, "that an advance army unit had reported seeing large merchant ships and three smaller ones fleeing the capital, loaded to capacity with Chinese troops. They were on the upper reaches of the Yangtze, the most advanced being about 20 miles from Nanking. Ground forces were unable to reach them, and so it was requested that the naval air arm make an attack. It was rumored that a successful attack might earn a citation." So the bombers took off. The pilots were under orders to dive with the sun at their backs.

The valley below them looked peaceful, Okumiya recalled, "the serenity of the vista broken only by bomb-born columns of smoke from Nanking. . . ." Since the bombers were not equipped with oxygen, they were flying at 10,000 feet, and thus they could make out forms on the river. Just above Nanking, Okumiya noted, the Yangtze "split into three streams . . . and it was there . . . that I spotted four or more ships." One of those ships was the *Panay*.

■　■　■

Fat and stubby, the *Panay* resembled a Mississippi River paddlewheel steamer without the paddlewheel. Its lowest deck was almost as low as the waterline and its topmost deck, which served as a roof for most of the cabins, ran almost the length of the vessel. Awnings shaded the top deck fore and aft and, painted across both awnings—thus lying flat and being plainly visible from overhead—were two large American flags. On the morning of December 12, 1937, as on every morning over the previous week, the *Panay*'s mast was flying the vessel's largest U.S. ensign. As the *Panay* moved upstream in the Yangtze River, its nationality was unmistakable.

Just beyond Nanking, the Yangtze River formed a vast bend, swinging southward for about fifty miles before it straightened again, and rose from there some 300 miles toward Hankow. But near Nanking, in that bend of the river, where several islands formed oblongs midstream and where the current ran brown and cold, the *Panay* dropped anchor. Hovering close by were three Standard Oil tankers, the *Mei Ping*, the *Mei An*, and the *Mei Hsia*. Although they bore Chinese names and carried Chinese crews, each of these three vessels had Western captains. Each also had a Standard Oil "S" painted on its smokestack; each had a mast from which an American flag flew; each displayed yet another American flag, painted horizontally along the superstructure. Each, for protection, was staying near the *Panay*.

The *Panay* had a strange encounter. Shortly after 9:00 A.M., on Sunday, December 12, 1937, Lieutenant Commander James J. Hughes, the commanding officer, spotted something moving on the bank of the river. He checked more closely through his binoculars. A Japanese unit was standing close to the bank; one of the soldiers was waving a flag; and a launch was putting out from the shoreline. Hughes ordered his engines stopped. As the launch reached the side of the *Panay*, a Japanese officer climbed on deck. He was short and bulky in a mustard-colored trenchcoat. He was toting a pistol.

On a pad of paper he wrote, "Where are you going?" The *Panay*, Hughes responded, was offering protection to American citizens and ships.

Another slip came. This time the Japanese wanted to know the names and locations of the ships. Hughes made no response.

The Japanese insisted on seeing Hughes's superior.

Hughes invited him to leave the vessel.

The Japanese retreated.

The *Panay*'s motors started to throb again and, by 11:00 A.M., the gunboat was about twenty-seven miles upriver from Nanking. Hughes checked the location. On both sides of the river stood forests of reeds, each reed as thick as a bamboo fishing pole. Reaching a broad, open spot in the river, Hughes was satisfied. There he had the boat drop anchor again. He chose that spot, as he wrote later in a report to the president, because he "wished to keep out of the way of the contending armies; this location seemed highly desirable. We were easily visible, especially accompanied as we were by three Standard Oil tankers, for miles around, on every side."

George Atcheson, the second secretary from the embassy in Nanking and now aboard the *Panay*, sent a cable to the U.S. Shanghai consulate:

> VESSEL IS NOW ANCHORED 27 MILES ABOVE NANKING. . . . STANDARD OIL COMPANY STEAMERS . . . ANCHORED NEARBY. . . . PLEASE INFORM JAPANESE EMBASSY OF PRESENT POSITION OF PANAY AND AMERICAN MERCHANT VESSELS, AND REQUEST THAT APPROPRIATE INSTRUCTIONS BE ISSUED TO JAPANESE FORCES.

The cable sent, Atcheson joined Hughes and the other officers of the *Panay* for Sunday dinner. The food was solid navy fare: meat, potatoes, vegetables, and ice cream. After the meal, most of the men retired to their bunks to take naps. A few, including Norman Alley, a newsreel cameraman for Universal Studios, went onto the deck for a stroll.

Alley happened to be carrying his Bell & Howell. The time was 1:37 P.M.

■   ■   ■

At 1:37 P.M.—he had just checked his watch—Okumiya Masatake was waving to his fellow pilots and pointing downward. He glanced about for possible Chinese aircraft, he wrote, and "seeing none, banked my plane . . . to prepare for attack." Overhead, another squadron of Japanese bombers had released bombs. As he was banking, Okumiya observed one of those bombs as it descended toward the river. It scored a hit on a boat below.

Then Okumiya dived. As he raced earthward, he "lost sight of the distant horizon, then the far reaches of the river, and by the time our 60-degree dive had brought me down to 1,000 meters my vision was completely filled with the ever-growing target on the yellow surface of the water as it filled and overflowed the viewer of my primitive bombsight. At 500 meters I released the bomb and pulled out of the dive."

As he climbed again, Okumiya looked back down, surprised to see a large water ring near the stern of the ship. He had missed; he had failed to strike his target, one of the Standard Oil vessels.

Nearby, however, one vessel was smoking. Okumiya later learned the name of that vessel . . . the USS *Panay*.

■   ■   ■

On the bridge of the *Panay* a spotter called out a warning—airplanes were approaching from the southeast! Down in his cabin where he had been taking a nap, Commander Hughes scrambled up from his bunk, put on his uniform cap, and headed out toward the bridge. As he bounded up the steps, he glanced around: All the American flags were in place and, to anyone approaching by air, would be plainly distinguishable. Reaching the pilot house he grabbed a pair of binoculars, then finished the climb to the bridge. The only cover

over the bridge was a strip of canvas. Hughes adjusted his lenses. He could make out six aircraft, strung out in a line, speeding toward the *Panay*; the first three of these aircraft were beginning to drop. They were starting to power-dive!

Standing beside Hughes, Chief Quartermaster John L. Lang cried out, "They're letting go bombs! Get under cover!" As Hughes scrambled back down to the pilot house, the first of the bombs went off. It seemed to hit directly overhead. Then the airplanes went away.

Commander Hughes, however, lay wounded. After the bomb exploded, he later testified, "I lost consciousness for what must have been . . . a minute or two; when I came to, I discovered myself on the deck . . . , badly stunned with my head covered with blood, and my right leg painfully injured at the hip, making it impossible for me to raise my feet. A hole had been broken in the deck of the bridge near where Lang and I had been standing. I asked Lang if he were injured, to which he replied, 'No, sir'. . . . I asked him to put a life jacket on me and help me down to the ship's galley which is on the main deck, and a good central point from which to direct operations. Before I was able to reach the galley, which was . . . a slow process . . . , I heard *Panay*'s machine guns firing."

The Japanese bombers were coming back.

Out on the lowest deck, Norman Alley began taking pictures. "My first reaction," he said later, "was that the Japanese, mistaking the *Panay* for an enemy ship, had realized their error and were leaving." This was wrong, however, as almost directly thereafter a squadron of six small pursuit-type bombers came over at a much lower altitude and immediately began to power-dive and release what seemed to be 100-pound bombs. A reporter later asked Alley if the Japanese had been making a mistake. "Hell no," Alley retorted, ". . . when they started dive bombing they would have had to see our flags. They came straight out of the sun. And they came over and over."

The *Panay*'s return fire did little good. One bomb blast, going off near the forecastle, stripped Ensign Dennis Biwerse of almost all his clothing; picking himself up, he mounted a ladder to the top deck, trying to get to the machine guns, but a second blast knocked him down again. Shrapnel hit Lieutenant A. F. Anders, the executive officer, in the throat and the fingers of his right hand as he was trying to fit a pan of ammunition into a gun. Shrapnel also struck Lieutenant (junior grade) J. W Geist, making his leg immobile. Bombs ripped a hole in the side of the *Panay*, wounding still more men below.

Down in the petty officers' wardroom, Luigi Barzini, the Italian journalist assigned to cover the war, heard two or three new bombs explode; even though they exploded several yards from the *Panay*, they pockmarked the ship "with fragments like a calendar." Barzini and a companion slipped into the engine room, where the walls were the thickest. The "wounded at our feet moaned," he went on, "and those who had been hit by flying fragments screamed with pain. . . . Between one onslaught and another by the Japanese planes, Norman Alley of Universal News and Eric Mayell of Movietone News [had] cameras glued to their cheeks to record a moment, stolen here and there, of that inferno. . . . The ship was filling with water, listing to one side."

Back in the galley, Commander Hughes "noticed Mr. J. Hall Paxton (a U.S. embassy official), one of the passengers, standing on deck just outside the galley. I asked him to please come in and hold me up, which he kindly did. . . . From then on planes bombed us continuously until about 14:25. They appeared to be attacking us in relays of two or three each. The first group that came over divebombed us from a considerable altitude which kept them beyond the range of our machine guns. Later when the *Panay* was visibly smashed up, they came much closer, and not only let go their bombs from . . . perhaps one or two hundred feet, but also machine gunned our decks, firing as they came down diving. I distinctly heard their guns which had a different sound from the *Panay*'s. According to my reckoning, the *Panay* must have received about 24 direct hits. . . . At 13:58 the ship appeared to be settling fast. . . . Ensign Biwerse, the communications officer, came into the galley . . . asked if he should throw overboard the confidential publications. I told him to get them all overboard as quickly as possible." Then Hughes ordered the crew to abandon ship.

A few hundred yards upstream by the south bank, where he had docked at a pontoon wharf, Captain Mender of the Standard Oil tanker *Mei Hsia* was surveying the scene. *Mei An*, his companion vessel, was smoking and steering slowly toward the north bank; the *Mei Ping*, also hit, and tilting, was threading its way past the *Panay*. Crewmen were lowering lifeboats into the current

Shortly after three o'clock, the boats reached the reeds on the north bank. As the men sloshed ashore, they glanced behind. The *Panay* was about half-submerged—and the bombers were coming back.

High over the pontoon, where the *Mei Ping* was trying to dock, a Japanese airplane was circling, circling, then swinging and diving; as it pulled upward again, two black objects, shaped like eggs with tails, drifted down, slowly at first, or so it seemed, and then appearing to pick up more and more speed until with a crash they slammed into the side of the *Mei Ping*. The tanker turned into a fireball.

In the reeds by the north bank, the *Panay* survivors, cold and soaked, were pulling themselves up the four-foot mudbank, straining to haul the wounded on stretchers up onto solid ground. Once out of the water, Commander Hughes, wrapped in blankets and laid out in the reeds, convened his aides for advice: Were Japan and America, he asked, at war? If so, were the Japanese likely to track down the men from the *Panay*, right here in the reeds? Hughes's officers had no answers. Even as they conferred, however, they heard the sound of something throbbing.

The throbbing was growing closer, ever closer.

It was the throbbing of two launches, both Japanese.

The launches, one of the officers said, were heading "straight for *Panay*. And when they were about 300 yards from her . . . there were several bursts of machine gun fire from one or both of the launches."

The *Panay* was nearly submerged, with practically nothing but its flags showing. The Japanese opened fire anyway.

Then the two launches crossed back toward the center of the river, cruising "so slowly," the officer said, "that they hardly seemed to move. We waited tensely, thinking that they would surely head toward us."

■ ■ ■

From late in the afternoon on, wireless messages flashed up and down the Yangtze River. "PANAY UNHEARD SINCE 1342," Admiral Harry E. Yarnell signaled from the *Augusta*. "WHAT IS NATURE OF CASUALTY. ARE YOU IN CONTACT WITH PANAY VIA BRITISH?" From Hankow, the USS *Luzon*, another gunboat, radioed back: "NO COMMUNICATION SINCE 1355. . . . BRITISH ENDEAVORING DETERMINE NATURE CASUALTY. BUT BELIEVE NO BRITISH SHIP IN SIGHT."

The *Luzon* did pass along one report from the British. Near Wuhu, about twenty miles upstream from the site of the *Panay* attack, Japanese shore artillery had opened fire on two British gunboats, the *Cricket* and the *Scarab*.

The Japanese, as U.S. Ambassador Nelson T. Johnson wired to Washington, had been trying to sink all ships not their own in the reaches of the middle Yangtze.

But were they also to kill foreigners?

To that question, the *Panay* survivors had no answer. Late in the afternoon, the two Japanese launches did retreat. But, in the morning, would airplanes fly over the reed bank? Commander Hughes had sent Yuan Te Erh, a mess attendant, on a scouting expedition; Yuan returned with the news that a village called Ho Hsien lay roughly five miles up the river and about three miles inland. Hughes decided that the survivors, a party of about fifty, had to set out for Ho Hsien. So, bearing the stretchers and what little gear they had been able to salvage, the men of the *Panay* started to walk—while in the lowering darkness the *Mei Ping* across the river was blazing away.

En route to Ho Hsien they encountered a hamlet and, after they had shouted and pounded, someone on the inside opened the gate. George Atcheson, the State Department official, found a telephone. Despite the static, he reached Hankow. Although they feared Japanese patrols, the group trudged on. "We were draped in blankets that made us look like a procession of sorry ghosts of some long vanished Indian tribe," Norman Alley remembered. Then, about three miles from Ho Hsien, the column ran into armed soldiers, strung out across the pathway. The soldiers were only Chinese and by daybreak the procession was inside Ho Hsien. Then, high overhead, Japanese planes appeared.

Early that morning, December 13, 1937, Admiral Yarnell received word from Hankow that Atcheson had been on the phone. "MESSAGE RECEIVED . . . ," Yarnell cabled to the White House. "PANAY BOMBED AT MILEAGE 221 ABOVE WOOSUNG, 54 SURVIVORS, MANY BADLY WOUNDED NOW ASHORE. . . . NAMES OF PERSONNEL LOST NOT KNOWN. ATCHESON SAFE. CAPTAIN HAS BROKEN LEG. FURTHER INFORMATION WILL BE FORWARDED WHEN RECEIVED."

Yarnell also arranged for three gunboats, the USS *Oahu*, the HMS *Bee*, and the HMS *Ladybird*, to steam up the Yangtze. The boats reached the men, just off Ho Hsien, and the Japanese airplanes backed off. The *Panay* crisis had come to an end.

■ ■ ■

At the great bend of Whangpoo River, the bend that formed the harbor at Shanghai, the USS *Augusta* on December 17, 1937, stood waiting to welcome the *Panay* survivors. "I was on the bridge . . . ," wrote Hallett Abend, the stringer with *The New York Times*, in a piece that made front-page news. "A strange hush had come over [the] busy waterfront, and the steamer and launch traffic of the great river was temporarily suspended. All eyes were focused down the Whangpoo, and a hushed expectancy seemed to hold the busy river and the great war-ruined city. The sunset paled and dulled. The light began to fade and cameramen muttered despairing curses. . . . [But when] the *Oahu* was first sighted a curious murmur of suppressed excitement was felt the whole length of the 10,000 feet cruiser, whose decks were crowded with officers, sailors, marines, and a few civilians. . . . [T]hose aboard the flagship stood . . . in silence when they saw the survivors on the *Oahu* decks, whose faces in most cases were drawn and lined, many suffering obviously from shell-shock; others had their hands in slings, while others wore conspicuous bandages. A few hands were raised in salutes and greetings, and a few almost hushed salutations were exchanged across the narrowing waters as the ships drew together. . . . A hastily improvised gangway, of unplaned and unpainted lumber, was shoved from the *Augusta*'s deck onto the *Oahu*'s top deck. . . . Dusk deepened into darkness during the silent period of waiting. Then the *Augusta*'s floodlights illuminated . . . the gangway. . . . The first survivors to come aboard . . . were George Atcheson, Jr., . . . supporting J. Hall Paxton. . . . Mr. Paxton was wounded in the shoulder and injured in a knee; he was limping badly. . . . Next came nearly half a hundred members of the *Panay* crew. . . . The more seriously wounded were later taken ashore in Navy launches. . . . By this time a full moon . . . made a broad path of silver across the sluggish, muddy Whangpoo."

The men on the gangway were carrying three coffins, one of Sandro Sandri, an Italian journalist, and the other draped with an American flag. Storekeeper First Class Charles L. Ensminger had died at Ho Hsien.

Then, as the last of the survivors hobbled on the gangplank, they all heard a roar. Directly overhead and no more than 30 feet high, a flight of Japanese naval aircraft was diving at full throttle. Japanese authorities later described the flight as a "salute."

■　■　■

"Untrue" and "fantastic": with these words, Henry L. Stimson, the former secretary of state, began a letter to *The New York Times*, published on December 22, 1937, just after the *Panay* crisis. The words applied, argued Stimson, to the notion that the Pacific Ocean alone would protect America from Japan. That notion had lain at the heart of a resolution, just introduced into Congress by Representative Louis Ludlow, an isolationist from Indiana. The Ludlow Resolution had called for a national referendum on whether America should go to war. Stimson—by this time leading a nationwide movement for boycotting Japanese goods—denounced the Ludlow Resolution as "disruptive of our national unity." America, Stimson insisted, should leave the determination of war or peace to the Congress—and to the president.

But what *would* the president determine? In a cabinet meeting just after the *Panay* attack, Harold Ickes, secretary of the interior and an ally of Stimson, demanded an immediate trade boycott. Roosevelt, however, was cautious. "There is no such thing," he admonished Ickes, "as using economic sanctions without declaring war." Yet F. D. R. had *not* said he would *not* use sanctions.

The president was keeping his options open. He also was waiting to see the films of the *Panay* attack.

■ ■ ■

Because of a storm in the mid-Pacific and gale conditions off the coast of California, said news reports two days after Christmas 1937, Pan American Airways was postponing for twenty-four hours its *China Clipper* flight from Honolulu to Alameda. One of the passengers on the flight was Norman Alley. He was carrying his footage of the *Panay* attack. On December 28, at last, Alley stepped out through the doorway of the *China Clipper* at the Alameda seaport, and descended the ramp. With one hand he held the railing; with the other he gripped a small zippered bag, containing his film, insured for $350,000. Armed guards from the insurance company followed him down the steps of the seaplane. Although haggard, he almost immediately boarded a flight toward the east. Bad weather forced a landing at Cheyenne. But the following morning he was able to take off for Newark. Late in the afternoon of December 29, 1937, Norman Alley reached New Jersey.

Speaking to reporters, he said he was sure that the Japanese had attacked the *Panay* deliberately. At one point, however, he feared, viewers might be skeptical. Nowhere in the newsreel would they see the two Japanese launches machine-gunning the nearly sunken *Panay*. Alley explained. When the launches appeared, he had been crouching in the reeds, trying to keep his camera out of sight. Only after the launches left had he dared take more pictures—but the newsreel would show the upper part of the port side of the *Panay*, riddled with bullet holes. Reporters raced to file the story.

By 8:30 A.M., December 30, 1937, even before the *Panay* newsreel reached the projectionist, a crowd had started to gather in front of New York's *Rialto Theater*. The doors finally opened. So many customers jammed their way inside that many of them had to stand. The theater went dark. Then the screen lights came on, the first of the footage appearing before the audience: the Yangtze River;

Commander Hughes, immaculate in his dress whites; shots of the cloudless sky; the decks of the *Panay*; the gunboat's ensign, high overhead; the American flags painted across the awnings.

Then *it* happened. High above the mast, the black cross of an airplane in silhouette was zooming across the screen. The *Panay*'s mast seemed to be turning in a circle. The airplane, followed by another, and yet another, was diving, and in a moment they all were diving, swooping, bombing; sometimes the airplanes zipped by so close to the lens of the camera that viewers in the *Rialto Theater* could see the helmets and goggles of the pilots. The *Panay*'s crewmen were trying to defend the gunboat with machine guns so old they looked straight out of World War I, which they were. Viewers then saw the riverside, the forest of reeds, the mud banks, and, finally, the top strip of the side of the *Panay*, pockmarked with bullet holes. They also saw a close-up of Commander Hughes, his leg shattered, his mouth making a smile despite the agony of his pain.

In another New York movie house, the *Trans-Lux* on Broadway, when the newsreel showed the coffin of Charles L. Ensminger being hoisted aboard the *Augusta*, a man in the audience rose from his seat and commanded, "Everybody stand up!"

Everybody stood up.

■ ■ ■

In time the Japanese government did apologize for the *Panay* incident and in time it did pay an indemnity. Two incidents, however, struck President Roosevelt as ominous.

On Christmas Day, 1937, the Italian premier, Benito Mussolini, gave America a present of sorts. Mussolini already had joined with Japan and Germany in the Anti-Comintern Pact—and had taunted the United States for the loss of the *Panay*. On Christmas, his Fascist government announced that shortly an Italian military delegation would depart on a visit of goodwill and friendship to Japan.

On December 23, 1937, Roosevelt met in the Oval Office with Secretary of the Treasury Morgenthau, Secretary of State Hull, Chief of Naval Operations Admiral William D. Leahy, and Captain Royal E. Ingersoll, head then of the navy's planning division. After meeting again that night in Morgenthau's house, at 2201 R Street off Massachusetts Avenue, Ingersoll set off by train for New York. On Christmas night he sailed on the *Normandy*, reaching Southampton on the last day of 1937. After a day of rest he opened talks with the British.

Ingersoll's instructions were to keep the trip as quiet as possible— for he was to arrange "parallel action in the Far East." If Britain and America were to go to war with Japan, *then* the navies of the two countries would plan to shut down Japan's trade abroad.

By the end of 1937, Roosevelt was considering exactly what, in his response to Harold Ickes, he had implied he would not consider: an economic blockade of Japan.

PART II

·

1938

6

THE RAPE OF NANKING

By the start of 1938, the life of Franklin D. Roosevelt, at least when he was in residence at the White House, had turned into a series of established routines. He would awaken every day at about eight in the morning; he would have his cloak thrown over his shoulders; he would eat breakfast in bed, eggs, toast, juice, and coffee, from a tray placed over his lap; he would skim the papers, the *Washington Post*, the *Baltimore Sun*, the *Chicago Tribune*, the *Herald Tribune*, *The New York Times*, early editions of the last three papers flown in just for his perusal; then he would be ready for talk.

People would always be present: some days Edwin M. "Pa" Watson or Marvin McIntyre, his close aides; or Ross T. McIntire, the presidential physician; or Henry Morgenthau, Jr., the secretary of the treasury, fussing about the misdeeds of one or another of his cabinet colleagues; sometimes one or more of those cabinet members themselves; some mornings Eleanor Roosevelt, pleading for this cause or that; or just Missy LeHand or Grace Tully, White House secretaries whose conversation Roosevelt invariably found more relaxing than that of Eleanor. Then, with the aid of Arthur Prettyman, his valet, he would rise and dress, a considerable task. At ten or ten-thirty, the president would sidle himself into his wheelchair (designed like a kitchen chair, F. D. R.'s wheelchair had no arms). Prettyman would steer him along the corridor, down the elevator, past the row of the secretaries' desks, and, finally, into the Oval Office.

The office was unmistakably Roosevelt's. Nautical prints hung all over the walls, and the desk, originally President Hoover's, was a clutter of miniature flags, cigarette holders, ashtrays and matchbooks, paperweights, pens in penholders and pens strewn around the blotter, and file folders brimming with letters and notes and cables, a mound of paper that managed to spill across most of the rest of the rubble on the desk. Poking up from the litter, by the right-hand corner of the desk, was a large note card, typed each morning by "Pa" Watson and inserted in a leather frame; the card divided the president's day into appointments.

At noontime, aides would bring in a hot lunch, served on a tray. At about 5:30 each afternoon, Prettyman, the valet, would wheel the president back to the upper story. There, in the study, and dominating the conversation as always, Roosevelt would measure out cocktails for his secretaries or a few favored guests. After dinner he usually would write a letter or two and then go to bed early.

To outward appearances, then, Roosevelt's world was that of a country squire of the nineteenth century, old-fashioned, homey, cozy, predictable. The appearance belied the reality. Roosevelt conformed to no pattern, or at least to no one else's. Sometimes, as one of his biographers has written, "he hurried through appointments on crucial matters and dawdled during lesser ones. . . . He took many phone calls . . . , refused others, saw inconsequential and even dull people and ignored others of apparently greater political or intellectual weight. . . . Yet if Roosevelt's working habits lacked system and plan, they bespoke a habit of mind, a style of intellect . . . that could be summed up in one word, 'accessibility.' " In 1938, Roosevelt was reaching out for ideas, selling his own and doing so perhaps as never before. But salesman Roosevelt's toughest customer was the Congress, suspicious as always of presidents in general and of F. D. R. in particular. That is why, on the last day of January 1938, he summoned the Senate's Military Affairs Committee to the Oval Office.

■　■　■

The "munitions boom which helped to make the last New Year prosperous has become a full war boom and the [Japanese] nation, exalted by a succession of victories and happy with prosperity, is preparing for the holidays in a spirit of hectic exuberance." So wrote Hugh Byas, a Scot, a Japanese-speaking journalist, and a reporter for both *The New York Times* and the *Times* of London. Byas filed the story from Tokyo, on New Year's Day, 1938.

Trying to understand Japan to Byas was like feeling organs through a membrane: He could often tell that something was there but usually he failed to tell quite what. From the time of his arrival in Japan, back in the 1920s, officialdom had kept him in tight control. Byas to be sure had an office. Adjacent to his flat in the Imperial Hotel, the office had "three tall windows that rattled like the devil." In winter, Byas wrote, those windows were "pasted up to keep the wind out. From them you could see half Tokyo and, on the horizon, a long saw-toothed ridge of mountains." Tokyo itself was a "great noisy city with eight- and ten-story buildings that look[ed] as if they had been imported from Seattle."

Byas must have spent a lot of time looking out at those buildings; his sources were censored. Police agents followed him everywhere, he believed, even when he and his wife ventured out from the swarming Shinjuku station and took a train out to the suburbs and the villages with their little inns beyond. Fearing what could happen if they talked with any openness to a Western reporter, Japanese passengers on the trains, and then the vendors and the hotel keepers, showed masks of politeness and little else. Back in the office, Byas had a Japanese assistant, a man he identified as "Ofusa-san." Ofusa-san was a hard worker, every morning combing through the papers for items that Byas could report.

Byas did what he could. He could peer from his office windows and translate posters outside, banners that proclaimed this victory or that of Japanese forces in China. He could walk in the streets below and observe the tractor-drawn artillery, the soldiers taking bayonet practice in the parks, the delegations parading with flags and bugles as they escorted new draftees to their barracks. He could go downstairs in the hotel—through a lobby usually packed with tourists with their cameras and Japanese businessmen in their Western suits—and sit at the bar with his fellow journalists, comparing notes.

On the morning of January 11, 1938, Byas and his colleagues realized that something big was going on. They had received invitations to a press conference, inside the walls of the Imperial Palace itself.

Within those walls, massive and mortarless, a hodgepodge of ponds, gardens, and stands of miniature trees gave way, suddenly, to the Outer Palace. Passing the sentries, Byas and his colleagues walked down a long hallway and entered the audience hall. There they sat, and waited. At last Emperor Hirohito entered the chamber, followed by Premier Prince Konoye Fumimaro and the rest of the top level of the Japanese government. They, too, sat. The scene before him, Byas reported, was "singularly characteristic of present-day Japan, with its mixture of ancient and modern. In the hall, decorated with gold screens and the famous wall painting called 'The Thousand Sparrows', the Emperor in khaki and his generals, admirals, and ministers in uniforms or frock coats sat stiffly before tables draped with priceless brocades. The few speeches were of extreme formality and the proceedings . . . a solemn repetition and ratification in irrevocable form of measures already agreed upon."

As they left the Outer Palace, Byas and his fellow reporters conferred. Trading translations of what they had heard, the reporters sensed that the Japanese government had been using a critical word, a word sanctioned by the presence of the emperor. The word was "annihilation." Japan intended to annihilate the government of Chiang Kai-shek.

■   ■   ■

On January 9, 1938, Tillman Durdin, special correspondent for *The New York Times*, filed a full-page article. His piece, confirming Yarnell's fears, bore the dateline Nanking.

To understand what had happened at Nanking, Durdin wrote, "it is necessary to note that the city lies in a bend of the Yangtze at a point where the river turns from a northward course and flows east. It can easily be seen that a defending force occupying only the area within the city walls, and the immediate suburbs, could be surrounded on three sides." This was precisely what happened.

Early in December 1937, the Japanese crashed in upon Nanking from three sides, forcing the Chinese government to flee and to leave the city defenseless.

As soon as the government left, on December 8, 1937, the terror began; Nanking, Durdin wrote, took on an "appearance of awesome frightfulness." The Japanese scaled the walls—and the Chinese troops panicked. The doors of the city were locked but some of the soldiers thought they knew a way out; off Chungshan Avenue, the main thoroughfare, lay a tunnel, some seventy feet long and leading under the Hsia Kuan Gate, and from there out to the riverbank. A few dozen soldiers, then hundreds more, then thousands, crammed themselves into the mouth of the tunnel. And behind them, more Chinese soldiers still were begging passersby for civilian clothing, or just stripping themselves to their underwear (despite the December cold), piling the pavements with guns, grenades, swords, knapsacks, helmets, coats, and shoes, and then joining the human tide almost three miles long that was pushing its way forward toward the aperture of the tunnel that was supposed to lead under the Hsia Kuan Gate and out to safety.

But the tide stopped moving. The gate of the tunnel was locked; inside the tunnel thousands of Chinese had crushed themselves to death. In the procession behind the tunnel, then, an ammunition truck caught fire and exploded; rickshaws, automobiles, and carts went up in flames and the momentum of the mob pushed hundreds into the roaring blaze. At just that moment, according to a Western eyewitness, "Japanese planes, sweeping low, mowed down refugees and soldiers alike with wide-open machine guns. For the weak and the aged there was no escape." The Reverend John Magee, an Episcopal medical missionary, climbed over what he described as "mountains" of the dead. Along Chungshan Avenue, he found "charred bodies . . . everywhere, in places six and eight deep."

By the following day—Tuesday, December 14, 1937, two days after the *Panay* assault—the Japanese control of Nanking was complete. What happened next, Tillman Durdin reported to *The New York Times*, resembled the "vandalism in the Dark Ages or the brutalities of medieval Asiatic conquerors." Dr. Magee remembered: "I saw the Japanese at their approach. . . . Many [Chinese]

were shot in seeming sporting mood by the Japanese, who laughed
at the terror plainly visible on faces of coolies, merchants, and
students. . . . Women were hunted down in all Chinese homes. If
resistance was offered against rape, the bayonet was theirs. Even
60-year-old women and 11-year-old girls were not immune. They
were thrown to the ground and raped openly in the December
sunlight. Many were horribly mutilated." When one American protested, two Japanese privates held him and a Japanese officer
slapped him on the face.

Old men, Durdin reported, "were to be seen face downward on
the pavements, . . . shot in the back at the whim of some Japanese
soldier." Japanese soldiers, according to reports, would tie up Chinese prisoners in bundles of forty or fifty, load them into the backs
of trucks, and drive them to the city walls, there to machine-gun
them to death. Japanese soldiers would enter houses, Chinese or
foreign, and loot. Some of the foreign houses bore American flags.
No matter. The Japanese would tear the flags down and trample
them into the dirt. Bloated "bodies," a foreigner wrote, "lay everywhere. Dogs wandered from carcass to carcass. The stench was
terrific."

On December 19, 1937, Japanese soldiers marched up to several
missionary establishments in Nanking and ripped down the foreign
flags. At the American School in particular, they trampled the Stars
and Stripes into the ground and told the Chinese caretaker that if
he tried to fly it again, they would kill him.

December 21, 1937: "This is the shortest day of the year," a
Western doctor wrote, "but still it contains 24 hours of hell on
earth. Yesterday a 17-year-old came to the hospital in the morning
with her newborn baby. She had been raped by a Japanese soldier
the night before." A few days later the girl developed a case of
venereal disease; doctors gave her baby away to another girl who,
because Japanese soldiers had bayoneted her in the abdomen, had
lost her own child.

And Christmas Day: From outside his hospital office, the doctor
heard a knocking. He turned the door latch. On the stoop outside,
he related, "two coolies were supporting the blackened body of a
man whose eyes, ears, and nose were burned beyond recognition.

He had been bound with 40 or 50 others in a compact bundle; tins of gasoline had been emptied over them until their clothing was saturated. Then torches [had been] applied. He had escaped death only by being on the outer edge. . . . That afternoon men were brought to the . . . hospital for what assistance we could give them; . . . they had been used for bayonet practice. They had been tied in pairs, back to back, and forced to wait as calmly as possible while instructors showed recruits just where to jab their points for the most effective strike. Many such 'guinea pigs' were left for dead and brought to the . . . hospital later. Most of them died." Magee also saw mothers being "raped while their children screamed in terror at their sides. [He] saw instances where three- and four-year-olds were bayoneted. Families . . . were boarded up in their homes and burned alive."

On January 3, 1938, Western doctors in Nanking lodged a complaint with Japanese authorities: "A woman who was taken with five others from Number 6 Chien Ying Hsien ostensibly for Japanese officers . . . came to the university hospital," the complaint stated. "She [asserted] that they were taken by Japanese soldiers to a house in the west portion of the city which she thought must be a Japanese military hospital. The women washed clothes during the day and were raped throughout the night. The older ones were raped from ten to 20 times; the younger and good-looking ones as many as 40 times a night. On 2 January, two [Japanese] soldiers took our patient with them to a deserted school house and struck her ten times with a bayonet knife—four times in the back of the neck, severing the muscles of the vertebral column, once on the wrist, once in the face, and four times in the back."

On January 10, 1938, the doctors filed another complaint: "Girls as young as 11 and women as old as 53 have been raped on university property. . . . In other groups of refugees are women of 72 and 76 years who were raped mercilessly. In the seminary compound, 17 soldiers raped one woman successively in broad daylight. In fact, about one third of these cases are in the daytime."

By the middle of February 1938, more than "10,000 unarmed persons have been killed in cold blood," calculated an American missionary-professor at Nanking University. "Practically every building in the city, including the American [and] British . . . embassies, has been robbed repeatedly by [Japanese] soldiers. There is not an [unmolested] store in Nanking, save [a] rice shop and a military store. Most of the shops, after free-for-all pilfering, were systematically stripped by gangs of Japanese soldiers working with trucks, often under the observed direction of officers, and then burned deliberately. Most of the refugees were robbed of . . . their scanty clothing, and bedding and food. . . . You can imagine the outlook for work and life in this city with shops and tools gone, everything else plundered, no banks or communications, the people facing starvation."

· · ·

These were the stories coming out of China. They were so numerous and, in some cases, supported by corroborating photographic evidence, that we must assume the truthfulness of most of them. On another point, however, evidence most likely was rigged. In all probability the *Tanaka Memorial* was forged.

Attributed to Baron Tanaka Giichi, Japan's foreign minister in 1927, this *Tanaka Memorial*, allegedly sent to the emperor of Japan, called for Japan to conquer Manchukuo today, and tomorrow the world. The section of the *Memorial* most frequently quoted read:

> In the future if we want to control China, we must first crush the United States, just as in the past we had to fight in the Russo-Japanese War. But in order to conquer China, we must first conquer Manchuria and Mongolia. In order to conquer the world we must first conquer China. If we succeed in conquering China, the rest of the Asiatic countries and the South Sea countries will fear us and will surrender to us. Then the world will realize that Eastern Asia is ours and will not dare to violate our rights. This is the plan left to us by the Emperor Meiji, the success of which is essential to our national existence.

But was the *Tanaka Memorial* real? Like the Protocols of the Elders of Zion, it cropped up in a host of "scholarly" tomes. One such book was *Machiavelli of Japan: Tanaka Memorial Proven Genuine*; another was *Japan's Dream of World Empire: The Tanaka Memo-*

rial. Yet the proof? "There is no known original document in the Japanese language," a recent study concludes, "the version that appeared in Japan having been translated from the Chinese."

Indeed, the *Tanaka Memorial* surfaced for the first time in 1929—in Peking and in Chinese; later that same year, it appeared in a Nanking monthly review; and after Japan's invasion of Manchuria, the text spread worldwide, coming out in French, Russian, and English. In America, pamphlets bearing the words of the "authentic" document found their way into schools and colleges, chambers of commerce, and the offices of newspaper editors from one side of the country to the other.

But on three occasions at least—in the aftermath of the Manchurian invasion; during the Tokyo War Crimes Trial that followed the war; and again in the early 1960s—Japanese officials denied that the *Memorial* was authentic. They had, of course, an interest, in denying its authenticity. No one, however, has ever produced the original version of the *Tanaka Memorial*. The document seems to have been a Chinese fabrication.

■ ■ ■

But China's war against Japan was all-out, a war without mercy. In north China especially, the Communist guerrillas—ragged, surviving on gruel and turnips, and trekking barefoot over the ice in remote mountain passes—were perfecting the art of the ambush. A Japanese column would ensconce itself in a village along the Yellow River and build fires for the evening rice—only to spot guerrillas swarming down from the hillsides, wielding swords, knives, clubs, and bare knuckles, and then, before Japanese aircraft could arrive, falling back toward invisible mountain retreats.

Falling back was China's strategy: The farther back the Chinese fell, the longer the Japanese had to stretch their lines of supply. Even though they seemed to be victors, the Japanese were starting to look like losers.

■ ■ ■

Desperate to cut off supplies into China, the Japanese attacked the rail line at Nanking, just inside the border from French Indochina;

the bombing attack destroyed a French Catholic mission. A week later, the Japanese opened an attack on Hainan, the island just south of China that stood like a boulder in front of the Haiphong harbor. The French lodged a protest, reminding Tokyo that back at the start of the war in China, Japan had promised to keep its hands off Hainan. Reminding France in turn that various parties were using the Gulf of Tonkin to route goods into China, Japan rejected the protest. Then, on January 21, 1938, Holland announced that it was increasing its forces in the Indies: The number of Japanese fishing boats around Java and Sumatra had risen sharply and aboard those boats, Dutch intelligence had learned, Japanese "fishermen" were operating geodetic equipment and powerful radio sets.

In China itself, Japanese relations with Westerners were worse than ever. In Shanghai, Japanese officials had closed the lower Yangtze to foreign shipping and, in an effort to wreck Western markets, had started to bring their own goods into the city duty-free. In Wuhu, upriver from Nanking, Japanese soldiers entered an American Methodist mission school, found a safe in the main building, and blasted it open. Then, atop a junk owned by the mission, they spied an American flag. They tore it down, hurling it into the river. A Japanese soldier brandished his sword at an American woman; she was trying to protect the mission's elderly Chinese gateman. In Nanking the same day, January 27, 1938, a Japanese soldier slapped an official of the U.S. Department of State, John M. Allison. Allison had been investigating a charge of rape in an American-owned building.

In Tokyo, U.S. Ambassador Joseph C. Grew formally protested the incident and on January 30, 1938, the Japanese government apologized. A cycle, nonetheless, had started: Japanese forces would abuse Americans; the American embassy in Tokyo would protest; Japanese forces would abuse Americans (and other Westerners) again.

■ ■ ■

The Japanese, Nelson T. Johnson cabled President Roosevelt from Hankow, were engaged in a concerted effort to eliminate "all [American] influence among the Chinese." Johnson was the U.S. Ambassador to China. He was as plump as a pillow, his hair, lashes, and brows were pale gold, and his face was perpetually pink. Tilted back in a rickshaw, Johnson, commented one American in Hankow, looked more like a tire salesman than an ambassador. The looks were deceiving: Fluent in Chinese and capable of quoting Confucian classics by the yard (Evans Carlson's expression), Johnson had served in China for nearly thirty years. His staff respected him and so did the Chinese, for Johnson was willing and able to lobby Washington on behalf of China. Hence Johnson's cable: The ambassador was trying to edge the United States out of its neutrality and into action against Japan.

Another official in China was also trying to instigate action. In a cable dated January 14, 1938, and sent to Admiral Leahy, the chief of naval operations, Admiral Yarnell aboard the *Augusta* stated:

> The policy of Japan was announced unofficially to a U.S. Naval Attache by a responsible official to be (a) to drive all whites out of China; (b) to destroy all Chinese industrialism; and (c) to obtain control of the customs . . . and other financial organs of the Chinese government. . . . Japan has many . . . who realize the dangers of the present policy . . . but [who] are powerless to make their influence felt.

But Yarnell had a recommendation. With "our allies," he cabled, referring to Britain, France, and Holland, "we could control roughly 90 percent of the world's resources of iron, coal, and oil, as well as a major portion of other raw materials." Japan, Yarnell concluded, "can be strangled to death."

"Yarnell makes a lot of sense," said President Roosevelt, after Admiral Leahy had brought the cable to the Oval Office. "[What he says] goes along with that word 'quarantine' I used in the Chicago speech."

■ ■ ■

"Now . . . a significant piece of hitherto untold history can be written." Thus began Drew Pearson's syndicated column, "Washington Daily Merry-Go-Round" on the morning of November 26, 1938.

"Admiral Leahy [at the time of the *Panay* crisis] prepared a plan for a joint blockade of Japan by American and British forces. . . . [The nub] of the plan was the placing of British ships at Singapore, plus U.S. ships at Panama, plus the cooperation of Russia at Vladivostok. By stationing ships at these three focal points it [would have been] possible to isolate Japan completely. 'No war plan was ever simpler,' Admiral Leahy [William Leahy, chief of naval operations] reported to the president. 'We place our fleet at Panama and Hawaii. The British place 24 ships at Singapore. The Russians have 50 submarines at Vladivostok. They send them down to harass Japanese lines of communication between Shanghai and Nagasaki. The Japanese cannot live without supplies. . . . Within three months . . . Japan will be broken economically. We tell the Japanese we are going to blockade you until you get out of China.'"

Nothing came directly of Leahy's proposal: Russia feared an involvement; Britain was unwilling to spare the ships; and Roosevelt thought a blockade premature.

In the Washington bureaucracy, however, no fight was ever over and Leahy was a classic Washington bureaucrat: He never gave up on a fight. Leahy may have looked "more like a ship chaplain than the commander of the U.S. fleet"—a newspaper described him as "small of stature, quiet, polite, informal, and friendly"—but he was a man the navy needed.

Leahy knew how to keep his wife and himself prominent in the society pages of the *Washington Post*. He knew how to use scare tactics—early in 1938, Leahy leaked word of a "mystery fleet," not American, and by implication, therefore, Japanese, lurking off the coast of the Philippines. He knew how to play tough with Congress. When David I. Walsh, a U.S. senator from Massachusetts, an isolationist, and chairman of the Senate's Naval Affairs Committee, demanded to know why Roosevelt had sent Captain Royal C. Ingersoll to London early in the year, Leahy refused to answer. He knew how to win the right friends on Capitol Hill: Leahy forged a special alliance with Representative Carl Vinson from Milledgeville, Georgia, the soft-spoken, tobacco-chewing chairman, or perhaps monarch, of the House Naval Affairs Committee; Vinson was all in favor of big spending for the navy. Leahy knew how to do favors for shipbuilding firms in Newport News and Savannah—he knew that contacts made for political backing. And he knew how to frame legislation: Working with Vinson and Senator Joseph Tydings from Maryland, Leahy helped draft the Vinson–Tydings bill, a measure designed to increase navy spending by 20 percent.

The bill passed—and produced a shock in Tokyo. "Our view," a Japanese navy spokesman told reporters on March 24, 1938, referring to what by then was the Vinson–Tydings Act, "is that if Americans are not thinking of naval operations against Japan, they would not need a fleet of that size."

Had the spokesman known of changes in War Plan ORANGE, he might have expressed even greater alarm. Dating back to the early twentieth century, ORANGE had provided the guidelines for the navy's Pacific strategy, and its emphasis had been on defensive war. Under Leahy, however, the navy was reviewing ORANGE: Now the stress was on an offensive war. A plan, of course, was just a plan. Still, the language of the new War Plan ORANGE was strong. The 1938 version of ORANGE called for broad "military and economic pressure"—a blockade—to be imposed in the event of war and increased in severity until the United States had attained its "national objective," the defeat of Japan.

CHAPTER
7

THE HSÜCHOW
HOLOCAUST

U nder a cloudless sky at Munich, midway through March 1938, a large German passenger airplane circled the airfield, descended, and taxied to a stop. As a huge crowd waited by the terminal, workers pushed a ramp to the fuselage and then opened the aircraft's door. The onlookers burst into cheers. Standing at the top of the ramp and raising his arm in salute was the führer, Adolf Hitler.

The moment was critical in Hitler's career. Only the month before, he had staged a major coup, dismissing Generals Blumberg and Fritsch, who had tried to apply brakes to his aggressiveness, proclaiming that Germany was ready for a new role in world affairs, and announcing that Nazi Germany forthwith would officially recognize Manchukuo. The führer had been angling for an alliance with Japan.

Hitler then turned his attention to the annexation of Austria: On March 11, 1938, German forces trooped into Vienna, in what turned out to be a bloodless conquest; and now, just before noon on March 14, 1938, Hitler's airplane touched down at the airfield by Munich. After striding down the ramp, he rode in triumph into the city, where he had lunch. Then he left by motorcade for Austria.

Soon after dark, he reached Linz, just across the border. Under the light of torches in the market square, a "crowd of 100,000 . . .

engulfed the caravan in a display of joyous hysteria. . . . When the *Führer* appeared on the balcony of the city hall . . . the people were in a frenzy. . . . Tears ran down Hitler's cheeks." That night, staying in a suite in the Weinzinger Hotel, Hitler made a fateful decision. Even as he crossed the border, he seemed to have had in mind a rather loose union between Germany and Austria, such as had once existed between Austria and Hungary. With the enthusiasm of the night, however, he was changing his mind. "It is fate, Linge," Hitler confided in his valet. "I am destined to be the führer who will bring all Germans into the Greater German Reich."

The next day, Hitler reached Vienna; as he did so, young Nazi toughs in the city hurled bricks and stones through the windows of shops owned by Jews. *Anschluss*, Germany's annexation of Austria, was complete.

■ ■ ■

"Having forced the hand of little Austria, [Germany] will move in due course against Czechoslovakia and perhaps Romania and some other countries." Just after the *Anschluss*, Harold Ickes wrote these words in his diary. Ickes was known in Washington as the "old curmudgeon," because he had a bulldog jaw, was churlish in manner, and, at a minimum, was opinionated. He was as hardline in foreign affairs as he was liberal in domestic affairs. And in the realm of foreign affairs, Ickes saw only trouble for America. If Germany was annexing and Japan was annexing, he wondered, how much more could they annex if they did so in tandem?

■ ■ ■

On the day of Hitler's entry into Vienna, W. H. Auden and Christopher Isherwood, the two English gentlemen of letters, took tea with Madame Chiang Kai-shek. They had gone out to China to write a travel book. Upon their arrival in Wuhan—Wuhan referred to the triad of Yangtze River cities, Hanyang, Wuchang, and Hankow, the capital—however, they had met W. H. Donald. Donald was a red-haired, bulbous-nosed Australian and an adviser to Chiang Kai-shek; and Donald arranged to have Auden and Isherwood meet Madame. The idea of a travel book gave way to reportage.

"We crossed the river into Wuch'ang in the lace-curtained cabin of a private government launch," Isherwood wrote. "The guards all sprang to attention and saluted as we stepped on board; Donald leading the way, looking very grand and ministerial in his fur coat with its black astrakhan collar. . . . The Generalissimo and Madame [were] living . . . in the old provincial army headquarters. Our car passed under a stone gateway, flanked by painted lions, circled a lawn beneath which a solid-looking dugout had been built, and stopped before the guarded doors of the villa. Donald took us straight upstairs to wait in a small sitting-room, furnished in sham walnut, like the interior of an English road-house. From the bare wall the photograph of Dr. Sun Yat-sen looked down, decorated with the crossed flags of the Republic and the *Kuomintang*. . . . A servant brought in the tea-things and, a few moments later, Madame herself appeared."

Auden and Isherwood were stunned. "Madame," Isherwood put it, "was . . . small, round-faced . . . , exquisitely dressed, vivacious rather than pretty, and possessed of an almost terrifying charm and poise. Obviously she knows just how to deal with any conceivable type of visitor. She can become at will the cultivated, westernized woman with a knowledge of literature and art; the technical expert, discussing aeroplane engines and machine-guns; the inspector of hospitals; the president of a mother's union; or the simple, affectionate, clinging Chinese wife. She could be terrible; she could be gracious; she could be ruthless."

Far north of Madame's temporary residence in Hankow, another Chinese, a middle-aged Communist named Mao Tse-tung, had brushed a slogan: "Make Foreign Things Serve China." Madame would have understood. She was about to make Auden and Isherwood serve China. Isherwood told how.

Folding her hands and "lowering her eyes to the table," he commented, "Madame now began to deliver what was evidently, to her, a familiar lecture. For centuries, she told us, the Chinese people had been ruled by a despotic governing class. Therefore, when China became a republic [in 1911], they had very little idea of how to govern themselves. The officials of the old imperial order had possessed a definite moral code . . . [but] this moral code had died with them. . . . And so the "New Life Movement" was inaugurated in a speech by the Generalissimo himself . . . in 1934." Themes of this New Life Movement were: no more corruption; no more filthy toilets; no more spitting in the streets. China, in short, was about to become Westernized.

What a seductive message! China, under attack from Japan, was about to become a part of the West. And the two English gentlemen of letters were to be the conveyors of that assurance. The English gentlemen had qualms about becoming propagandists. Then they became witnesses to war, and they put their qualms aside.

Back in Hankow that evening, as they neared their hotel, the air raid sirens began to scream. The police, Isherwood wrote, "began to clear the streets, hustling rick-sha boys into the cover of archways and doors. The abandoned rickshas were lined up, like kneeling camels, along the gutters." Joined by a few other Britishers, Auden and Isherwood climbed to the roof of an American bank near their hotel. Since the electricity was off, they had to grope their way up a staircase. But the moon was out, and once they were on the rooftop, they could see below them the Yangtze and Hankow. The sirens had sounded for the second time. In twenty minutes or so, Japanese bombers would be overhead.

A "pause," Isherwood noted. "Then, far off, the hollow, approaching roar of the bombers, boring their way invisibly through the dark. The dull, punching thud of bombs falling, near the airfield, out in the suburbs. The searchlights criss-crossed, plotting points . . . ; and suddenly there were six of them, flying close together and high up. . . . The searchlights followed them right across the sky; guns smashed out; tracer bullets bounced up towards them, falling hopelessly short, like slow-motion rockets. . . . If you looked closely you could see the dull red shrapnel-bursts and red sparks, as the Japanese planes spat back. Over by the aerodrome a great crimson blossom of fire burst from the burning hangars. In ten minutes it was over, and they had gone. . . . We heard later that six Chinese planes had been destroyed before they had time to take to the air."

● ● ●

The Japanese controlled the air, but not necessarily the ground. Their forces, Isherwood and Auden heard, were "thrusting forward like the spokes of an irregularly shaped fan. To the northwest the fan covered Nanking; to the west it approached Wuhu . . . ; to the southwest it touched Hangchow. [But about] the country which lay between these points information was contradictory and vague. The [Japanese] would advance along a valley and retreat again. They would occupy a village or a railway station, and hold it like a fort in the midst of an area overrun with hostile guerrilla units. It was even said that with a knowledge of the lie of the land you could easily penetrate their lines, unchallenged, even to the very outskirts of Shanghai."

Already vulnerable, the Japanese in the spring of 1938 actually lost a battle. The place was called Tai-er-chwang, a junction on the rail line that ran southwest from Tientsin. The time was the morning of April 7, 1938.

Evans Carlson witnessed the battle; his report to Roosevelt reads almost like one from Vietnam: "The Chinese proceeded systematically to seize the villages around Tai-er-chwang. Heavy fighting occurred during these operations. Success attended the Chinese efforts, but apparently they did not effectively close the gaps between the villages, for it was through those gaps that the Japanese remnant made good their escape on the night of 6 April. On the nights of 4 and 5 April the Japanese used tear gas. . . . Tear gas containers were seen at Tai-er-chwang after the battle. Doctor Mac-Fadden, of the Presbyterian Hospital at Hsu-chow-fu, reported that soldiers suffering from gas were brought to his hospital. . . . The use of gas indicated to the Chinese that the Japanese situation was desperate, and the commander decided to attack on the night of the 6th. The Chinese assault on the night of the 6th was made almost exclusively with hand grenades and big swords. In this connection, it is interesting to note Chinese comments on the effectiveness of weapons. They rate machine guns as effective. But, say the Chinese, 'our' hand grenades are more effective than the Japanese machine guns, and 'our' big swords are the most effective of all." Japan's technological advantage over China had reached a point of diminishing returns; as Carlson observed.

"It was nearing nine o'clock," Carlson wrote then in his memoirs, "and a brilliant sunlight suffused the plain around Tai-er-chwang, bringing into sharp relief the greens and yellow of early spring. . . . Overhead three Japanese observation planes droned back and forth. . . . Along the railroad an armored train inched its way ahead, preceded by a pilot engine and a squad of soldiers who examined the roadbed for landmines, and flanked by infantry who proceeded on foot in single file. Columns of stretcher-bearers plodded across the fields bearing the wounded towards the dressing station at the rail head."

Everything seemed to be going in slow motion. Then, suddenly, from the rice paddies that flanked the railroad, the guerrillas arose en masse, opening fire. The train stopped and Japanese soldiers, at least those who had survived the gunshots, scrambled in behind the wheels. The Japanese soon brought in armored units and airplanes, the Chinese slipped in more and more guerrillas, and the battle lasted eight days. "The nearer I came to town," wrote a Japanese correspondent for *Asahi Shimbun*, the Tokyo daily, "the more bodies I saw lying about, like dots on a green carpet." The Grand Canal, which lay nearby, was "red with blood"—Japanese blood.

In time the Chinese guerrillas did fall back, permitting the Japanese to take possession of Tai-er-chwang. But the Japanese had lost the fight. Their war machine no longer looked invincible.

■ ■ ■

Springtime had come to the Yangtze Valley and in Hankow, Christopher Isherwood wrote, the trees "are all in leaf, the gardens are full of blossom. The rickshas have folded back their hoods and the ricksha coolies run sweating, stripped to the waist. The troops have removed the padding from their uniforms or exchanged them for light cotton clothes. The civilians have begun to appear in white drill jackets and shorts." The sky by day was a silken blue and by night all a-twinkle with stars. Hankow had taken on an idyllic appearence—but the war still raged. The Chiangs were activating every possible source of appeal for help.

Early in April 1938, Robert McClure, a Canadian medical missionary who ran a clinic near Hankow, received a mysterious message: The following afternoon, he was to make himself available, waiting at such and such a street corner in Hankow. McClure "kept the appointment," his biographer wrote. He "had no sooner arrived at the designated corner than a green Chevrolet drove up, the back door swung open, and the driver gestured him to step inside. He was driven along what appeared to be a random route and was transferred to a truck. The random ramblings and sudden transfers continued for the better part of an hour, until he found himself being escorted inside the perimeter wall of a Chinese suburban house. Here he was greeted by a small, exquisitely dressed Chinese lady who spoke flawless English with a trace of an American accent." The lady was Madame Chiang Kai-shek.

McClure was middle-aged, red-haired, wiry, blunt to the point of rudeness; he had been born in China and had come back after medical school in Toronto, dedicated utterly to his life's calling, the saving of Chinese lives. Madame knew exactly how to handle him.

In the presence of the good Dr. McClure, she was all kindness and humanity, and brilliant besides, for she could rattle off statistics on per-capita rice requirements as well as McClure could. As she was doing so, the generalissimo entered the room. The three of them had dinner. Chiang Kai-shek was gentler than McClure had expected, "slight, bald, and almost shy. He was wearing his uniform, but without giving the impression of ramrod starchiness that appeared in newsreels. The Generalissimo preceded the meal with a simple grace. The food itself was unpretentious and was served in just sufficient quantity for . . . nourishment. The couple apologized for the cloak-and-dagger way in which McClure had been brought to see them, but explained that the Japanese had the idea that if the Generalissimo and his wife could be eliminated the war would be over." General Chiang Kai-shek and his wife, therefore, kept constantly on the move; as a rule they never slept twice in the same house.

After dinner, the three of them walked outside into the garden; they had heard the air raid alert. Far in the distance McClure could see the flashes of bombs. "They are one day late," said Madame. She and her husband had slept right over there, she said, just the night before.

In the weeks that followed, Madame spent more and more time with McClure; down in Cheng-chou, where he had his clinic, she turned up regularly. She would appear unannounced, "disguised as a working woman, or a Chinese grandmother, and have [Dr. McClure] take her on a whirlwind tour of orphanages or hospitals. Then she would vanish again, with a security man close in her wake. One day in Hankow, she insisted on being escorted . . . to an orphanage in a large Roman Catholic mission. She went just as 'a friend' of Dr. McClure. The Mother Superior, who thought the worst of all Protestant missionaries . . . miffed at Dr. McClure's having the effrontery to visit her orphanage accompanied by his loose woman."

Loose woman or not, Madame had got her hooks into McClure. Late in the spring of 1938, she summoned him to Hankow again. This time she made a proposition. She wanted McClure to go to England, Canada, and America, to lecture on behalf of the cause of China. McClure went.

■   ■   ■

Another North American also toured Hankow. This was a bespectacled, square-jawed, highly intelligent, if more than a bit ponderous, Wall Street lawyer. The lawyer had aspirations beyond Wall Street, so he was educating himself in matters of foreign policy: That was the reason for his visit to Hankow. He was John Foster Dulles.

Upon his return to New York, late in April 1938, Dulles spoke to the Lunch Club. Standing on the dais, he praised the Chinese Communists—this was Dulles!—as the "most effective fighting portion and the most patriotic" of the Chinese troops; and he expressed his conviction that the Japanese would never topple Chiang Kai-shek.

Henry L. Stimson was in the audience. Dulles's words impressed him: Perhaps, Stimson concluded, Japan could be beaten after all.

■   ■   ■

Right after hearing Dulles, Stimson and his wife, Mabel, took the afternoon train, the Congressional Limited, down to Washington. Their "primary purpose," Stimson wrote in his diary, was to see

Woodley, his estate, "in all the full richness of its spring beauty." But he had another purpose as well. He went to Washington to receive a briefing from Stanley Hornbeck.

Tall, big-faced, and balding, Hornbeck was smart and aggressive enough to win Stimson's respect. As a Ph.D. in political science from Wisconsin, then professor, author, and government expert on Far Eastern diplomacy, Hornbeck had served a twenty-year apprenticeship for his current position: State Department adviser on political affairs. Hornbeck was opinionated, forceful, and blunt; and his style has led scholars to see him as a renegade within the State Department, almost a gun-toting desperado out of the west, ready at a moment's notice to set his sights on Japan and pull the trigger. Actually, Hornbeck was a man of his times and his background. During his student years, he had absorbed—as had Stimson and Roosevelt—a nineteenth-century brand of internationalism, the conviction that if nations would only display goodwill, they would find they had interests in common. So even after the Manchurian crisis, Hornbeck had tried to treat Japan evenhandedly. But Japan, in Hornbeck's judgment, was refusing to display goodwill; therefore, he concluded, Japan and America were going to collide. And this was precisely what Hornbeck conveyed to Stimson.

Stimson had spent the first part of the morning photographing his tulips and dogwood blossoms, using color film, he noted, "for the first time." Then he had gone up to the porch to talk with Hornbeck. Hornbeck was as blunt as ever: The Japanese were predators, he stated, and the time was coming when America would have to stop them or "back down."

But what, Stimson queried, should America do to stop them?

Hornbeck ticked off his answers. Repeal the neutrality acts; renounce the 1911 United States–Japan trade treaty; slap embargoes on Japanese goods; place U.S. naval vessels along a lookout line far out in the Pacific, with warning stations in Alaska, Hawaii, and Samoa. Thus, he said, "we would show the Japanese government . . . that we mean business."

■ ■ ■

In Tokyo, one personage at least feared that America meant business: Premier Prince Konoye Fumimaro. Konoye was an aristocrat and, as a young man, he had been appropriately elegant, even foppish. But the premiership, a post he had held since early 1937, had aged him. He had grown haggard, for he had grown convinced— or so he wrote in his postwar memoirs—that the policy of annihilation in China was mistaken. Japan, he believed, was heading for disaster. Yet what could he do? As a civilian politician, Konoye had to face the fact that in the Japanese system of politics, the real power lay in the hands of the industrialists, the generals, and the admirals. The premier was at best a broker, his authority restricted largely to shuffling and reshuffling cabinets. So late in May 1938, Konoye did what he could. He shuffled the cabinet. He dismissed Foreign Minister Koki Hirota, a hard-liner with regard to China, and he brought in General Ugaki Kazushige, a moderate.

Believing the war in China to be futile, Ugaki bustled about, holding meetings, sending out cables, and hinting to his embassies in London and Washington that Japan was about to wear a new face. He even tried to lure Chiang Kai-shek into talks.

Ugaki's initiatives died aborning. His enemies in industry and the military engaged in a shuffle of their own: They took China policy out of his hands. So Ugaki was foreign minister with little over which to minister. He soon resigned.

■　■　■

Japanese tactics in China were always the same, noted a foreign reporter. Whenever "they were about to launch a concerted drive against a city, they unleashed their air force as an advance guard to break down the morale and order of the people and troops in the Chinese rear." Hsüchow was "no exception."

Lying just about straight north of Nanking, Hsüchow commanded a major rail junction and thus was the gateway through which Japanese columns in the north could link with their counterparts in the south. After the Japanese had recovered from Tai-er-chwang, therefore, they turned on Hsüchow.

From the end of May 1938 on, the air attacks on Hsüchow became increasingly fierce, and the flight from the city turned into a mighty migration, a huge swollen and swelling column of refugees, all heading inland, all heading westward, all heading away from the Japanese. A British journalist observed the columns: "Dainty Chinese girls in silken semi-modern dresses and slippers, older women hobbling along . . . on their bound feet with the aid of long poles on which they balanced; occasional old men; rich wives of merchants in rickshas; peasant girls plodding stolidly; . . . whole families in heavy oxcarts with solid wooden wheels . . . ; babies in boxes on tiny wheels or strapped to the backs of tottering older children; . . . farmers lifting the handles of gigantic loaded wheelbarrows. . . . There were almost no motor vehicles, and the few were piled to the sky with women and goods. . . . An occasional horseman trotted by; a few officers and officials pedalled along on bicycles. But . . . most of the soldiers, like most of the refugees, simply walked. . . . Soldiers in every shade of khaki, from dust yellow to pale green and blue, peasants in everything under the sun, all were mingled in one endless procession."

The route of the refugees lay through Cheng-chou and there, before he set off on his lecture tour, Dr. Robert McClure did what he could to help. Later he remembered "thousands of refugees fleeing in panic; haunting memories of wide-eyed orphans waiting trustingly to do whatever the adult world decreed they should do; memories of typhus, gangrene, and death."

Yet the refugees were the lucky ones. On May 21, 1938, the Japanese entered Hsüchow.

As he stood on a hill of pomegranate trees, a Japanese soldier recalled in his diary, "the order to depart [for Hsüchow] was given. Soldiers got up from under willow trees, yawned and stretched themselves. Soldiers who had been in houses, on the [Li] mountain, or in the rye fields, gathered in straight lines, and taking up their guns, soon began to march. I watched them from my hill. Far to the right a unit was advancing through the . . . sea of rye fields along the foot of the mountain. To the left, too, marching soldiers stretched as far as the eye could see. Even down in the center of the rye fields they formed a long line. The advancing army gave me the impression of steadily increasing power."

From inside the city, a foreigner described the Japanese entry:

"Appropriation of houses begins, officers and soldiers alike breaking from one house into the next to choose a place of shelter to their taste. A certain sense of power seems to sweep over them, of power unopposed to break the bonds of civilized restraint."

With Hsüchow captured and raped—Hsüchow was almost a rerun of Nanking—the Japanese resumed their drive to the interior. Soon they were menacing Hankow.

■ ■ ■

They were also menacing Westerners; incidents were piling up.

Late in February 1938, a Japanese destroyer a mile off Gap Rock, part of Hong Kong, and thus within British territorial waters, seized *Asian*, a British-owned tramp steamer, and hauled it off to Port Mako in the Pescadores. Only after the British protested extensively did the Japanese let the steamer go.

Early in March 1938, Grace Brady, an American teacher at St. Mary's Hall Episcopal School—the school stood inside the Hongkew sector of Shanghai—crossed the line from the British zone. A Japanese sentry stopped her, demanding that she open her handbag. She complied. As she was doing so, however, he slapped her across the face. The U.S. Consulate protested.

Early in April, ten American missionaries in China signed a petition and sent it to Secretary of State Cordell Hull. Ever "since the Japanese occupation of the lower Yangtze Valley," the petition stated,

> we have been generally forbidden access to our property by the Japanese Army. . . . In our enforced absence nearly all [our] buildings have been looted and damaged and many of them have been destroyed by fire. . . . [F]rom three to six months have passed since the first Japanese occupation of these properties and there seems little hope of any change.

In June 1938, Japanese airplanes descended from the skies over the south of China and bombed the American-endowed Lingnan University and, in Canton, a Standard Oil Company storage plant. At the T'aining Presbyterian mission in Shantung, Dr. Frederick

Scovel tried to protect his Chinese nurses from rapacious Japanese; a Japanese soldier shot him in the side. In Nanking, Dr. J. C. Thompson tried to stop a Japanese soldier from beating a rickshaw puller; the soldier slapped him. At Tsingtao, the port city of the base of the Shantung Peninsula, Mrs. Thomas H. Massie, wife of an American naval lieutenant, was returning to land after visiting her husband aboard the USS *Tulsa*. As she reached the pier, a Japanese sentry demanded to know who she was; when she failed to respond immediately—in Japanese—he slapped her across the mouth. In Tientsin, Japanese customs officials at the railway station harassed foreigners, insisting that they fill out page after page of entry forms and following them to their hotel rooms if they refused to do so.

Piling on top of each other, these incidents spelled a direct Japanese challenge to the status quo. For close to a century, Western commercial interests in China had centered their activities on the treaty ports, a string of cities that ranged all the way from Tientsin and Tsingtao in the north to Shanghai in the middle and to Amoy, Swatow, Hong Kong, and Canton in the south. Each of these cities, which China had signed away in part or altogether to foreigners (usually to the British), had its seamy side, with opium dens and beggars, and derelicts from all over the world. Each also had its respectable side, with parks, clubs, churches, banks, hotels, and manicured lawns, virtual copies of suburban London. Most important, each represented Western control—in the treaty ports of China Westerners controlled the currencies, the exchange rates, the tariffs and quotas, the regulations over shipping and navigation, the rates and symbols of the power of the West. And the Japanese were determined to end all that.

Premier Konoye said as much. In a late May 1938 statement that reflected the resurgence of hard-liners in his cabinet, he said: "Japan's primary object in China" was the "driving out of foreign influence . . . and supplanting it by Japanese influence."

■   ■   ■

Inside the arched and colonnaded facade of the old State Department Building, just to the east of the White House, and down at the end of an echoing marble corridor, in the secretary's office, a critical meeting took place. The date was June 10, 1938. The tall windows by the office corner overlooked the First Division Monument, down at the corner of E and 175th Streets. Secretary of State Cordell Hull was behind the desk and, seated in leather chairs in front of him were two top aides, Stanley Hornbeck, the political adviser, and Maxwell Hamilton, chief of the Far Eastern Division. The issue before the men in that meeting was how tough America should get with Japan.

Hornbeck thought "very"; Hamilton was more moderate. And Hull, as was his wont, listened to both men with care.

White-haired and handsome, Cordell Hull, his eventual successor, Dean Acheson, remembered, "looked like a statesman in the classic American tradition—the tradition of the great Virginia dynasty, of Henry Clay, of Daniel Webster (but much handsomer, more like Warren Harding). His well-structured face was sad and thoughtful, his speech slow and gentle, except when he was aroused. . . . Suspicious by nature, he brooded over what he thought were slights and grievances." His brooding led, in accordance with the traditions of his native Tennessee, to feuds; and in the nation's capital, Cordell Hull had plenty of feuds. A former representative and then U.S. senator from Tennessee, he had been around Washington for a generation and, like many others with long tenure in the capital, he had mastered the art of caution. Hull even looked cautious. Starched, pressed, buttoned, and scowling, he resembled a grandfather in someone's Victorian photograph; and with his ever-exacting search for precisely the right word, he drove the president wild. Over cocktails in the White House, the evening ritual to which the secretary was never invited, Roosevelt sometimes mimicked Hull's lisp.

As F. D. R. knew full well, however, people around Washington trusted Hull. "You must realize," Roosevelt once said when asked why he kept Hull on at State, "that Cordell Hull is the only member of the cabinet who brings me any political strength that I don't have in my own right." Although Hull and Roosevelt differed in style and even in culture, furthermore, they both thought Japan barbaric and dangerous. They differed not over ends, but means. Hull wanted to creep and Roosevelt, much of the time, wanted to march. But both men above all else were politicians, watching events, heeding constituents, and calibrating as best they could just how far they could go and when.

For Stanley Hornbeck, during the meeting of June 10, 1928, the time to go was right then. The public, he pointed out, was restive; and he did have a point. Movie newsreels were showing horrific pictures from China and, in a rising tide of opinion, Americans wanted Japan to get its due. In fact, hoping to end what they termed "this cruel invasion of China," prominent citizens, including Nebraska's Senator George W. Norris, Professor John Dewey, Alma Gluck Zimbalist, Paul Robeson, and Dr. Reinhold Niebuhr, had signed an appeal, demanding a boycott of Japanese goods. Labor unions, too, were demanding boycotts and longshoremen were refusing to handle Japanese products. Across the spectrum of American politics—Democrats and Republicans, northerners and southerners, interventionists and isolationists—people were starting to demand an end of cotton, oil, machine tool, and scrap iron sales to Japan. These sales were called the "blood trade."

At least, Hornbeck told Hull, the government could block the sale of airplanes to Japan. Hull, at last, agreed. Hull chose the middle ground. The State Department, a spokesman announced the next day, would be reluctant to "issue any licenses authorizing exportation . . . of any aircraft . . . to countries the armed forces of which are making use of airplanes for attack upon civilian populations." The restriction clearly applied to Japan.

CHAPTER
8

MONROE DOCTRINE

Streaking over the bridge that crossed the mouth of the St. Lawrence River, President Roosevelt's train reached the exact point where America and Canada touched, then slowed, and in the station of Kingston, Ontario, came to a halt. Accompanied by his son James, the president appeared in the door at the rear of his car. The crowd of onlookers applauded. As Roosevelt clambered down the steps and onto the platform, a pudgy little man stepped forth from the crowd. This was William Lyon Mackenzie King, the prime minister of Canada. King was thought peculiar: A bachelor, he lived along in a three-story Ottawa house, the upper floor of which looked like a medium's parlor—complete with heavy draperies, a crystal ball, and a candle, ever lighted, placed under an oil portrait of his dead mother. What she told him was uncertain. But Mackenzie King would come down from his seances with her and then stage this or that maneuver to perfection.

In inviting Roosevelt to Kingston, Mackenzie King was doing just that—staging a maneuver to perfection. More exactly, he was building political support for what would become a military alliance among America, Britain, and Canada.

As Mackenzie King approached him from across the Kingston train platform, Roosevelt flashed his great electrifying smile. The two men shook hands, the president towering over the prime minister. Mackenzie King almost bowed. Then, as a regiment of the Royal Canadian Mounted Police snapped to attention, Roosevelt and

King entered the rear seat of a waiting limousine. The limousine, Canadian, started; and at the command of Roosevelt, it stopped. Inside the station, a band had struck up "The Star-Spangled Banner" and "God Save the King." To the accompanying cheers of the crowd, the limousine finally proceeded to its final destination, the stadium at Queen's University.

All this took place on the morning of August 18, 1938. As Roosevelt said to an interviewer, the date for him marked a turning point.

Standing under a canopy on the floor of the stadium and donning the robes of a Queen's University doctor of laws, Roosevelt gripped at the lectern. "To have the pleasure of being once more on Canadian soil, where I have passed so many happy hours of my life," Roosevelt began, "there is added today a very warm sense of gratitude for being admitted to the fellowship of this ancient and famous university."

So far his speech was standard. Then, thrusting his jaw forth and looking out over the packed seats of the stadium, he got to the point.

"We in the Americas are no longer a faraway continent to which the eddies of controversies beyond the seas could bring no interest or harm," the president declared. "Instead, we in the Americas have become a consideration to every propaganda office and to every general staff beyond the seas. The vast amount of our resources, the vigor of our commerce, and the strength of our men have made up vital factors in world peace whether we choose or not." Oceans no longer were barriers to aggression. F. D. R. continued, "Happily, you and we can look clear-eyed at these possibilities, resolving to leave no pathway unexplored . . . which may, if our hopes are realized, contribute to the peace of the world. Even if these hopes are disappointed, we can assure each other that this hemisphere at least shall remain a strong citadel wherein civilization can flourish unimpaired."

To this point, Roosevelt had been reading from prepared text by speechwriters. But now came a zinger—and as the typescript itself shows, Roosevelt had inserted the next few words with his own pen.

"The Dominion of Canada is part of the . . . British Empire,"

Roosevelt stated. "I give you the assurance that the . . . United States will not stand by idly if domination of Canadian soil is threatened by any other empire."

"ROOSEVELT ASSURES CANADA OF OUR HELP IF ATTACKED," said *The New York Times* the next morning in a banner headline. "Roosevelt carried his good neighbor policy to Canadian soil," the article below explained. President Roosevelt had "extended the Monroe Doctrine to Canada."

In his Doctrine of 1823, President James Monroe had denounced any attempt by the great powers of Europe "to extend their system to any portion of this hemisphere as dangerous to our peace and safety." The words had been brave—and without effect. What had early nineteenth-century America been able to do to keep the great powers of Europe out of the Western Hemisphere? Nothing. Throughout the nineteenth century, the Monroe Doctrine had done little more than gather dust on State Department shelves. President Theodore Roosevelt, of course, had shrieked forth his "corollary" to the Monroe Doctrine: The "United States," T. R. had told the Senate in 1905, ". . . under the Monroe Doctrine . . . cannot see any European power seize and permanently occupy the territory of one of [the Latin American] republics." The words were still brave; furthermore, now the United States had the power to back them up. But Theodore Roosevelt's adaptation of the Monroe Doctrine did not apply to Canada or to the Pacific.

With his Queen's University speech, Franklin D. Roosevelt changed all that, and with good reason. Japanese fishing boats, already busy taking photographs off Panama, El Salvador, and Mexico, had been showing up near Alaska, Vancouver, and Victoria according to intelligence reports that reached his desk with regularity. So, in Kingston, Roosevelt promised to defend Canada against "any other empire."

The promise made Mackenzie King nervous. Even though Canada and America had been growing closer diplomatically, he believed Washington all along had exaggerated the Japanese danger. Still, with Britain declining in power, he needed the American shield. Besides, Roosevelt's speech could only help Mackenzie King, because the Canadians loved it.

After the speech, Roosevelt lunched with the trustees of the university: Crowds peered in through the refectory windows and Roosevelt waved with his tall silk hat. As the limousine took him away from the campus after lunch, more crowds still lined the streets, cheering and holding up little Union Jacks; some people were waving the Stars and Stripes. Canada and America were drawing closer together; an English-speaking bloc was coming into existence.

And another bloc, that of Germany, Italy, and Japan, also was coming into existence. But where, in the formation of those two blocs, would the Soviet Union fit?

• • •

Close to the point at which the borders of Russia, Korea, and Manchuria came together, a mist-filled lake called Chasen gave way to sloping meadows and then to a range of heavily wooded mountains. The largest of those mountains bore a Chinese name, Changkufeng. Changkufeng was wild and uninhabited, but it had its strategic importance. A Japanese naval base lay just to the south and a Russian naval base—at Vladivostok—lay just to the north. The lake at Chasen and the mountain at Changkufeng had become a no-man's land, under mutual and constant observation. On July 13, 1938, Japanese scouts sent out the alarms. Through their binoculars, they had seen Soviet troops digging in on the hillside at the opposite side of the lake.

Japanese agents slipped across the border into Russian territory and, crawling along the hillside, took pictures. But a Soviet patrol caught them, executed one of the Japanese, and then destroyed the films.

Two weeks went by—two weeks during which Japanese forces were reinforcing their side of the lake but little else took place. Suddenly, however, the Japanese opened fire. Then they marched around the lake, dug in for themselves, and started up the slopes of Changkufeng. There they ran into a nasty surprise: In a battle that lasted until August 11, 1938, Soviet aircraft and armor were able to throw the Japanese back. Japanese forces on the spot had to agree to a cease-fire. The battle had been no more than a border squabble. But it signified, as the French put it, that "the enemy of my enemy is my friend."

Russia was becoming Japan's enemy. America was becoming Japan's enemy. For reasons of state, therefore, Russia and America were growing closer.

. . .

A new crisis erupted between America and Japan. This crisis bore a close resemblance to the *Panay* incident.

Just after 8:00 A.M. on August 23, 1938, Captain Hugh Woods, an American pilot, took off from Hong Kong's Kai Tak airport. Although Hong Kong now is so built up that when your airplane lands, you can see people typing beyond the windows of the sky-scrapers, Kai Tak in 1938 was almost in the countryside. As Captain Woods taxied down the runway, preparing to fly his DC-2 to Chungking, therefore, he could plainly see the rims of the moun-tains of China proper—and over those mountains he could see a cluster of eight Japanese fighter planes. He was not particularly worried. He had encountered such formations before and, besides, his own airplane, with fourteen passengers aboard, was marked clearly, in both letters and characters, with CNAC, China National Aviation Corporation, a commercial operation. Just to be safe, how-ever, he stopped his DC-2, waiting until the Japanese fighters were out of sight. Then, finally, he taxied again and took off.

When he was just inland from the mouth of the Pearl River, however, he spotted three Japanese pursuit planes swooping down on him. Some 5,000 feet below and to the left, a bank of clouds covered the tops of several small mountains. Diving for the edge of those clouds, he wrote in his report later, he "was in there for a few seconds and emerged on the other side. Directly ahead of me all was clear, so I started to turn to re-enter the clouds when I heard machine gun bullets striking inside the control room. I immediately started descending in a tight spiral. During this spiral I could see the shadow of my plane, also the shadow of another plane directly at my rear. The terrain immediately underneath consisted of small rice paddy fields surrounded by dykes. I considered it extremely hazardous to attempt a landing on land due to those dykes, so I headed for a river a short distance to my right. I shut off the engines, cut the motor switches, and disconnected the battery, and glided into a landing on the water. During this time the plane was being struck by machine gun bullets. The plane was landed safely near the right hand side of the river. By the time the water cleared from the windshield, however, the current had caught the plane, and swept it into the middle of the current."

None of the passengers was injured. But since the Japanese pursuit planes were hovering overhead, Woods ordered all aboard to get beneath the plane, down in the water. Woods himself began to swim toward a sampan, tied up on the opposite bank.

As he approached the shoreline, the airplanes dived on him, letting loose with their machine guns. At first, Woods recalled, "[I] submerged myself when they started shooting, but later became so exhausted I could not do this. Many bullets came extremely close; so close in fact that it left no doubt as to whether they were aiming at me or the ship. After what seemed an endless time, I reached the shore in a state of complete exhaustion. . . . It was probably over an hour before I could stand. I was violently ill at my stomach."

He was able to glance back toward the river. There, as the DC-2, half-submerged, floated downstream, the Japanese fighters resumed their attack. All but two still out on the river died in the machine-gun fire.

Normally slow to anger, Cordell Hull flew into a rage when he learned of the incident. "You may state" to the Japanese government, he cabled Ambassador Grew in Tokyo,

that the attack upon the plane has aroused public feeling in this country. . . . You should express the emphatic objection of this government to the jeopardizing in this way of the lives of Americans as well as other non-combatant occupants of unarmed civilian planes engaged in clearly recognized and established commercial services over a regularly scheduled air route.

By the way of retort, the Tokyo government said that its own pilots suspected the DC-2 of miltiary activities and that the DC-2, furthermore, was legally Chinese. America, in short, should mind its own business.

There the affair ended—except that America *was* minding its own business. The trail of that business revolved around the pipe-smoking, intense figure of Juan T. Trippe, president of Pan American airlines, whose office was high in the Chrysler Building in New York City. Pan Am received a federal subsidy for carrying mail internationally and had two prominent military officers, Admiral W. H. Standley, a former chief of naval operations, and General W. C. Ilner, a former chief of staff of the U.S. Army Air Force, on its board of directors. In part, therefore, Pan Am was an instrument of the U.S. government; Trippe himself had close buddies in Congress. Pan Am, in turn, had acquired the American interest in the China National Aviation Corporation, and thus was part owner of the shot-down DC-2. So, by extension, what had happened to the airplane was the affair of the American government.

Was CNAC nonbelligerent? Captain Woods's DC-2 was unarmed. But other CNAC planes, DC-2s, *had* been flying into Chungking with tanks of fuel for military use.

∎ ∎ ∎

By late August 1938, Washington was sweltering. The heat and the humidity were awe-inspiring, and, in the hot sun of the afternoons, the asphalt drives around the U. S. Capitol were melting and gooey. Under the dome, too, the atmosphere was hot, although not just from the weather. A debate was heating up over American neutrality.

Should America stick to the neutrality acts? Many in Congress—and outside—thought yes: Irish-Americans had little wish to sacrifice sons for England; German-Americans still retained a degree of sympathy for their ancestral homeland; Swedish-Americans were happy to milk their cows and fly their planes; left-wing isolationists thought intervention abroad had to stem from a capitalist plot; right-wing isolationists thought intervention abroad would turn Roosevelt into a dictator—or into even more a dictator than to them he already was; and the American mood in general found its expression in the popular slogan of the 1930s, "No More Foreign Wars." Like a huge old sounding box, furthermore, Congress picked up, amplified, and distorted the welter of views.

And in Congress, the isolationists were many and loud: Senator Gerald Nye, a North Dakota Republican who resembled the later movie actor Kirk Douglas; Senator William Edgar Borah, the Idaho Republican, with his old, lined face, his unkempt black suit, and his straggling black tie, a cartoonist's version of a senator; Senator Hiram Johnson, a nouveau riche from California and an old foe of the League of Nations; Michigan's Senator Arthur Vandenberg, with quivering jowls; Senator Robert M. La Follette, Jr. from Wisconsin; Senator Burton K. Wheeler from Montana, a Democrat but an implacable foe of Roosevelt; and Representative Hamilton Fish from Roosevelt's own Dutchess County in New York. Here were the banner holders of isolationism. Under their leadership, Congress had passed the neutrality laws. But was Congress to preserve these laws?

The isolationists said yes.

Or sort of said yes. The isolationists, after all, were politicians, and politicians listened to voters, and the voters back home were angry. They were angry over Japanese bombings: angry over the Japanese bombing, in mid-June 1938, of an American Southern Baptist mission at Pingtu; angry over the Japanese bombing, in early July 1938, of the residence of a Dr. Gillette, an American citizen, in Fukien Province on the south coast of China; angry over repeated Japanese bombings, in early August 1938, of American mission properties at Wuchang; angry over the Japanese bombing, in mid-August 1938, of the St. Hilda's School for Girls, property in central China of the American Christian Missionary Alliance.

Voters were angry—and so were investors. The Japanese had lowered booms across the waters at Shanghai, refusing to raise them for American vessels; the Japanese had seized, without payment, such goods as the tobacco stock of the Carolina Leaf and Tobacco Company and a lighter belonging to the U.S.-owned Shanghai Lumber and Coal Company; the Japanese had prevented salesmen from the Singer Sewing Machine Company from docking at Shanghai; the Japanese had shut off two American oil companies from their long-standing markets in China; the Japanese had severed American exporters, based in China, from their sources of fur and wool.

With all this anger boiling up, would Congress back off from neutrality? One senator certainly thought it should do so.

■ ■ ■

In the echoing rotunda of the Capitol, when the footsteps of the tourists had faded away, when Capitol policemen had unbuttoned their collars and opened their law books for night school, and when the rats had begun scuttling over the bases of statues of dead politicians, then, according to legend, the ghosts of the greats of the past met to consider the state of the Union. If they did convene during the stifling hot month of August 1938, they would have observed a tall, slender man pacing along the marble floors almost every night. He might have weaved as he walked, for he had more than just a taste for fine old whiskey; he might have been smoking, renowned as he was for his skill at cadging cigarettes from reporters. That month, in fact, he was drinking and smoking even more heavily than usual. He was Senator Key Pittman, a Democrat from Nevada and chairman of the Senate's Committee on Foreign Relations. He was also conscious of bearing a great burden. He had taken on the role of leader in the fight to change the neutrality laws.

Pittman was an obvious candidate for the job. He was a jingo, even a Japan-basher, at least when he was drunk, which was a good deal of the time. Back in 1935, just before Christmas, he had spoken to the Las Vegas Rotary Club, likening the leaders of Japan to Kaiser Wilhelm II of Germany and suggesting that Japan wanted nothing less than to conquer the world. Pittman's speech had kicked up a furor. The government in Tokyo had been indignant and Father Patrick J. Byrne, head of the Maryknoll mission in Japan, said that someone should "strangle Pittman immediately." Pittman had dried out in time and toned down his language. He had left no doubt, however, about where he stood. By February 1938, Pittman was advocating a U.S. naval arms race with Japan—to him, Japan was the enemy.

So, as leader of the interventionists in Congress, Pittman was swinging into action. As his committee members, fanning themselves and sweating, convened around their baize-covered table, Pittman laid a resolution before them. He wanted a Senate select committee to investigate the Far Eastern crisis and he wanted that committee to recommend military action against Japan. The committee amended the wording, toning it down. But Pittman did get a part of what he, and Roosevelt, wanted. Midway through August 1938, the U.S. Senate called for fortification of Midway, Wake, and Guam.

Pittman was addictive and ill, but he was also smart: He had hooked up with Sol Bloom in the House of Representatives—Bloom, a short, quick-witted character out of the Lower East Side of Manhattan, had made a fortune in music publishing and then in a few real estate deals, and in 1940 was to become chairman of the House Committee on Foreign Affairs—and Bloom, ever the driver, pushed the Pittman bill forward.

■ ■ ■

In Tokyo, the prestige of Joseph C. Grew, the American ambassador, had never been higher. Athletic and big, he frequently appeared, unlike most other diplomats, out in public, strolling in the parks or towering above the crowds in the Ginza. His courtesy was legendary. One afternoon, while Grew was walking his spaniel near the grounds of the Imperial Palace, the dog got away and fell into the moat. A passing taxi driver stopped, clamored down the wall, and, risking his neck, rescued the pet. Before the ambassador could thank him, however, the man drove away. Grew took out advertisements in the papers, offering the driver money, gifts, whatever. Embassy personnel finally located the man but he insisted on anonymity. He explained that he respected the American ambassador too much to wish a reward for his unworthy deed.

Many Japanese thought they owed Grew thanks. After the *Panay* crisis, as the Japanese saw it, Grew, and Grew alone, had kept America from striking back.

They had a point. Grew had worked day and night to keep mutual relations peaceful—but the task was becoming impossible. To the Japanese he had to keep explaining away the bombast of figures like Key Pittman; to the Americans he had over and over to present the Japanese view; namely, that Americans in China were acting in ways that were anything but neutral. Here is a sample of Japanese accusations that Grew forwarded to Washington: In Hopeh Province, American Presbyterian missionaries had allowed Chinese troops to use their church as a sanctuary; in Shansi Province, Chinese troops had used an American-owned church as a fortress. Near Hsüchow, American missionaries had let Chinese soldiers use their establishment as a communications center. At Tsingtao, Sen Chih-ti, head of a Chinese secret police unit, had taken sanctuary in a middle school run by the American Presbyterian church.

Were these allegations true?

■ ■ ■

"Father," wrote Frances Roots, the daughter of the American Methodist bishop in Hankow (as Frances Hadden, she was to become a professional dual pianist), in a letter in January 1938 to her brother back in America,

> is right now in an adjoining room talking with Chou En-lai, the Communist leader who has been conferring with Chiang Kai-shek this afternoon. He is coming to supper with his wife here Saturday evening after another talk with Father. . . . The Chiangs' Australian adviser, W. H. Donald, came yesterday and the day before, and had a long talk with Father.

In a later letter, Miss Roots described the family circle:

> Our luncheons swell from a planned six to an unexpected twelve. At teatime there are several parties going on at once. Dinner may find anyone here, from Chou En-lai to Minister of Finance H. H. K'ung. Chou's secretary, Ch'ang Tsz-hua, General Teddy Wu who supervised filming *The Good Earth*, English and Chinese newsmen, government officials including Mayor K. C. Wu. . . . Father has seen a lot of the Eighth Route Army [the Communist guerrillas] here. . . . We lunched at the Chiang K'ai-shek's—a delightfully informal family meal.

And the main topic of all these talks? How to embroil America in the war.

Such contracts between Americans and Chinese were common—

a point that Grew felt obliged to make to Washington. But he also had to make a point to Tokyo.

Certain words were creeping into Grew's conversations in Tokyo: words like "gravely," "in no uncertain terms," and "with the utmost emphasis." In his genteel way, Grew was trying to convey the idea that even he found Japanese actions in China to be "sickening." Grew was discouraged. He saw himself as "forever mopping up." He was ready for a trip back home.

■ ■ ■

Roosevelt also was discouraged. By late summer 1938, he was nearly halfway through his second term, a point at which, traditionally, the power of two-term presidents began to vanish. Presidents by this point had proffered their programs, delivered their speeches, tendered their deals, and expended their patronage. So it was with Roosevelt. In the autumn of 1936 he had won a landslide victory over the Republican nominee for president, Kansas Governor Alf Landon; in the autumn of 1938 he was about to be a lame duck.

During his second inauguration, early in January 1937, the weather itself seemed an omen. Bursts of "cold rain soaked in inaugural decorations, furled the sodden flags around their staffs, and drenched dignitaries and spectators alike while they gathered below the Capitol Rotunda. The rain drummed on the cellophane that covered Roosevelt's old family Bible, as he stood with upraised hand facing Chief Justice Charles Evans Hughes." Hughes had been the leader of the "nine old men." Now they glared at each other, the "old judge, his wet whiskers quivering in the wind, the resolute President, jaw stuck out. Hughes read the oath with slow and rising emphasis as he came to the words, 'promise to support the Constitution of the United States.' Roosevelt gave the words equal force as he repeated the oath. At this point, he said later, he wanted to cry out, 'Yes, but it's the Constitution as *I* understand it, flexible enough to meet any new problem.' "

Roosevelt certainly moved fast to solve one problem, the problem of the "nine old men." Early in 1937, after the Supreme Court had struck down a key new agency, the National Recovery Administration, he sent Congress his Court-packing plan, a scheme that would have allowed him to add to the Court new justices, younger and Democratic justices, *his* justices. But, to Roosevelt's shock, Congress rejected the scheme; even Democrats voted against him.

Roosevelt swore revenge. Setting out by train in mid-1938, Roosevelt spoke at Georgia Military Academy, insulting Senator Walter F. George, seated a row away; George won the primary. Passing back through Greenville, South Carolina, Roosevelt took a dig at Senator Cotton Ed Smith. "I like the way you look," F. D. R. said to a crowd. "You don't impress me as being people willing to work for 50 cents a day as one of your senators has said"; Smith won the primary. Traveling finally to Maryland, to Denton on the Eastern shore, the president denounced Senator Millard E. Tydings as one of "those in public life who quote the Golden Rule but take no steps to bring it any closer"; Tydings won the primary. Only in New York did Roosevelt enjoy success: Thanks to the string-pulling of Thomas Corcoran, John O'Connor, chairman of the U.S. House Rules Committee, went down in defeat.

F. D. R. had managed to split the Democratic party, the very foundation of his political power, and he knew it. By the end of the summer in 1938, people around him commented that he seemed to have lost his drive; certainly the lines around his mouth had deepened to furrows and the circles under his eyes had turned dark and brown. Speaking to Harold Ickes, his secretary of the interior, F. D. R. talked about what he might do in retirement. To a journalist, Anne O'Hare McCormick, who described her interview with Roosevelt in the October 16, 1938, issue of *The New York Times Magazine*, the president admitted that he had nothing new to offer in domestic policy. No "surprises" lay in store, he said; no "new departures." In effect, the administration of President Franklin D. Roosevelt was almost over.

■　■　■

But events, and possibly a member of the cabinet, took a hand. Europe was on the brink of war, and the British were distributing gas masks in London; the French were boxing up the stained glass windows of Chartres; and the Germans were preparing to break the

Czech nation in two. And then Henry Morgenthau, secretary of the treasury, urged an idea on Roosevelt: "You know, Mr. President," he said just after the McCormick interview appeared, "if we don't stop Hitler now he is going on down through the Black Sea. Then what? The fate of Europe for the next hundred years is settled. There is no question in my mind that if the countries around Europe would establish a blockade, we could choke Germany to her knees."

A blockade!

The British had blockaded Germany in World War I, and ever since Hitler's seizure of Austria, the idea of a blockade had been floating around Washington. Cautious, and, as always, keeping his options open, Roosevelt made no commitment to a blockade. But neither did he rule the idea out.

CHAPTER
9

NEW ORDER FOR
EAST ASIA

"It is my great pleasure, on this occasion of the birthday anniversary of the late Emperor Meiji and once more remembering the high virtues of the emperor, to enunciate the views of the government in connection with the establishment of peace in the Far East."

The speaker was Premier Prince Konoye, his voice crackling out of Tokyo radio sets at breakfast time, on November 3, 1938. Up in the U.S. Embassy, translators were listening closely, scribbling as fast as they could, preparing to show a transcription of the speech to Ambassador Grew. Konoye's speech, embassy officials realized quickly, was going to be a big one. He was proclaiming what he called a "New Order in East Asia."

What Japan "sincerely desires," Konoye was stating, "is the development and not the ruin of China. It is China's cooperation and not conquest that Japan desires. Japan desires to build up a stabilized Far East by cooperating with the Chinese people who have awakened to the need of self-determination." China's "true" self-determination, Konoye made clear, could emerge only through tutelage by Japan, only through union with Japan. In that union China would be purged of "communism" (Mao Tse-tung, Chou En-lai, and the Eighth Route Army), "colonialism" (the government of Chiang Kai-shek), and "Western influence" (the special rights and interests of

115

France, Britain, and America). All this Japan was willing to bring about, at great sacrifice, for China. But China was going to have to do its part. China, Konoye insisted, must recognize Manchukuo; allow Japan to station troops in China indefinitely; let Japanese citizens set up special zones of business and residence in China wherever they wished; and grant to Japan exclusive rights to the exploitation of China's natural resources. Japan, of course, would cooperate with others—the Western powers—but only as long as those others recognized that Japan had first claim to China's assets.

Ambassador Grew was shocked. Here, on the typescript, he believed, was the arrogance of Japan unmasked. As always, Grew was judicious; he wondered if he was being unjust and went to talk with Arita Hachiro, Japan's new foreign minister. His conversation with Arita left him more shocked than before.

Arita was square-faced, with a bristling crew-cut. "It is the firm conviction of the Japanese government," he snapped at Grew, "that now, at a time of continuing development of new conditions in East Asia, an attempt to apply to present and future conditions without any changes concepts and principles which were applicable to conditions prevailing before the present incident [the Japanese called the war in China the "China Incident"] does not . . . contribute to the solution of immediate issues." Grew understood the meaning: As far as Japan was concerned, the Open Door policy was dead, the Washington Conference system was dead, Japanese cooperation with the West was dead. Because of America's support for China, Japan had come to see America as the enemy; yet Japan pushed on into China nonetheless.

■ ■ ■

Canton, a tropical city in the south of China, lay inland from the coast. Its distance from the mouth of the Pearl River was about the same as that of Philadelphia from the mouth of the Delaware or of Washington from that of the Potomac. Unlike those American rivers, however, the Pearl, just in from Hong Kong above and Macao below, spread out in a delta, the main channel meandering among a host of swamps and islets and fields that sloped to the water. Winding between two ancient structures, the Boca Tigris (or

"Mouth of the Tiger") forts, the channel widened to form the Canton harbor. Great junks, sampans, and skiffs, creaking and bumping together, caused a perpetual traffic jam. Steamers coming from Hong Kong had to barge their way up to the shore.

Shore was a long, narrow island called Shameen. The houses on Shameen Island, with their high windows and sweeping verandas, looked as if they had been transplanted directly from South Carolina's port of Charleston; and in a sense they were. British imperial architecture had long since spread around the world and, as early-nineteenth-century British and Americans reached Canton, confined there by the Chinese authorities to Shameen Island, they built the kinds of structures with which they were familiar. But whereas in Charleston the verandas faced the sea and its breezes, in Canton they faced a channel, rows of warehouses, and beyond the sprawl of the city, with its occasional pagodas.

On October 12, late in the afternoon, an armada of Japanese airplanes roared over Shameen and swooped down on the warehouses and city. A foreign journalist, Edna Lee Booker, saw the attack. Staying at the Victoria Hotel on Shameen Island, she was seated in a wicker chair outside, looking out over the channel. A waiter came with a drink. As she was lifting her glass, a siren sounded. She went to the railing. Just in front of her, Japanese planes started diving so low that they were almost level with the tops of the banyan trees.

When the airplanes left, she crossed a bridge. A "peculiar, awesome silence hung over the scene," she wrote. "Where one might have expected screams, agonized cries, all was hushed. My first thought was that *all* of those . . . Chinese were dead. Then, here and there, I became conscious of movement. But there were no cries, no moans—just dumb silence." She looked more closely. "A man," she wrote, "was fitting a dangling arm back into place. Close to a wall a woman, in a last feeble effort, was trying to draw back to herself her poured-out entrails. A ricksha stood intact, the coolie sprawled between the shafts; but his head was gone, his torso putty-gray and naked. Nearby lay a dead mother, mangled and torn, the body of her baby crushed to her own. A woman stumped along on bound feet, her face smoke-smeared—but her head was entirely hairless, one of the weird tricks of explosions. Then, almost at my feet, was the body of a young girl who seemed to be sleeping, but was dead from concussion."

Four days later, the main Japanese force blitzed into Canton; Japanese soldiers started again with their looting, burning, and raping. But in seizing Canton, the Japanese had achieved something new: They had blocked China's last point of access by sea to the world outside.

· · ·

The balance of power in Europe, too, was shifting; Germany already had annexed Austria. Now, in August and September 1938, a new annexation was in the offing—that of the Sudetenland. In creating Czechoslovakia, the framers of the Versailles Treaty in 1919 had lumped together three distinct ethnic groups, the Slovaks in the east, the Czechs in the middle, and the Germans in the north and west, the mountainous region that flanked Germany and was called the Sudetenland. Some people who spoke German lived in Prague and some who spoke Czech lived in the Sudetenland, but such proximity often just exacerbated tensions and mutual stereotyping.

By the autumn of 1938, the Sudenten issue had come to a boil. Agents from the Third Reich had helped light the fire. Responding to the crisis, Adolf Hitler had begun to demand self-determination (a Wilsonian principle) for the German Sudetenland. In effect, self-determination meant unification with Germany and the dismemberment of Czechoslovakia, a dismantling of a major part of the Versailles Treaty. So ethnic rivalries in the mountains of central Europe had international implications.

In late September 1938, a four-power conference took place in Munich. From Italy came Benito Mussolini, with his black shirts and his incredible jaw; from France came Edouard Daladier, snuffling around with his moustache; from Britain came Prime Minister Neville Chamberlain, with his umbrella tightly rolled and his usual air of condescension manifested toward all; from Germany, of course, came the führer, Adolf Hitler. The upshot of the Munich Conference is well known. Faced with Hitler's threat then and there to invade the whole of Czechoslovakia, Daladier and Chamberlain agreed, in return for a German pledge to refrain from an all-out invasion, to grant Hitler the go-ahead to annex the Sudetenland.

■ ■ ■

Hankow also fell—the Hankow that since springtime had become a city of refugees, of peasants bent low under their loads, of soldiers with wounds and in rags, of Hunanese and Cantonese and Sichuanese, people from Shanghai and Peking, each group speaking a different dialect or even tongue. Hankow was a city of refugees; and on top of all those refugees the bombs had started to fall. After one Hankow bombing raid, late in the summer of 1938, a foreigner "almost stumbled over the body of a man lying by the waterside, his entrails exposed. He was still breathing. No one had time to attend to him, apparently, or he was regarded as a hopeless case. Perhaps he was unconscious and could feel no pain, as my companion assured me, but as we passed one [such] sight after another, I wished above all things that there had been morphia for the wounded."

The Chinese had an expression, *"mei you."* It meant, "There isn't any," or "We're out of it." So, *mei you* morphine.

But the Japanese had mustard gas, and by late September 1938, they were using it. "We haven't got gas masks, and the Japanese are now using gas constantly," declared T'an En-po, the Chinese general in charge of the Hankow theater. "It lays our men out for long enough to enable the enemy to come and bayonet them as they lie gasping for breath. A few days ago two whole battalions of my troops were wiped out in a gas attack."

The Japanese army may have used even more than gas. Headed by Ishii Shiro, an army surgeon, Japanese technicians in the lower Yangtze Valley had built at least one laboratory, called a "water purification unit." Code-numbered Unit 731, this laboratory, set up in Nanking, was "capable of breeding, in the course of one production cycle, lasting only a few days, no fewer than 30 billion microbes." Unit 731 was experimenting with the insertion of microbes into porcelain bombs. "Water purification," in short, meant germ warfare.

Did the Japanese drop their germ-filled bombs in Hankow—as

they did later, and elsewhere, in China? We have no proof. But we do know that just before its collapse, Hankow did experience several outbreaks of the plague.

Hankow fell to the Japanese on October 25, 1938. The Chinese government moved even farther upriver, to Chungking.

■   ■   ■

"Unless the Japanese march is halted by the Chinese or by some other nation, the time will come when Japan and the United States will be face to face and definitely opposed to each other in the international political arena." So said Stanley Hornbeck, after the fall of Hankow; and even Cordell Hull, the ever-cautious secretary of state, agreed. "I have proceeded here on the theory," Hull stated to the Canadian minister, "that Japan definitely contemplates securing domination over as many hundreds of millions of peoples as possible in eastern Asia and gradually extending her control through the Pacific Islands to the Dutch East Indies and elsewhere, thereby dominating . . . that one-half of the world; and that she is seeking this objective by any and every kind of means."

Did Roosevelt agree? Maybe, because he was also hearing from Evans Carlson and Carlson, just before leaving China late in 1938, wrote, "what I have seen convinced me that the military-naval group which controlled Japan [is] possessed of an insatiable appetite for power which would inevitably bring that nation to the point where she would one day challenge the United States in the . . . Pacific, unless she were stopped."

These beliefs amounted to a domino theory—*they* will come, and come and come, unless *they* are stopped.

"PACTS TO FREE TRADE SIGNED AT HISTORIC TABLE," proclaimed the November 18, 1938, edition of the *Washington Post*. As the four great mirrors of the East Room of the White House reflected the scene, five men sat around a battered walnut table, the same table at which Abraham Lincoln conferred with his cabinet. The five men were Sir Ronald Lindsay, tall, gray-mustached, and then the ambassador of the United Kingdom; Arnold E. Overton, young, wavy-haired, and permanent secretary of the British Board of Trade; William Lyon Mackenzie King, bald, plump, and bland, and the prime minister of Canada; Cordell Hull, the white-haired secretary of state; and, wheeled in after everyone else had taken his place, President Franklin D. Roosevelt. Roosevelt sat at the table, facing the news cameras.

Seldom, commented the *Washington Post*, had the East Room, even when the Kellogg–Briand Peace Pact was signed there in 1928, "witnessed a scene of greater international moment. . . . There was no fanfare. The only glitter came from the three huge chandeliers and from the golden epaulets of the British, American, and Canadian military and naval aides who stood near the door. In a semicircle around the old walnut table sat a varied audience of the Cabinet members, Senators, Representatives, . . . women in silver fox capes, girls in sports dresses, reporters in old tweeds. . . . As Roosevelt entered, the assemblage went quiet. The dignitaries around the table took up pens, affixing their signatures to pages in huge, gilt-edged, ribbon-bound volumes. Then Roosevelt himself signed; and when he had finished, he rolled his pen in his fingers and, smiling, said, 'I want to recall that this signing takes place precisely on the third anniversary of the first great trade agreement between the United States and Canada.' "

With this ceremony in the East Room, the English-speaking democracies of the North Atlantic region had signed two trade agreements, one between the United States and Great Britain, the other between the United States and Canada, designed, the press proclaimed, to achieve world peace through free trade. The Roosevelt administration in general and Secretary of State Cordell Hull in particular believed that free trade was good for America and that what was good for America was good for the world. But the pacts were actually aimed against Germany and Japan.

And Japan fired back.

In mid-September 1938, Japanese airplanes bombed Standard Oil Company property at Hoilow, on Hainan Island; the manager's house had been flying an American flag and it had displayed two more Stars and Stripes, painted across its rooftops. The U.S. embassy in Tokyo protested again and, again, the Japanese refused to apologize. In Tokyo, in fact, Tohokai, a small but potent political party, demanded that Westerners leave China altogether. A Japanese Foreign Office spokesman repeated the demand.

It "can no longer be doubted that Japan aspires to rule all Asia,

put the white races in retreat, and finally dominate the world,"
Edgar Snow wrote, summarizing such events in an article for *The
Saturday Evening Post*: "Preposterous? Incredible? We may think
so. But after a decade in the Orient I have been convinced by
the Japanese—by their candid declarations and repeatedly by their
actions—that this is the logic of their programs. . . . But everything
by degrees. . . . In south and central China, Japan would, perhaps,
be satisfied just now with protectorates or semi-protectorates. But
serious . . . competition everywhere must be annihilated once and
for all, as in Manchukuo, and Japanese monopoly established over
China's natural resources and communications, her labor power,
and her markets. Politically, the objective had enlarged to desire
the destruction of all genuine sovereignty in China and the reconstruction of all its material and human resources *for conscription
under Japanese leadership in future offenses against the great western powers* [emphasis added]."

Was Snow, in these words that reached millions of Americans
readers, exaggerating? Perhaps so. To many, however, his words
rang true: Late in 1938, Secretary of State Cordell Hull sent a note
to Japan that spoke of a "great and growing disparity" of Japanese
and American interests. If Japan continued its suppression of American interests, Hull implied, the United States might retaliate.

■   ■   ■

"I am taking the liberty of pleading China's cause so earnestly
because you have three times instructed me to proceed with the
proposals for assistance to China."

So went part of a memorandum late in 1938 from Secretary of
the Treasury Morgenthau to President Roosevelt, complaining about
Secretary of State Hull. Morgenthau detested Hull, partly because
Morgenthau was high-strung, New York, and quick, while Hull was
phlegmatic, Tennessee, and slow; and partly because Morgenthau
and Hull were rivals for access to the president. Morgenthau was
ever alert for a chance to undercut Hull. Hence the memorandum.

"All my efforts," Morgenthau's lament continued, referring to his
hope to extend credits to China,

have proved to no avail against Secretary Hull's adamant policy of doing nothing which could possibly be objected to by an aggressor nation. I need not tell you I respect Secretary Hull's integrity and sincerity of belief . . . , but the issues at stake go beyond any one of us and do not permit me to remain silent. It is the future peace and present honor of the United States that are in question. It is the future of democracy, the future of civilization that are at stake.

Roosevelt agreed, but he was subtler than Morgenthau. He knew how to wait. In November 1938, Hull was out of the country, flying down to Peru for a conference on hemispheric relations. Sumner Welles, the undersecretary of state, became the acting secretary.

A Harvard graduate, rich, and once altar boy at the wedding of Eleanor and Franklin Roosevelt, Sumner Welles was the quintessential diplomat. Said *Time*: "He . . . is absolutely precise, imperturbable, accurate, honest, sophisticated, thorough, cultured, traveled, financially established." Six feet three inches tall, outfitted in Saville Row suits, and possessed of a deep and mournful voice, Welles could have been one of those pompous lawyers standing behind desks in the black-and-white movies of the 1930s and 1940s. A reporter likened him to a "tall glass of distilled water." As a friend of Roosevelt, Welles was able to pop across Executive Avenue and into the Oval Office practically whenever he pleased. Welles treated protocol, and Hull, with contempt. Hull hated Welles.

On the morning of November 28, 1938, Sumner Welles placed a telephone call to Henry Morgenthau's office, high in the Treasury Building across the White House complex. Welles wanted Morgenthau's support on a matter having to do with Latin America. Morgenthau assented and, of course, asked for a favor in return. The Chinese needed credits, he told Welles, and the president approved, but Hull kept blocking the deal. Would Welles use his personal channel to Roosevelt and help? Welles promised he would. That afternoon Sumner Welles, tall and elegant, strode along the walkway and entered a back door of the White House. That evening Welles called Morgenthau at home: Roosevelt had given the go-ahead.

Just before Christmas Day 1938, Morgenthau had his deal,

sealed, signed, and about to be delivered. A dummy corporation, entitled the Universal Trading Company and registered in Delaware, with headquarters in New York, would import tung oil from China. Whether or not the tung oil actually materialized, Universal Trading would hand the Chinese $25 million in cash—money obtained from the Export-Import Bank. Through the Universal Trading Company, China in turn would purchase American trucks and supplies.

The response in Tokyo was sharp. Morgenthau's action, declared the Foreign Ministry, represented interference in the "China Incident" and a danger to Japanese-American relations.

■   ■   ■

Tokyo had another reason to be irate. An American citizen, one Herbert Osborn Yardley, had gone to Chungking.

"We flew above the clouds all the way [from Hong Kong] to Chungking," Yardley wrote in his memoirs, "and I saw nothing of China until, miraculously, we came out of the clouds and landed on a little sandy island in the middle of the Yangtze River. To the north, on its rugged promotory . . . sprawled the city of Chungking, a scurf of mud and bamboo huts and low, dull-colored stone buildings. I was depressed. It was a dreary prospect, which stirred in me dark premonitions of evil to come. There was nothing to dispel this oppressive mood when we [Yardley was accompanied by a Chinese secret agent] arrived in the city itself. The sampan ferried us to the foot of a cliff, and sedan chairs bore us up a flight of 300 steps to the muddy streets at the top, where a car awaited us. A winding, narrow highway flanked by lines of rickshas brought us past the western gate to a small, four-story apartment building." Yardley's culture shock only deepened. His apartment building, he wrote, "is infested with rats. . . . Only a few days ago, a rat killed the newborn baby of one of our guards, tearing out his testes before the mother could interfere. Despite traps set at my insistence, rats gallop in the attic, and scarcely a night passes that I am not awakened by one or two running over me." Outside his window, he added, "lay the dark, crowded, fog-wrapped city."

Rats, fogs, and all, however, this was Chungking, the newest capital of China; and Yardley was present on a clandestine mission.

Born in Worthington, Indiana, where as a youth he had worked as a railroad telegrapher, Herbert O. Yardley became the State Department's premier decoder. Established in a New York brownstone at 3 East 38th Street, Yardley ran the Black Chamber, a cluster of cryptanalysts who during the Washington Conference of the early 1920s read Japan's most secret messages. Within the closed world of official espionage, Yardley became a hero.

Then his world fell apart. Midway through the 1920s the State Department cut his budget, and with the stock market crash of 1929, dismissed him altogether. Out of a job, Yardley went back home to Indiana. There he struck it rich: His book about his exploits, *The American Black Chamber*, became a best-seller. Yardley had become famous, or infamous, and later China hired him. Arriving in Chungking, he went to work on Japanese cipher scripts, learning to plot out just when the Japanese would bomb Chungking.

But Yardley still wanted the glory. He wanted to meet personally with Chiang Kai-shek.

"Honorable Foreign Expert," went a note from Yardley's secret agent-assistant. "Your coming to China is appreciated. . . . Now that you are living in Chungking, I am concerned to know whether food and quarters are suitable. The Generalissimo is directing operations at the front and will not be able to come to Chungking for the time being. But when he does come I will take you to see him." Chiang at the time actually *was* in Chungking. Like many foreigners in China, before and after, Yardley was encountering the classic method of barbarian control: isolate; promise; isolate; promise; and then toss in a banquet. Yardley became the victim of many a banquet.

Yardley, in Chungking, was a private citizen. But he was an American, and he *was* working against Japan.

■ ■ ■

In Manila, the American military adviser's office resembled a formal drawing room of the nineteenth century. Inlaid bookcases and cabinets of dark Filipino woods lined the walls. The "shelves were crowded with volumes whose titles ranged over many fields of learning; a large number of the books had been dated before 1900. Here and there lay mementos of the early years of the American occupation of the archipelago. In prominent display were framed pictures of the [adviser's] wife, parents, and brother. The furniture in the spacious room included a long sofa, several well-padded chairs, a screen decorated with a Chinese brush-stroke painting, military and national flags on stands, and a large Chippendale desk. A calling fan droned monotonously, stirring the hot air of this upstairs office. The windows of the office opened out onto the bustling thoroughfare below, and beyond that, gave a view of Manila Bay, Corregidor, and, outlined against the cloudbanks on the horizon, Bataan." In 1938, the man who occupied the office was Major General Douglas MacArthur.

MacArthur's career had blazed like a star. He graduated first in his class at West Point in 1903, and became an aide to President Theodore Roosevelt. Showing up on the fields of France in World War I wearing a heavy muffler and a turtleneck sweater, he acquired the nickname "the Dude": He came out of that conflict the youngest American brigadier general. Moving back to West Point as superintendent, he modernized the academy. In 1932, however, a major general, he besmirched his own reputation by suppressing the march of the Bonus Army in Washington. His star sank. Roosevelt made him chief of staff for one year, but then MacArthur went out to the Philippines as military adviser to the Commonwealth government. In 1937 he resigned from the U.S. Army. Events, however, kept him in the picture.

In 1938, MacArthur was worried. He already had described the Philippines as lying "on the flank of Japan's vital sea lanes, as forming a barricade that, for the moment, denied Japan access to the teak, quinine, tin, rubber, and oil of the Dutch East Indies." MacArthur believed, furthermore, that Japan had designs on the Phillippines: Japanese shopkeepers, barbers, bicycle salesmen, sidewalk photographers, tourists in Manila, all of them, intelligence had told MacArthur, had been studying the defenses of the Philippines and sending their reports to Tokyo. MacArthur could draw but one conclusion: The Philippine archipelago was the door to the Pacific and the Japanese were squinting through the keyhole.

Could America hold the Philippines? In a letter to William Allen White, the Kansas editor, MacArthur wrote: "The history of failure in war can be summed up in two words: Too Late. Too late in comprehending the deadly purpose of the enemy; . . . too late in preparedness; too late in uniting all possible forces for resistance; too late in standing with one's friends."

MacArthur had no wish to be too late. In late 1938, he sent one of his staff officers to Washington to drum up support for the Philippines' defense. The officer was Lieutenant Colonel Dwight D. Eisenhower.

· · ·

Another American trying to drum up support was Claire Chennault in China. His problems were legion. His planes were damaged; his spare parts were few; and his Chinese pilots were worthless. A cabal of Chinese generals, furthermore, had tried to fire Chennault—he was, after all, a foreigner, and a particularly outspoken foreigner at that—and Chennault had remained head of the Chinese air force only through the intervention of T. V. Soong. Soong, the brother of Madame Chiang Kai-shek, was rich and powerful; in August 1938, he moved Chennault and what remained of the Chinese air force to southwestern China.

The place was Kunming, in Yunnan Province. Kunming lay at the end of the Burma Road.

"Kunming," Chennault wrote home, "is . . . about 6,000 feet above sea level with higher mountains all around. . . . It is near a very large lake on which thousands of people live all their lives in sampans and small junks. They have no radios and they can't read, so they know nothing about the world except such rumors as they hear." Kunming did have its natural beauty; the hills around the city were dotted with temples and huge, moss-covered trees; but Chennault was unimpressed. Nearly "all the natives" of the region, he noted, "smoke opium and opium smokers are always lazy and dirty." Kunming itself was a jumble of walls with gates, mud-brick houses, and "narrow, dirty, and rough" streets. Chennault himself had a bathtub and a toilet, "very rare conveniences in Kunming." But his Chinese aviation students were "behind badly" and the flying field was wretched. Chennault was begging for supplies.

Late in the year, an angel of mercy, William D. Pawley, came to the rescue. Big, bluff, and aggressive, and a representative of the Douglas and Curtiss-Wright aircraft companies, Pawley was a supersalesman. He thought big, he worked hard, and usually he got what he wanted. The war in China, he had calculated, was bound to be a boon for U.S. airplane-makers, just as long as China could get credits; but he did have a problem. America's neutrality laws forbade the direct sale of armaments to China. For Pawley, however, a problem was practically the same thing as a solution. And the solution was simple: build the damned airplanes in China itself.

And in December 1938, Ambassador Nelson T. Johnson went down the Burma Road. He did so in the company of James M. McHugh, a marine and the U.S. assistant naval attaché. Fluent in Chinese and lunching almost every day with Chiang Kai-shek, McHugh had been sending letters regularly to General Thomas Holcomb, commandant of the U.S. Marine Corps. In these letters, which Holcomb showed to Roosevelt, McHugh had been adamant on the need for more aid to China. Roosevelt, in turn, wanted to consult with McHugh, and Johnson, in Washington. The two men set off from Chungking by car.

"We started our . . . trip," McHugh jotted down in his diary on December 12, 1938, "from the south bank of the Yangtze River at Chungking. The whole embassy staff was there to see us off. Mr. Johnson and I left Chungking at 7:30 A.M. Driving was very difficult. It had rained all night and soon started again. We crossed five passes—the last 3,500 feet above Chungking." Then McHugh and Johnson reached the start of the Burma Road—if, indeed, it could be called a road. Some stretches, McHugh wrote, were "little more than bullock paths, without any metal surface; others were footpaths ages old, trodden by the foot of man and beast for generations, too narrow for any large vehicles." But McHugh and Johnson did manage to inch their Chevrolet along as far as the start of the British rail line in Burma. By New Year's Eve 1938, they were in Washington.

On New Year's Day, Ambassador Johnson spoke with President Roosevelt. "Unless we begin to show our teeth and indicate to the world and specifically to Japan that we mean business, we may forever find ourselves stopped from taking action." So Johnson remembered his conversation. "Time is with China in its conflict with Japan, but time is with the totalitarian states in their relations with the democracies. We should do what we can to assist and encourage the Chinese in their fight for an independent national existence."

●　●　●

In 1938 another American took a trip, then consulted with Roosevelt. William J. Donovan was a New York lawyer, a Republican, a hero from World War I, and a dabbler, or more than a dabbler, in matters of intelligence. He sailed to Europe. There, on a mysterious trip, he toured the defenses of Czechoslovakia, made notes on conditions in Italy and the Balkans, and went to Nuremberg, where he saw the German army in "exercises and maneuvers." Not long after his return to America, Donovan saw Roosevelt. They discussed the need, in America, for a centralized intelligence agency.

A member of the U.S. consular service, Ralph Coy, resigned his position in October 1938, and returned to America. He had served for thirteen years in China, Korea, and Japan. Soon after he came back to Washington Coy went to work for Donovan in that centralized intelligence agency.

PART III

·

1939

10

FRONTIER ON THE RHINE?

Snow had fallen the night before; by noontime, America's capital, with its new monuments and buildings of marble, gleamed in the sunshine. The senators who entered the row of limousines waiting at the top of Capitol Hill must have blinked and squinted their eyes. These men were the members of the Senate's Military Affairs Committee, four Republicans, eleven Democrats, most of them from the southern and western states. The chairman was Morris Sheppard from Texarkana, in the northeastern corner of rural Texas. Just that morning, Sheppard had gone to the White House, where Roosevelt had urged him to bring the full committee down. Roosevelt wanted to speak to them in confidence. Complying, Sheppard had rounded up his charges and joined them as they rode down the Hill. As the automobiles stopped under the North Portico, a guard directed the senators to the Oval Office. Seated behind his desk, the president had just finished a tuna sandwich and an apple.

He boomed out a cheery hello. The senators all sat.

"Morris came in this morning," Roosevelt began, nodding toward Senator Sheppard. "And we got to talking about national defense and the general world problem. . . . Of course, as you know, I am very much exercised over the future of the world [Roosevelt had already spelled out his fears early in January in his State of the Union message] and I do not belong to a school of thought that says we can draw a line of defense around this country and live completely and solely to ourselves. I always think of what happened in another administration. I think it was in 1807, before Bob Reynolds was born."

The men in the chairs around Roosevelt's desk yukked it up. Democratic Senator Robert Reynolds, a North Carolinian, a member of the Military Affairs Committee, and even in Congress renowned for his garish neckties and the plugs of tobacco in his cheek, had been born in 1884. He grinned at Roosevelt's crack. A White House stenographer was getting all this down.

"There was a hell of a row going on on the other side—Europe," Professor Roosevelt was explaining, ". . . between Dictator Napoleon and the antidictators [the Austrians, the Prussians, and the British]. In 1807, the British, trying to strangle Napoleon, issued . . . the 'Orders in Council' [forbidding] American ships . . . to trade with any port . . . dominated by Napoleon. . . . A few months later Napoleon . . . issued the 'Decree of Milan' in which [he] forbade any . . . commerce between the United States and any of the anti-Napoleon nations. . . . So Congress did what it thought was a very intelligent thing."

Pausing, Roosevelt shook a Camel from its pack, inserting it in his cigarette holder.

". . . It passed the Non-Intercourse and Embargo Acts, which said to American shipping, 'By God, as long as these fellows issue decrees, we will issue a decree that no American commerce can trade with anybody.' "

The president inhaled through his cigarette holder. Then he continued.

"Of course the damned thing didn't work," he said. "In the first place it was practically unenforceable and, in the second place, the country began to strangle. . . . All the ships were tied up and we began to strangle. . . . The net result was that . . . we got into the War of 1812, largely because we had accepted strangulation by legislation. . . ."

"Well," Roosevelt concluded, punctuating his lines like an actor, "so much for an illustration from history." He had made his point: Neutrality was impossible. Now his face turned grave.

"About three years ago," the president stated, "we got . . . pretty definite information that there was in the making [a] policy of world domination between Germany, Italy, and Japan. . . . They would move simultaneously, or they would take turns in aggressive operations against other nations. So it is not a new story at all. But during [the past three years] that pact has been strengthened almost every month. . . . There exists today, without any question whatsoever . . . an offensive . . . alliance."

The room was still. Roosevelt let his words sink in.

"There are two ways of looking at it," he resumed. "The first . . . is the hope that somebody will assassinate Hitler or that Germany will blow up from within; that somebody will kill Mussolini or that he will get a bad cold in the morning and die . . . ; that the Japanese people will say, 'We can't stand that tightening of the belt much longer; we have got to do something; we won't fight or march.' " As Roosevelt reminded the senators, however, "it took seventeen years, 1798 to 1815, before [Napoleon's enemies] finally threw him out."

And the second way? The way of preventing Italy, Germany, and Japan from dominating the world?

"It may come to you as a shock and it should not be talked out loud . . . ," Roosevelt said, but "what is the first line of [our] defense? . . . [In] the Pacific [it] is a series of islands, with the hope that through the navy and the army and the airplanes we can keep the Japanese—let us be quite frank—from dominating the entire Pacific Ocean. . . . [In] the Atlantic, our first line is the continued independent existence of . . . France and England. . . . [But] we cannot assume that they would defeat Germany and Italy. The best opinion is that it is a 50–50 bet, and that is too serious to be overlooked. [And if France and Great Britain fell?] Then the next most obvious step, which Brother Hitler [has] suggested, would be Central and South America. . . . We have definite knowledge today that in Brazil the Germans have an organization which, probably on pressing a button from Berlin, would be put into operation and would constitute . . . a very serious threat to the Brazilian government. . . ."

Luridly, Roosevelt was conjuring up the fall of Brazil, then of Venezuela and Colombia, and of Central America. "How far is it

from Yucatan to New Orleans or Houston?" the president was asking, rhetorically. "How far from Tampico to St. Louis or Kansas
City? How far?"

His greatest fear, F. D. R. declared, was the "gradual encirclement of the United States by the removal of the first lines of
defense. . . . Therefore," Roosevelt said, getting at last to his point,
"we do want to see if privately owned [airplane] plants are capable
of mass production." America, the president believed, needed more
fighter planes and bombers, lots of them, and needed them soon.
Here, in this moment, probably, we find the conception of what
we now call the military–industrial complex. The senators in the
Oval Office, all of them, Democrats and Republicans alike, burst
into applause.

Yet soon thereafter, one of these senators, or possibly more than
one, went to the press, leaking an alarming version of Roosevelt's
words. Roosevelt, reporters stated, had proclaimed that the "frontier of America is on the Rhine."

■   ■   ■

Clustering around the president's desk for their news conference of
February 3, 1939, the reporters could hardly contain themselves.
A few exchanged wisecracks with Roosevelt. Then one of them burst
out with *the* question of the week. "One of the principal items of
the conference [with the Senate Military Affairs Committee]," the
newsman said, "is that you are supposed to have [said] that the
Rhine was our frontier. . . ."

"What shall I say?" Roosevelt shot back. "Shall I be polite or call
it by the right name?"

"Call it by the right name," came the response.

"Deliberate lie," the president stated.

Was Roosevelt's statement itself a lie? Was the stenographic
record of Roosevelt's meeting with the Military Affairs Committee
of the U.S. Senate doctored? Who knows? What *is* clear is that in
Roosevelt's judgment, America was vulnerable to attack: Neither
the Atlantic nor the Pacific sufficed any longer as shields for the
nation's protection. Like it or not, Roosevelt believed, America was
going to have to take unprecedented steps to defend itself.

■ ■ ■

Joseph P. Kennedy, the ambassador to Great Britain, was relaying the viewpoint of his hosts—the British fear, dating back at least to Napoleon, of one great power or a coalition of great powers, hostile, able to conquer the Eurasian land mass, and thus positioned to threaten sea lanes from the Atlantic to the Pacific. Events only seemed to be confirming these fears. Early in February 1939, the Japanese had seized Hainan Island, off the southern coast of China; late the same month, Japanese airplanes had bombed a railroad station well inside Hong Kong; and, in Europe, Hitler's armies had seemed ready to move.

It "is not improbable," Kennedy concluded in his warning to Roosevelt,

> that America might find it impossible to maintain the strategic triangle Dutch Harbor–Hawaii–Panama against a [German–Italian–Japanese] coalition. . . . Also, without sufficient bases of its own, the United States Navy would be unable to protect American trade routes across the Pacific and Atlantic and could be cut off from vital sources of supply in Malaya and Dutch East Indies. . . . The air factor, also, cannot be overlooked. The effective radius of bombers is increasingly rapidly and to this danger must be added the potential threat of aircraft carriers and of air raids from bases in Latin America. . . . In short, America alone in a jealous and hostile world, [might] find that the effort and cost of maintaining "splendid isolation" [might] be such as to bring about the destruction of all [America's] values.

What was Kennedy up to? He had the reputation, well deserved, of being isolationist. But here, in his letter to Roosevelt—implying the need to build up America's defenses—he seemed interventionist. Perhaps eying the White House, if not for himself then for his son, Joseph P. Kennedy was trying to be all things to all people. But certainly he was conveying the sense that America was in danger; he was underlining Roosevelt's own fear of an encirclement of America.

■ ■ ■

"[The] automatic telephone rings at 2:30. I stumble out of my bunk and grope . . . in the darkness. 'Steve speaking. . . .' 'Squadron Duty officer. Reveille, son!' I . . . put on my flying clothes, fumbling around in an early morning stupor. . . . In the wardroom the sleepy mess boys seem to be wandering aimlessly. . . . As I sit down and pick up the morning press report, the familiar odor of scrambled eggs begins to bring me to life. While I'm eating, the other pilots drift in. Nobody tries to talk.

So began an account in *The Saturday Evening Post* by Lieutenant Stephen Jurika, Jr., a pilot with the U.S. Navy. Jurika was aboard the aircraft carrier *Saratoga*, at sea off Oahu.

"The alarm bell ends breakfast," the author continued, "sending its clanging echoes through the ship. . . . Juggling our flight equipment, we start for the Ready Room. . . . [Soon] the loudspeakers up on the flight deck begin blaring commands: 'Stand by. . . . Start the engines.' From up on the flight deck came a coughing explosion, a dozen of them, a hundred, and then the *Saratoga* is engulfed in a roaring wave of sound. . . . Leaving the Ready Room, we grope about in the dark for the stairs leading up to the flight deck. Outside it's still dark. . . . An occasional star peeps out from between the low clouds and is quickly blotted out by the huge stack as the *Saratoga* rolls in the long Pacific swells. A mechanic with a shaded flashlight guides me to my . . . bomber. I climb in. . . . [M]y turn comes. Guided by signalmen . . . I taxi . . . up to the take-off spot. . . . The mechanic and the second of my two passengers nod. [The mechanic's] flashlight makes a circle. I advance the throttle. . . . We start rolling fast. . . . A moment later, we're off the end. . . . I begin to find the lights of the planes ahead. After a wide easy turn we slide into formation. [Climbing] to 12,000 feet, we pick up light on the horizon, and the clouds below . . . begin to take on the colors of dawn. Off in the distance, massed cloud banks mark the island of Oahu and the city of Honolulu. . . . The sun is red through the cloud tops now, though it is still dark on the sea below. . . . Just off the nose and through a large hole in the cloud, I can see Diamond Head and a twinkling fringe of Honolulu.

Suddenly the . . . pattern of our flight breaks to pieces. The dive bombers and fighters move over and drop from our flanks at terrific speed, shrinking quickly to small silver darts which finally sink into the obscuring shadows of the Hawaiian dawn. [Then] our signal comes and . . . nose down in a howling dive, we head for Pearl Harbor. Green hills and red roofs flash by beneath us; then the Punchbowl, the Aloha tower, and the big tourist hotels at Waikiki. The air-speed drops to 200 as we level off and zoom over the Army's Hickam Field and the Navy base at Pearl Harbor. . . . After the [mock] attack . . . the squadrons re-form and fly past the beaches and the coral reefs, around Diamond Head, and stream out past Mokapu Point for the *Saratoga*." The U.S. Navy itself had staged a preview of the coming disaster at Pearl Harbor.

Did someone in Tokyo clip the article, file it away, and pull it out later for detailed study? Possibly. But about the article itself, three points are clear: The author of the article was a regular officer on active duty with the U.S. Navy; accompanying the article were two pictures (one of six U.S. patrol bombers off Oahu, the other of an airplane taking off from the flight deck of the *Saratoga*), both of which bore the credit, "Official U.S. Navy Photograph"; and in late January 1939, when the article appeared, *The Saturday Evening Post* boasted a circulation in the millions. Conclusion? Written, prepared, and placed by the American government, the article was propaganda. It may have been a warning to Tokyo. It certainly was an attempt to sell the American public on the glamor of air power.

The article was scarcely unique. On February 8, 1939, for example, the *San Francisco News* carried a photograph of the U.S. cable station on Midway, a map of the island, with its lagoon and coral atoll, and a headline that proclaimed, "GOVERNMENT BLASTING OUT CHANNEL FOR SUBMARINE BASE AT DROWSY MIDWAY HALFWAY BETWEEN NORTH AMERICA AND CHINA!"

■　■　■

Dark and heavy, the clouds of January had been scudding down from the north, obscuring the tops of Tokyo's skyscrapers and covering the city with snow. Bicycles and autos stood abandoned for a week; lone, dark figures trudged through the drifts. The atmosphere was foreboding and so was the mood, for times in Japan were tough. Raw numbers told the story. In the Bank of Japan, in the government ministries, in the great industrial houses of Mitsubishi and Sumitomo and Matsui, the ledgers all were making one point: Japan was going broke! Debts were growing; exports were falling; raw materials such as iron, lead, copper, nickel, rubber, and oil were in short supply; and ordinary Japanese were reduced to eating boiled cabbage, pickled relish, and fish soup without the fish.

The war in China was taking its toll. Japan had reached the point where, Hugh Byas reported, "the length of a matchstick and the skin of a rat are important economic factors in continuing the war with China. So [are] toothpaste, toy balloons, tin foil and chocolate bars, freckle cream and caviar, bathing suits and chewing gum, bookbindings and teacup decorations, golf balls and patent medicine and a thousand and one other things which might seem far removed from the 'sinews of war.' The materials that go into these things must be imported, paid for abroad. . . . Not even Germany [in World War I] could have been so tightly laced as Japan is today. Chemists in the Ministry of Agriculture are tanning rat skins to find a leather substitute. Major commodities such as metals, oil, wool, cotton, leather, and chemicals . . . [are] marked for removal from the market. . . . Iron is scarcer than gold. It is hard now to buy a frying pan; [soon] it will be impossible."

Japan, to be sure, *could* have recouped its losses. By saving and investing, it could have gotten back on the road to prosperity it had started to follow in the nineteenth century. In 1939 the country *could* have created the "Japanese miracle." Doing so, however, would have meant getting out of China. And *that* Japan was unwilling to do: No politically significant anti-China war movement had surfaced; no such movement had been allowed to surface.

Even more than before Japan was mobilizing for total war. Under Premier Hiranuma Kiichiro—early in January 1939, Prince Konoye resigned as premier—Japan had tightened its controls. Censorship was stricter; political indoctrination in the schools was shriller; mass meetings were larger; and the shoutings of slogans were louder. From every corner of the Japanese islands, propagandists were scattering sparks, fanning them far, and from every corner of Japan the hatred of things Western was blazing forth. "War on Russia!" mobs were screaming. "War on France!" "War on Great Britain!" And "Smash the American fleet!"

• • •

Early in March 1939, Key Pittman of Nevada, chairman of the Senate's Committee on Foreign Relations, authored and introduced a congressional resolution. Intended to safeguard America by strengthening friendly belligerents, the Pittman resolution would have allowed those countries—France, Great Britain, and China—to purchase American arms.

Pittman's resolution, however, went nowhere fast. Congress was still in an isolationist mood and, besides, Europe at least seemed calm. From Paris, William C. Bullitt, America's ambassador to France, wrote to Roosevelt, saying that it "is unquestionable that your acts [Bullitt apparently was referring to the start of America's naval and air rearmament] have had a cooling effect on Hitler." From London, Winston Churchill, still just a member of parliament, encouraged F. D. R. to "keep on beating the drums and talking back to the dictators." And in Washington, Roosevelt himself remarked that "our policy during the past month . . . has had a definite effect."

Despite Hitler's blandishments, furthermore, Japan had held back from an open alliance with Germany. So Americans had a sense of reprieve. But the reprieve proved short-lived.

• • •

Seated at the head of the green baize-covered table in the Cabinet Room at Number Ten Downing Street, Neville Chamberlain, the prime minister, put a question to his ministers. This was the Chamberlain of the tightly rolled umbrella, the Edwardian wing-tipped collars, and the tiny pin head; this was Chamberlain the appeaser. Actually, Chamberlain was through with appeasement. All through the depression years of the 1930s, Chamberlain and, to be fair, most other British leaders, had refused to face a fact—that Britain's power was declining and that Germany's was rising. Germany's challenge, they had hoped against hope, was merely ethnic, a desire to embrace under the aegis of one nation all those central Europeans who could be defined as German.

But neither the Czechs nor the Slovaks nor the Poles were German. Chamberlain and others in Britain could no longer see any justice in Hitler's acquisitive claims. Now, late in March 1939, Hitler had invaded Czechoslovakia and taken Memel on the Lithuanian coast. Chamberlain was prepared at last to raise the issue in cabinet: Should Britain stand up to the Reich? The answer was yes.

On the evening of March 31, 1939, Chamberlain addressed the House of Commons. If Hitler invaded Poland, he declared, Great Britain would declare war on Germany.

∎ ∎ ∎

Japanese forces, furthermore, had invaded the Spratlys, just west of the Philippines. In themselves, the Spratly Islands, an archipelago of nearly uninhabited rocks, reefs, and lagoons, were useful only as docks and airstrips. But they also straddled the shipping lanes around Indochina; they lay within striking distance, by air and sea, of the Philippines; and they provided take-off points from which Japanese bombers could depart, reach the Dutch East Indies, and return with fuel to spare. To the State Department, the seizure of the Spratlys indicated that Japan had in mind a future struggle in the Southwest Pacific.

CHAPTER
11

THE WORLD OF TOMORROW

Sound the brass, roll the drum
To the world of Tomorrow we come.
See the sun through the gray,
It's the dawn of a new day.

Thus began the words of the hymn of the New York World's Fair, which opened in Flushing Meadows, New York, on April 11, 1939. That date was special. It was the sesquicentennial, exactly, of George Washington's first inauguration as president, right there, in New York. On the opening day of the fair, in fact, a George Washington look-alike led the parade into the grounds, riding past the pedestal of a towering statue of the first president. Past the statue, however, the fair looked nothing like the late eighteenth century: Its buildings and free forms and pylons resembled nothing so much as the sets of the hit movie of the year, *The Wizard of Oz*. For the World's Fair of 1939 was a big, fanciful, and garish monument to dreams—the dream of progress, the dream of peace, the dream of "the dawn of a new day."

The dawn, alas, proved false. Sometimes "I lie awake . . . and try to recapture the vision and the sound of the World of Tomorrow," wrote Meyer Berger, who had covered the fair for *The New York Times*. "I try to remember . . . the pastel lighting. . . . I think . . . of nights when I sat by the Flushing River and saw the World of Tomorrow reflected on its onyx surface, in full color, and upside down." The world was just about to be turned upside down.

. . .

A detail from that 1939 New York World's Fair: Near the middle of the fairground stood the Perisphere, a huge globe that housed a futuristic and utopian city, in the form of an architect's model. Foreign dignitaries made beelines for the Perisphere; the king and queen of England showed up. But in a kind of dress rehearsal for their arrival, another head of state put in an appearance. He was short, dumpy, dark-haired, and double-chinned; despite the heat and humidity, he wore a top hat, striped trousers, and a woolen morning coat. His wife sported a flamboyant Latin dress and hat. He was the U.S.-installed dictator of Nicaragua, Anastasio Somoza.

Six years before, President Roosevelt had proclaimed the Good Neighbor policy, a promise that the United States would refrain from its customary and usually grisly Marine Corps interventions in places like Haiti, the Dominican Republic, and Nicaragua. American-perpetrated atrocities had been legendary. With families like Somoza's entrenched in power, of course, the United States had no need—for the time being—to stage any further interventions. On the eve of Somoza's visit, Roosevelt is alleged to have said of the Nicaraguan, "He may be a son of a bitch, but at least he's our son of a bitch."

Roosevelt is alleged to have made the same comment about other Latin American dictators—but therein lies the point. Somoza traveled from Managua to New Orleans, and from New Orleans via Washington to the World's Fair and back, at the expense of the U.S. Treasury. In gratitude, Somoza brought with him as a gift for Roosevelt a table made of Nicaraguan hardwood and inlaid, in gold, with an image of Theodore Roosevelt, a bas-relief of the head of Franklin Roosevelt, and two maps, one of the Panama Canal and the other of a proposed canal across Nicaragua. Somoza also brought with him a set of Nicaraguan postage stamps. And on his return to Managua, Somoza did two more things: He took down a portrait of

Adolf Hitler from his office wall and put up four pictures of Roosevelt; and he renamed his capital city's main street the Avenida Roosevelt.

In return for what we now call foreign aid and military assistance—America's propping him up in power—Anastasio Somoza was aligning his republic with the United States and its allies-to-be, and against Nazi Germany and its allies-to-be. This was the Good Neighbor policy. Through aid, assistance, bribery, or all three, the Roosevelt administration was rallying its side against Germany and Japan.

■   ■   ■

Just as the World's Fair was opening, Theodore H. White, a young, short, intense stringer with *Time*, reached Chungking. White had just graduated from Harvard, but not even his Chinese-language course there had readied him for this moment. Chungking practically hit him in the face. The city was packed, filled everywhere with "new stores and signboards. Each store proclaimed its origins: Nanking Hat Shop, Hankow Dry Cleaners, Hsüchow Candy Store, and Shanghai Garage and Motor Repair Works almost by the dozen . . . ," he wrote. "In squalid, hastily built sheds you could buy Fukienese-style fish food, Cantonese delicacies, peppery Hunanese chicken, flaky Peking duck. . . . All the dialects of China mixed together in Chungking in a weird, happy cacophony of snarls, burrs, drawls, and staccatos." People milled around and the buildings jammed ever closer together. Chungking, White noted, had "no steel, so bamboo was sunk for corner poles; little wood, so bamboo was split and interlaced for walls. Then the ramshackle boxes were coated thick with mud and roofed with thatch or tile—and just sitting there, open targets for the bombs from the Japanese airplanes."

Herbert O. Yardley, the American cryptographer who also was in Chungking, finally met the generalissimo, Chiang Kai-shek. Chiang's house was on a hillside, surrounded by an unmortared brick wall. The inside, Yardley commented, "was unpretentious. . . . The walls were painted white and the windows were draped with cheap black-out cloth. There were no flowers, pictures, or scrolls. . . . At the far end [of a large room] beside an open fireplace, stood a thin man in yellow khaki and black-cloth

Chinese slippers. He wore no military belt, decorations, or insignia of any kind. This was Chiang Kai-shek. Through an interpreter, Chiang asked Yardley to explain his work. Yardley did so, and Chiang expressed his appreciation.

Yardley's work, ostensibly, was that of a teacher: He was instructor to about thirty Chinese students, some of whom knew some Japanese. They were learning, or trying to learn, how to unravel Japanese Morse-coded radio broadcasts. Yardley had shown his class how to translate the dots and dashes into *kana*, Japanese-written combinations of consonants and vowels. The students, by Yardley's standard, were making slow progress.

Soon after his meeting with Chiang Kai-shek, Yardley made a breakthrough. Working away at his desk one evening, he noticed something peculiar: Of the forty-eight *kana* in the Japanese syllabary, the messages his agents interpreted were using only ten. Why, Yardley wondered, only ten? He made an educated guess. Perhaps those ten *kana* stood for the numbers one through ten. The guess was right. The messages his receivers had picked up were coming from somewhere close by; Yardley surmised that a Japanese telegrapher-spy in or around Chungking was tapping out a series of numbers in clusters three times a day, and the clusters of numbers were always the same in length. Experience told him that those clusters were "meteorological messages, giving the weather, ceiling, visibility, barometer readings, dew point, and wind direction and velocity."

Yardley went back to his clusters of numbers. One column for several days had consistently read 459, except for one day, when the number was 401.

Yardley checked his calendar. The month was February 1939, and as usual for Chungking in February, just about every day had been foggy and rainy—except for the one day when the column had read 401. And on that day a few bombers had appeared overhead.

The conclusion was obvious. The telegrapher was sending out weather reports for use by the Japanese bombers.

In March 1939, vegetables started to break through the soil and the clouds over Chungking began to thin. Soon the weather would be consistently good and the airplanes would appear en masse. Yardley knew what he had to do: He had to find the Japanese spy, and fast. He got lucky. With the aid of a direction finder scrounged up by Chinese associates, he located the source of the broadcasts, a shack behind a pagoda a few hundred yards up a slope from Chungking. In a burst of derring-do, Yardley and a handful of Chinese secret service agents surrounded the shack and captured the Japanese spy—before the spy had a chance to destroy his transmission set. Yardley himself took over the radio. Using the code he had constructed from *kana*, he proceeded to send out his own weather reports, conjuring up continued fog and rain and hoping thereby to postpone the inevitable air assault.

His ruse, however, could work for only so long. On May 3 and 4, 1939, the Japanese unleashed the first two of their great aerial attacks on the Chinese capital. The holocaust of incendiary bombing had reached Chungking.

■   ■   ■

Two bombings of Chungking are "now forgotten milestones in the history of aerial terror," Theodore white was to recall, "but at the time they marked the largest mass slaughter of defenseless human beings from the air in the rising history of violence."

Late in the afternoon of May 3, 1939, White and some friends spotted a "formation of 27 Japanese bombers, a serene and unbroken line of dots in the sky . . . ," White wrote. "I made my way back to the . . . Friends Mission, deep inside the walled city, where I was then lodging. By this time it was full dark, and what I was seeing was the reaction of a medieval city to the first savage touch of the modern world—which was total panic. Behind the slope, as I climbed up, was the red of spreading fire; and from the red bowl beyond the rim, people were fleeing. They were trudging on foot, fleeing in rickshas, riding on sedan chairs, pushing wheelbarrows; and as they streamed out, an occasional limousine or army truck would honk or blast its way through the procession. . . . At the crest, where one began the descent into the old city, I could get a larger view. The electric power lines had been bombed out; so, too, had the trunk of Chungking's water system. . . . There was no light but that of the fires, no water to fight the fires, and the fires were spreading up and down the alleys of old Chungking. One could hear the bamboo joints popping as the fire ate the bamboo timbers; . . . women keened, men yelled, babies cried. . . . I could hear screaming in the back alleys; several times I saw people dart out of the alleyways . . . , their clothes on fire."

Herbert Yardley observed the next night's bombing. As he watched from what he called his "hut," a hillside house to which he had moved, he could see "geysers of smoke and debris . . . , followed by the thunderous crashes of the exploding bombs. The earth heaved beneath our feet. From the city's tip at the confluence of the rivers the silver birds swept over the business section toward . . . the foreign embassies, the red flashes and columns of debris rising in their path. Into the southwest they swept, over the Yangtze, and vanished beyond the mountains. Throughout Chungking a . . . wake of slow, creeping fires marked where they had passed."

All this reached America in pictures. Rather like the before and after of the old magazine advertisements, *Life* ran vivid photographs from Chungking: an aerial view of the city as it jabbed like a fingernail between the Chialing and Yangtze rivers; a few downtown buildings such as the Bankers' Club and the Bank of Chungking, modernish structures that could have been lifted whole from Omaha or Kansas City, but that instead were silhouetted against distant Chinese mountains; then the same buildings as nothing but shells; and the rubble; and then, at the base of the rubble, a row of corpses, sprawled, naked, and blackened.

■ ■ ■

Moving to the slow beat of muffled drums, a funeral procession made its way through the grounds of the U.S. Naval Academy at Annapolis. Starting near the brick and white tower of the Maryland State House, the cortege followed a walkway around the gray-stone dormitories and the training boats lined up by the quay, and, finally, reached the end of a pier. There the marchers stopped, under a sky that was threatening squalls. The date was March 18, 1939. Bringing up the rear of the procession were officials from the U.S. State Department, Maxwell Hamilton and Joseph Ballantine; in the middle, decked out in ribbons and braid, Rear Admiral Wilson Brown was escorting a Japanese widow and her two small daughters; and in the lead, a contingent of U.S. Marines was carrying a wooden pagoda. In the pagoda were the ashes of Saito Hiroshi, Japan's late ambassador to the United States. A band of the pier played solemn music. Then the marines placed the pagoda on a launch and, when the widow and the daughters were aboard, the launch put out to the USS *Astoria*, a cruiser anchored in the Annapolis harbor. Weighing anchor, *Astoria* shortly slipped down the Severn River, toward Chesapeake Bay, and out into the Atlantic Ocean. Its destination was Japan.

Succumbing to the first stages of lung cancer a few months before, Saito resigned his ambassadorship. He stayed on in Washington, however, getting treatment at the Walter Reed Hospital. He died on February 26, 1939; according to Japanese custom, his body was cremated.

Within twenty-four hours of the death, officials on both sides of the Pacific started grasping at what they saw to be a chance of making a good-will gesture. In Tokyo, Baron Yoshida Shigeru, recently resigned as Japan's ambassador to Great Britain, sought out U.S. Ambassador Joseph C. Grew, hinting that Japan would welcome a token of friendship; in Washington, Joseph Ballantine, assistant head of the State Department's Far Eastern Division, wrote a memorandum in which he suggested the return of Saito's ashes to Japan on a warship. The State Department's protocol officer objected, pointing out that such an honor normally went only to those who died while actually in office. But Stanley Hornbeck, then Hull, and finally Roosevelt, all signed on Ballantine's memo. so under the command of Captain Richmond Kelly Turner, the *Astoria*, bearing the ambassador's ashes, set off for Japan.

During the first legs of the *Astoria*'s voyage, Japanese–American friendship seemed to blossom. In Panama, the Japanese consul treated the crew to a lavish party; in Honolulu, Japanese nationals, clustering along the pier, waved up their greetings and cheered. During a party aboard the ship, the *Astoria*'s officers reciprocated, inviting Japanese aboard and even donning kimonos.

Even before the *Astoria* could finish the trip, however, the goodwill began to fade, for the news turned grim. Hitler seized Prague; Mussolini invaded Albania; Roosevelt asked Congress to fortify Guam; Japan announced that it would spend 1.7 million yen on its navy; France beefed up the harbor at Cam Ranh Bay; Roosevelt ordered a major part of the U.S. Fleet to Pearl Harbor; and Japanese naval forces occupied the Spratly Islands. While the *Astoria* was still at sea, furthermore, Ambassador Grew had occasion to submit a new protest to the Japanese government. "I am directed," Grew wrote, "to invite [your] attention . . . to the ever lengthening list of instances in which, as a result of air raids by the Japanese air forces [in China], American properties, although clearly marked . . . have been damaged and in some cases destroyed." Since his last protest, Grew pointed out, "there have occurred not less than 135 instances of aerial attacks by Japanese forces endangering American lives and resulting in damage to American property." Grew cited cases:

> three bombings . . . of the property of the Christian and Missionary Alliance at Taiping; bombing of the Missionary Home at Sai Nam, Kwangtung . . . ; bombing . . . of the property of the Standard Vacuum Oil Company at Nanchang; bombing . . . of buildings of the Christian and Missionary Alliance at Kweilin, which resulted in the killing and wounding of members of the staff . . . ; the bombing of the American Southern Baptist Mission hospital, also at Kweilin, and the bombing . . . of the American Presbyterian Mission, North, at Hengyang, Hunan; . . . of the Suteh Girls' School of the American Methodist Episcopal Mission at Chungking; the American Church Mission at Kuling; the American Catholic Mission at Loting, and the serious wounding of Father Kennelly; . . . the American Southern Baptist hospital at Chengkow [which] was bombed twice, causing six casualties.

The last bombing in Grew's list, of the Convenant Missionary Society at Siangyang, in Hupeh Province, took place on March 20, 1939, two days after the USS *Astoria* had steamed out of Annapolis.

These bombings, Grew warned the Japanese government, "have . . . resulted in death and injury to American citizens . . . and, if continued, could not fail to have . . . deplorable effects. The

Government and the people of the United States are becoming increasingly perturbed."

The *Astoria* reached the mouth of Tokyo Bay in the predawn hours of April 17, 1939.

As the cruiser slipped up toward Yokohama, a light stabbed out through the darkness. Another light blinked from far away, then another and another, and soon lights were twinkling all around the *Astoria*. Then the darkness gave way to grayness, and finally to daylight. The light brought a shock. When they spotted Japan for the first time the afternoon before, the *Astoria*'s crew members had been enraptured by the physical beauty—the slatted sails of fishing boats, the blue coastline of the island of Honshu, the distant peak of Mt. Fuji, with its covering of snow.

But daylight brought a view of the ugliness. Passing the *Astoria* was a battle division of Japanese cruisers and destroyers, squat vessels, and the Americans could see the faces of the Japanese crew members as they moved about the decks or polished the gun sights; the Japanese vessels were en route to somewhere in the south. Then Yokohama itself rose into sight. It was a grim jumble of shipyards, cranes, steel mills, smokestacks, all of it overlaid by smog. Escorted by three more Japanese destroyers, the *Astoria* anchored off the Yokohama bund.

There the ceremonies began. Captain Turner of the *Astoria* had chosen his tallest and brawniest marines to serve as pallbearers. Carrying the dark, wooden pagoda with Ambassador Saito's ashes inside to a launch, and from there to a pier, they handed their charge over to a row of Japanese Bluejackets—who, stepping up to the marines, looked like midgets. Ambassador Grew was standing by; he was as tall as any of the marines.

Marching through a large crowd of onlookers, the new funeral procession left the pier and reached the Sakuragicho railroad station, boarding a special train for Tokyo. At the Honganji Temple the next day, Foreign Minister Arita delivered the eulogy; in his conclusion he pronounced the *Astoria*'s visit a "token of growing friendship between the United States and Japan." Grew responded, addressing an audience of Japanese army and navy men as well as two former prime ministers; he said that there was "no irreconcilable divergence in the interests of our two nations."

The celebrations went on for a week. Up in the U.S. embassy, Grew hosted receptions for top Japanese officials. Down on the Ginza, a store window displayed an American flag and, in English, the words "Hearty Thanks to the Astoria"; another shop collected 5,000 signatures on a scroll that gave thanks to Roosevelt; a Tokyo theater staged a week's worth of shows for the benefit of the Astoria's seamen; and the sailors got souvenirs, tram tickets, sightseeing tours, all free.

The Astoria reciprocated. On the cruiser's last night in Japan, April 25, 1939, Captain Turner put on a banquet. Cherry blossoms festooned the wardroom and long tables sagged under the weight of "2,000 sandwiches, 20 platters of luncheon meats, 20 pounds of chili, one dozen hams, and an equal number of turkeys, 30 pounds of prawns, twice as much lobster, seven types of salad, ice cream, hundreds of cookies, two kinds of cake, and three varieties of cheese." Grew congratulated Turner for a job well done; and through the ship's intercom, the captain passed the compliment along to the crew. The next morning, accompanied by shouts of "banzai" from the piers, the Astoria set off for Long Beach.

But trouble surfaced even before the Astoria was clear of Tokyo Bay. Camouflaged "by wearing a machinist's mate's insignia," according to one account, a U.S. Navy photographer "placed a camera with a powerful telephoto lens atop one of the [Astoria's] masts. [He had hoped] to photograph the Yokosuka dry dock where Japan's newest battleships were being built. Just as the Astoria reached the appropriate point, however, two ancient coal-burning tugs passed between ship and shore, belching enough black smoke to render any photographs useless."

Back in Tokyo, furthermore, Ambassador Grew picked up a disturbing report: During the Astoria's visit, Italian and German diplomats were closeting themselves with certain high-ranking Japanese; and these Japanese started lobbying for their country's participation in a tripartite alliance. Indeed, virtually ignoring the Astoria's visit, Japan's ultranationalist press was playing up evidences of American hostility. And in Shanghai at the same time, Japanese authorities announced that to control Western "subversion," they were going to exercise their "right" to seize foreign vessels as far as 100 miles out to sea.

The *Astoria's* visit had provided a moment of friendship. By friendship, however, Japan and America meant quite different things. Japan wanted America to accept the New Order for East Asia; America wanted Japan to end the war in China, or at least to respect the rights and lives of Americans there. Japan refused to acknowledge America's righteous anger; America refused to acknowledge Japan's great fear, that of encirclement by American planes and ships and bases. Despite the *Astoria's* visit, therefore, Japanese–American relations only settled further into a deadly pattern—action–reaction, tit for tat, a closing of choices.

The *Astoria* left Annapolis amid certain hopes of goodwill. It returned to Long Beach in a "farewell to friendship."

■ ■ ■

Friendship indeed was gone. In Honolulu, in the middle of April 1939, A. L. Patterson, the Chungking representative of the United Aircraft Corporation, told reporters that he was taking the Pan-Am Clipper to San Francisco. In his briefcase, he said, he had a contract calling for the purchase, by China, of $15 million worth of American war planes; China had specified "rush construction." The planes were to reach China by an undisclosed route.

Two days later—according to the Tokyo newspaper *Asahi*—Japan announced that it was going to extend its "nautical line" 1,000 miles beyond the Spratlys. Such a line would cut across the shipping lanes of Indochina, the Philippines, and Singapore.

■ ■ ■

On April 20, 1939, while the *Astoria* was still at port in Japan, a tall, slender, brown-haired, still boyish-looking man in his late thirties entered the Oval Office in the White House. Roosevelt leaned forward from behind the desk—only later did the man stop to realize that the president was crippled—and extended his arm for a handshake. "How's Anne?" Roosevelt asked; "she knew my daughter in school, you know." A part of Roosevelt's charm lay in his efforts to find points in common with others. Anne was the man's wife; the man himself was the Minnesota farmboy turned famous aviator, Charles A. Lindbergh.

After the kidnapping and death of their son, Charles and Anne

Lindbergh fled to Europe. Visiting Germany, Lindbergh, quite to the detriment of his reputation, had praised Hitler as a "great man" and had touted the Nazi air force as "unbeatable." He earned his due: The Nazis rewarded him with the Service Cross of the Order of the German Eagle. Back in America, Interior Secretary Ickes excoriated Lindbergh as the "Knight of the German Eagle." Ickes had a point: Coming home at last in the spring of 1939, Lindbergh lost little time in making himself the leading spokesman of the isolationist cause.

Lindbergh's meeting with Roosevelt was tense. There "is something about [F. D. R.] I did not trust," Lindbergh recorded in his journal, "something a little too suave, too pleasant, too easy." From his own side of the desk, the president found Lindbergh honest, but to the point of fanaticism, a real-life version of James Stewart in the 1939 movie *Mr. Smith Goes to Washington*. In Roosevelt's view, Mr. Smith and Mr. Lindbergh were naive and, therefore, dangerous.

■   ■   ■

"You see two or three of them behind every bar," Christopher Isherwood wrote of the White Russians who, stateless, sought refuge in Tientsin, "a fat, defeated tribe who lead a melancholy indoor life of gossip, mahjong, drink, and bridge. They have all drifted here somehow . . . and here they must stop; nobody else will receive them. They have established an insecure right to exist . . . Chinese nationality-papers of doubtful validity, obsolete Tsarist identity-certificates as big as tablecloths. . . . Their great, pallid faces look out into the future, above innumerable cigarettes and tea-glasses, without pity or hope."

This was Tientsin, a haven for refugees and a Chinese city about to become the focus of a new Far Eastern crisis. Inland from the sea by a score or so of miles—a channel linked Tientsin to Taku, the seaport—the place had been a walled city once. But in 1858, the British, alongside the French, had come with their guns and, in the Peking Convention of 1860, had taken as their own a strip of Tientsin called the Purple Bamboo Grove. Two miles long, a few hundred feet wide, and lying along the bank of the River Hai, the grove had become, by treaty, a zone of extraterritoriality: The foreigners, that is, had gained a title to what in effect had been clumps of their own national territory.

By 1900, others—the Germans, the Austrians, the Italians, the Belgians, and the Japanese—had claimed their own zones in Tientsin. And each zone looked like home: the French with their cafés; the Germans and the Austrians with their beer gardens; and the British with their window boxes and their manicured lawns. Of all these zones, or concessions, as they were also called, the grandest was the British, with a great department store, Whiteway and Laidlaw—the Harrods of Tientsin—and Gordon Memorial Hall. The latter was a high Victorian architectural horror, replete with finials and battlements, and named after Charles "Chinese" Gordon. Gordon, who had served in China, was the British officer who had died in the siege of Khartoum.

Gordon Hall was a communal center. In the summer of 1939, the British were going to need a communal center, because the old Purple Bamboo Grove had become a center of anti-Japanese terrorism. A pattern had established itself. Slipping into the foreign concessions, a band of Chinese would murder a Japanese—or a wealthy Chinese who was collaborating with the Japanese; the assassins then would slip out to hide in a nearby village; Japanese launches would churn up the Hai River; soldiers would sweep out to villages, sometimes even the right one, and with their machine guns mow down peasants in retaliation, then retire to the launches.

Tientsin would be quiet for a few days. Then the cycle of violence would start again—except that, on April 9, 1939, a change did take place. Entering the foreign zones, four Chinese guerrillas burst in upon the home of Ch'eng Hsi-keng; Ch'eng was the customs inspector for Tientsin—that is, a Japanese puppet. The Chinese left him dead, stabbed, his blood forming a puddle in the midst of his expensive Oriental carpet. This time, however, the killers fled not to their village but to the British concession.

The crisis came fast. The Japanese demanded that the British hand the assassins over; following instructions from London, the British authorities in Tientsin refused to do so. The Japanese then announced that they were going to blockade the British concession.

The Japanese produced a full litany of accusations. The British concession, they claimed, had become a virtual sanctuary, a honeycomb of hideouts for Chinese guerrillas, not to mention propaganda presses and secret radio stations. All these accusations contained a great element of truth—but were equally a pretext. The British banks in Tientsin held reserves of Chinese silver the Japanese wanted—and British authorities had maintained the *fapi*, the northern Chinese currency, refusing to give preferences to Japan's own bank notes. So the real issue in Tientsin was one of power and control.

The British concession in Tientsin had remained a citadel of Western interests on the north China coast. And the Japanese intended to storm the citadel.

They struck on June 13, 1939. On that day, with their launches massing along the Tientsin bund, Japanese troops ringed the British and the French zones with an electrified barbed-wire fence; anyone who wished to go in and out of those zones would have to cross a Japanese-manned barricade.

CHAPTER
12

THE DARK SUMMER

As the special train with its blue and silver central car started over the Niagara bridge, the young couple inside the car pressed their faces to the window. He was fine-boned; she was plump but pretty. Peering out at the floodlights at the crest of Niagara Falls, he felt a thrill, for he had not seen that sight since his days as a young British officer. His wife was Queen Elizabeth and he himself was King George VI, about to be the first British monarch on this, the night of June 7, 1939, to set foot on American soil.

Guns boomed forth as the train reached the station on the American side. A red carpet stretched to the edge of the platform; Secretary of State and Mrs. Cordell Hull stood at mid-carpet, waiting. The train came to a halt. As flash bulbs popped, King George VI, followed by Queen Elizabeth, stepped down from the car. As the king and the secretary shook hands, Hull extended a formal welcome. The king bent forward shyly, but the queen raised two fingers, as *Time* put it, "in a greeting as girlish as it was regal." Joined then by Canada's prime minister, William Lyon Mackenzie King, the royal couple mounted the steps of the railroad car again, and the train left the station, heading for Washington.

Three governments, American, British, and Canadian, had a stake in the success of this visit. Those three countries had been edging ever closer to alliance, and the royal couple's presence in Washington was to be a symbol of that amity.

157

Just before 11:00 A.M. the next day, a Friday, the presidential limousines reached Union Station, pulling in and onto the platform. Standing beside Mrs. Roosevelt, the president balanced himself on the arm of Brigadier General Edwin Watson. The train arrived and its distinguished visitors alighted. Stepping forward, Hull spoke to Roosevelt: "Mr. President," he drawled, "I have the honor to present Their Britannic Majesties."

"Well," Roosevelt said, beaming his great smile, "at last I meet you."

"Mr. President," the king said, sweating already in his full-dress admiral's uniform, "it is indeed a pleasure for Her Majesty and myself to be here."

As they shook hands all around, a marine band played "God Save the King" and the "Star-Spangled Banner." The president and the king then entered one limousine, Mrs. Roosevelt and the queen a second, and, preceded and followed by Secret Service autos, the motorcade left Union Station, rounding Massachusetts Avenue, outside the plaza, and proceeding to a point on First Street, just below the Capitol dome. Two huge American flags flew in front of the Capitol. King George VI snapped off a salute—and the American crowds went wild. The motorcade proceeded then for the White House.

The following morning, the Roosevelts accompanied the king and queen to Mount Vernon, where George VI laid a wreath on George Washington's tomb. The press loved the moment: The king of England was paying tribute to the leader of the American Revolution; the roles of master and dependent had switched.

The royal couple finished their American trip at Hyde Park, and there they spent an all-American Sunday afternoon. After services just up the road at St. James's Episcopal church, the President took them for a spin in his open-topped shiny blue Ford. A photograph shows the king in the rear seat, his shirt collar outside his jacket collar, in the style of an English gentlemen at play; but in the picture he is leaning forward, obviously forcing a smile, his neck muscles taut with anxiety. And small wonder! After all, Franklin D. Roosevelt, a polio victim, was at the controls—the car was equipped with a hand throttle and brake—and as he sped merrily along the lanes around his estate, he chattered away at a steady pace and kept throwing his head backward in laughter. But no accident occurred.

Back at the house, the king at last relaxed. After strolling to the edge of the bluff, from which they could look up and down the long valley of the Hudson River, their highnesses joined the Roosevelts and Mackenzie King on the lawn above the orchard for a picnic. Crowded behind barriers, onlookers could scarcely believe their eyes. There, right in front of them, seated in a weathered wooden armchair, George VI, king of England, Wales, Scotland, Northern Ireland, and all the rest, was eating a hot dog, drinking a beer, and asking for seconds of both.

Late in the afternoon, the king and queen boarded their train again, and pulling out of the Hyde Park siding, started on the trek that would take them to Canada, then back to the British Isles. Their American sojourn was over.

Their visit had been a smashing success—and in one way the public knew nothing about. On the night of Saturday, June 10, 1939, Roosevelt stayed up late for once, chatting with George VI and Mackenzie King in the library of the Hyde Park mansion. The room was spacious, and comfortable in an old-fashioned way, with old naval pictures on the walls and deep-seated, tall leather-backed black chairs. There the king, the prime minister, and the president huddled until 1:30 A.M. Finally, Roosevelt leaned over from his own chair, patted George's knee, and said, "Young man, it's time for you to go to bed." The king retired to his bedroom upstairs.

But he was too keyed up to sleep and in his diary, two days later, he revealed why. His notes are preserved in the Royal Archives.

"[Roosevelt] was very frank and friendly," the king wrote, "& seemed genuinely glad that I had been able to pay him this visit. . . . We talked of the firm & trusted friendship between Canada and the U.S.A. F. D. R. mentioned that . . . he had already laid plans for the defense of the Pacific Coast of Canada, especially Vancouver Island." The king noted that Roosevelt also spoke of wanting access to Trinidad. "From this base," Roosevelt's navy could "patrol the Atlantic with ships and aeroplanes, on a radius of approximately 1,000 miles. . . . If he saw a U-boat he would sink her at once and wait for the consequences."

Then came the zinger. Roosevelt had promised no alliance. "If London was bombed," however, the president told the king, "the U.S.A. would come in."

■ ■ ■

Would the United States come in? A growing network of lobbyists, strange bedfellows that they were, certainly hoped so; blending public relations and enticements, even bribes, this network was unrelenting. Samuel Untermeyer, the liberal lawyer, had been urging an anti-Japanese, as well as an anti-German, boycott. Walter Judd, a medical missionary who had worked in Shansi Province, was hitting the lecture circuit, describing in graphic detail how he had removed bomb fragments—"those things," as he called them—from Chinese bodies; he conjured up for his listeners vivid pictures of how their very own automobiles were being scrapped and reforged as Japanese bombs. Other missionaries campaigned for sanctions against Japan, sanctions "backed up by naval force."

Chinese lobbyists were active, too: Alben W. Barkley of Kentucky, a Democrat, the majority leader, and a member of the Senate's Committee on Foreign Relations, accepted a packet of valuable Chinese postage stamps; Treasury Secretary Morgenthau accepted, from K. P. Ch'en, a financial official from China, a "beautiful embroidered coat," for Mrs. Morgenthau; for himself he accepted a "magnificent carved ivory boat and [a] beautiful pair of jade cuff links."

Lobbyists kept the pressure on the president. "If the United States carries out her . . . China policy [the Open Door and the treaty abrogation], then she is bound to clash with Japan." Thus began an article, quoted from Chiang Kai-shek's *China Weekly Review* and mailed to Roosevelt by the Chicago-based American Association for China Famine and Flood Relief. The group was a nonprofit missionary coalition; the document being quoted supposedly was from a Japanese newspaper. "We shall have to settle the question by force . . . ," the document continued.

[T]here can be no doubt that Hawaii will be the most important strategic point. . . . WITH THE HAWAIIAN ISLANDS AS HER BASE

OF OPERATIONS, AMERICA COULD BOMB TOKYO OR OSAKA WITH-
OUT MUCH DIFFICULTY. . . . BUT IF, ON THE CONTRARY, JAPAN
OCCUPIES THE ISLANDS, her fleet [could] BOMB CITIES ON THE
WEST COAST OF AMERICA. . . . Japanese forces would undertake,
AS THE NEXT STEP, THE TASK OF DESTROYING THE PANAMA CANAL
AND THE MAIN SQUADRON OF AMERICA. . . . THE THIRD PERIOD
would begin with a landing of Japanese forces on the western
coast of the American continent and the work of destroying the
cities and naval ports on the West Coast.

Was this document, sent to Roosevelt late in the summer of 1939,
a forgery? Perhaps. But the document itself, preserved in the Roosevelt Library at Hyde Park, shows someone in the White House
took the pains to underline the capitalized words with a crayon.

■ ■ ■

Question time came to the House of Commons on the evening of
June 22, 1939, and Geoffrey L. Marder, a Liberal backbencher,
rose to direct his question at Prime Minister Chamberlain. "How
many British subjects," Marder demanded, "will have to be
insulted, stripped, and killed before the British Government will
do anything?" Chamberlain stood, mumbled some vagaries. Marder
was referring to Tientsin.

Tientsin had come to the point of crisis. For the crime of passing
a basket of vegetables over the barricade, Japanese soldiers shot
two Chinese peddlers to death. The Japanese were harassing the
residents of the British concession as well. Cecil G. Davis, a colonial
official from New Zealand, approached the barricade: In a nearby
examining shed, Japanese policemen detained him, forcing him to
strip and to stand naked; one of them slapped him across his mouth
with his passport. John Anderson, a newspaperman who had been
born in Tientsin, set out to visit his mother, who lived out in the
former German concession. Japanese soldiers forced him to strip,
and slapped him, too, with his passport. As Anderson dressed again,
a Japanese soldier said, "You think because you're British you
needn't be afraid."

Also, Japanese soldiers forced Mr. and Mrs. D. Finlay, a British
couple employed by the International Country Club, situated in the

Japanese sector, to strip. Mrs. Finlay was permitted to retain only the girdle on her hips. A Chinese policewoman searched her, but in full view of a male Japanese soldier. Japanese soldiers arrested, then released, E. T. Griffiths, second officer of the Chinese coastal steamer *Yoochow*; in speaking to a group of Japanese soldiers, he seemed to have used "insulting language." Japanese soldiers stopped and strip-searched a Mrs. Fink, principal of the American school in Tientsin, along with her twelve-year-old daughter; the girl became hysterical. And a Chinese taxi driver solved the problem of having constantly to undergo Japanese-conducted strip searches: Whenever he drove his taxi, he wore nothing more than his underwear. This way he saved time, he told reporters, whenever he had to take a fare into the Japanese zone.

As Vice Admiral Hibino Masahuso, chief of the Japanese naval forces in the north China region, put it, any foreigner in Tientsin who opposed the New Order for East Asia would suffer "chastisement." And in Tokyo, a mob gathered in front of the British embassy. Shouting and sweating in the mid-July heat and waving banners, the throng charged the embassy gates; only after a series of skirmishes with the Royal Marines did the demonstrators retreat. As they departed, they left behind a traditional East Asian funeral wreath, done up in black and white. Its characters said: "Britain Is Dead!"

■   ■   ■

"I ask myself whether any Prime Minister ever had to contend with such a series of critical events as I have," Neville Chamberlain wrote to his sister on June 17, 1939. "The behavior of the Japs has been increasingly insolent and aggressive . . . , and the Tientsin incident is only the culmination of successive acts of provocation. . . . How it [the Tientsin crisis] will turn out," he added, "I don't know."

He soon found out. Seated across from Foreign Minister Arita, at a desk the size of a card table, Sir Robert Craigie, the British ambassador in Tokyo, had been trying for days to settle the Tientsin issue. The late June weather was hot and Arita was making things even hotter: A cartoonist portrayed Craigie hunched over that tiny table, shoeless, pantless, shirtless, indeed except for his bowler and his heavy horn-rimmed glasses, stark naked.

The cartoonist had hit on the truth. The best Craigie could extract from Arita was a face-saving formula. "His Majesty's Government," a communique finally stated,

> recognize the actual situation in China, where hostilities on a large scale are in progress. . . . The Japanese forces in China have special requirements for the purpose of safeguarding their own security and maintaining public order. . . . His Majesty's Government have no intention of countenancing any acts or measures prejudicial to the attainment of the above-mentioned objects.

In plain language, the British caved in. In the hope that the Japanese now would behave, they were going to hand over the Chinese terrorists, sequestered in Tientsin. Trumpeted a Tokyo newspaper, "A SECOND MUNICH!"

■ ■ ■

The Tientsin crisis did come to an end. The British, by the time the new year came, had conceded to most of Japan's demands, including the handing over of the Chinese terrorists based in Tientsin; but the significance of the Tientsin issue persisted. The British—connected as they were in the real world with the Americans—had presented the Japanese with the specter of Anglo-American support for China. And the Japanese were, at a minimum, resentful.

■ ■ ■

The Tientsin episode set off alarms in Washington. So did a letter to Roosevelt, from Colonel Joseph C. Fegan, Commandant of the Fourth U.S. Marines in Shanghai. Back in 1936, Fegan had accompanied Roosevelt on an official trip to Ottawa and, as with Evans Carlson, F. D. R. used Fegan as a source of confidential advice. Fegan's letter, therefore, was disturbing. "We hear," he wrote to the White House, that negotiations are underway in which the British are offering to share with the Japs their wharves located along the Yangtze in exchange for certain trade privileges. This yield on the part of the British is but an example of what is being carried on sub rosa. There is no question but what the British are selling the Chinese out down the river.

Like many Americans, Roosevelt had hoped that the British Empire could serve as a shield against Japanese aggression. Now the truth was evident—the shield had fallen. America, the president was growing convinced, was going to have to carry its own shield.

■ ■ ■

Roosevelt shared his concern with the cabinet. Seated in the brass-studded leather chair at the head of the table, he spoke of his talk with Grew. According to Ambassador Grew—this from the published diary of Harold C. Ickes—"there is a group of young Japanese officers in the Army and Navy who really dictate to the higher command and to the government what they shall do. Grew suspects that this group was responsible for the sinking of the *Panay*. It was trying to create an incident that would involve us. He is fearful that it will now try to create an incident that will involve England, with what consequences no one can predict."

That was the problem; the consequences of Britain's precipitous decline in the Far East were unpredictable. Addressing the cabinet, Roosevelt hinted at new measures.

Memorandum for the Attorney General:
. . . As you know, the V.P. [Vice-President John Nance
Garner from Texas] takes the definite position that the
President shall not be bound at all by [the neutrality]
legislation, as such legislation offends his constitutional
powers. If we fail to get a [new] Neutrality Bill, how far do
you think I can go in ignoring the existing act—even
though I did sign it?

—F. D. R.

In this letter, classified until 1972, Roosevelt was writing to Frank Murphy, once the governor of Michigan and now the attorney general of the United States. Murphy's response, if any, seems to have vanished—even though Roosevelt did soon elevate him to the U.S. Supreme Court. But the point of Roosevelt's mission was clear: In the interest of the security of the nation, as he saw that security, the president of the United States was asking his attorney general whether he, as president, could evade the law.

■　■　■

For the moment, Roosevelt contented himself with a step indisputably within his powers. On July 26, 1939, following the president's instructions, the State Department gave formal notice that in six months the United States could abrogate the 1911 Japanese–American Treaty of Commerce. The United States would renew the treaty, a spokesman in Washington said, if and only if Japan ceased its maltreatment of Americans in China.

Cheers went up. "I am extremely glad to hear that America has decided on the abrogation of the commercial treaty with Japan," Madam Chiang Kai-shek wrote to James McHugh, the U.S. Marine who was back in Chungking. "This attitude on America's part," she said, "should have some salutary effect on the dwarfs." (Chinese, of whatever stature, referred to the Japanese as dwarfs; one Chinese character stands for "bandit," "dwarf," and "Japanese"). "In rejecting the American–Japanese treaty," the Confederation of Chinese Patriotic Associations wired Hull from Saigon, "you have delivered a grievous blow to the aggressors. Your gesture is greatly appreciated by the civilized world." Even Senator Arthur Vandenberg of Michigan, the owl-eyed and hidebound isolationist, applauded the administration's action.

The Japanese reaction was different. In Tokyo, a Foreign Office spokesman called the treaty abrogation "unthinkable." And more: "There is authoritative reason for believing," Rear Admiral Walter S. Anderson, director of naval intelligence, wrote to Roosevelt on August 25, 1939,

> that the Japanese are concerned with regard to their future supply of oil, in connection with the United States' notice of abroga-

tion of the treaty, and they intimate that it will have a serious effect on their supply if the United States places an embargo on oil, scrap iron, lead, copper, [and] steel.

The Japanese government, in short, saw the treaty abrogation as a prelude to economic war.

Here we see again the pattern of action and reaction. Japan's actions in the Far East—the *Panay* attack, the atrocities, the bombings, the insults, the humiliations, the besieging of Tientsin—all led to America's reaction, the treaty abrogation. In turn, that American reaction raised fears, in Tokyo, that the United States in time would strangle Japan, or at least try to do so. So a new possibility was arising: that in response to the American reaction, Japanese forces would begin fanning out toward the south.

In August 1939, a question mark hung above the Pacific. Would America impose sanctions on Japan?

■ ■ ■

But two events were obscuring that question mark. One of those events was taking place in Central Asia.

Out on the distant frontier, where the borders of Manchuria and Inner and Outer Mongolia merged invisibly on the vast grasslands called the steppes, a war of some sort had been going on since springtime. Just what kind of war was vague. Since Western reporters were unable to get anywhere near the region, the world knew only that *something* was going on.

At a Manchurian outpost called Nomonhan, on the eastern bank of the Halha, which was sometimes a river, sometimes a stream, sometimes a trickle, and sometimes just dust, a series of skirmishes had taken place: Soviet-supported Mongols had crossed the Halha from their side and Japanese units had crossed it from theirs; both had sallied back and forth several times. These clashes produced scant result. By midsummer 1939, in fact, the area had become almost peaceful. In a contemporary photograph, steppe grasses in the foreground frame a wide valley; the valley is treeless and dotted only with Japanese armored cars and tents; and beyond a bend in the Halha River, the steppe extends into the distance and then rises, at the horizon, to a cloudless sky. The scene looks almost serene.

Late in July 1939, however, that bend in the Halha exploded with action. At dawn on the morning of July 24, Japanese sentries scanned the horizon. There, silhouetted against the sky and packed together from north to south as far as the eye could see, was one long row of the boxlike forms of Soviet Russia's tanks. The battle that ensued became known as Zhukov's Masterpiece. In what one Russian observer called a "perfect battle of encirclement," Soviet General Georgi K. Zhukov, whose armored forces held a 4 to 1 numerical advantage, entrapped the Japanese units in a wide-sweeping pincers movement. By August 24, 1939, the battle was over. Most of the Japanese in the valley were dead, and their corpses lay facing the river. The valley of the Halha was now Soviet.

Despite its remoteness, the significance of the Halha River war was vast. In the words of a Russian historian, the battle "deprived [the Japanese] of the basis of their anti-Soviet designs"—it showed them that no longer could they hope to win a war against Russia. And in the judgment of the International Military Tribunal for the Far East (the Tokyo War Crimes Trial), Japan had found that "as the door of opportunity closed in the North, the southern gates began to open."

■ ■ ■

The moon, on the night of September 3, 1939, rode high over a darkened city of London; Hitler had invaded Poland and Britain had declared war on Germany. Thin crosses cut into black paper covered the traffic lights and dim blue bulbs enabled commuters to find their way to the Underground. In Buckingham Palace, King George VI, Queen Elizabeth, and their daughters, the princesses Elizabeth and Margaret Rose, prepared to move to Windsor Castle, twenty miles west of the city. The Foreign Office received a report from Canberra: "If Britain is forced to war, she will not go alone," Prime Minister Robert Gordon Menzies declared; "Australia stands where she stood 25 years ago."

■ ■ ■

On a bright Sunday morning, exactly one week after the British declaration of war, a sports car pulled away from the drive of a country house, just outside London. As the car skirted the city, the driver could see huge barrage balloons floating in the cloudless blue of the sky; London was readying itself for air raids. Reaching the entrance of Windsor Castle, the car entered the Great Park and followed the twisting course of the roadway. Parking in front of the lodge, the driver walked inside. Since the occupants had just moved in, the furniture in the dining room was still sheeted with dust covers. The driver of the sports car apologized for the Sunday morning intrusion, then handed over a slip of paper.

The occupant of the lodge was King George VI. The driver, who in haste had to borrow his son's sports car, was Vincent Massey, the Canadian high commissioner. And on the slip of paper, in words telephoned to Massey only that morning from Canada House, on Grosvenor Square, was Canada's request for permission to declare war on Germany. "It is expedient," the slip of paper stated, "that a proclamation should be issued in the name of His Majesty, in Canada, declaring that a state of war with the German Reich has existed as of and from September 10th."

The king wrote "Approved" and affixed his signature, "George R.I." Canada now had entered World War II, bringing the war to the very northern border of the United States of America.

■   ■   ■

At 2:50 A.M. on September 1, 1939, the telephone in President Roosevelt's White House bedroom started to ring. The president must have been deep into sleep, for of late he had shown signs of profound fatigue. Only days before he had been cruising off Newfoundland, fishing and trying to rest. With the news of the Nazi–Soviet Pact, however, he had rushed back to Washington. When he reached Union Station, reporters noticed, his seersucker suit was soiled and his face was creased in an unaccustomed frown. Now, as Roosevelt lifted the phone receiver, he found that the connection was poor. For a moment or two he failed to make out who was calling. Then he figured it out. It was Ambassador William Bullitt, calling from Paris.

Bullitt had bad news. The Nazis, he had just learned from his counterpart in Warsaw, had begun their invasion of Poland.

Now it was Roosevelt's turn to telephone. Placing the calls himself, he got in touch with Undersecretary of State Sumner Welles, Secretary of War Harry Hines Woodring, Secretary of the Navy Charles Edison, and, at the Carlton Hotel, Secretary of State Hull. Limousines raced out to meet each of these men and, in the dark of the late summer night, the White House turned aglow with light.

After breakfast that morning, Roosevelt met in the Oval Room with reporters. He dispensed with his usual banter, simply expressing the hope that the countries now at war in Europe would refrain from bombing civilians. Phelps Adams uttered the question that was uppermost on all reporters' minds.

"Mr. President," he asked, ". . . can we stay out of it?"

Eyes down, the president sat in silence for many long moments. Then he answered, saying only, "I sincerely hope so."

■ ■ ■

In Tokyo, the government's first reaction to the Nazi–Soviet Pact was "like opening a mail box and having a pack of hornets dash out." To Japanese officialdom, the world seemed turned upside down: The Germans had seemed to be friends; the Russians had seemed to be enemies; but now friends and enemies were friends of each other. It made no sense.

In the midst of this confusion, the Japanese cabinet resigned. A new premier, General Abe Nobuyuki, took office. Japan had no interest in the European war, he declared at a press conference.

Tucked into his statement, however, was a piece of advice for the British: The time had come for the British to withdraw altogether from the East Asian theater.

Recovering with celerity from its shock over recent events, the Japanese government had seen its opportunity—and was ready to take it. With the forces of Britain now needed in Europe, Japan at last could realize its most treasured objective: the creation of a greater East Asian zone of autonomy.

Only America stood in Japan's way.

■ ■ ■

Behind the ornate façade of America's State Department building, a top-level meeting took place on September 12, 1939, in strictest secrecy. Closeted with Secretary Cordell Hull, Undersecretary Sumner Welles, and Assistant Secretary George Messersmith, a private citizen, Hamilton Fish Armstrong, had taken the train from New York to lay out a proposal. A man of moderate height, with brown hair, brown eyes, and a brown moustache, Armstrong was a scion of America's aristocracy, second cousin of a congressman, grandnephew of a secretary of state, and direct descendant of Peter Stuyvesant, the peg-legged governor of old New York. He also was editor of *Foreign Affairs,* the major publication of the New York-based Council on Foreign Relations—which, in turn, financed by the biggest New York banks and by the Rockefeller Foundation, represented the nation's foreign policy establishment. Armed with these credentials, Armstrong had ready access to the State Department. His proposal: a Council–State Department committee, called "War Peace Studies," designed to report to the president on America's coming role in the world.

Hull thought the group a good idea. The Rockefeller Foundation kicked in $44,500 to pay for the study. And, in mid-December, 1939, the committee got to work. It was going to recommend that Roosevelt pursue a "new world order," an "order with profound implications for Japan."

CHAPTER
13

THE AMBASSADOR'S WARNING

While the armies of Germany blitzed into Poland, the world watched transfixed. A huge war map went up on one wall of Roosevelt's White House office, pins stuck in it giving him an up-to-the-hour view of the fighting. As for the American public, the battle of Poland was the biggest news event since the end of World War I. The story was unprecedentedly dramatic. "Horses against tanks!" wrote William Shirer, Berlin correspondent for the *New York Herald*. "The cavalryman's long lance against the tank's long column. Brave and valiant and foolhardy though they were, the Poles were simply overwhelmed by the German onslaught. This was their—and the world's—first experience of the blitzkrieg: the sudden surprise attack; the fighter planes and bombers roaring overhead, reconnoitering, attacking, spreading flame and terror; the Stukas screaming as they dived; the tanks, whole divisions of them, breaking through and thrusting forward 30 or 40 miles in a day; self-propelled, rapid-firing guns rolling 40 miles an hour down even the rutty Polish roads. . . . This was a monstrous mechanized juggernaut such as the world had never seen."

■ ■ ■

"I awakened at 5:30 in the morning." America's ambassador to Poland, Anthony J. Drexel Biddle, Jr. was keeping a journal; this was his entry for September 1, in Warsaw.

171

At first I did not understand what had disturbed me. I went to the window and peered over the tranquil city. All was quiet—and yet I felt trouble was in the air. (It was only later that I ascertained it had been Warsaw's first air alarm that had disturbed my rest—I had evidently been subconsciously aroused by the sirens, which had ceased by the time I awoke. The plane which had caused the sounding of the siren had bombed the race course at the edge of town.) When I put in a telephone call for Mr. Jan Wrszlacki [an official at the Polish Foreign Office], the night operator (still on duty) informed me his line was busy. It remained busy so long that I felt confident something was wrong. Finally I succeeded in getting through to him, and in response to my question, he said I was correct in my expressed suspicion that the Germans had attacked.

As quickly as he could, Drexel, via Ambassador Bullitt in Paris, relayed the word to President Roosevelt; he also cabled long and detailed reports to the White House.

■ ■ ■

September 11, 1939

My dear Churchill:
It is because you and I occupied similar positions in the World War that I want you to know how glad I am that you are back again in the Admiralty. Your problems are, I realize, complicated by new factors but the essential is not very different. What I want you and the Prime Minister to know is that I shall at all times welcome it if you will keep in touch with me personally with anything you want me to know about. You can always send sealed letters through your pouch or my pouch.
    I am glad you did the Marlboro [sic] volumes before this thing started—and I much enjoyed reading them.
                                             —Franklin D. Roosevelt

Soon after the invasion of Poland, Winston Churchill had gone back to being first lord of the admiralty; and with this letter, F. D. R.

opened a correspondence with Churchill that lasted throughout the war. The tomes to which the president referred were Churchill's six volumes entitled *Marlborough—His Life and Times*. The first duke of Marlborough, who had won great victories over the French in the War of the Spanish Succession, was John Churchill, Winston's famous ancestor; and one suspects that the publication of these volumes suited the descendant's political purposes. Certainly the biography illustrated the principle of strategy that Churchill pressed on Roosevelt: the gradual encirclement of the enemy, and strangling him by means both military and economic.

■ ■ ■

Upon his ascension to power in 1933, Adolf Hitler stripped "non-Aryan" academics of their German university posts. More than 100 Jewish physicists had to leave the Reich, some of them finding their way to America. There they found a champion, Alexander Sachs.

Although no scientist himself—he was a philosopher and an economist—Sachs had been a Roosevelt speechwriter and had access, therefore, to the Oval Office. So late in the afternoon of Wednesday, October 11, 1939, he went to the White House. Entering the West Wing, he approached the desk of General Edwin "Pa" Watson. Positioned in the outer office, Watson's role was that of chief dragon, designated to hiss flames on those who presumed to waste the president's time. The last thing on earth Sachs was doing, however, was wasting the president's time. Watson let him in.

"Alex!" came the cheery voice from behind the desk in the Oval Office. "What are you up to?"

With curly hair and a receding chin, Sachs resembled Harpo Marx; and with Roosevelt especially he often played the clown. Now Sachs proceeded to warm up his audience of one. He had a yarn for Roosevelt, he said, the tale of a young man from Pennsylvania more than a century before. Writing a letter to Napoleon, the young man had laid out a scheme whereby a few French ships, without sails, could attack and destroy the Royal Navy. Napoleon had only scoffed. The young man had gone ahead to build those kinds of ships anyway—they were the submarine and the steamboat—and the young man, of course, was Robert Fulton. Roosevelt laughed.

Sachs then advised the president to listen with care. Respecting Sachs, Roosevelt took the advice; he even called on his valet, Arthur Prettyman, for two snifters and a bottle of prized Napoleon brandy. Passing one glass over to Sachs, Roosevelt sat back in his chair to listen.

After a concise explanation, Sachs handed Roosevelt a letter from Albert Einstein. Einstein, the world's leading theoretical physicist, recently had immigrated from Germany and was fully abreast of developments there. Because of scientific advances, in fact, Einstein's letter informed Roosevelt, Hitler's Third Reich soon would be able to build "bombs of hitherto unenvisaged potency and scope." A "single bomb of this type," Einstein foresaw, "carried by boat and exploded in port, might well destroy the whole port together with some of the surrounding territory." Einstein's next words were even more alarming. "I understand," he wrote, "Germany has actually stopped the sale of uranium from the Czechoslovakian mines which she had taken over. . . ."

Roosevelt looked up.

"Alex," he said to Sachs, "what you are after is to see that the Nazis don't blow us up."

"Precisely," Sachs responded.

Roosevelt buzzed the intercom and "Pa" Watson appeared at the door. Handing him Einstein's letter, Roosevelt said, "This requires action." F. D. R.'s comment was the start of the Manhattan Project, the building of the atomic bomb.

■   ■   ■

Shortly after Sachs's conversation with Roosevelt, Lieutenant General Yasuda Takeo started to worry. A short, stocky man, and an electrical engineer by training, Yasuda was the director of the Japanese army's Military Aeronautic Technical Laboratory in Tokyo. Although an administrator, Yasuda had retained his interest in physics. Following journals from abroad with care, he, like Einstein, realized that the Germans had made a momentous discovery in late 1938: When fissioning, uranium atoms gave off neutrons; and the neutrons could split other atoms; an ensuing chain reaction could trigger a gigantic explosion. Someday, somewhere, Yasuda knew, somebody was going to build a bomb of unparalleled power.

But who?

Yasuda knew of Germany's progress; but he also knew that at Berkeley, Ernest O. Lawrence had won the Nobel Prize for the invention of the cyclotron. So America, as well as Germany, had the potential for building that bomb.

Yasuda was worried. Suddenly, late in 1939, the American journals that had dealt with physics were saying nothing further about fission. What, Yasuda wondered, was wrong? Yasuda believed that America must be building a bomb.

■ ■ ■

Under another veil of silence, cryptographers in Washington were on the trail of breaking the Japanese codes. They had made one breakthrough already—back on the evening of July 26, 1935. Captain Yamaguchi Tamon, Japan's naval attaché to the United States, was living then in a suite in the Alban Towers, a chic apartment building on Wisconsin Avenue; his office and his living quarters were adjoining. There he had been having a problem. During the evenings his duplex often lost power. The lights would "flicker, grow dim, then go out altogether," even though lights elsewhere in the building were still on. He would call for an electrician, but by the time the repairman could arrive, the power would have returned. All this was mysterious but not mysterious enough, apparently, for alarm.

So on the night of July 26, 1935, Captain Yamaguchi and his aides went to a dinner party, leaving only one person, a file clerk, on duty behind. The host and hostess for the evening were Ellis and Claire Zacharias, whose house on Porter Street was close to the Washington Cathedral. Zacharias, a U.S. navy commander in intelligence, had returned recently from Tokyo, where he had served as the American naval attaché: Yamaguchi and Zacharias thus were counterparts, acquaintances. And to renew that acquaintance, they said, the Zachariases had invited Yamaguchi and his staff for dinner; the occasion, ostensibly, was *chugen*, a Japanese midsummer festival. Yamaguchi agreed to come.

When the guests arrived, Commander Zacharias mixed martinis, ladling out the gin and holding back on the vermouth. As Captain Yamaguchi was imbibing his first martini, the lights back in his Wisconsin Avenue suite flickered again and went out. As he was downing his second martini, his file clerk was telephoning the desk downstairs, asking for the electrician. As Yamaguchi was gulping his third martini, two men dressed in overalls showed up at the apartment door, identifying themselves as the electricians; this time the lights still were down. And as Captain Yamaguchi was staggering to the dinner table, the two men in overalls were starting to check everything, sockets, switches, wiring, and, in the office next to the living quarters, a typewriterlike device that sat uncovered on a work table. The men happened to have a powerful flashlight and its beam happened to settle on that typewriterlike device. Then the yellow disk of light moved on, lit up a socket, and the two men in overalls actually found a short circuit. Captain Yamaguchi's electrical trouble was over.

The two men, assistants to Commander Zacharias, soon sequestered themselves in a locked room of the Navy Building on Constitution Avenue, sketching everything they could remember about the machine their beam had illuminated. The machine was a coding device, known to the Japanese as Type No. 91-A; Zacharias, who had suspected its presence in the Wisconsin Avenue duplex, gave it the arbitrary name of "RED machine." The "RED machine" was an early computer; within months of the episode in Captain Yamaguchi's flat, U.S. Navy cryptanalysts had figured out how to reconstruct it. Now operatives in Washington could read the reports, sent back to Tokyo, by the Japanese naval attaché.

And more: By the autumn of 1939, from listening posts scattered around the Pacific—Seattle's Bainbridge Island, Pearl Harbor, Wake Island, and Cavite in the Philippines—the U.S. Navy was eavesdropping on naval messages out of Tokyo. From that eavesdropping, one point became increasingly clear: The Japanese navy was going to move south, and soon.

■   ■   ■

The Japanese, too, had been gleaning intelligence. From the mid-1930s onward, Japanese agents, many of them working as fishermen, dentists, and barbers, had reached Central America, finding their way into Costa Rica, Nicaragua, El Salvador, and Mexico. Based in Mexico, on the west coast port of Guaymas, Japanese fishing fleets, equipped with radios, ship-to-shore telephones, and cameras, were observing U.S. naval maneuvers.

Japanese agents were even present in California. There, in 1939, two spy scandals erupted.

Lieutenant Commander Miyazaki Toshio, an official with the Japanese consulate in Los Angeles, found an American recruit—Harry Thomas Thompson, a twenty-eight-year-old former farmhand from Maryland who had become a yeoman in the navy. His tour over, Thompson was unemployed. Miyazaki met him on the San Pedro docks, offering an advance and $500 a month if Thompson would spy for Japan.

Thompson accepted the offer. Buying himself a fresh uniform and posing as a seaman still on duty, he wandered around San Diego and onto the warships. He must have been a good actor, for he asked questions, took photographs, and even snitched codebooks, all of which he passed along to Miyazaki without once being challenged. Unfortunately, for himself at least, Thompson was unable to keep his mouth shut. To his San Diego apartment mate, Willard James Turntine, another former yeoman, Thompson bragged that he was in contact with a mysterious Japanese named "Tanni."

Alarmed, Turntine got in touch with the Office of Naval Intelligence. Investigating, the Office of Naval Intelligence discovered that "Tanni" was Miyazaki; in Thompson's garbage can, furthermore, detectives found the draft of a letter Thompson had sent to Miyazaki, quitting his work as a spy. Miyazaki, investigators concluded, must have received the original: He had left the country posthaste. Found guilty of espionage, Thompson got fifteen years in prison.

John Semer Farnsworth, formerly a lieutenant commander in the U.S. Navy, also got caught. To the members of the class of 1915, back at Annapolis, the nicknames "Dodo," "Si," "Charlie," "Mayevsky," and "Johnny" all designated Midshipman Farnsworth, happy-go-lucky, good-natured, extremely intelligent, and hard-drinking. Graduating high in his class and going into naval aviation, Farnsworth rose rapidly through the ranks.

Then, however, his career went sour. He had married a Maryland debutante and, whether to keep up with her family or to pay for his own boozing, or both, he extorted money from an enlisted man. Apprehended, he lied about it. A navy court-martial sent him packing. Out of a job, he offered his services to several countries, always without success, until he approached Japan. The Japanese hired him eagerly, starting him with a cash advance of $50,000—on condition that he obtain and deliver a copy of the U.S. Navy handbook, *The Service of Information and Security*.

The handbook, containing photographs of all the battleships in the U.S. Navy, was classified; Farnsworth nonetheless did the job. Scurrying about the Navy Department in Washington, he located a copy, photocopied it, and delivered the copy to the Japanese embassy, the two-story, yellow brick structure on Massachusetts Avenue. He did more. Pretending to be drunk, which he usually was, he donned the uniform of an American naval commander, boarded a destroyer at Annapolis, fooled an ensign into showing him maneuver data, and, information in hand, drove again to the Japanese embassy.

Still on the trail of money and perhaps notoriety, Farnsworth then did himself in. Contacting Fulton Lewis, Jr., the columnist and crack Washington reporter for the Hearst newspaper chain, he proposed a deal: For $20,000, he would write a series of articles entitled, "How I Was a Spy in the American Navy for the Japanese Government." He added a condition: Because he intended to sail for Germany, he wanted three days' lead time before publication. Lewis notified the Office of Naval Intelligence; in 1937, a federal court imprisoned Farnsworth on the charge of espionage.

Late 1939 brought a new revelation. A Mexican peasant, walking along the shore of Lake Texcoco, found a pigeon that lay exhausted alongside the water; attached to the pigeon's leg was a narrow, tubular box. According to *The New York Times* of November 11, 1939, the campesino delivered the pigeon plus box to authorities in Mexico City and the Mexican government showed the contents of the box to officials at the U.S. embassy. Inside the tube were three messages: One, written in pencil on a rectangular sheet of yellowish white paper, twice said "J. V."; the second, written in pen and also on yellowish white paper, bore the designation "U2–69"; and the third, written in the margin of a clipping from a German newspaper, gave a nautical position fifteen miles off Tampico. A notation read: "October 17, 4:00 A.M." A German submarine in the Gulf of Mexico, the U.S. embassy concluded, had been trying to make contact with someone on shore. Who?

As Undersecretary of State Welles already had intimated to Roosevelt, Friedrich Karl von Schleebruggs, a German intelligence officer, had set up shop in Mexico City. His task there was severalalfold: to buy oil from America; to spy on America; and to cooperate with the Japanese intelligence apparatus, widespread along Mexico's Pacific coast—where Yaqui Indians, recruited by Japanese agents, kept watch on the American navy.

By the end of 1939, then, two sets of intelligence services, the American versus the Japanese and German, were circling each other like wrestlers. The overt war would not start for another two years. The covert war, however, was well under way.

■　■　■

Japan faced a distinct disadvantage: The country even *looked* poor. John P. Marquand, the American novelist, visiting Japan, had noticed how the landscape looked "anciently worn and brown." As he peered from his train window, "human figures appeared and vanished, caught in the immemorial attitudes of old paintings: men and women bending over mattocks or bearing baskets or walking with the long pole from which two buckets hung. The scattered farm houses, mostly thatch-roofed, looked as though faintly sketched on an endless faded scroll." A drive through Tokyo itself looked Marquand through "streets of . . . crowded wooden bungalows, lightly impermanently constructed, as though solider homes were not worth building in the face of the earthquakes that so frequently visit these islands. I could understand," Marquand here was speaking through the voice of one of his fictional protagonists, "Japan's sensitiveness to any enemy threat from the air. A sight of those unpainted matchboxes of dwellings, with hardly air space between them . . . explained why Japan watched with unconcealed misgivings the construction of our airplane carriers and the development of Chinese . . . aviation. A few incendiary bombs were all that would be needed to bring about almost unimaginable disaster, and I have been told that the inflammability of Osaka and other great industrial nerve centers of the Empire was even more pronounced." Japan, in short, was vulnerable.

Vulnerable was precisely the word being used, in the autumn of 1939, by the planning board of the Japanese cabinet. That planning board had already reached conclusions that were, at best, baleful. To continue the war in China, the board stated, Japan needed to build up precision in industrial machinery, gas separators, and mercury rectifiers; chemicals in bulk, from ammonium sulfate to caustic soda; scrap iron; and lubricants, oil, and gas. Malaya and the Philippines did produce iron ore and the Dutch East Indies did produce petroleum. The preponderance of these products, however, came from America. But America had become the great Pacific antagonist, and the war in China was going nowhere.

• • •

"Mr. Chairman, Ladies and Gentlemen: First of all, permit me to express my great satisfaction on returning from leave of absence. . . ."

The speaker, Ambassador Joseph C. Grew, had just returned to Japan from his sojourn in America. He had long looked forward to going home, for the strain of being ambassador in Japan, a hostile country, had taken its toll. Grew's trip, fortunately, had proved refreshing. Home in Boston's Back Bay, in his family's three-storied house on Marlborough Street, he had relaxed at long last; reuniting himself with his grandchildren at a cottage in New Hampshire, he had been able to put the cares of his post aside altogether. But not for long. As Grew traveled a bit, he was struck by the "steadily hardening" views toward Japan, not only of his friends but also of the people at large—"shop clerks, gas station attendants, taxi drivers, and Pullman passengers."

In Washington, the administration was clearly determined not to let Japan squeeze Americans out of China. On the contrary: President Roosevelt spoke "confidently" to Grew of "intercepting the Japanese fleet as it moved southward, of reinforcing Manila and Pearl Harbor, and of holding naval maneuvers in Hawaiian waters." The president, Grew noted in his diary, had finished with "gestures of welcome"—gestures such as the voyage of the *Astoria*—and was quite prepared to slap an embargo on Japan.

Now, back in Tokyo, Grew decided to speak frankly. The occasion was an after-dinner speech to a meeting of the American–Japan Society. The Society was prestigious; the banquet would include American businessmen and their wives, along with Japanese from the highest financial, diplomatic, and court circles. So in preparing his speech, Grew chose not to list specific Japanese atrocities in China—anything that smacked of an attack would offend the Japanese in his audience, he believed, and would make a dialogue impossible. He delivered the speech in a Tokyo banquet hall on the evening of October 19, 1939.

Stepping to the lectern, Grew, dressed in white tie, took off his horn-rimmed glasses, using them for emphasis. He began diplomatically, saying how glad he was to be back in Japan. He also praised the Japanese pavilion at the New York World's Fair.

Then he changed his tack. What he had to say next, Grew stated, came "straight from the horse's mouth"—he was going to relay the thoughts of the president of the United States.

On "returning from a long stay in America," Grew told his listeners, "would it not insult your intelligence if I were to talk of trivialities?" He proposed instead to speak of important things—of how and why Americans so strongly resented Japan's actions in China. Grew allowed that many "of you who are listening to me may well be thinking: 'There are two sides to every picture. . . .' Granted. In America . . . I did my best to show various angles of the Japanese point of view. But here in Japan I shall try to show the American point of view. . . . Let me therefore try to remove a few utterly fallacious conceptions of the American attitude as I think they exist in Japan today." Any thought of America's hostility to Japan being based on misunderstanding, Grew held, was mistaken. There were no misunderstandings: "The facts as they exist today are accurately known by the American people. I do not suppose any country in the world today is better served by the press and radio with accurate foreign information than the United States. . . ."

Grew now became even franker. The Japanese in his audience were attending his every word.

"Many of you," he stated, "are not aware of the increasing extent to which the people of the United States resent methods which Japanese armed forces are employing in China, and what appear to be their objectives. The American people regard with growing seriousness the violation and interference with American rights by Japanese armed forces in China in disregard of treaties and agreements." His compatriots, stated Grew, were being more than just "legalistic." They were, rather, angry and fearful. Japan's New Order for East Asia, Americans feared, would leave their own Open Door principle "truncated and emasculated"; the injuries suffered by Chinese—and by Americans—appeared "wholly needless."

Grew paused, putting his glasses back on. For his audience he had some words of warning.

When "such opinion tends toward unanimity," he stated, "it is a force which a government cannot possibly overlook and will not fail to reflect in its policies and actions." America, that is, was likely to do more than just abrogate a treaty. So Japan had better change its ways.

Back in America, the reaction to Grew's speech was ecstatic. *The New York Times* praised the talk as "the strongest ever made by a diplomat in Japan"; editorial writers in other papers described Grew's message, variously, as "a . . . thunderbolt," "good if bitter medicine," "bare-knuckle diplomacy," and, of course, "straight from the horse's mouth"; the *Washington Star* ran a cartoon, showing Grew in his tuxedo, wagging his finger at a toothy and sinister little Japanese soldier. In the States, in fact, Joe Grew became a national hero. After all, without firing a shot, he seemed to have persuaded Japan to mend the errors of its ways.

Indeed: Japanese airplanes stopped bombing American missions in China; Japanese authorities in Shanghai promised to reopen the Yangtze to foreign shipping; Japanese soldiers evacuated certain American properties in China; and Japanese officials initiated investigations into American complaints, piling their desks high with stacks of reports and, in a few cases, actually offered compensation. As if suddenly converted, the Japanese seemed to be seeking atonement for their sins.

■ ■ ■

Yet soon after Grew's speech, Japanese propagandists began blasting away at the United States, warning America against meddling in Asia. "We possess the strongest Navy in the Far East and dominate the South Seas markets," warned the Institute of the Pacific from Tokyo. "The South Seas belong to the Far East and Japan is entitled to share the wealth of those regions, which Europe snitched while Japan was self-isolated [before Commodore Perry's visit to Tokyo Bay]. It is necessary to rectify Japan's economic portion, and now is the . . . moment, while European powers with interest in the South Seas are preoccupied. . . . It is sometimes proposed that Dutch oil be forcibly seized, but other methods can be tried *at first* [emphasis added]. . . . We do not expect Britain, France, Holland readily to accept our demands, but the longer the war lasts, the more certain it becomes that our ideas will materialize." The Institute of the Pacific attacked the United States especially for trying to preserve the "status quo."

And exactly one day after Grew gave his speech, Nomura Kichisaburo, just confirmed as Japan's foreign minister, spoke to reporters. The "determination of the entire Japanese nation to bring about a New Order in East Asia," he announced, "is too strong to be changed or affected by the interference of a third power." By "third power" he meant the United States.

In the end, therefore, Ambassador Grew's warning met with defiance. One threat had engendered another.

■ ■ ■

The threats, or what seemed to be threats, were mounting like storm clouds in summer. Japan, the U.S. Army attaché reported from Tokyo, was planning to exploit the bauxite, aluminum, and nickel reserves in their League of Nations–mandated islands, just above Australia. From Chungking, moreover, H. H. K'ung, serving then as China's prime minister, raised questions that *Time* passed along to its American readers: "Why should Japan build a great Navy if her territorial ambitions are confined to China? Why should they have established in the United States, Panama, and elsewhere in the Americas, an espionage system from coast to coast? Why, also, should Japanese fishing fleets congregate in [great] numbers off the

Pacific Coast of the United States; and why should Japanese fishermen ply their craft in every bay and inlet of the Hawaiian Islands?"

. . .

Just after dusk on September 19, 1939, a small slender man darted out of the State Department building, heading across Executive Avenue to the White House. He was Assistant Secretary of State A. A. Berle, Jr. Berle always seemed in a hurry; an acquaintance dubbed him a "ball of intellect and nervous energy." But on this evening he had a special reason for haste. As he read the latest diplomatic cables, his own worst fear seemed to be coming true: Reports suggested a joint German–Russian–Japanese division of the Eurasian landmass "from Manchuria to the Rhine," a power bloc that might well dominate the rest of the world. Berle knew his duty. He had to bring his forebodings to the attention of President Roosevelt.

As they met at the president's bedside, Roosevelt seemed "very sleepy." He agreed with Berle, nevertheless, that Hitler, Stalin, and the Japanese would "keep on going while the going was good," meaning that at a minimum the Nazis would be seeking bases on the shores of the Atlantic.

Continuing the conversation the next afternoon, Berle and Roosevelt were joined by Samuel Rosenman, a presidential speechwriter, and by Secretary of State Hull. Roosevelt, Hull suggested, might state publicly that the United States would never declare war; Hull may have been thinking of his own presidential bid, and of throwing his lot in with the isolationists. Whatever his motivation, the Oval Office for a few moments, Berle recorded, was a tomb of "dead silence." At last Roosevelt turned to Hull and asked, "Can you guarantee that? Can I guarantee that?" The answer, clearly, was no. Having "in mind the discussion of the night before," Berle wrote in his diary, "in which the President had indicated that [America might go to war if] the sweep of German arms finally indicated the establishment of a naval base in the Atlantic islands, say the Azores, there was not much question what was in the President's mind." The danger was coming closer and closer.

Still hoping that the friendly countries—Britain, France, and

China—could tie the aggressors down, Roosevelt appeared the next day before Congress. He was going to ask for a repeal of the arms embargo.

■　■　■

Filing into the House gallery, diplomats from nearly every country save Italy, Germany, and Japan peered toward the floor below. Called by the president into special session, senators and representatives, many of them back from far-flung places, were finding their chairs and sitting. Positioned in front were some of Roosevelt's closest allies: Representatives Sol Bloom from Manhattan; Claude Pepper, the wiry, red-haired senator from Florida; Senator James F. Byrnes of South Carolina. *Time* called Byrnes so slick that he could "charm snakes without a flute"; from behind the scenes in Congress, Byrnes was going to lead the floor flight for Roosevelt.

Months before, the Senate had received the Pittman resolution, a measure that, amending the neutrality laws, would have overturned the embargo on arms sales to friendly belligerents abroad. The bill had gone nowhere, partly because Congress was not yet ready for it and partly because Pittman's grasp on leadership, indeed on himself, was slipping. Now, however, with Byrnes's help, Roosevelt intended to jolt Congress into action. For the first time since becoming president, he entered the House chamber without smiling.

After a brief preamble, F. D. R. asked Congress to (1) forbid Americans to travel in danger zones or aboard belligerent ships; (2) restrict the movements of American ships in danger zones, such zones to be defined by the president; (3) allow ninety-day credits for friendly belligerents; and (4) repeal the arms embargo. "It has been erroneously said that [the embargo repeal] might bring us nearer to war," Roosevelt said, anticipating his opponents' objections. "I give you my deep and unalterable conviction . . . that by repeal of the embargo the United States will more probably remain at peace than if the law remains as it is today."

Many of those seated in the House chamber stirred uneasily, for Roosevelt's voice had lingered over the word "probably." As if in reassurance, he added a warning: "We know what might happen to us . . . if the new philosophies of force were to encompass the other continents and invade our own. We, no more than other nations, can ill afford to be surrounded by the enemies of our faith."

■   ■   ■

After giving his speech, Roosevelt set off for Hyde Park. There he received a note from Lord Tweedsmuir, the governor general of Canada; Tweedsmuir wanted to know if he might "slip down inconspicuously." In private life, Tweedsmuir was John Buchan, the Scottish soldier, statesman, and writer of thrillers. One of Buchan's novels, *The 39 Steps,* had been turned into a movie by Alfred Hitchcock. After his move to Ottawa, Buchan—Tweedsmuir—had become one of Roosevelt's closest friends. F. D. R. nevertheless asked him to wait. A visit from so prominent a personage as Tweedsmuir, a Briton to boot, was bound to become public knowledge, cannon fodder for the isolationists. "I am almost literally walking on eggs," Roosevelt wrote back to Lord Tweedsmuir, "and, having delivered my message to Congress, . . . I am at the moment saying nothing, seeing nothing, and hearing nothing."

Tweedsmuir stayed in Ottawa. Roosevelt was involved in the fight of his political life.

■   ■   ■

At the behest of Fulton Lewis, Jr., the commentator, Colonel Charles Lindbergh went on the air. America had no need to repeal the arms embargo, "Lindy" claimed: "What more could we ask than the Atlantic Ocean on the east, the Pacific on the west? . . . Our civilization is [not] defending itself against some Asiatic intruder. . . ." For Lindbergh, rather, the war was the result merely of "greed, . . . fear, and . . . intrigue. . . ."

Supporting Lindbergh was the panoply of America's isolationists. David Brinkley, the television commentator, has described them thus: "There were beer hall fascists who, not always secretly, admired Hitler and would not have minded slipping into brown shirts of their own and taking to the streets with flaming torches and swastika flags and truncheons to break the heads of those they despised. There were communists who opposed Hitler until he signed [the] non-aggression pact with the Soviet Union and overnight did a 180-degree turn when orders came from Moscow. There were Irish-Americans still unwilling to forget or forgive Britain's exploitation of Ireland. A few industrial tycoons saw Hitler as eminently reasonable in his treatment of business, which was more than they could say for Roosevelt. . . . There were those who believed any enemy of Roosevelt must be a friend of theirs. And still others, many of them in Congress, . . . felt that Roosevelt had an appetite for dictatorship and that in the strains of a war with Hitler he might become one. In their view, anything he wanted, including going to war, should be denied him."

In whatever way they could, the isolationists in Congress were going to deny the president. The day after Roosevelt's address, their leaders met to plot strategy in the office of California's Senator Hiram W. Johnson. Johnson's office, which overlooked the Supreme Court and the Capitol Plaza, had special significance: In this very office President Woodrow Wilson's opponents had planned their successful attack on his League of Nations treaty; now the isolationists hoped to repeat the success. They were mostly Republicans, but they came from every region of the country save the south— John G. Townsend, Jr. of Delaware, D. Worth Clark of Idaho, Homer T. Bone of Washington, Henrik Shipstead of Minnesota, Bennett C. Clark of Missouri, David I. Walsh of Massachusetts, as well as the big five, Johnson, Gerald P. Nye, Wisconsin's Robert M. La Follette, Idaho's William E. Borah, and Vandenberg of Michigan. Speaking with reporters after the meeting, Senator Vandenberg said: "This bill [Senator Pittman's] has upon its face the trademark of unneutrality and malice." Peering over his spectacles from just behind Vandenberg, Senator Johnson added, "We are going to have a bully fight."

And so they were, for Roosevelt himself was pulling no punches. Senator Pat Harrison was a Mississippi Democrat, leaning toward the isolationists; Roosevelt phoned him twice, personally soliciting his support. Georgia's Senator Walter George was in the hospital, undergoing an eye operation; the president sent him a get-well card, signing it himself. James Elliott Heath, a Virginian, had been a crony of Virginia's Democratic Senator Carter Glass for thirty years; Roosevelt appointed Heath to the post of federal customs inspector in Norfolk. Alf M. Landon had been the G.O.P.'s presidential candidate in 1936 and Frank Knox, a Chicago newspaper publisher, was a Republican; Roosevelt invited them both to the White House for chats. Roosevelt thus was reaching out to opponents—midwestern Republicans and Democratic southerners who had opposed him on the Court-packing plan; he was sallying forth into the citadels of the enemy.

On October 2, 1939, the full Senate sat to debate. Positioning themselves on the carpeted floor, Senators Pittman and Borah had a go at each other, letting loose floods, torrents, cascades of words. Offstage the two men were friends; onstage they were the bitterest of enemies. Their words persuaded no one, probably, but the isolationists did pull off a maneuver. Gaining the floor, Senator Nye proposed that President Roosevelt act as mediator in the European war and Senator Edwin C. Johnson, an isolationist from Colorado, introduced a resolution: While F. D. R. mediated, the resolution declared, Congress could recess. The purpose here was obvious. Events in Poland had tilted public opinion toward embargo repeal, so the isolationists were hoping to buy time. From the State Department building, however, Cordell Hull cut them short. The administration, he announced, had no intention of mediating in Europe.

Counterpunching, the isolationists went public; going on the radio, Senator Rush D. Holt, a West Virginia Democrat, denounced the embargo repeal. But Senator George W. Norris, a Nebraska Democrat, rebutted. Although a Roosevelt ally, Norris until this moment had stayed neutral on repeal. Now, on radio, he spoke out. Norris was blunt. The real issue, he stated, was whether America would do what was right—go to the aid of the allies. And back in the Capitol, two more orators, Senator Tom Connally from Texas, a cosponsor of the Pittman bill, and Senator Arthur H. Vandenburg, turned against each other. Vandenberg said repealing the embargo was like "monkeying with a buzz saw." "Why change?" he demanded. "Why take a chance?" Connally took the floor. With his string tie and curly locks, he looked like a cartoonist's caricature of a southern senator; and, in fact, deserting his notes, he drawled and twanged his way into an old-style stump speech that lasted for more than two hours. He stood four-square behind repeal.

The isolationists maneuvered again. Senator Charles W. Tobey, a New Hampshire Republican, moved to separate embargo repeal from the rest of the Pittman bill. His resolution lost, 65 to 26, but it did eat up a few days. Worried by the delay, Roosevelt discreetly compromised: The White House dropped the ninety-day credit clause as well as the limits on shipping.

But having yielded, Roosevelt then struck back, striking as only Roosevelt could strike, indirectly but effectively. Under a provision of the Neutrality Law of 1935, F. D. R. barred belligerent submarines from American ports except through *force majeure*—diplomatese for "acts of God"—and emergencies not due to warfare. Roosevelt's action, following repeated reports of submarines off Maine, Florida, and Alaska, was good public relations. It reminded Americans that in 1916, just a year before we went to war with imperial Germany, a German U-boat had shown up in the Baltimore harbor. Roosevelt's gesture was a reminder that such danger remained.

The isolationists then made a mistake. Late in October 1939, they turned Charles Lindbergh loose once again. Speaking on a nationwide radio hookup, he urged the ban of all "offensive" weapons; and he implied that Canada should sever its Commonwealth ties with the United Kingdom. He should have stuck to his planes. Walter Lippmann, the columnist, held that no one in 100 years had done as much to harm relations with Britain. Dorothy Thompson, the journalist, sputtered that "nowhere on this soil has the Nazi concept of imperialism been so clearly stated as in Colonel Lindbergh's second speech." (At a dinner party once, an affair attended by Dorothy Thompson, Lindbergh, who was a practical joker, had poured Listerine in a decanter of burgundy; Miss Thompson, a respecter of wine, now paid him back.)

Other reporters got wind of the rumor that, in making his speech, Lindbergh actually was trying to set himself up to run for the Senate from New Jersey—for the seat once held by his father-in-law. But Lindbergh's balloon exploded even before he could get it blown up. Upon hearing his second radio address, his mother-in-law, Mrs. Dwight Morrow, the acting president of Smith College, repudiated it in public.

Then, on October 27, 1939, the time came for the Congress to vote. As twilight settled on the Capitol dome, Senator Clark of Missouri rallied the troops for one last charge against repeal. As a substitute for the Pittman bill, he offered a new measure, a total arms embargo; but the Senate repudiated it, 60 to 33. Soon thereafter the real vote came: By 63 to 30, the Senate decided in favor of embargo repeal. On November 2, 1939, the House of Representatives, too, voted for repeal. The Pittman bill at last could go to the White House.

At 10:00 A.M. on November 3, 1939, Roosevelt staged a little ceremony in the Oval Office. Roosevelt himself sat behind the desk, covered as it was with the usual clutter, books, stacks of papers, figurines of Democratic donkeys, ashtrays, flags, and letter knives. The president was wearing a gray, chalk-striped suit. In front of the desk, a photograph shows, stood Senator Pittman, tall and wan. Ranged around from Pittman's left were House Foreign Affairs Committee chairman Sol Bloom, short, smiling, and wearing a pince-nez; Speaker of the House (and father of Tallulah, the actress) William B. Bankhead, sharp-eyed and watchful; Cordell Hull; Vice-President Garner, with cigar and white eyebrows; and Kentucky's Alben Barkley, majority leader of the U.S. Senate. Roosevelt signed the Pittman bill and passed out pens all around.

Everyone present understood the ceremony's significance. As a supplier of weaponry, the United States now was a participant in the war, even without a formal declaration.

■ ■ ■

Out in the Atlantic Ocean, although far to the south of the United States, a battle was shaping up that would hint further at America's lack of neutrality. This battle involved the German pocket battleship, the *Admiral Graf Spee*.

The first grayness on the south Atlantic, on December 13, 1939, showed nothing to the lookouts high in the crow's nests above the *Graf Spee*. With the dawn itself, their visibility increased to twenty miles, and still they saw nothing. The breeze was light and the swells were calm; all signs pointed toward another beautiful, and perhaps profitable, day. The *Graf Spee* was a raider, larger than a cruiser and faster than a battleship; the vessel had been harassing

Allied commerce in the Indian and the Atlantic oceans for two months already.

Now the ship was positioned off the estuary of the River Plate, that great body of water that flows between Argentina and Uruguay, and goes into the Atlantic Ocean at Montevideo. The River Plate for a century was a major carrier of foodstuffs, especially Argentinean beef and wheat, to northwestern Europe; thus the sea-lane between Montevideo and Liverpool was vital to Great Britain's survival. The *Graf Spee*'s assignment was to break into that sea-lane, to strangle it. The ship's lookouts were scouting for prey.

Just after dawn one of them did notice something. Dead ahead on the horizon and cutting smack across the *Graf Spee*'s course, two tiny masts came into view. Four more masts then appeared. The *Graf Spee*'s electronic gear went into action, measuring the distance to those masts as seventeen miles. Captain Hans Langsdorff increased his speed and ordered the battle ensigns hoisted.

Langsdorff peered ahead from the bridge, identifying the British cruiser *Exeter* and then two destroyers. Surely, he assumed, these British ships were hiding a convoy of merchantmen, and those merchantmen were steaming northward, just beyond the horizon. The faster the *Graf Spee* sped, the more distinctly the forms of the British vessels loomed.

Then, for Captain Langsdorff, the truth hit home. There was no convoy. He had raced right into a trap.

The *Graf Spee* had speed and firepower, but it was only one ship, and the British had three, *Exeter* and the two destroyers, *Ajax* and *Achilles*. Gunfire and torpedoes flew back and forth and smoke screens spread out, rendering any accuracy a matter of chance.

At the heart of the action was the *Graf Spee*, twisting this way and that, dodging, lashing out blindly, striking now and then with a hit, but receiving two scores for every one it delivered. All in all, the *Graf Spee* suffered more than twenty blows, some of them insignificant, but others killing thirty-six men and wounding fifty-eight, including Captain Langsdorff, wrecking the upper works and the galleys. Light German cruisers had been trailing the *Graf Spee*, but as darkness fell, they held back, trying to stay out of danger. The HMS *Exeter*, too, had been hurt, and made off slowly toward the Falkland Islands, with fifty-three dead and many crewmen wounded.

But what would happen to the *Graf Spee* was the critical issue. Although in great pain, Captain Langsdorff was lucid enough to realize that he could never make it to Germany. He turned down toward Montevideo, the capital of Uruguay. Uruguay was neutral; his ship and his crew, he hoped, might find succor there. The *Graf Spee* arrived in the port. Government and apartment buildings rose against the hills in the background. In the Parliament building in the foreground, close to the water's edge, local politicians were anguishing over what to do. Faced with a variety of international pressures, they finally reached their decision: *The Graf Spee* was entitled to repairs; but it could only stay for three days.

Repairs were one thing but escape was another. A number of Uruguayan mechanics did come aboard. While they were doing so, however, the sharks, otherwise known as the British, smelled blood and were gathering, with more and more warships, at the mouth of the River Plate, just waiting.

Cables flashed back and forth between the *Graf Spee* and the admiralty in Berlin. Hitler had no idea what to do; neither did Admiral Erich Räder, the navy's chief of staff, so the decision flew back to Captain Langsdorff, wounded, perhaps delirious, but on the spot and, therefore, a likely scapegoat. The captain made his choice. Early in the evening of December 17, 1939, the *Graf Spee*, blackened and scorched but with its battle colors up and followed by the German steamer *Tacoma*, slipped out of its berth in Montevideo.

Just inside international waters downstream, a trio of British warships, *Ajax*, *Achilles*, and *Cumberland*, pointed their guns and waited for the Germans to cross the invisible line. Uruguayans by the thousands stood on the riverbank, watching in silence. The sun was setting behind the *Graf Spee*. The pocket battleship stopped just before the three-mile limit. Crew members transferred to the *Tacoma*. For a few moments the estuary was hushed. Then, in the darkness, a flame or two flicked up from the *Graf Spee*, by order of the Germans themselves, some more flames, followed by an explosion, and another explosion, and another and another, until finally the *Graf Spee* was a ball of fire, all red and yellow against the black of the late December South American night.

The administration in Washington had drawn a "neutrality zone" around the American republics, in both the Northern and Southern Hemispheres; the zone extended 200 miles out to sea, and so the British warships off Montevideo were far within the United States' self-proclaimed limits. Indeed, the U.S. State Department duly filed a protest.

But British officials in London noted the tone of the protest. The Americans had filed their complaint with a wink.

PART IV

·

1940

CHAPTER

14

PHONY WAR; REAL WAR

The Oval Office was quiet, without visitors for once. A winter storm had blown through Washington in the night, and as workmen outside cleared the White House walkways, the scrapes and clunks of their shovels were muffled by the fresh fallen snow. Inside the president was working at his desk. Just in front of the lamp a plume of smoke from a cigarette in an ashtray spiraled upward toward the ceiling. The cigarette went out; Roosevelt lit another, and it too went out. Roosevelt was deep in concentration, reviewing a draft of what would be his seventh State of the Union Address, organizing, revising, going over the passages just given him by Sam Rosenman, his speech writer, getting the words just right. "It becomes clearer and clearer," the critical lines went, and he would read this passage to a somber Congress, "that the future world will be a shabby and dangerous place to live in—yes, even for Americans to live in—if it is ruled by force in the hands of a few. . . ."

On the afternoon of New Year's Day, 1940, putting the finishing touches on the speech he would deliver three days later, President Franklin D. Roosevelt was hinting at what lay ahead: war against the "few," Italy, Germany, and Japan.

No available evidence shows that F. D. R. was planning a conventional war yet. The isolationists still packed political punch and America was still weak militarily. Enlistees were few; officers were old; equipment was scarce and out of date, even with the previous

197

year's rise in defense spending. Too rapid a growth in that spending, furthermore, was bound to cause inflation. Roosevelt was hardly jumping into war.

He was, rather, easing into war. With the turn of 1940, he was president over a government that had been, was, and would be, increasingly, confronting the "few" with psychological war, clandestine war, and economic war. Such forms of war were undeclared, and intended perhaps as mere deterrence. However, they still amounted to war.

■ ■ ■

But how to conceal that war? On January 21, 1940, Roosevelt spoke with Edwin "Pa" Watson—tall, bluff, overweight, and a general from Alabama, Watson was one of the White House secretaries—asking to see a packet that, in 1915, President Woodrow Wilson had ordered concealed in the archives of the Treasury Department. The packet contained the bill of lading, undoctored, of the British ship *Lusitania*, sunk by a German submarine off the coast of Ireland. When the British published the bill of lading, it contained only civilian goods; the original, however, as Wilson knew, listed contraband. Watson sent F. D. R. the document, along with the following note.

THE WHITE HOUSE
WASHINGTON
1–26–40
MEMORANDUM FOR THE PRESIDENT:
This is from Mr. Durning [Harry M. Durning, collector of customs], and is the original manifest of the S. S. Lusitania. He wanted me to open it, but I was afraid to do it until you had seen it. I have contacted Mr. Durning.
—E. M. W.

Roosevelt had the original—a carbon copy actually, since the true original had gone down with the ship—bound in a leather case. Roosevelt was studying how a previous president, his mentor, had covered over his own route to war.

. . .

Looming up out of the snow only a few blocks from the White House, at 1439 Massachusetts Avenue, stood the embassy of the Third Reich, a brownish red-brick architectural horror out of the deepest nineteenth century, replete with parapets, cast-iron railings, and closed draperies of a heavy purple velvet, all of it contriving to give the impression of Teutonic foreboding going on inside. The impression was close to the truth. Hans Thomsen, the tall, blond, handsome chargé d'affaires, who had been running the embassy since Crystal Night, was worried. The outbreak of war in Europe, he cabled Berlin, probably had been "decisive in making up Roosevelt's mind [to run again for the presidency]. In addition to his strongly developed pretensions to leadership and his vanity vis-à-vis world opinion, he believes that in these critical times he must 'make the sacrifice' of another four-year term to the American people."

Thomsen and his wife, Bebe, were good at their job. He was dashing and she was gorgeous and they both were so charming, so honest. At diplomatic receptions, she even could burst into tears at a moment's notice, sobbing on and on about those "awful Nazis." People around the Washington cocktail circuit, especially after some cocktails, would give her solace, comforting her, consoling her, making her feel at home, letting her in on the latest gossip. And according to the gossip that winter, Thomsen wired back to Berlin, Roosevelt, once reelected, would lead America into the war.

. . .

The sandy-haired man with round horn-rimmed spectacles reached the White House early on a January morning, and was whisked immediately to the second floor; this was Ambassador Joseph P. Kennedy, back from Britain for a much needed rest. Taken to the presidential bedroom, he expressed doubts about Britain's ability to survive. Kennedy went on to propose, therefore, that America take over some of Great Britain's shipping, thus helping both Britain and America and keeping trade channels open. Roosevelt listened with interest.

Kennedy then handed the president a message from the first lord of the admiralty, Winston S. Churchill. As Roosevelt read, Kennedy walked over to the highboy, and with his forefinger traced a sea route on the veneer; Churchill wanted to disrupt German ore shipments by mining Norwegian waters, and he wanted Roosevelt's permission. Roosevelt nodded.

As Kennedy knew, Roosevelt and Churchill had already been in touch; the ambassador asked Roosevelt what was going on. Said Roosevelt: "I have always disliked him since the time I went to England in 1918. [As assistant secretary of the navy, Roosevelt had gone on a junket to France and Great Britain.] He acted like a stinker at a dinner I attended, lording it all over us. . . . I've given him attention now because there is a strong possibility that he will become the prime minister and I want to get my hand in now."

■ ■ ■

The war in Europe had settled into a stalemate. The Russians, to be sure, at last were crunching their way to victory in Finland; but the rest of the Continent had bogged down into what people called, variously, the "*Sitzkrieg*," the "*drôle de guerre*," the "Phony War."

In France, soldiers manning the Maginot Line, that vast and seemingly impregnable barrier fortress, had grown complacent. Under orders to hold their fire and to avoid provoking the Reich, they had become accustomed to standing about with their arms folded while German convoys—where the Maginot Line ran beside the Reich's frontier—rumbled along on the opposite bank of the Rhine.

In Germany, people appeared almost unaware of the war. "It was difficult to believe in Berlin on this Sabbath day that a great war was on," William Shirer noted in his diary entry of January 28, 1940. "The streets and parks are covered deep with snow and in the Tiergarten . . . thousands were skating on the ponds and lagoons. Hundreds of children were tobogganning. Do children think about war? I don't know. This afternoon in the Tiergarten they seemed to be thinking only of their sleds and skates and the snow and ice."

In Great Britain, on the afternoon of Christmas Day, 1939, King George VI had addressed his subjects on the wireless. "A new year is at hand," he had broadcast, keeping his stammer under control. "We cannot tell what it will bring. If it brings peace, how thankful we shall all be. If it brings us continued struggle we shall remain undaunted. In the meantime I feel that we may all find a message of encouragement in the lines which, in my closing words, I would like to say to you." Here the king quoted Minnie Louise Haskins, a lecturer at the London School of Economics and a poet.

> "I said to the man who stood at the Gate of the Year, 'Give me a light that I may tread safely into the unknown.' And he replied, 'Go out into the darkness, and put your hand into the Hand of God. That shall be to you better than light, and safer than a known way.'"

The Phony War, however, was about over. Urged on by Churchill, as John Colville, private secretary to Prime Minister Chamberlain, recorded in his diary on New Year's Day, 1940, the British cabinet was

> considering a daring offensive scheme in northern Scandinavia, which they think might bring Germany to her knees but which also, to my mind, is dangerously reminiscent of the Gallipoli plan [the ill-fated British attack on the Turkish shoreline in World War I, when Churchill also had been first lord of the admiralty]. Briefly, they have decided that if Germany could be denied her Scandinavian supplies of iron she would have to give up the struggle. They contemplate either (a) blockading Narvik, in northern Norway, by means of destroyers and mine fields, or (b) more boldly, landing a force in northern Norway to take possession of the ore deposits and thus prevent shipments to Germany. . . . The effects are likely to be (i) a German invasion of southern Scandinavia. (ii) a violent air attack on this country by way of reprisal.

Or both.

> To the Editor:
> Now we are approaching [a] national problem brought about by war. . . . For three years the great resources of our

country to a major degree have been thrown continuously to
the aid of wrong-doing in the Far East. They have been
used . . . to facilitate acts of inexcusable cruelty toward
unoffending Chinese civilians, women and children. They
have been used to promote the violation of treaties which
we initiated and which represent the hope of modern
civilization in the Far East. They have been used to destroy
the humanitarian work carried on in China by American
churches, missionaries, and educators. . . .

With these words, printed on January 11, 1940, Henry L. Stimson, the former secretary of state, began a long letter to *The New
York Times*. Receiving front-page coverage, he proceeded to
denounce sales by Americans to Japan of iron ore, steel, scrap iron,
and oil, the very stuff of the Japanese war machine. Stimson wanted
an immediate embargo on those goods. But he went further still.

The "stable equilibrium of Eastern Asia," he averred, "in which
the United States is so deeply interested and which is now menaced
by Japan's attack on China, cannot be restored without a complete
reversal of the conduct followed over several years by the leaders
of the Japanese Army. . . ." The United States could restore "law
and order" in Asia only if it were willing to "act," and to act "along
several lines."

Thus spake Stimson. Like his counterparts across the Atlantic,
the sea lords of Britannia, Stimson espoused what he assumed was
an unassailable syllogism: The security of the Anglo-American world
lay in the preservation of international stability; Germany and Japan
had threatened that stability; America therefore must "act" against
them, and do so "along several lines." What he meant by the words
in quotations he left to his readers' imaginations.

■　■　■

Although out of office, Stimson was not out of power. He was the
powerful leader of a powerful political coalition, one we might think
of as an iron triangle—a network of interests demanding intervention abroad. At one corner of the triangle stood the private lobbies:
Chinese-Americans, Czech-Americans, Serbian-Americans, and Pol-

ish-Americans; southerners; Jews; Methodists, Episcopalians, and Presbyterians; Catholic leaders such as New York's Francis Cardinal Spellman; and above all a coalition of missionaries who had been in China.

Headed by Roger Sherman Greene, a New Englander who had done consular duty in China, and headquartered on the White House side of the New York Avenue Presbyterian Church, this coalition called itself the American Committee for Non-Participation in Japanese Aggression. Its honorary chairman was Henry L. Stimson; its principal publicist was Walter Judd, later a congressman from Minnesota; its board included such notables as Helen Keller, Reinhold Niebuhr, the theologian, Dr. Paul H. Douglas, economics professor at the University of Chicago and a future senator from Illinois, Dr. A. Lawrence Lowell, president emeritus of Harvard, Dr. Robert E. Speer, former president of the Federal Council of Churches, Jonathan Daniels, editor of the *Raleigh News-Observer*, Mrs. J. Borden Harriman, the American minister to Norway, Frederick McKee, a Pittsburgh industrialist, and the editor of the *Emporia Gazette*, William Allen White.

An even larger organization was the Committee to Defend America by Aiding the Allies. Headquartered at 8 West 40th Street in Manhattan, the board of this larger committee overlapped with the board of the first: It included the same Mrs. J. Borden Harriman, the same Frederick McKee, and the same William Allen White, this time as honorary chairman. Ellsworth Bunker, who showed up later as U.S. ambassador to Vietnam, chaired the Finance Committee; Clark M. Eichelberger, a Chicagoan who ran the League of Nations Association, was the national director. The board included the actor Douglas Fairbanks, Jr. This was the American way of lobbying: Set up a national headquarters, form alliances and interlocking directorships, show off the film star or the athlete, set up local chapters, and penetrate Washington.

This point of the triangle also included foreigners. China sent Hu Shih, the famous intellectual, as its de jure ambassador and soon would send T. V. Soong, Chiang Kai-shek's brother-in-law, as its de facto ambassador. Australia sent Major Richard G. Casey as its own first ambassador to Washington: handsome, mustachioed, superbly dressed, a World War I hero, and a former Rhodes scholar at Trinity College, Oxford, Casey affected being more English than the English; his job, however, was to woo America as Australia's defender.

Canada sent Arthur Purvis, the long-faced ecclesiastical-looking Montreal munitions maker; his job, at which he succeeded brilliantly, was to work hand in hand with Treasury Secretary Morgenthau, evade the neutrality legislation, and purchase material. This was the so-called "Morgenthau–Purvis channel." Under the neutrality acts, Britain could purchase U.S. munitions only with cash on the barrel; but Britain was low on cash. Working with Purvis, therefore, Morgenthau's task was to find ways—such as a loan from the Reconstruction Finance Corporation and Treasury purchases of British assets—for the British to get their hands on cash.) France sent Jean Monnet, later founder of the European Community but, early in 1930, a partner of Purvis in the purchasing business.

And Great Britain sent, as ambassador, Philip Henry Kerr, Lord Lothian. Fifty-eight years old, Lothian was tall and big-boned, with a high forehead and a Roman nose; although a member of the British aristocracy and the owner of huge estates in Scotland and Norfolk, Lothian sensed exactly how to appeal to democratic-minded Americans. When on the road to give speeches, which he did frequently, selling Americans on the need to defend Great Britain, he traveled informally. In a most "unambassadorial manner," his biographer wrote, "he would put his head round the door [in the British embassy in Washington] while a subordinate was working and say, 'I am off to New York!', then just get into his own car and actually buy his own ticket. Returning from an air journey, he [was] remembered stepping out of the airport with a disreputable gray hat over one eye and his coat thrown over his shoulder." Lothian was not always informal. Hosting white-tie dinners in his embassy at 1300 Massachusetts Avenue—*Time* described the building as a "huge, spreading million dollar red-and-white Queen Anne palace"—he cultivated the high and mighty of Washington, including especially Henry Morgenthau. In Morgenthau he found a natural ally: Like Lothian and the government Lothian represented, Morgenthau was enamored of the idea of economic warfare against Germany and Japan.

At a second corner of the triangle stood executive branch officials: Morgenthau; Interior Secretary Ickes; the State Department's Stanley Hornbeck who, although an official, served as adviser to the Committee for Non-Participation in Japanese Aggression. No longer on active duty, Captain Evans F. Carlson and Admiral Harry E. Yarnell were retired but hardly retiring: Both had become publicists for the Chinese cause.

And at the third corner of the triangle were the relevant members of Congress: Key Pittman, chairman of the Senate Foreign Relations Committee; Sol Bloom of the Lower East Side of Manhattan and chairman of the House Foreign Affairs Committee; Senator Byrnes from South Carolina; Congressmen Adolf Sabath (Czech-American), Anton F. Maciejewski (Polish-American), and Leo Kocialkowski (Polish-American) from Chicago; and Congressmen Rudolph G. Tenerowicz, John Lesinkski, and John Dingell, all Democrats and all from heavily Polish-American Detroit. Dingell was a high-ranking member of the powerful Ways and Means Committee.

These three points of the triangle—the interest groups, officials, and members of Congress—represented a huge and potent political force. The leaders moved from office to office with ease; they dined together at the Mayflower Hotel or in private homes in Georgetown; they played golf together at the Burning Tree Country Club or met for croquet at Woodley. They had access to the major media of mass communications of the era—*Life*, *Time*, and *The Saturday Evening Post*. They even had access to the White House.

Late in March 1940, the *Washington Post* carried an item of significance. T. V. Soong, who controlled China's finances, had left Hong Kong and was coming to town. Soong would show what "access" really meant.

■ ■ ■

What could be drearier, wrote Hallett Abend, *The New York Times* reporter in the China that Soong was leaving, "than a land long occupied by a hated and arrogant enemy, a land with half-ruined cities, with farms laid waste, with sullen men and thousands of shamefaced women? A conquered land, with trade throttled, with insecurity on all sides." This was China in the dark winter of early

1940. "From Harbin . . . in the far north to Canton in the far south the story is the same," Abend went on, "except that the far north is a frozen land in winter. . . . The winter . . . is the worst Peking and Tientsin have known for decades. . . . Dust and sand from the Gobi Desert are whirled across the empty courtyards of the one-time Forbidden City by winds cutting chill. In great mat-shed structures thousands of beggars and homeless Chinese are given one bowl of millet gruel a day, but scores die of hunger and cold on the streets every night. The Legation Quarter, deserted by diplomats of higher rank than secretaries, waits, powerless and unimportant. About 500 American Marines, divided half-and-half between Peking and Tientsin, are the only remaining symbols of the power of the western world. In Tientsin, foreign business is dead. The Japanese Army monopolizes the trade in the exports of [the] hinterland, whether it be sausage casings, furs, or wool from Inner Mongolia."

Yet these Japanese efforts at control were hollow. To achieve a real victory in China, the Japanese needed one thing and that one thing they could never win—the hearts and the minds of the people.

They certainly could not—at least not without an all-out war—quench the flow of goods into China. Down in the Hong Kong harbor, where the ferries plied the waters between the island and Kowloon, Hallett Abend had a good look at the piers. Along the waterfront, he cabled the *Times,* "block after block . . . was piled high with goods ordered by Chungking"—machinery, tires, huge coils of barbed wire, and, he estimated, 2,200 motor trucks. These goods represented a major fact of the China war: Fueled with funds from abroad, especially from the overseas Chinese communities, China was purchasing material, storing it in Hong Kong, shipping it down to Haiphong, and hauling it by rail in through Yunnan and up toward Chungking.

■ ■ ■

As if to taunt Japan, the Chinese early in March released a report of a banquet in Chungking. A many-coursed affair with dishes of fish, crayfish, pork, and snake, both stir-fried and crisped, and with the participants gulping down their countless *kanpei,* or toasts, the banquet really was a feast, a commemoration, an appreciation.

Chungking had reason to express gratitude. In New York alone, the General Relief Fund Committee of the Chinese Consolidated Benevolent Association had just raised $40,000 for use by the republic of China; and from Chicago, three trucking experts, Maurice L. Sheehan, A. S. Bass, and C. W. Van Patten, had come to give advice on transportation problems. Most important, the Chinese government wished to make public the fact that leaders of the leading secret societies were present in the banquet hall, had formed a "Citizen's Self-Strengthening Society," and were officially joining the Kuomintang in an anti-Japanese "united front."

The secret societies had been collaborating with Chiang Kai-shek for years. Yet the announcement of that collaboration, reported in Tokyo dailies and in *The New York Times*, said point-blank to the Japanese: "You may have invaded. But you will never win."

· · ·

On the cold and misty morning of March 30, 1940, Japanese soldiers lined the walkway to a simple hall in Nanking. Trudging between them, a compactly built, round-faced Chinese man approached the doorway. He was Wang Ching-wei, a defector from the government of Chiang Kai-shek: By becoming a collaborator with the enemy, by serving as a puppet leader in Nanking, Wang seemed to have persuaded himself, he would be in a position at least to end the warfare in China. So once inside the building, he mounted a platform and introduced his new "ministers." They stepped forward, all stopping in a circle chalked on the platform and making a bow, Japanese-style. Japanese soldiers had chalked in the circles. Wang then gave a speech—written by the Japanese—calling on all China to unify behind his new presidency.

China unified all right. A secret society contract went out on Wang's life.

The United States and Japan had drawn their lines in the dirt. In fact, they were already engaging in one kind of war, a currency war.

To help legitimize their occupation, the Japanese issued their own banknotes, drawn on the Central Reserve Bank of Shanghai and designed by Chinese engravers. The engravers subverted the currency. On the new five-dollar bills, according to one account, the "pattern of intricate sketched lines surrounding the middle part of the large figure '5' on both sides of the note formed two small, white-rimmed circles which together definitely resembled the eyes and even the head of a fox"—in the Chinese tradition, a malevolent goblin. Then "along the edge of the etched frame on the reverse side of the $10 notes, people began to make out the ominous silhouettes of turtles—winged turtles at that. . . . These animals symbolized in Chinese eyes a person without legal parents, an imbecile capable of the dirtiest acts of disloyalty. . . . But the most striking and sensational discovery was made on the 50 cent notes. . . . Some patient soul while examining the front side with a magnifying glass noticed something odd about the picture of Dr. Sun Yat-sen's mausoleum. Among the bushes and shrubbery on both sides of the great stone stairway leading to the tomb were six distinct and neatly drawn Chinese characters, skillfully hidden. At first no particular significance was attached to this because the characters were placed in deliberate disorder, but after a little experimenting the following sentence was formed: 'Chung yang ma hsanglai chia'; meaning 'Central, or Nationalist, government soon will be here.' The 50 cent notes disappeared from circulation."

Underlying such trickery was the indirect but real conflict between Japan and America: Japan was underwriting the Nanking, or puppet government's, currency; America, through an Export-Import Bank loan, was supporting the Chungking, or Nationalist government's, currency. Two years before Pearl Harbor, the United States and Japan were fighting with money.

■ ■ ■

They were also fighting a trade war. With no more formality than the midnight striking of the grandfather clock in Secretary of State Cordell Hull's office, the 1911 United States–Japan commercial treaty expired. The Japanese had worried about this. Horinouchi Kensuke, the Japanese ambassador, had called on the State Department, asking for "information on future relations." The American officials had been curt. Trade would have to proceed on a day-to-day basis, they informed him, and its continuation would be tied to Japanese behavior.

America already had subjected Japan to a "moral embargo." Now the way was clear for mandatory embargoes.

Then, to the consternation of the Japanese, three omens appeared, almost simultaneously.

First, Senator Key Pittman began calling for sanctions against Japan. Second, the U.S. Commerce Department issued a report filled with telling statistics. In the first ten months of 1939, the United States had taken 33 percent of Japan's "foreign currency" exports (to countries, that is, outside the "yen bloc," Japan–Manchukuo–China) and supplied 44 percent of Japan's imports. From America, Japan had purchased 40 percent of its cotton, 65 percent of its oil, 70 percent of its scrap iron, and 95 percent of its automobiles and automobile parts. Japan, in short, was dependent on the United States and, therefore, economically vulnerable. And third, the American Friends of the Chinese People, headquartered at 168 West Twenty-third Street in New York, urged President Roosevelt to end Japan's most favored trading relationship with the United States. The board of directors of this group included Clark M. Eichelberger, Franz Boas, a professor at Columbia University, Rockwell Kent, the artist, Dr. Mary E. Woodley, the president-emerita of Mount Holyoke College, and Mrs. James Roosevelt, the very mother of the president.

■ ■ ■

Japan resorted to threats. If "the United States imposed an embargo on the exportation of war materials, including petroleum, to Japan, that country would be confronted with the necessity of obtaining its petroleum supplies from the Netherlands Indies," the Japanese government warned. And so that everyone would get the point, Tokyo placed a list of demands on the Dutch colonial government in the Indies. Japan wanted "a lowering of trade restrictions; greater facilities for Japanese enterprise in the Indies; easier entry for Japanese merchants, employees, and workers; mutual control of the press." Sending a cable to Washington, Dutch officials stated that if "we give in on the so-called less important points, if we give the

Japanese even a finger's breadth of their demands, they will quickly ask the whole of our country."

In Washington, Hull and Roosevelt were worried. If Japan was looking toward the Indies today, where would it look tomorrow? Toward Australia? New Zealand? Wake Island and Guam? Hawaii? Beyond?

An article appeared in U.S. newspapers in the middle of March 1940. In a previously undisclosed mission, the announcement went, six U.S. Navy bombers had landed at Canton Island, controlled jointly by the United States and Britain and lying southwest of Hawaii. The bombers next were going to make a run up to Johnston Island, where the navy was building a seaplane base. Together the two legs of the flight would equal 3,750 miles, roughly the distance from Honolulu to Tokyo.

■   ■   ■

Just before Easter, 1940, a propaganda bombshell exploded. The Germans published a White Book, an official compilation of documents which, the Reich claimed, proved American complicity in starting the war in Europe.

In 1939, the allegation went, William C. Bullitt, America's ambassador to France, had returned to Washington, meeting there twice with Jerzy Potocki, Poland's ambassador to America. Potocki had cabled his version of the interviews to his foreign minister, Józef Beck, in Warsaw—hence the German claim that when they took Warsaw, they uncovered the now-published documents. After conferring with Roosevelt, the published version of the cable showed, Bullitt went to Potocki, making the following pledges:

> First, activation of foreign policy under the leadership of President Roosevelt, which will sharply and unequivocally denounce the totalitarian states. Second, war preparations of the United States on sea, on land, and in the air, which are soon to be realized in accelerated tempo. . . . Third, the decided opinion of the President that France and Britain must put an end to all policy compromises with the totalitarian states. They are not to enter into any discussions with them that aim at any territorial changes.

Hirohito, the Emperor of Japan, bemedalled and riding at the head of a military parade during the Lunar New Year, 1937, shortly before the outbreak of the Sino-Japanese War. *(Life Photos)*

Shanghai harbor, August, 1937. This photo was taken from near the roof garden of the Palace Hotel. The smoke against the skyline is from the *Izumo*, a Japanese warship. *(AP/Wide World Photos)*

Colonel Evans Carlson, the U.S. Marine who, during the Sino-Japanese War, toured the Far East as President Franklin D. Roosevelt's secret agent, and returned to America to serve as publicist for China. *(UPI/ Bettmann)*

Claire Chennault, the aviator who led the American Volunteer Group (later the Flying Tigers) in China. This picture was taken in July, 1941, by International News Photo. The original caption said Chennault "will direct a Chinese aerial offensive against Japanese bases which military sources said might now be expected 'at any time.'" *(UPI/Bettmann)*

Generalissimo and Madame Chiang Kai-shek outside their Nanking residence in late 1937. This photo was taken just before the Rape of Nanking. (*UPI/Bettmann*)

King George VI and Queen Elizabeth, seated with the First Lady (far left), the President's mother (center), and Franklin D. Roosevelt (right), June 11, 1939, on the veranda of the Roosevelt home in Hyde Park, New York. The party had just returned from church services. The night before, F.D.R. had promised King George that if London were bombed, America would go to war. *(AP/Wide World Photos)*

William J. Donovan, President Roosevelt's special envoy to Europe and Coordinator of Information. This photo was taken in late 1940, just before Donovan's first trip abroad as Roosevelt's special envoy. *(UPI/Bettmann)*

Viscount Halifax, the British ambassador to America, and Dorothy, his wife, aboard the *King George V*, en route to Washington in early 1941. (*The Earl of Halifax*)

T. V. Soong, Chinese lobbyist, and Henry Morgenthau, Jr., U.S. Secretary of the Treasury, signing an agreement of financial aid to China. (*UPI/ Bettmann*)

The Burma Road. *(AP/Wide World Photos)*

President Franklin D. Roosevelt and Prime Minister Winston S. Churchill during shipboard religious service at the Argentia Conference, 1941. *(Franklin D. Roosevelt Library)*

The secret map of South America, President Roosevelt's "proof" that the Axis powers had designs on the Western Hemisphere. The handwritten notes, penned in German, are about the production, storage, and shipment of fuel. *(Franklin D. Roosevelt Library)*

Friends and their stamp collections: President Franklin D. Roosevelt (left); Postmaster General Frank C. Walker (center); Dr. T. V. Soong (right). The photo was taken in 1942. *(UPI/Bettmann)*

A map of the Pacific, carried by United States News in the autumn of 1941, showing flight times from various U.S. bases (real and potential) of bombers of Tokyo. *(Los Angeles Times)*

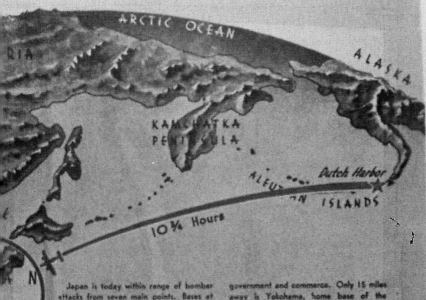

Japan is today within range of bomber attacks from seven main points. Bases at those points are being kept at wartime strength and readiness by the United States, Britain, China and Russia.

In airline miles, distances from the bases to Tokyo are as follows: Unalaska—2,700; Guam—1,575; Cavite, P. I.—1,860; Singapore—3,250; Hongkong—1,825; Chungking—2,000; Vladivostok—440.

Comparable figures for flying time from the bases are shown by the Pictogram. These figures are based on the use of a bomber with a flying range of 6,000 miles at an average speed of 250 miles an hour, a type representative of those to be turned out on a large scale for American air forces, and for shipment to Britain and China.

Principal targets for enemy bombers attacking Japan would be the Tokyo-Yokohama area, and the city of Osaka, 240 miles southward. These two areas are the head and the heart of industrial Japan.

Tokyo, city of rice-paper and wood houses, is the center of transportation, government and commerce. Only 15 miles away is Yokohama, home base of the Japanese Navy. Damage to the repair and supply facilities there would seriously cripple the fleet, Japan's main striking force.

At Osaka is concentrated most of the national munitions industry. Hastily expanded during the last three years, the arms factories are built of wood. Acres upon acres of these wooden buildings in and near the city present a highly vulnerable target for incendiary bombs. This same strategic liability is true of other cities, making it imperative to keep attacking planes at a distance. Use of aircraft carriers by hostile forces would intensify the difficulty of this task for the Japanese Navy and air force.

These facts influence the decisions of Japan's leaders today. And the facts are made ever more pointed for them by the spectacle of American-produced bombers, aviation gasoline and supplies flowing into Vladivostok, nearest source of danger to their capital.

President Franklin D. Roosevelt asking Congress to declare war on Japan, December 8, 1941. *(Franklin D. Roosevelt Library)*

The Poles had the "moral assurance," furthermore, "that the United States would leave the policy of isolation and be prepared to intervene on the side of Britain and France in case of war." Bullitt, the Germans were charging, had played the role of incendiary.

Another incendiary, in the German White Book's version, was Ambassador Joseph P. Kennedy, in London. On June 11, 1939, according to the White Book, Kennedy had spoken to Jan Wazelaki, Poland's trade councilor to Great Britain, for three-quarters of an hour. "Even if war were not to come this year"—this from what the Germans presented as Wazelaki's subsequent cable to Warsaw—

> [Ambassador Kennedy said] neither Britain nor the United States would interrupt or limit their arms programs. As a result, Britain had in secret introduced foreign exchange restrictions. It was no longer possible, [Kennedy] said, to invest or transfer British capital to a foreign country without permission of the government. . . . In further course of the interview Kennedy questioned me concerning the situation in Poland and our needs. . . . He added that he would see the Prime Minister and Lord Halifax [the foreign secretary] on the necessity of aiding Poland immediately. In conclusion the ambassador stated that his two sons [Joseph P. Kennedy, Jr., and John F. Kennedy], who had recently traveled all over Europe, . . . intended to make a series of lectures on the European situation . . . after their return to . . . Harvard University. The ambassador places great importance on these lectures as an element in forming American public opinion.

Did Kennedy actually say these things? After a conversation with Kennedy much later, Colonel Charles A. Lindbergh recorded in his journal: "He [Kennedy] said the reports . . . which were captured and published by the Germans, . . . were almost entirely correct as far as the parts which concerned him. . . . He laughed and said he didn't know about what Bill Bullitt said (but I gathered he felt that was pretty accurate, too)."

And Bullitt?

As ambassador to France, he had without question made commitments of U.S. aid to France. Equally without question, in 1938, he had proposed a scheme whereby American-made sparkplugs, magnetos, cylinder blocks, wood and steel castings for engines, and metal plates for wings would all be shipped to Canada and, in an evasion of the neutrality laws, be assembled there as airplanes for sale to Britain, France, and Poland. In a congressional hearing, Bullitt did deny having the alleged conversation with the Polish ambassador; but his biographers believe that he perjured himself. The documents captured in Warsaw, concludes a British historian, "left little doubt as to what had stiffened Polish resistance to German demands during the August 1939 crisis."

. . .

The Bullitt affair, however, soon faded from view. The world's attention now focused on Norway. During World War I, after all, the country had been neutral; and even after the Soviets invaded Finland, late in 1939, giving the French and the British a pretext for moving across the North Sea, Hitler had paid little attention to Norway. But February 1940 changed his mind. Undeniable reports were flooding into Berlin: The Allies were cooking up a Scandinavian invasion.

If successful, such an invasion, from Hitler's point of view, could have three results, all of them dire. First, the British could base bombers at Oslo, and Oslo is closer than London to Berlin. Second, the British could bottle up the Reich's submarine force in the Baltic. And third, the British could deprive Germany of Swedish iron ore, thus crippling the Reich's war production and depriving Hitler of the gains he had made so far on the Continent.

. . .

The British, to be sure, also had their eyes on the Germans—from Norway, the German navy would have a straight shot at Scapa Flow, the great British naval base in the Orkneys, high above Scotland. As early as Christmas Eve, 1939, Churchill had cabled Roosevelt that, fearing a German assault on Scandinavia, Great Britain might well have to mine the Norwegian harbors; and on February 5, 1940, Britain's Supreme War Council decided to have a go at the Swedish ore fields. If the British waited until the ice broke, they might find the Germans in Norway already.

By the end of March 1940, therefore, a British task force was ready to move, but not completely prepared. Supply problems were great and cooperation with the French, who were going to join in the mission, was almost nonexistent. But if the invasion failed, Britain might still turn to America.

. . .

Easter came early in 1940, on March 24, and in all the great cities of the Western world, people turned out as if in celebration of the last moment of any hope of peace. French and British soldiers, decked out in their dress uniforms, mingled with the civilian crowds on the Champs Elysées, and throughout the cafés and theaters of Paris, throngs of holidaymakers created an atmosphere of gaiety and cheer. Out on the Heath in London, the crocuses had just pushed up through the grass, and in the sunshine of the afternoon, owners of the Queen Anne-style houses in nearby Hampstead and Golders Green walked their dogs down the pathways, or strolled by the portraits in Kenwood House.

Children in Washington rolled Easter eggs on the south lawn of the White House. And in New York's Town Hall at 2:00 P.M., John Charles Thomas of the Metropolitan Opera gave a recital. In a gesture of patriotism, he performed wholly from the American repertory, MacDowell, Ives, and, finally, Stephen Foster's hauntingly beautiful song, "Gentle Annie." "Thou wilt come no more gentle Annie," Thomas sang, with his crystalline diction and ringing high baritone:

> Shall we never more behold thee,
> Never hear thy winning voice again?
> When the spring-time comes, gentle Annie,
> When the wild flowers are scattered o'er the plain.

CHAPTER
15

THE SCANDINAVIAN INVASION

"As left off in my diary of yesterday, I was awakened by the telephone ringing at about half-past twelve [at night, on April 9, 1940] to say that a message . . . had been received from Daisy Harriman [Florence Harriman, the American minister to Norway] that . . . German ships were proceeding up the Oslo fjord, were being fired on by the Norwegian batteries, and that Norway was now in a state of war with Germany."

The diarist was Jay Pierrepont Moffat, a descendant of John Jay (the first chief justice), young State Department protocol officer—colleagues had dubbed him "Pierrepontifex Moffaximus of Protocol"—an outstanding official, and a reliable scribe. At "about half-past eleven [the next night]," he recorded, "the Norwegian minister called. . . . He confirmed that the Germans had taken Bergen and other Atlantic ports, though how they were able to do so in the face of the British blockade and the presence of British warships he was unable to understand. He pointed out that Norway could at best put up merely a *pro forma* resistance. . . . [T]he German troops were admirably prepared and equipped, and were not 'inefficient' like the Russians."

Moffat understood the meaning of the message. The Phony War was over and the real war had started. And, in Scandinavia, Germany had beaten the Allies to the punch.

214

■ ■ ■

"It is fantastic that none of the things which happened in the week preceding the fatal daybreak of April 9 [1940] awakened us to the danger," wrote Florence Jaffray Harriman, America's minister to Norway. Mrs. Harriman—Mrs. J. Borden Harriman, née Hurst— had been a clubwoman, a suffragette, a Washington hostess, and an ardent supporter of Democrats for President. F. D. R. had repaid her in the time-honored way.

"A hundred incidents should have prepared us," her memoirs continued. "One afternoon in February, a Nazi plane landed, without warning, just outside Oslo. Without a by-your-leave, 30 passengers were disgorged who scattered over the field with cameras, taking photographs, making memoranda. . . ." Then, on Friday, April 5, 1940, all officials of the Norwegian Foreign Office received invitations from the German minister to see a "peace film." It turned out to be a "film, terrifyingly documentary and horrible, of the bombing of Warsaw. The audience was shocked . . . still puzzled as to why the film had been shown to *them*, to Norwegians."

When the Oslo air raid alarms finally sounded, Minister Harriman and her staff roused themselves from bed, jamming what possessions they could grab—clothing, typewriters, codebooks—into the trunks of their automobiles. Approaching Lillestrom, on the outskirts of Oslo, the American diplomats heard the snap, snap, snap of machine-gun fire overhead. A small Norwegian airplane was giving chase to a German Heinkel. "We craned to watch," Mrs. Harriman wrote. "Drivers pressed forward, not exactly frightened, but we all breathed more easily as we moved out from under those dark outlines in the sky. . . ."

But what was happening was unmistakable. In a coordinated motion that resembled the releasing of a spring, German air and ground forces surged up and across from the islands of Denmark. German destroyers simultaneously materialized out of the mists and fogs, striking at all major points along the Norwegian coastline, Oslo and Stavanger in the south, Bergen, Trondheim, and Namsos in the middle, and Narvik in the north; Narvik lay at the end of the rail line that reached the ocean from the Swedish iron ore mines at

Gallivare. In London, the speed of the fall of Narvik seemed unbelievable: Newspaper readers thought that Narvik must be a misspelling of Larvik, a town just below Oslo.

The truth finally sank in. After several changes of plans and a great deal of muddled thinking, the British and the French tried to take Trondheim, but they failed; and by early May 1940, the Germans were in complete control of central Norway. The Allies tried again, and failed again, at Narvik; the British admiralty, under Churchill's command, proved so paralyzed by fear of German bomber attacks that it held back the main parts of the fleet. Thus Scandinavia was lost.

■　■　■

"BETRAYAL OF NORWAY!"

"Amazing Acts That Gave Oslo to Hitler; Norse Traitors Helped Nazi Spies Silence Forts." With these words blazing as its headline, the April 15, 1940, edition of the *Chicago Daily News* announced to its readers that Norway had fallen because of fifth column activities.

The publisher of the *Daily News* was Colonel Frank Knox. Sandy-haired and beefy, Knox had been a Roughrider with Theodore Roosevelt in the Spanish-American War; after roaring his own way up the hillsides of the U.S. newspaper world, Knox gained control of the *Chicago Daily News* and turned it into an organ of interventionist bellicosity. Always looking for a chance to get a leg up on the *Chicago Tribune*, his isolationist rival, Knox hired the services of Leland Stowe, known throughout the nation as a crackerjack foreign correspondent. Setting out for Knox to cover the wars in Poland and Finland, and then hearing rumors that the British were up to something funny in Norway, he fled to Sweden. His sensational *Daily News* story of April 15, 1940, was datelined Stockholm.

For "the first time," Stowe reported, "the story behind Germany's paralyzing 12-hour conquest of Norway on Tuesday, April 9, can be told. Between midnight and noon of that bewildering day, Norway's capital, all her principal seaports and her most strategic coastal defenses fell into German hands like an overripe plum. By bribery and extraordinary infiltration on the part of Nazi agents, and by treason on the part of a few highly placed Norwegian civilians and defense officials . . . the German dictatorship built a Trojan horse inside of Norway." Introducing American readers to the name of Major Vidkun Quisling, undeniably a Nazi collaborator, Stowe termed the German victory "among the most audacious, most perfectly oiled political plots of the last century."

Minister Harriman, who had also escaped to Stockholm, took issue: "There has been a good deal written about how the easy occupation of Oslo was due to treachery. What we have to call 'the Fifth Column' had indeed been busy; the Nazis were indefatigable in an infinite variety of ways, from defamation of the British to a thousand minor tricks and courtesies of propaganda, in an effort to make the Norwegians German-friendly. There was trade acceleration. There was interchange of tourists and students. But not a bit of real evidence has been adduced, apart from Major Quisling [who headed up Norway's pro-German puppet regime] and his small group who moved swiftly to obtain possession of telephones, telegraph, and radio, that the Norwegian people, for a moment, welcomed the invasion. Everything in the Norwegian democracy was opposed to Nazi brutality. . . . As for Quisling, many people had for a long time regarded him as of unsound mind."

Despite Mrs. Harriman's testimony, however, the Overseas Press Club, over luncheon at the Gladstone Hotel in New York, lauded Stowe for revealing the "true" method, the Trojan horse, the fifth column by which the Germans overran Norway.

■ ■ ■

On the afternoon of May 5—three days after Norway fell—Prime Minister Chamberlain entered the House of Commons. The House was crowded and Chamberlain, Harold Nicolson recorded, was "greeted with shouts of 'Missed the bus!' " The prime minister made a short, ineffective speech. Then Leo Amery, a backbencher and, like Chamberlain, a Conservative member from Birmingham, rose from his seat. Referring to Oliver Cromwell and the English Civil War three centuries before, he looked down toward Chamberlain and stated: ". . . This is what Cromwell said to the Long Parliament when he thought it was no longer fit to conduct the affairs of the nation: 'You have sat too long for any good you have been doing.

Depart, I say, and let us have done with you. In the name of God, go!' "

At 11:10 the next evening, pale and angry, and picking his way over the outstretched legs of his former followers, Chamberlain went. And on the morning of May 10, 1940, King George VI called for Winston S. Churchill. Churchill now was the prime minister.

In what was virtually his first act, he fired off a cable to Roosevelt, trying to link America to Britain's own war. "Immediate needs," he wired the president,

> are:
> First of all, the loan of 40 or 50 of your older destroyers. . . .
> Secondly, we want several hundred of the latest types of aircraft. . . .
> Thirdly, anti-aircraft equipment and ammunition. . . .
> Fourthly, . . . steel. . . .
> Fifthly, we have many reports of . . . possible German parachute or airborne descents in Ireland. The visit of a United States squadron to Irish ports, which might well be prolonged, would be invaluable.
> Sixthly, I am looking to you to keep that Japanese dog quiet in the Pacific, using Singapore in any way convenient.

■ ■ ■

"I went up to my father's bedroom. He was standing in front of his basin and was shaving with his old-fashioned Valet razor. He had a tough beard, and as usual he was hacking away." The author of these words was Randolph, Winston Churchill's son; on the morning of May 18, 1940, he had gone to visit his father at Ten Downing Street. Randolph Churchill continued:

" 'Sit down, dear boy, and read the papers while I finish shaving.' I did as told. After two or three minutes of hacking away, he half-turned and said: 'I think I see my way through.' He resumed his shaving. I was astounded, and said, 'Do you mean that we can avoid defeat (which seemed credible) or beat the bastards (which seemed incredible)?'

He flung his razor into the basin, swung around, and said:—'Of course I mean we can beat them.'

Me: 'Well, I'm all for it, but I don't see how you can do it.'

By this time he had dried and sponged his face and turning around to me, said with great intensity:—'I shall drag the United States in.' "

John Colville, by this point Churchill's private secretary, corroborated this account. "Indirect attempts are being made, through the Dominion's High Commissioners, etc.," he wrote in his diary, "to bring the U.S. into the war by painting to members of the Administration the most somber portrait of what we expect from Germany."

■ ■ ■

During the first days of the Norwegian invasion, the tulips on the south lawn of the White House were starting to bloom. The petals were a sign of springtime. But what would the springtime bring? Was America, reporters asked Roosevelt in the wake of the German invasion of Norway, in any danger?

"You can put it this way," Roosevelt said, as he sat behind his desk in the Oval Office, "the events [in Scandinavia] will undoubtedly cause a great many more Americans to think about the potentialities of war."

The administration, he then announced, was freezing Danish and Norwegian accounts in America, shutting those funds off from use by the Germans. Most Americans, he added, regarded Greenland as "inside the Monroe Doctrine." Greenland was Danish; and Roosevelt, by implication, was warning Germany to keep its hands off the overseas territories of the defeated European powers. The same point would apply to Japan.

■ ■ ■

And Japan was in a squeeze. All around southeast Asia, from Indochina and the Philippines down to Thailand, Malaya, Singapore, and the Dutch East Indies, Chinese chambers of commerce—and the tongs, or secret societies, with which they were hooked up—were persuading indigenous Chinese to take action against the Japanese.

The society's methods were often unsubtle; uncooperative Chinese sometimes found their ears sliced off or their doors smeared with dung; but they *were* effective. Secret society fund-raising had produced millions of dollars for the motherland, enabling China to stay in the war; and secret society–induced boycotts of Japanese goods reduced Japanese exports to southeast Asia to about half of what they were before 1937. Despite repeated representations from Tokyo, furthermore, European colonial authorities in Indochina, Malaya, and the Indies had been unable—or, the Japanese suspected, unwilling—to suppress the societies. And in the Philippines, Chinese boycott leaders substituted U.S. goods for Japanese, thus buying American sympathy for China.

At the time of the Scandinavian invasion, Tokyo was asking how Japan could break out of the ever-tightening encirclement. The answer was threefold.

In response, first, to what he was sure was an American atomic bomb program, Lieutenant General Yasuda Takeo, director of the Japanese Military Aeronautic Technical Laboratory, summoned a young staff officer, Suzuki Tatsuaburo. A graduate of Tokyo University in physics and X rays, Suzuki went directly to his former professor, Sagane Ryokichi. Sagane, in turn, had studied with Ernest Lawrence at Berkeley, then at the Cavendish Laboratory in Cambridge. Back in Japan, he had built the largest cyclotron outside the United States. In America, Sagane told Suzuki, Lawrence and others most certainly were working on a bomb—but Japan could, too, especially if it exploited uranium deposits in Korea. Suzuki went right to work.

In response, second, to America's naval buildup—the Vinson Bill of 1938, itself a response to *Japan's* naval buildup—Japan had already launched a renewed ship construction program, intended to produce eighty fresh vessels of war. But now, in the spring of 1940, Admiral Yamamoto Isoroku, chief of staff of the Japanese First Fleet, began to toy with an idea—a Japanese carrier attack on the American ships at Pearl Harbor.

And in response, third, to the problems it faced in southeast Asia, the Japanese government began to prepare its people for what was to come. "With the South Seas regions, especially the Netherlands

East Indies," Foreign Minister Arita Hachiro asserted at a press conference on April 15, 1940, "Japan is economically bound by an intimate relationship of mutuality in ministering to one another's needs. Similarly, other countries of East Asia maintain close economic relations with those regions. That is to say, Japan, these countries and these regions together are contributing to the prosperity of East Asia through mutual aid and interdependence. Should hostilities in Europe be extended to the Netherlands and produce repercussions . . . in the Indies, it . . . would give rise to an undesirable situation from the standpoint of the peace and stability of East Asia. . . . The Japanese government cannot but be deeply concerned over any development accompanying an aggravation of the war in Europe that may affect the status quo of the Netherlands East Indies."

If Holland fell and Roosevelt extended the Monroe Doctrine as far as the Indies, Japan would regard it as an act of aggression.

■ ■ ■

Ambassador Grew was turning sixty. His face, his biographer wrote, "was less sinewy and his hair was nearly white and thinning on top." He still was the consummate diplomat, as charming as always, and as dedicated to bridging the chasm that divided Japan and America. That chasm, however, seemed wider than ever. Back in Washington, "Mr. Stimson and his satellites," as Grew called them, were renewing their clamor for embargoes. And over in China, Japanese soldiers were at "it" again.

In Macao, the Portuguese enclave south of Hong Kong, situated on the mouth of the Pearl River, Japanese soldiers swaggered into the gambling houses, flourishing revolvers and coercing croupiers into accepting Japanese military notes. In Shanghai, Japanese authorities announced their intention of taking control of the International Settlement's Council; Japanese in Shanghai did outnumber Europeans and Americans. And in Tientsin, Americans at the barrier were under orders to alight from their cars—and bow to the Japanese sentries.

All this left Grew tense and exhausted. "Dear me," he wrote to his daughter in mid-April 1940, "I must be getting dreadfully morose."

■ ■ ■

And small wonder.

Although still based at San Diego, the bulk of the United States Pacific Fleet was out on maneuvers hundreds of miles to the west of Hawaii. Talking with reporters, Rear Admiral James O. Richardson, chief of the Pacific Fleet, declined to give details about those maneuvers: He said only that they had "involved more steaming about than he had seen on any others in the Pacific area." But one point was clear. On their eastward return, these ships, about forty of them, put in for an indefinite period at Pearl Harbor. Admiral Richardson then did call Pearl Harbor the "Gibraltar of the Pacific;" and as the returning ships rounded Diamond Head at night, great spotlights from the shoreline illuminated each vessel and some 100,000 spectators who had gathered on the beaches clapped and cheered.

Once the American ships were inside and at berth, antisubmarine nets closed off the mouth of the harbor. Four Japanese sampans, nonetheless, somehow got inside. Apprehended, the crewmen claimed that a high sea had swept them in. But U.S. authorities arrested them, charging them with espionage.

Simultaneously, the U.S. Navy created a "security patrol" around Oahu. Aircraft carriers now regularly "disappeared" into the Pacific and naval patrol bombers began making daily flights 300 miles off Hawaii.

Tokyo's government-controlled newspapers charged that these activities were aimed against Japan. American officials claimed that they were only defensive.

■ ■ ■

But the line between offense and defense was blurring. Glance "at the map of the Pacific," C. Hartley Grattan, a journalist, wrote in the May 1940 issue of *Harper's Magazine*, "and you will see that Japan, by taking over the German islands north of the Equator, gained control of a curtain of islands which hangs directly between the United States and the Philippines and the Dutch East Indies, the bottom of the curtain being dangerously close to the northern boundary of the Australian possessions. . . . [T]he Japanese [further-more] have strengthened the worth of [those islands] in recent years by developing them, by pouring Japanese nationals into them until they outnumber the natives, by establishing an airline down through them, and by fortifying strategic points. . . . In addition, the Austra-lians think that Japan . . . has built strong bases at Truk in the Carolines and Jaluit in the Marshalls." The latter islands, the author noted, "are . . . 4,000 miles from Singapore, and hence beyond the easy reach of the British. In short, the Australians see the islands as a finger which points threateningly at them."

A particular item in the news gave rise to this article. The Civil Aeronautics Board in Washington, according to a piece in *The New York Times*, approved a new Pan American Airways line from Hawaii to Pago Pago, then on to Auckland and Sydney. The Civil Aeronautics Board, in fact, called this new air route "valuable to the national defense." Why? Because, Mr. Grattan pointed out, such an air link would give America "an almost unseverable contact with Australia." America, in brief, was moving toward a de facto alliance with Australia—further tightening the circle around Japan.

■   ■   ■

Pan American was receiving a federal subsidy; the U.S. Navy fig-ured that it, too, should be getting more money. Late in April and early in May 1940, Admiral Harold R. Stark, Admiral William D. Leahy's successor as chief of naval operations, testified on Capitol Hill in favor of the latest naval expansion bill—a measure introduced by Representative Carl Vinson that would increase the size of the navy by 25 percent. Stark was a good navy bureaucrat and certainly available to administration wishes; Roosevelt had picked him over fifty-nine others who outranked him.

Like Defense Department spokesmen in our own time, Stark knew how to deal with Congress: He scared the committee mem-bers. Japan, he was "reasonably certain," was secretly building eight new dreadnoughts. The Japanese government, to be sure, denied the charge. But Stark swore that since Japanese authorities allowed foreigners nowhere near their naval yards and since those naval yards were partially camouflaged with bamboo and branches, Congress ought to assume the worst.

And just to make sure that Congress was listening, Stark's deputy, Rear Admiral Joseph K. Taussig, used one more tactic. He presented Congress with figures about how many workers, back in the home states and districts, the navy bill would put to work.

It worked. Congress increased the navy's appropriations by a fourth.

■   ■   ■

Roosevelt, too, was selling the cause. Shortly before dinnertime on May 10, 1940, he invited Harry Hopkins, the secretary of commerce, to the Oval Office for cocktails.

Thin and sunken-looking, and an inveterate chain-smoker, Hopkins came to politics from a background of social work: For a time he worked in New York as the national president of the Anti-Tuberculosis League. Because of that background, he may have been skeptical about the need for massive military spending. But Roosevelt wanted Hopkins on the team wholeheartedly. After he mixed martinis for Hopkins and Missy LeHand, therefore, the president treated them both to a lecture. Hopkins's notes are preserved at the F. D. R. Library at Hyde Park, and they present a picture of America surrounded by enemies.

"The Atlantic and Pacific," Roosevelt reflected aloud, while Hopkins scribbled away, "were adequate defensive barriers while fleets under sail would move at an average speed of five miles an hour— the sudden forays like the burning of our national capital [in the War of 1812] were possible. The oceans gave strength to defense as long as steam fleets and convoys [attained only] fifteen or twenty miles an hour—

"But the new element—air navigation—steps up the speed of possible attack enormously—to 200 or 300 miles an hour. Furthermore, it brings new possibilities of the use of much nearer bases from which to attack the continent itself.

"The fjords of Greenland are only x miles from Newfoundland, x from Nova Scotia, New Brunswick, and Quebec, only x miles from New England.

"The Azores are but. . . .

"The islands of the South Pacific are not too far removed from the west coast of South America to prevent them from becoming bases of enormous strategic advantage to attacking forces.

"People assumed last year—there would be no war—and when it came they thought [it] would be conducted like World War I—there would be impregnable lines and [it would] settle down to long contests of endurance.

"Our whole concept revamped.

"Today we see motorized armies moving 200 miles a day—we see air armadas successfully landing thousands of troops—miles in rear of the defending front. We see attacks capable of destroying airplane factories—munitions—hundreds of miles [behind the lines].

"Complete reorientation."

■   ■   ■

Ten days *before* Roosevelt gave his little lecture, the French military attaché in Switzerland sent an urgent cable back to Paris: Between May 8 and May 10, 1940, the message warned, the Germans would launch an attack toward France. Two days before, British reconnaissance planes over the French border spotted, on the winding roads of the Ardennes Forest below them, a vast armada of German tanks. On the morning before, a huge headline in *The New York Times* proclaimed: "NAZIS INVADE HOLLAND, BELGIUM, LUXEMBOURG. . . ." And by the time Roosevelt was pooring martinis for Harry Hopkins and Missy LeHand, talking with them, and then sharing dinner with them, German tanks were crossing the frontier into France.

■   ■   ■

Six days after his lecture, Roosevelt addressed a joint session of Congress, calling for the sale of airplanes to Britain and France and the production, in America, of "at least 50,000 planes a year." Dramatizing his point, the president referred to the fact that airplanes could launch "swift and deadly" attacks across vast global expanses.

Then he pulled back, focusing the members' attention on "the possibility of attack on vital American zones." This, as always, was Roosevelt's style—couching new proposals in old terms.

CHAPTER
16

THE FALL OF FRANCE

Late in the hot, steamy afternoon of May 21, 1940, in Washington, a young American journalist-lawyer, his wife, and a group of their friends met for a picnic supper on a clump of rocks overlooking the Potomac rapids. The occasion was a birthday, but hardly anyone in the party felt any joy. The news was too grim for gaiety. Eleven days before, the Germans had launched their invasion of France and now, German armored divisions had reached the coast of the English Channel, splitting the armies of France and Great Britain asunder. The "waters of the Potomac danced in the setting sun," the journalist-lawyer wrote later; someone "hopefully recalled the miracle of the Marne in World War I. His optimism was not catching. Day by day the newspaper maps had shown the ominous lengthening of the needlelike [German] salient that had started as a tiny bulge at Sedan. Now it had reached Abbeville; only the ocean had stopped the assault that the French were helpless to check. The world we had known had lost its underpinnings, and we sat silent and stunned."

The group was aware of an unassailable fact. Germany was going to defeat, and occupy, France.

. . .

From a point in the Maginot line close to Strasbourg, in France, a pair of young French sentries hunched down to peer through the slot in their pillbox. The sun was about to peek over the hills of

227

Germany to the east, for the time was shortly before dawn on May 10, 1940; and the bridge that led across the Rhine toward the German fortifications at Kehl was glittering with innumerable little lights. Soon the river would ripple and flash in the sunshine, and the sky would grow blue and cloudless and warm. Soon the sentries would be off duty and, having retired to the underground barracks far below, would be able to sleep soundly under the covers on their bunks. Already their comrades down there were stretching and yawning as they climbed out of bed, waking to another morning of boredom and ease, and certain that all they would have to do that day would be to sit in their canteen, drinking beer or wine, and listening to the radio from Paris. Like the sentries in the pillbox above them, these men felt restless but safe.

Before dawn that same morning, the panzer tanks of the Nineteenth German Armored Corps, under the command of General Heinz Guderian, were rumbling along with their lights extinguished through the Eifel Mountains, just east of Luxembourg and just north of a break in the Maginot line. In the lead came tanks, armored cars, and reinforced motorcycles; next came troop trucks, heavy artillery, and supply echelons; and finally, stretching fifty miles to the rear, marched columns of infantry. Since the mountains were still pitch dark, the various drivers had to exert their utmost powers of vision to avoid collisions, or end up in the roadside ditches. Yet more and more troops quartered in the Eifel were up and under way; more and more armored vehicles were clattering from the approach roads to join the main columns of tanks. The noise of the motors was getting on everyone's nerves. The men were uneasy and nervous; tempers were beginning to flare.

Far to the rear, Luftwaffe pilots, too, were up and about, tumbling from their bunks, scrambling into their flight jackets, racing to their briefing sessions. Even before sunrise, German bombers and fighters had climbed to the sky, most of them droning off toward Holland and Belgium, hoping thus to divert Allied attention from where the main armored thrust was aimed.

The German code name for the operation was *Sichelschnitt*, the cutting motion of a scythe. The idea was to pull off a great big trick.

When the Germans invaded France in 1914, they marched across the fields of Flanders, swinging their infantry down through Belgium so that, in theory at least, the last man on the right would brush the English Channel with his sleeve. Throughout the years that followed their defeat in 1918, German General Staff officers kept working on contingency plans that foresaw their armies once again crossing the plains of Belgium. Early in 1940, however, during the time of the Phony War, the airplane of a German officer who was carrying a copy of such a plan crash-landed behind the Maginot line; French intelligence officers, Berlin suspected, were pouring over the documents. So the Germans hastily developed a new plan, Operation *Sichelschnitt*.

Deciding this time only to feign going toward the Channel, the German high command sent waves of airplanes to bomb Rotterdam and a few panzer columns toward the Albert Canal in Belgium— while ordering most of the armored units elsewhere, down from the Eifel Mountains, in through the duchy of Luxembourg, and out across the Ardennes Forest toward France, toward Sedan. Sedan was just a town, but it possessed great significance, because near Sedan there was a breach in the Maginot line. Above Sedan stood the ninth French Army and below Sedan stood the Second French Army, the two least trained units in the French military; beyond Sedan stood nothing at all, nothing, that is, but rolling hills, the shores of the English Channel, and then the city of Paris. But first the Germans had to reach Sedan, and blocking their way was the Ardennes Forest. Its trees were thick, its hills were steep, its valleys were narrow, and its twisting roads could hold a tank to a pace both slow and vulnerable to assault. A few antitank cannons hidden among the trees or a few airplanes swooping down through the valleys could destroy a division of panzers within moments. Marshal Philippe Pétain, a commander in chief of the French army in World War I, had called the Ardennes Forest "impenetrable."

As he led the German column over the border of Luxembourg on the morning of May 10, 1940, therefore, General Heinz Guderian looked nervously out of the cockpit of his tank toward the end of the bridge below. He was, as always, expecting trouble. No Luxembourgeois soldiers appeared and so, for a time, he could relax. Through the slit in his turret he could see cows munching and farmers trudging into their fields. By 10:00 A.M., Guderian had crossed Luxembourg and was moving over the tip of Belgium. He was still nervous. Occasionally one of his tanks would stall or run out of gas, and other tanks from behind would have to spend precious minutes pushing it into a ditch. Such slowdowns seemed increasingly frequent; and the slower the German units went forward, the more inviting they became as targets for the bombers of the French air force.

But to Guderian's surprise, no such bombers appeared—the only aircraft he saw that day bore the reassuring black crosses of the Luftwaffe—and by nightfall he was encamped on the western slopes of the Ardennes, overlooking France. Just a few miles to the north, the Seventh Panzer Division had reached even farther into France than Guderian had. The commander of the Seventh Division was General Erwin Rommel.

On the morning of May 11, 1940, warnings did begin to reach the French high command: Overnight air reconnaissance had revealed a heavy concentration of German motorized elements pushing through the Ardennes Forest. Having snapped at the German bait, however, the strongest of the French armies had shifted northward, up toward the Channel, moving away from the scene of the main action.

"Keep going! Keep going! Don't stop!" As anxious as ever, General Guderian even before dawn on May 12, 1940, was standing with his head and shoulders above the turret of his tank, shouting down orders, waving his forces ever forward into France and toward Sedan. Belgian airplanes had found him by this time, and from across the Meuse, a few miles to the southwest, French artillery was starting to lob up its shells. But Guderian kept moving and, by the end of the afternoon, had stopped his tank on a hillside. Before him were the medieval spires of Sedan. He had done it! He had done the impossible! He had penetrated the Ardennes Forest. With a yell and a wave, he led his tanks down the slope, across the valley of the Meuse, and into Sedan. Rommel had beaten him there.

In 1940, General Erwin Rommel accomplished in three days what the previous generation of German generals, in World War I, had failed to accomplish in four years. On May 13, he forded the Meuse;

on May 14, he broke through at Sedan; and on May 15, he struck forth again, leading the way for all the other panzer units up to the English Channel and closing a trap behind the Allied forces located in Belgium. On May 23, General Guderian himself entered the French channel town of Gravelines, only ten miles from Dunkirk. The bulk of the British force was holed up in Dunkirk.

Hitler, however, was beside himself. Still far back in Germany, he had been hunching over a table set up in his special train car and pouring over a large map of France. Staff officers had stuck pins in the map, the pins representing the panzer progress; on Hitler's map, the pins, radiating from the lower reaches of the Rhine River, were curving rows up into Holland, along the Albert Canal in Belgium, over the coastline past Antwerp; another row led up through eastern France to the channel coast just west of Belgium. The pins, in short, described a rapidly shrinking pocket from midway up the Belgian border to Dunkirk. The trouble was, it all seemed too easy. The führer was fretful.

"Rather unpleasant day," recorded General Franz Halder on May 17, 1940; as chief of staff, Halder was accompanying Hitler in the train car. "The Führer is terribly nervous. Frightened by his own success, he is afraid to take any chance. . . . Führer unaccountably keeps worrying about the southern flank. He rages and screams that we are on the best way to ruin the whole campaign."

Fearful, Hitler issued a fateful command. He ordered the panzer columns, about to close in on Dunkirk, to pause. They did so for three days. By May 24, 1940, 400,000 Allied troops, some of them French but most of them British, were pinned in a strip of territory, the bottom of which touched Lille and the top of which stretched about thirty miles from Ostend on the Belgian coast to a point about five miles below Dunkirk, in France. Inside this corridor, the land was flat and, aside from marshy patches, easily passable. Gathered along the perimeter, the panzers would reach Dunkirk quickly; and once they came, Dunkirk would be defenseless. The British government, nevertheless, decided to evacuate its troops.

Across the English Channel from Dunkirk, near the base of the white cliffs of Dover, a small entranceway in the chalk wall led to a honeycomb of underground passages. Offices adjoined the passages and the largest of these offices, that of Vice Admiral Bertram Ramsay, looked out again from the face of the cliff. From that window, on the morning of May 25, 1940, Ramsay witnessed a "strange fleet of ferries, hoppers, dredges, barges, coasters, and skoots," all converging on Dover, all preparing to cross the channel for an attempted rescue at Dunkirk. The boats were varied in type but skippers all had but one thought: watching the sky for any signs of the Luftwaffe.

In Dunkirk itself that night—the Allied perimeter had shrunk to the outskirts of the town itself—the piers and the warehouses were blazing, for the Luftwaffe was already at work there, demolishing much of the harbor front and missing only two long breakwaters, moles that stuck out like arms to enfold the harbor's entrance. Those moles were the salvation of the troops on the shore. First singly or in pairs, then in larger groups, and finally in a swaying, serpentine column, the men began to wade out into the water, some of them until they were neck deep, until they had reached the end of the eastern mole. There in the cover of the night, the first of the boats were pulling in from Dover.

The next day, and the next and the next, dawned drizzly with fog, to the consternation of the German pilots but much to the joy of the troops in Dunkirk. Despite the poor visibility, soldiers on the beaches could see the sea, and out of the sea each day materialized a fleet of vessels—steamers, ferries, "fishing smacks, drifters, excursion boats, glittering white yachts, mud-spattered hoppers, open motor launches, tugs, towing ships, life boats, Thames sailing barges with their distinctive brown sails, cabin cruisers, their brass work gleaming, dredges, trawlers, and rust-streaked scows." This was the evacuation of Dunkirk, with long lines of men curling out into the water and thousands more waiting on the beaches behind them. Best of all the clouds were so thick, a German pilot wrote, that "you can learn on them."

But the bad weather did not hold. Early in the afternoon of June 1, 1940, two British patrol boats left Dover, heading for Dunkirk. The sea was calm, the air was clear, and the sun was bright. The war even seemed far away. Suddenly, however, a lieutenant aboard the second of the boats heard a "roar, a rattle, and a bang." Just ahead, a Stuka dived toward the first boat. Machine guns blazing, seven more Stukas appeared, plunging fast toward the two British boats. The boats did survive; in fact, they drove the Stukas away. But midway through the afternoon of June 3, 1940, the panzers broke through Dunkirk's perimeter.

By dawn the next morning, German marines were pouring into Dunkirk's outlying streets; and shortly after 8:00 A.M., a German colonel in an armored car rolled into the center of town, stopping in front of the red brick Hotel de Ville. There he met the senior French officer in Dunkirk, who, decked out in a gold-leafed kepi, formally surrendered the city. German troops meantime were racing toward the waterfront, passing the burnt-out warehouses, reaching the rubble of the docks, and pulling up behind long rows of soldiers who were wading out toward the tip of the eastern mole.

To the surprise of the Germans, however, these soldiers were French. The British had gone.

That evening Prime Minister Churchill addressed the House of Commons. The galleries were packed and, as Churchill entered, the crowd cheered. He delivered the bad news: Holland and Belgium had fallen and now France itself was in peril. But we, Churchill declared, shall "go on to the end. We shall fight in France, we shall fight on the seas and oceans, we shall fight . . . in the air, we shall defend our island, whatever the cost may be. We shall fight on the beaches, we shall fight on the landing grounds, we shall fight in the fields and in the streets, we shall fight in the hills; we shall never surrender, and even if, which I do not for a moment believe, this island or a large part of it were subjugated or starving, then our Empire beyond the seas . . . would carry on the struggle until, in God's time, the new world, with all its power and might, steps forth to the rescue and the liberation of the old."

So there it was. Churchill was looking to America for succor. He had no choice.

■　■　■

"Dearest Lu," General Rommel wrote to his wife on the morning of June 5. "Today the second phase of the offensive begins, . . . I shall be observing the attack from well back in the rear. A fortnight,

I hope, will see the war over on the mainland. . . . The whole world is sending its congratulations. I've opened nowhere near all the letters yet. There hasn't been time."

After the British escape from Dunkirk, the German armies had regrouped, refueled, and resumed their drive toward Paris. But contrary to what he had written his wife, Rommel was in the lead again. His first objective was the Somme River, seventy-five miles north of Paris. A few French calvary units threw themselves in the panzers' path, but Rommel's units quickly overpowered them. "Over to the left," Rommel wrote to his wife again, "a giant pillar of smoke belched up from a burning [gasoline truck] and numerous saddled horses stampeded riderless across the plain." At 9:00 P.M., on June 5, Rommel sent a message back to divisional headquarters: "All quiet forward, enemy in shreds." He was thirty miles from the Somme.

At dawn on June 6 the panzers moved forward again; French resistance was scattered and feeble. Rommel's units, forming a column 2,000 yards wide and twelve miles deep, "moved as if on an exercise. In this formation we advanced up hill and down dale, over highways and byways straight across country." The next day's advance, Rommel wrote,

> went . . . over roadless and trackless fields, uphill, downhill, through hedges, fences, and high cornfields. . . . We met no enemy troops, apart from a few stragglers, but plenty of indications in the shape of military vehicles and horses standing in open country that they had left shortly before our arrival. . . . Sometimes we even surprised refugee trucks in open country, their occupants, men, women, and children, underneath the vehicles, where they had crawled in mortal fear.

Rommel reached the Somme on the evening of June 7, 1940. At daybreak his columns launched their encirclement of Paris.

On the move again, the German armored units, like Caesar, divided Gaul into three parts: One column headed southeast, striking toward the rear of the Maginot line; a second turned westward toward the mouth of the Seine; and a third went streaking across the flat coastal plain of Picardy toward the city of Paris.

"Dearest Lu," Rommel wrote on the morning of June 10: "I'm

in fine form, although I'm on the go the whole time. Our successes are tremendous and it looks to me that the other side will soon collapse. We never imagined that war in the west would be like this. . . ." Although Rommel himself had veered away from the main units, intent on cutting a British division off from the coast— he captured 40,000 prisoners—other panzer units pushed along the Seine toward Vernon, a small, tree-shaded town just twenty miles above the Paris–Brittany rail line.

War came to Vernon with a sudden brutality. At midday on June 10, a huge, limping column of refugees crossed the bridge that led to the town. Slowly, with babies in wheelbarrows, grandparents in pushcarts, youngsters on bicycles, soldiers on foot, children and women in carts, the procession plodded toward the center of the town. Some of these people had spent days on the road, some had been bombed, some had been strafed, and all of them bore on their clothes the dust and grass that bespoke the days of tramping and the nights of sleeping in fields. But now they were in Vernon. There, under the arch of the elms that crossed over streets, they felt safe from attack. The Luftwaffe hit the town with shattering blows. Trees toppled, houses caved in, and the old Norman church blazed into an inferno of flames. By the middle of the afternoon, the panzers, having swarmed around Vernon, started southward again, heading directly for Paris.

Robert Murphy, an American diplomat in Paris, walked out of the U.S. embassy on the afternoon of June 13, 1940, making his way past the Obelisque in the Place de la Concorde. He looked up the broad expanse of the Champs Elysées toward the Arc de Triomphe. "As every visitor to Paris knows," Murphy wrote, "this is one of the world's greatest traffic hazards. But now the only living creatures in sight were three abandoned dogs cavorting beneath the large French flags which still hung [over] the great concourse." Three days before, the government and much of the populace had departed from Paris; and one day later, on June 14, 1940, Germans tore the French flags down. From the top of the Eiffel Tower fluttered a swastika.

■ ■ ■

As the Germans were closing in on Paris, an operator at the British Embassy in Washington placed a call to Walter Lippmann. Lippmann, the hawk-nosed, hawk-browed syndicated news columnist, was the dean of America's journalists and a proud wielder of political influence. Policymakers did not always follow Lippmann's advice. But "they listened to him and sought his support," his biographer has noted "—and they learned not to take his opposition lightly. Lippmann commanded a loyal and powerful constituency, some ten million of the most politically active and articulate people in America. Many of these people literally did not know what they ought to think about the issues of the day until they read what Walter Lippmann had said about them. A politician could ignore that kind of power only at his own risk." Hence the telephone call from the British Embassy to the Lippmann home in Georgetown: Lord Lothian, the British ambassador, wanted Lippmann's help.

Once inside the British Embassy, Lippman found Lothian pacing. If France fell, and it appeared likely to do so, Lothian said, Britain could fall as well; and the collapse of Britain would give Hitler control of the seas. So something had to be done, and fast. Britain might survive if it could get destroyers, Lothian pointed out, but Britain could get those destroyers from one place alone, the United States; and the laws of the land forbade the sale of such things to belligerents. Did Lippmann understand the danger?

Lothian was preaching to the choir. Lippman had already argued that the fall of France would overturn the balance of power, and placed the Anglo-American democracies in peril.

But what to do? Lothian and Lippmann hit on a scheme: The United States would turn over a number of destroyers *in a swap* for British bases in the Western Hemisphere. Lothian would present the idea to the foreign policy establishment and Lippmann would sell it to the public. As part of his sales pitch, Lippman paid a call on America's favorite hero from World War I, General John Pershing, and he prevailed on the old man to make a speech on the radio. "Today may be the last time," Pershing soon broadcast, "when by measures short of war we can still prevent war." Lippmann liked the words: He had written them.

Word got out that Lippmann was behind the Pershing speech

and a reporter for the *St. Louis Post-Dispatch* made his way to Lippmann's summer home in Maine. Was the rumor true? Lippmann confessed that it was—whereupon the journalist accused him of being a "warmonger," and threatened to start a congressional investigation of an Anglo-American "plot to get America into the war."

Lippmann took care of the matter with dispatch. Getting on the telephone, he called his summer neighbor, Joseph Pulitzer, who owned the St. Louis paper, and told the publisher to lay off. Pulitzer dropped the investigation—Walter Lippmann and, behind him, the interventionist lobby, had that much power.

■ ■ ■

A tide of repression was flooding America. The U.S. House of Representatives already, in 1938, had created a select committee to investigate "the diffusion within the United States of subversion and un-American propaganda"—this was the House Un-American Activities Committee (HUAC), by 1940 intimating that subversives were under every bed. And more: Fearing fifth columnists, E. D. Rivers, the governor of Georgia, ordered all aliens in his state to undergo fingerprinting. The Federal Bureau of Investigation sent eleven agents, "experts on sabotage and espionage," to keep watch on the Philadelphia Navy Yard: Fifth columnists were rumored to be lurking about. In New York City, Mayor Fiorello La Guardia's office announced the assignment of extra policemen to protect the new airport at North Beach, in Queens. Obviously the fifth columnists could strike in the urban north as well as in the rural south—indeed, anywhere.

So just before the end of June 1940, Congress passed the Smith Act, the nation's first peacetime sedition measure since 1801. It stated: "Whoever knowingly or willfully advocates, abets, advises, or teaches . . . overthrowing . . . the government of the United States. . . ; whoever . . . prints, publishers, edits, . . . or publicly displays any written or printed matter advocating, advising, or teaching [the overthrow of] any government in the United States . . .; whoever organizes . . . any society, group, or assembly of persons who teach, advocate, or encourage the overthrow . . . of any such government; or becomes or is a member of . . . any such society . . . knowing the purpose of [such a society] shall be fined . . . or imprisoned . . . or both. . . ." Two prominent House members, Howard W. Smith of Virginia, chairman of the Rules Committee, and John McCormack of Massachusetts, later Speaker of the House, had led the fight for these provisions, and the intent of their work was clear: to restrict the free speech, free press, and free assembly clauses of the First Amendment to the U.S. Constitution.

Even the U.S. Supreme Court was having a go at the First Amendment. In their last appearance of the 1939–1940 session, the Justices ruled in a case called *Minersville School District* v. *Gobitis*.

When you drive past Minersville on the interstate highway, you feel that you are passing by the middle of nowhere. Located in northeastern Pennsylvania, between Harrisburg on the one side and Allentown and Bethlehem on the other, Minersville is stuck down in a mountain range so thinly settled that you suspect there must be more bears than people.

Minersville was little more than village—so everyone there knew about it when the Gobitis family ran into trouble. For the Gobitises were Jehovah's Witnesses. Back in 1936, Lillian Gobitis and William, her younger brother, both of them pupils in the public grade school, had gone home with distressing news. Their principal had expelled them. He refused to allow them back unless they agreed to salute the flag at the patriotic exercises that began each school day.

As Jehovah's Witnesses, the Gobitis family took seriously the strictures of the Book of Exodus: "Thou shalt have no other gods before me; Thou shalt not make unto thee any graven image . . .; Thou shalt not bow down thyself to them. . . ." A national flag, to Jehovah's Witnesses, was a graven image and, for reasons of religious conviction, not to be saluted. The Gobitis parents had so instructed their children. But the principal of the grade school, supported by the Minersville school board, viewed the children's refusal to salute as a sign of disloyalty. On that ground, he had expelled them from school.

The Gobitis appeal reached the U.S. Supreme Court. On June 3, 1940—Flag Day—the Court made known its decision. Felix Frankfurter wrote the opinion.

"The ultimate foundation of a free society is the binding tie of cohesive sentiment," Frankfurter declared. Small, wiry, intense, brilliant, dark-eyed behind his pince-nez, Frankfurter had been an immigrant from Austria; he had risen rapidly, becoming a law professor at Harvard, the protector of dozens of young students whom he placed in key jobs in Washington, and, finally, a justice, appointed by Roosevelt. Frankfurter spoke for much of official Washington. The flag, he continued in the *Gobitis* opinion, is "the symbol of our national unity . . . the emblem of freedom in its truest, best sense. . . . The influences which help toward a common feeling for the common country are manifold. Some may seem harsh and others no doubt are foolish. Surely, however, the end is legitimate." So saying, Justice Frankfurter and the U.S. Supreme Court upheld the expulsion of the Gobitis children from school.

"Surely, however," Justice Frankfurter had stated, "the end is legitimate." In a climate of fear, in a springtime so rife with rumors of spies, saboteurs, and traitors that dissidence of all sorts was suspect, even the United States Supreme Court could declare that the end—the inculcation, by government, of national conformity—justified the means. As France fell, America became hysterical.

At least that was the opinion of Colonel Charles A. Lindbergh. Going on the air again, he argued that enemy armies in no way would be able to cross the oceans, by ship or by plane. Lindbergh, however, left himself open for raillery. This time his attacker was Jimmy Byrnes, the slick, quick-witted little senator from South Carolina. Byrnes just happened to be the Senate's sponsor for the new navy authorization bill; money for the navy would be the foundation of Charleston's prosperity. Going on CBS radio, Byrnes accused Lindbergh of aiding fifth columnists. "Fifth Columnists are already active in America," Byrnes maintained. "And those who consciously or unconsciously retard the efforts of this government to provide for the defense of the American people are the Fifth Column's most effective fellow-travelers."

■ ■ ■

Roosevelt himself got into the suppression business.

"When I spoke to J. Edgar Hoover" Henry Morgenthau recorded in his diary entry of May 20, 1940, and asked him whether he was able to listen in on Nazi spies by tapping the wires, . . . he said no; that the order given by Bob Jackson [Robert H. Jackson, the new U.S. attorney general] stopping him had not been revoked. I said I would go to work at once. He said he needed it desperately. He said there were four Nazi spies working in Buffalo across the Canadian border and the Royal Mounted Police had asked for his assistance and he had been unable to give it. I called up General Watson [General Edwin M. "Pa" Watson on the White House staff] and said this should be done, and he said, "I don't think it is legal."

I said, "What if it is illegal?"

He called me back in five minutes and said that he told the President and the President said, "Tell Bob Jackson to send for J. Edgar Hoover and order him to do it."

In a follow-up memorandum to Attorney General Jackson, Roosevelt stated:

I have agreed with the broad purpose of the Supreme Court decision [limiting] wiretapping. [Roosevelt probably had in mind the 1928 *Olmstead* case, in which the Court had stopped the federal government from tapping the telephone lines of a Seattle bootlegger.] However, I am convinced that the Supreme Court never intended any dictum in the particular case which it decided to apply to grave matters involving the defense of the nation. It is, of course, well known that certain other nations have been engaged in the organization of . . . "fifth columns" in other countries in preparation for sabotage. . . . It is too late to do anything about it after sabotage, assassinations, and "fifth column" activities are completed.

Justice Oliver Wendell Holmes, Jr. remarked once that the Constitution meant what the Supreme Court said that it meant. In his memorandum to Attorney General Jackson, in asserting his own reading of what the Supreme Court really thought, Franklin D. Roosevelt was suggesting that the Constitution meant what the *president* said that it meant.

Roosevelt went further still. Was there "any law or executive order," he asked Jackson, "under which it would be possible for us to open and inspect outgoing . . . or incoming mail to and from certain foreign nations?" A mail-opening campaign, the president indicated, would pick up messages pertaining to " 'Fifth Column' activities—sabotage, antigovernment propaganda, military secrets, etc." Jackson's answer was negative. That response, however, was no deterrence. Even without the sanction of law, the FBI, apparently at Roosevelt's request, proceeded to train agents in the techniques of opening the mail.

Whose mail? Among others, that of Colonel Charles A. Lindbergh. Lindbergh and his supporters, the president was convinced, were part of a fifth column. "Today's threat to our national security is not a matter of military weapons alone," Roosevelt said on May 26, 1940. "We know of new methods of attack. The Trojan Horse. The Fifth Column that betrays a nation unprepared for treachery. Spies, saboteurs, and traitors are the actors in this new strategy. . . . But there is more in an added technique for weakening a nation. . . . The method is simple. It is . . . a dissemination of discord. A group—not too large—a group that may be sectional or racial or political—is encouraged to exploit its prejudice through false slogans and emotional appeals. . . . Sound national policies come to be viewed with a new and unreasoning skepticism. Singleness of national purpose may be undermined." And the principal underminer, thought Roosevelt, was Lindbergh. "If I should die tomorrow, I want you to know this," Roosevelt confided in Morgenthau over a lunch. "I am absolutely convinced that Lindbergh is a Nazi."

Lindbergh may have been foolish and Lindbergh may have been wrong. Germany, furthermore, *did* have spies in America; so did Japan. But no one in 1940, and for that matter no one in the half century since, has proven Lindbergh to be a Nazi. But, of course, he *was* opposed to the president's new defense program, and its cost of millions upon millions of dollars.

■   ■   ■

Francis and Helen Miller were members in good standing of the interventionist lobby: He was an executive of the Rockefeller-supported Council on Foreign Relations; she was the Washington correspondent of the prestigious London journal, *The Economist*. And they lived on an estate in Fairfax, Virginia, horse country for the elite of the nation's capital. Urged on, furthermore, by a Baltimore attorney named Richard F. Cleveland, son of President Grover Cleveland, they decided to put their estate to the service of their cause: an American declaration of war against Germany.

An initial meeting at the Miller home took place on June 2, 1940, and it embraced among others the Millers, Cleveland, M. L. Wilson of the Department of Agriculture, and Edward P. Warner of the Civil Aeronautics Board. The conversation lasted all day. To their astonishment, the guests realized that they held identical views— to a person they believed that American democracy was in mortal danger—but what, they wondered, could they do to move America toward a war declaration? At last they hit on an answer. They would draft a letter to the public, attract prominent signatures, and release the document to the papers.

Entitling their letter "A Summons to Speak Out," they did get some of the signatures they wanted. The list included Herbert Agar, the Louisville editor; John L. Balderston, the Beverly Hills playwright; Henry W. Hobson, the Episcopal bishop of Cincinnati; Lewis Mumford, the writer; and Admiral William H. Standley of New York, a retired chief of naval operations. Some of the signers already belonged to the Committee to Defend America by Aiding the Allies; Admiral Standley served on the board of directors of Pan American Airways.

Only a handful of newspapers, however, carried the "Summons" and Helen Miller was prepared to let the matter drop. But a friend, Dr. Henry Pitt Van Dusen of New York's Union Theological Seminary, intervened.

Determined to keep the drive for war going, Van Dusen arranged for an appointment with Lord Lothian at the British Embassy. How, Van Dusen asked, could he, his friends the Millers, and the others help? America, Lothian replied, might send over some overaged destroyers; he would do, he added, whatever he could to assist Van Dusen and the Millers.

So a deal was cut. Lothian wrote Churchill of "encouraging" changes in "American opinion"; Van Dusen set up a meeting to be held early in July in New York's Columbia Club, putting the Millers in touch with more movers and shakers.

■ ■ ■

For the occasion of the University of Virginia's commencement exercises, June 10, 1940, President Roosevelt took the train up to Charlottesville to give a speech. He had already spoken to Congress, asking for 50,000 new airplanes. Now he was prepared to go further.

Rain clouds had obscured the mountains around Charlottesville and when Roosevelt rode from the station, the streets were drenched. The exercises took place inside the gymnasium. Donning a cap and gown and a crimson Harvard hood, Roosevelt made his way to the temporary platform. The band struck up "Hail to the Chief"; and 500 undergraduates in their own caps and gowns cheered him wildly.

Then Roosevelt spoke. Starting with a denunciation of isolationism, he interjected a comment that produced a flinging of mortarboards and a chorus of rebel yells. "On this 10th day of June, 1940," the president said, "the hand that held the dagger had stuck it in the back of the neighbor." Italy had just declared war on France and Great Britain. Roosevelt then went on, likening isolationism to a dream of "a lone island in a world dominated by force," a "nightmare of people lodged in prison, handcuffed, hungry, and fed through the bars from day to day by the contemptuous, unpitying masters of other continents." Nothing short of "victory over the gods of force and hate," he concluded, could preclude such imprisonment.

On "this 10th day of June, 1940," President Franklin D. Roosevelt spoke of "victory."

■ ■ ■

Without victory, Roosevelt believed, America would face defeat. Roosevelt's America would face no middle ground—as two prominent guests surely helped to convince him.

The first guest was a novelist, rough of face, gentle of manner, passionate of style—John Steinbeck. The year before, Steinbeck's most famous book, *The Grapes of Wrath*, had won the Pulitzer Prize and, in the spring of 1940, Steinbeck had been on location with Henry Fonda, making parts of the movie in Mexico. "In light of this experience," he had written to Roosevelt, "and against the background of the international situation, I am forced to the conclusion that a crisis in the Western Hemisphere is imminent, and is to be met only by an immediate, controlled, considered, and directed method and policy." Roosevelt took time out to chat with Steinbeck.

The second guest was Roosevelt's neighbor from up the Albany Pike Road in Hyde Park, Cornelius Vanderbilt, Jr. Embarking on a tour of Latin America, Vanderbilt had promised to keep Roosevelt informed on whatever he saw. The Germans were coming, the Germans were coming, Vanderbilt reported to Roosevelt: "In Colombia, Costa Rica, and Mexico," Vanderbilt stated, "I saw advance preparations for the Nazi invasion—private Nazi airports—private Nazi bombers—German civilians training natives. . . . It is not impossible that the United States might be conquered in a few weeks after England falls."

Were Steinbeck and Vanderbilt exaggerating the menace to America? We know—with hindsight—that Hitler had developed no great *plans* for an invasion of the Western Hemisphere. Roosevelt himself knew, however, that millions of persons of German, Italian, and even Japanese blood lived in Latin America, that Germany had strong economic ties with Argentina, Brazil, Venezuela, Colombia, and Mexico, and that German airlines were operating in every South American country from Cape Horn to the Panama Canal. And if Pan American country from Cape Horn to the Panama Canal. And if Pan American Airlines represented an unofficial but actual American form of pressure on Japan, Nazi-controlled airlines in Latin America represented an unofficial but actual German form of pressure on the Americas.

■ ■ ■

In preparation for that victory, Roosevelt reorganized the government.

He appointed Robert Sherwood, the gaunt, six-foot seven-inch playwright who resembled, some thought, a "walking coffin," as a speechwriter. Sherwood was well equipped for the job. In his 1938 play, *Abe Lincoln in Illinois*, still running on Broadway in the summer of 1940, he portrayed Abe Lincoln as overcoming fears and doubts, moving from a tolerance of slavery to an acknowledgment of its evil, gradually willing to accept, even at the cost of war,

America's need "to state and restate the fundamental virtues of our democracy, which have made us great, and which can make us greater." Sherwood was perfect for portraying Roosevelt-the-reluctant-war-leader.

Roosevelt brought Archibald MacLeish, the editor and poet, into the administration to run an Office of Facts and Figures, that is, of propaganda.

He established a National Defense Commission, a board of directors for the burgeoning military–industrial complex. This commission included Harriet Elliott, dean of women at the University of North Carolina, to advise on "consumer protection"; Leon Henderson, the scruffy, plump, New Deal economist who was to keep his eye on price stability; Sidney Hillman, founder of the Amalgamated Clothing Workers union, who was to keep on top of employment figures; and Chester Davis, an expert on farm production.

So far the board looked just like one of the alphabet soup agencies of the depression era. But now came the surprise. Roosevelt also brought in the captains of industry. For transportation: Ralph Budd, president of the Chicago, Burlington, & Quincy Railroad. For airplanes: William S. Knudsen, solid, honest, still talking in the quaint brogue of his native Denmark, and president of General Motors. For steel: the white-haired, Hollywood-leading-man-handsome, forty-year-old Edward R. Stettinius, Jr. For planes, again: Donald Nelson, the big, jovial, red-faced executive vice-president of the Sears, Roebuck Company. For oil: a young man named Nelson Rockefeller. For ships, Floyd B. Odlum, the financial wizard who held stocks in all of the above, as well as in Electric Boat at Groton, Connecticut.

Soon renamed the Office of Production Management and situated in the white marble temple on Constitution Avenue, the Federal Reserve Building, the group multiplied and gave seed. Its job was to control defense contracts and it did so, with defense dollars now flowing into precisely the industries from which these captains had come. The Office of Production Management, in fact, represented the mightiest iron triangle of all—the alliance among the armed forces committees of the Congress, the executive branch of the government, and the leading producers of guns and munitions.

Roosevelt was not finished yet. Easing incumbents out, he brought in Frank Knox, the Chicago publisher, as secretary of the navy, and Henry L. Stimson, the squire of Woodley, as secretary of war. (They in turn brought in, as special assistants, leading lights of the legal establishment, Adlai Stevenson of Chicago to the Navy Department, Robert A. Lovett and John McCloy of New York to the War Department.) Knox and Stimson had three things in common: Both were interventionists; both were wired into America's highest circles; and both were Republicans. On the eve of the Republican national convention, held in July 1940, Roosevelt had staged a raid, bringing two prominent members of the GOP into his own, Democratic, administration. Republicans, not surprisingly, shouted, "Dirty politics!" But Roosevelt got what he wanted: a government that was liberal and conservative, Democratic and Republican, pro-labor and pro-business. It was a coalition government.

The government reconstituted, Roosevelt made a series of new moves. He extended the Monroe Doctrine to include Danish-owned Greenland. He ordered the strengthening of bases in Alaska and Hawaii, as well as new airplane and warship construction at factories and shipyards across the continent. He encouraged the Treasury to work out a new loan for China.

America's response to the fall of France, then, looked like that of almost any nation gearing itself up for war: a cracking down on domestic dissent; a shifting of power into the hands of the executive; a buildup of arms; an expansion of buffer zones; and talk about victory.

■　■　■

For Japan, the fall of France was a kind of solution. The war in China had been dragging on for nearly three years; and although the Japanese had bombed, raped, pillaged, imprisoned, tortured, and bribed, no end seemed in sight. Suppressing the Chinese guerrillas was like trying to hold a dozen Ping-Pong balls under the surface in a tub of water: Aid from abroad, not much but enough to sustain a war of terror, kept trickling into China, in from Mongolia, in from Hong Kong, in from Hanoi, up along the Burma Road. Whatever Japan did in China, the foreign powers counterbalanced.

But now the balance shifted. Britain pulled ships back from Singapore to defend the home islands; and France fell, leaving Indo-China an orphan.

Japan lost little time moving into the vacuum. The Japanese government demanded that the British close the Burma Road, and Great Britain complied; to weaken the British still further, Tokyo sent agents into Rangoon, hoping to stir the Burmese people to rebellion and riot. Foreign Minister Arita spoke on the radio, picturing a vast new aggregation of satellite states in East Asia and the South Seas, all revolving harmoniously around Japan. The satellite region, *Nichi Nichi,* the Tokyo daily, explained, would include French Indo-China, the Dutch East Indies, British Hong Kong, Singapore, Malaya, Burma, and the remaining foreign concessions in China.

On June 18, 1940, the day of France's formal capitulation to Germany, a group of Japanese officials marched up the steps of Government House in Hanoi. The colonial government already had agreed to staunch a flow of material to China. Distrustful, however, the Japanese delegation now demanded the right to station observers at the border. If the French refused, the delegates made plain, Japan would invade.

■ ■ ■

Adolf Hitler had won the war—in France. Pacing about in his headquarters deep in the Black Forest, he was still profoundly worried. Late in June, he offered peace of a sort to the British, but they spurned the overture. His future looked ominous. Intelligence reports had turned grim: Britain had long-range bombers, and was planning to use them to level the Ruhr; British emissaries were starting to collude with the Soviets, and the Soviets were preparing to strike into Romania; British agents in Washington—this from the German Embassy—were working hand in glove with the Roosevelt administration, biding their time, waiting for Roosevelt's reelection, planning with the turn of the year to bring the weight of America against Hitler's Third Reich. These reports were nightmarish. The Ruhr housed 60 percent of Germany's industrial production. Romania was the Reich's only sure source of oil. And an American entry presaged Germany's loss of the seas, and of coal down through Norway.

At the end of June 1940, the führer reached two strategic and fateful decisions. First, he would launch an aerial assault on Britain, hoping to knock the British out before America came in. Second, in the springtime, once the winter season had passed and the snow was gone, he would invade Russia.

■ ■ ■

One item may have escaped the German intelligence network. Doing the rounds of the Washington cocktail parties, Constantine Alexandrovich Oumansky, the Soviet ambassador to the United States, was trying to build up his own network of political allies. (Roosevelt had recognized the Soviets officially in 1933, but relations remained chilly.) Oumansky faced obstacles; his country was suspect and he himself was squat, nearsighted, and obnoxious; he was, Cordell Hull was to write, "one of the most difficult foreign diplomats with whom we ever had to deal."

Oumansky, nonetheless, did have his uses. Undersecretary of State Sumner Welles spoke to him, conveying the message that the administration wanted a better relationship with Moscow. That relationship would be aimed against the Reich.

CHAPTER

17

THE BATTLE OF BRITAIN

The morning after the British evacuation of Dunkirk, two high-ranking German officers walked on the beach. The sand beneath their boots was littered with tin cans, empty bottles, thousands of shoes, military staff papers blowing in the wind, all the flotsam and jetsam left behind by an army in retreat. One of the Germans pointed out toward the channel. "There," he exclaimed, "is the grave of British hopes!" The other German was not so sure. "They are not buried yet," he commented. This second German was Colonel General Erhard Milch, deputy to the chief of the Luftwaffe, Hermann Göring. Milch turned to leave the beach. "We have no time to waste," he said.

Within a few hours, Milch was aboard Göring's armored train, several miles outside Dunkirk. Göring had lost some of his blubber, and a nurse, with him aboard the train, had cut his intake of pills, paracodeine, to thirty a day. But he was still grotesquely huge. Making his way around the table in his command car, he hugged his generals and slapped them on their backs. Then, waddling to the head of the table, he proclaimed that victory was at hand and that, at Dunkirk, the British army had been "wiped out."

"The British army?" General Milch queried. "They have got practically the whole of their army back across the channel, and that's worrying."

Göring's fat face fell.

What, he asked Milch, should Germany do next?

Milch was emphatic. "I strongly advise the immediate transfer to the channel coast of all available Luftwaffe forces . . . ," he stated. "The invasion of Great Britain should begin without delay." That was the beginning of Operation Sea Lion, Germany's halfhearted effort to invade Great Britain.

Germany's effort was halfhearted because Hitler's desire was halfhearted. Out of the jumble of his hatreds, prejudices, and illusions, one dream for twenty years had held constant: that Germany and Britain would form an alliance in which Germany would control the land and Britain would control the seas. Even as France was falling, accordingly, Hitler, through a series of intermediaries—including the duke of Windsor, the former Edward VIII, who was residing in Lisbon—still expressed hope that Germany and Britain would reach an amicable settlement. Churchill, to be sure, spurned all such offers; we shall not know exactly why until the twenty-first century, when his relevant papers are declassified. But Hitler held on to enough of his dream, even in July 1940, to make him pall before the idea of invading Great Britain.

Göring noticed Hitler's hesitation and drew the only possible conclusion. If Germany was going to defeat Great Britain, it was going to have to do so quickly.

Beginning in the middle of July 1940, Göring put out the word that he wanted a victory, and fast; so, even when cold rains scudded in from the Atlantic, German airplanes went up from their bases far down in France, dogfights raging over the English Channel itself, and over the counties of Hampshire, Sussex, and Kent. The two sides, the Royal Air Force and the Luftwaffe, were evenly matched; the Germans had more and better planes, but the British had radar. The British and the Germans both suffered losses; pilots were blown up, fried, drowned, or rescued, or returned to their landing strips in triumph. By the end of July, the Battle of Britain was a draw.

August 15, 1940, was the day of the *Adlerangriff*, the Eagle Attack; and as hundreds of Ju-88s, Heinkels, and Stukas shuttled back and forth across the channel, British hangars burst into flames, and in aerodromes from Portsmouth to London, bomb holes appeared on the runways. But the British held on.

Then the nature of the war changed. Up to the end of August 1940, Göring on Hitler's instructions had kept London itself off-limits to bombing. We enter here into a fog thicker than those off the Thames. Hitler's reasoning remains unclear—and so does Churchill's. What *is* clear, however, is that on the night of August 25, 1940, the British began bombing Berlin, and soon thereafter the Luftwaffe began bombing London, and nothing could have been better calculated to arouse American sympathies for the plight of Great Britain than reports of the bombing of London.

As afternoon gave way to evening on Saturday, September 7, 1940, spotters in Kenwood House, a mansion on the edge of Hampstead Heath, commented on the beauty of the red glow of the setting of the sun. Then they wised up. The red glow was emanating not from their right, off to the west, but rather from their left, to the east. London's East End was on fire.

The bombing of London, and especially of the East End, with its rows upon rows of tenements near the city's docks, warehouses, and factories, went on without letup for the next seven days. Churches collapsed, fires spread, sirens shrieked, and within that week some 12,000 Londoners died, were wounded, or found themselves entrapped in the rubble. And then Göring decided to hit them harder than ever.

Sunday, September 15, 1940, known in the annals of the Royal Air Force as Battle of Britain day—dawned sunny and bright. By mid-morning, British radar screens were jammed, packed as tight as they could be with masses of blips; and within the hour, some 400 German bombers, accompanied by even more German fighters, were sweeping in from over the channel. British Hurricanes went up to meet them. By late in the afternoon, people standing outside their cottages from Seven Oaks to Dover could look up and see vapor trails in every direction crisscrossing the clear blue sky. After it was all over the results of the fight proved modest: The British lost twenty-six airplanes and the Germans fifty-six. But several dozen of the German bombers suffered serious damage; their undercarriages were shot up or their engines were ablaze; about twenty splashed into the channel.

The Luftwaffe had not lost, but neither had it won. On September 15, Hitler brought Operation Sea Lion to an end. He started firebombing by night; he began U-boat warfare against British food-stuffs. But he directed the most attention toward the USSR, where he reckoned he might have a chance of winning.

■ ■ ■

"This is London. . . ."

And this was the voice, resonant, deep, ever so slightly sardonic, of the CBS radio news correspondent in London, Edward R. Murrow. Murrow lived with his wife, Jane, in a flat on Hallam Street, just below Portland Place, the location of the British Broadcasting Corporation. Churchill had made sure that Murrow could speak from the BBC. Hallam Street itself, however, was a bit of a risk. Knowing the propaganda value of the BBC, the Luftwaffe had made the area around Portland Place, including Hallam Street, one of their primary targets.

From the biography, we have a picture of Murrow making his way to work in the dark—"groping, striding, running, throwing himself flat as recommended when a bomb went off, arriving finally at the Bronze Doors of Broadcasting House, often out of breath, occasionally dusty, very occasionally on all fours." Behind the Bronze Doors, "guards with live ammunition and orders to shoot on sight if necessary, okayed passes." Propaganda, obviously, was all-important.

Murrow's studio was in a subbasement; sitting behind a microphone, loosening his necktie, and pulling out his notes, he would start his nightly broadcasts.

"This is London [September 10, 1940]. . . . Larry LeSueur [another CBS reporter] and I have spent the last three hours driving about the streets of London and visiting air-raid shelters. We found that like everything else in this world the kind of protection you get from the bombs depends on how much money you have. . . . We looked in on a renowned Mayfair hotel . . . and found many old dowagers and retired colonels settling back in the overstuffed settees in the lobby. It wasn't the sort of protection I'd seek from a direct hit of a half-ton bomb, but if you were a retired colonel and his lady, you might feel that the risk was worth it because you would at least be bombed with the right sort of people, and you could always get a drink if you were a resident of the hotel. If you were the sort of person I saw sunk in the padding of this Mayfair mansion, you'd be calling for a drink of Scotch and soda pretty often—enough to keep these fine uniformed waiters on the move. . . ."

"This is London [September 13, 1940]. This has been what might be called a 'routine night'—air-raid alarm at nine o'clock and intermittent bombing ever since. . . . Only two small fires can be seen on the horizon. . . . [T]he Germans have been sending their bombers singly or in pairs. . . ."

"This is London [September 18, 1940]. There are no words to describe the thing that is happening. Today I talked with eight American correspondents in London. Six of them had been forced to move. . . . I may tell you that Bond Street has been bombed, that a shop selling handkerchiefs at $40 the dozen has been wrecked, that these words were written on a table of good English oak which has sheltered me three times as bombs tore down in the vicinity. But you can have little understanding of life in London these days—the courage of the people, the flash and roar of the guns rolling down the streets where much of the history of the English-speaking world has been made, the stench of air-raid shelters in the poor districts. These things must be experienced to be understood."

"This is London [September 22, 1940]. I'm standing . . . tonight on a rooftop looking out over London, feeling rather large and lonesome. In the course of the last fifteen or twenty minutes, there's been considerable action up there, but at the moment there's an ominous silence hanging over London. . . . Just on the roof across the way I can see a man wearing a tin hat, a pair of powerful night glasses to his eyes, scanning the sky. . . . Down below in the streets I can just see that red and green wink of the traffic lights; just one lone taxicab moving slowly down the street. Not a sound to be heard."

"This is London [October 10, 1940], ten minutes before five in the morning. . . . London is again the main target. Bombs have been reported from more than fifty districts. . . . For three hours after the night attack got going, I shivered in a sandbag crow's nest atop a tall building near the Thames. . . . A stock of incendiaries bounced off rooftops about three miles away. . . . Five minutes later, a German bomber came boring down the river. We could see his exhaust trail like a pale ribbon stretched straight across the sky. Half a mile downstream there were two eruptions and then a third, close together. The first two looked like some giant had thrown a huge basket of flaming golden oranges high in the air. The third was just a balloon of fire enclosed in black smoke above the housetops. . . . There was peace and quiet . . . for twenty minutes. Then a shower of incendiaries came down far in the distance. They didn't fall in a line. It looked like flashes from an electric train on a wet night, only the engineer was drunk and driving his train in circles through the streets . . . Half an hour later a string of fire-bombs fell right beside the Thames. Their white glare was reflected in the black, lazy water near the banks and faded out in midstream where the moon cut a golden swathe broken only by the arches of famous bridges. . . ."

Broadcasting to an audience 3,000 miles away, Murrow once said, was like leaving letters in a log. He need not have worried. More than any other foreign correspondent, Edward R. Murrow, direct, plainspoken, vivid, concrete, invisible but audible, brought home to Americans the horror, and the thrill, of air power. Archibald MacLeish, the poet turned propagandist, put it best: "You," he wrote, referring to Murrow, "burned the city of London in our homes and we felt the flames that burned it . . . You destroyed the superstition of distance and of time." After listening to Murrow, Americans began to think of the Battle of Britain as a prelude to a Battle of America.

Lord Lothian, Great Britain's ambassador to the United States of America, stayed away from overt propaganda. He could afford to do so. From across the Atlantic Ocean he had the broadcasts of Edward R. Murrow and the romanticizing of the use of air power.

■　■　■

Air power meant *offensive* air power, as Harry Hopkins, the hollow-cheeked, ash-flecked, wisecracking Roosevelt aide soon found out. Like many Americans, Hopkins had believed that "national defense meant just that. If an enemy fleet approached our shores, we would merely line up our own . . . like a football team defending its goal line . . . ; any hostile ships that might break through . . . would be handled by our coastal defenses."

On the evening of August 15, 1940, however, Roosevelt went to work on Hopkins again. They were sitting in Roosevelt's upstairs White House study; the windows were open and, because the air was sultry, electric fans were turning. Taking a sheet of White House stationery, Professor Roosevelt sketched a map of the American East Coast and located the principal military bases with a series of Xs. These bases, Roosevelt told Hopkins, covered less than one and one-half percent of the coastline. So if war did come, the president said, America would have to reach out to enemy shores first, by sea and by air.

■ ■ ■

Having finished their highballs, eleven people sat down to dinner in a secluded room of New York's Columbia Club. It was Friday, July 11, 1940; the host was Lewis W. Douglas, president of the Mutual Life Insurance Company and a former director of the budget; the guests included Herbert Agar, Bishop Henry Hobson, Francis Miller, and Admiral William Standley, all signers of "A Summons to Speak Out." To each of these people, time was of the essence: France had fallen; Britain might be next; and then America. America could save itself, therefore, only if it went to war against Hitler and defeated him as soon as possible. Lewis Douglas's guests in the Columbia Club were the war hawks of 1940.

In the weeks that followed, the war hawks met regularly in the nearby Century Association—they took on the name of the Century Club—and expanded their roster. Situated on West 43rd Street and designed by the society architect Stanford White, the actual Century Club was classically designed, with a Palladian facade. By the advent of autumn, the group that called itself the Century Club included:

• Francis P. Miller, a Virginian, a graduate of Washington and Lee, a Wilsonian, a veteran of World War I, an official of the Council on Foreign Relations, a Democratic member of the Virginia House of Delegates, and coauthor, along with his wife, Helen Hill Miller, of a 1930 book entitled *The Giant of the Western World: America and Europe in a North-Atlantic Civilization*. The "price of beef in Kansas City affected the cost of living in London," they had written, "and the cost of steel from Birmingham, England, meant more work or less pay in Birmingham, Alabama. A symphony composed in New York was acclaimed in Berlin and Paris, while a novel written on *la rive gauche* was praised in Boston or Savannah." The North Atlantic nations had become as one; their every interest lay in their staying as one. The Millers were the ideologues of the Century Club.

• Dr. Henry P. Van Dusen, a Philadelphian, a member of the faculty at the Union Theological Seminary, a member of the Committee to Defend America by Aiding the Allies, and a liberal Protestant activist. During the 1930s, Union had been a hotbed of social reformism—along with his students and colleagues, Van Dusen had joined picket lines and participated in marches of protest—but in one vital respect Van Dusen was the odd man out. He believed that to defend his faith a Christian should be prepared to take up arms—"Onward Christian Soldiers!"

• Lewis W. Douglas, a native of Arizona, a graduate of the Massachusetts Institute of Technology, a World War I veteran, a member of the Committee to Defend America, and a businessman. To the United States Chamber of Commerce, he had asserted that to "retreat to the cyclone cellar . . . means, ultimately, to establish a totalitarian state at home."

• Ulric Bell, a hard-drinking newspaperman, Washington correspondent for the *Louisville Courier-Journal*, and one hell of a political operator. On behalf of the Century Club, he "saw people in Washington; he made contacts; he got things done." He had little interest in the ideology of the Millers or the theology of Van Dusen. He was, however, a buddy of "Pa" Watson in the White House.

• Ward Cheney, a Yale graduate, a Republican who in 1940 was prepared to vote for Roosevelt, and the president of Cheney Brothers, manufacturers of silks. He was the group's bankroller.

• Herbert Agar, a figure, along with Thomas Wolfe, William Faulkner, Tennessee Williams, and Robert Penn Warren, in the South's literary renaissance, and an editor with access to the Oval Office.

• Will Clayton, a Mississippi-born cotton executive and in 1940 a vice-president of the Export–Import Bank.

• James P. Warburg, a native of Hamburg, a Harvard graduate, and a prominent New York banker.

• Henry Sloane Coffin, president of the Union Theological Seminary.

• James Bryant Conant, a chemist and the president of Harvard.

• Harold Guinzburg of New York, president of Viking Press.

• Henry R. Luce of Shantung Province, China, publisher of *Time*, *Life*, and *Fortune*.

• Admiral William H. Standley and Robert E. Sherwood.

• Allen W. Dulles, later director of the Central Intelligence Agency, but in 1940 a forty-seven-year-old New York attorney and the grandson of Robert Lansing, President Woodrow Wilson's second secretary of state. Dulles was an avowed interventionist.

• Dean G. Acheson, a Groton, Yale, Harvard Law graduate, clerk to Justice Louis D. Brandeis, representative of clients as diverse as the Soviet Union and the Morgan bank, and a Democrat. "Nothing seems to be more foolish," Acheson said to a group of Yale undergraduates, "than a policy designed to assure that if we must fight, the fighting shall be done on our own territory." Acheson, who sported a British guardsman–style moustache, was a critical figure in the Century Club. He was the one to find legal justification for the bases-for-destroyers deal.

• George Watts Hill, a Presbyterian, a Democrat, and a banker in Durham, North Carolina. Through his financial interests, Hill was allied with the Bull Durham Tobacco Company; Bull Durham's founder had been "General" Julian Carr; Carr had been the protector of a Chinese immigrant named, in North Carolina, "Charlie" Soong; Carr indeed had bankrolled the Soong fortune in China; George Watts Hill was one of the multiple entry points into the American foreign policy establishment of Charlie Soong's son, T. V. Soong.

■ ■ ■

The embodiment of the foreign policy establishment was in New York, a townhouse just east of Central Park at the intersection of Park Avenue and 68th Street; corner lamps marked the building, and behind its glass front doors lay the headquarters of the Council on Foreign Relations. In the inner sanctums, far from the public view, the Council's War Peace Studies Committee had been working for nearly a year. The committee's members included: Owen Lattimore of the Johns Hopkins University; Hanson W. Baldwin of *The New York Times;* John Foster Dulles, New York attorney and future secretary of state; Allen W. Dulles, New York attorney and future director of the C.I.A.; General George V. Strong, chief of Army intelligence; and Launchlin Currie, an adviser to Roosevelt. Chairing the group was the short, white-haired Norman Davis, once a businessman and now President Roosevelt's ambassador-at-large. The committee took its lead from Davis, Davis took his lead from Roosevelt, and from the committee Roosevelt got a rubber stamp on the policy he wanted to follow anyway—the containment, even the defeat, of Japan.

The "foremost requirement of the United States in a world in which it proposes to hold unquestioned power," the committee recommended to Roosevelt, "is the rapid fulfillment of a program of complete re-armament." Japan represented a threat to America's unquestioned power. The threat, therefore, had "to be dissipated through peaceable means if possible, or through force."

■ ■ ■

"Think of it," *Life* quoted an official with the Reconstruction Finance Corporation as saying. "A Chinaman comes flying into Washington. He takes a room in a hotel, he talks to a couple of people, he tells a story, and he sticks to it. And the first thing you know, that Chinaman walks off with $100 million in his pocket. $100 million! Just think of it!"

The "Chinaman" was T. V. Soong, Harvard graduate, one-time operator on Wall Street, brother-in-law of Chiang Kai-shek, scion of China's wealthiest family, director of the Bank of China, and now, Washington lobbyist; and what he did *was* amazing. Upon his arrival in Washington in the summer of 1940, as *Life*, again, put it, Soong "engaged a suite at the Shoreham, shaved and bathed, and took a taxi to the White House to see his old friend, the President of the U.S. After a chat with the President, Soong called on Henry

Morgenthau and Jesse Jones [head of the Reconstruction Finance Corporation]. He explained that he wanted money in vast amounts [for China, of course] but that he did not propose to beg for it. Told that it might be a good idea to contact a few Congressmen . . . T.V. Soong snorted. He had come to Washington with a business proposition and the President, the Congress, and Mr. Jones could take it or leave it." They took it.

For Soong, the "Mr. Jones" connection was critical. Jones, who had taken over from Harry Hopkins as secretary of commerce, was a Texan, a Democrat—rather than a New Dealer—and as large in body as he was vast in power. At six feet two inches, he was heavy but solid, and his blue eyes, white hair, and dimpled cheeks were familiar all over Washington. So was his reputation for work; after twelve or fourteen hours a day he would still be going strong.

The work had paid off. Starting as a developer in Dallas and Houston, he went to Washington in the Hoover years to head the Reconstruction Finance Corporation, through which he lent money to thousands of enterprises. With the interest that came back in, he expanded his fiefdom, adding the Federal Housing Administration, the Electric Home and Farm Authority, the Home Owners' Loan Corporation, and the federal Home Loan Bank system; he controlled the Export–Import Bank. So powerful was Jesse Jones that when Roosevelt nominated him as commerce secretary, no one in the Senate so much as peeped. So when Mr. Soong went to Washington, he checked in first with America's triumvirate, Roosevelt, Morgenthau, and Jones.

Soong was slick, hard to follow, like a carp in a muddy stream. When he did surface, in Washington, he could have given classes in how to manipulate the American political system. He had networked superbly already: Admiral Thomas C. Hart, current chief of the U.S. Asiatic Fleet, was a friend; so was Admiral Harry E. Yarnell, Hart's predecessor and now, ostensibly, in retirement; so had been Admiral Mark Bristol, one of Yarnell's predecessors and a guest at the Chiang–Soong wedding in Shanghai, but Henry Luce had used *Fortune* to run an article in praise of Soong.

At the start of the Sino-Japanese War, Soong purchased an estate in Hong Kong on the Peak, overlooking Repulse Bay; living there among rare knickknacks, rich brocades, and massive furniture, and protected by the British police, he directed his country's economy. Atop the radio in Soong's mansion stood a photograph of Franklin D. Roosevelt, with the inscription, "To my friend, T. V. Soong."

Once in Washington, furthermore, Soong used his ties to cultivate new ones: The admiralty connection—and Roosevelt—led to Frank Knox, the secretary of the navy; the Knox connection led to Felix Frankfurter who, as a Harvard law professor, had been a one-man employment agency for the New Deal and who, as a justice of the U.S. Supreme Court, was up to his eyeballs in foreign policy formulation; the Frankfurter connection led to Thomas "Tommy the Cork" Corcoran, Frankfurter's protégé from the Harvard Law School, the Mr. Fix-It of the Roosevelt administration, and now lobbyist; the Corcoran and other connections led to Edward Stettinius, formerly the head of United States Steel.

To stir-fry these ingredients, then, Soong and his wife bought a large fieldstone house at 2871 Woodland Drive, just below the Washington cathedral; decorating the place with rare Chinese paintings, they entertained lavishly, inviting such people as Jesse Jones, the Morgenthaus, and Warren Lee Pierson of the Export–Import Bank to elaborate dinners, often with Peking duck as the *pièce de résistance*.

Soong even had the services of a private agent, a Pole named Ludwig Rajchman. A physician by training and then head of the League of Nations' public health office, Rajchman during the Manchurian crisis had gone out to China; there he had hooked up with Soong. Like Soong, Rajchman left few tracks. All the record shows, therefore, is that he turned up again in Washington, in 1940, as the unofficial representative of the London-based Polish government-in-exile. That government's figurehead, although old and dying, was still a legend in America: Ignace Jan Paderewski. Rajchman's position in Washington derived in part from Paderewski's unrivaled prestige among Polish-American voters. Rajchman, a reporter commented, was a "Pole with a long, clever face . . . who loves intrigue as a drunkard his brew . . .;" allying himself with Soong, and serving as a conduit of information from inside the administration, Rajchman worked simultaneously for a free Poland and a free China.

This was T. V. Soong's operation in Washington—and it proved effective indeed. Along with his allies, Soong—bespectacled and corpulent, he resembled a blimp in a frock coat—worked the system so skillfully that he won two $50 million loans for China. One was for currency stabilization; the other was for food, gasoline, trucks, ammunition, machine guns, and pursuit planes. America's neutrality in the Sino-Japanese War was now purely illusory.

■ ■ ■

The Japanese knew it. How they managed to keep Soong under observation is unclear. They were, however, watching closely. A cable picked up by War Department cryptographers read as follows:

> In summarizing the confidential conversations between AM, KO KAI JIN, and TO MEI JI: Although T.V. SOONG, at first, made every effort to secure a loan from the United States of $25,000,000, because of the question of security, negotiations were deadlocked. With England's help, however, he has succeeded at last in getting a loan. . . . As security for this loan, China has offered rights for the development of mines in Szechuan, Unnan, Kweichow, and Shansi Provinces, as well as tung oil, tin, tungsten, and tea. The United States has contracted to make deliveries of airplane parts, miscellaneous machines, and cash. . . . It is understood that the first allotment of American goods will be delivered in October.

In view of Japanese intelligence, Soong had mastered the secret of lobbying success in Washington. He had aligned himself with the British.

■ ■ ■

An observer out for a stroll or a horseback ride among the cherry trees in East Potomac Park, on the afternoon of Saturday, July 13, 1940, would have seen the masts of a yacht easing its way out of the Washington navy yard and sliding down the Anacostia River, and from there into the Potomac. The vessel was the *Sequoia*, the official yacht of the secretary of the navy. The observer might have made out the figure of the secretary himself, Frank Knox; Knox's picture was often in the papers. But a second man on the deck of the yacht kept himself out of the news and so would have been unfamiliar; this second man was gray-haired and ruddy, with the build of an overweight boxer. Early in the evening, a pedestrian on Constitution Avenue would have noticed a limousine pulling away from the Navy Building, streaking westward in the direction of Georgetown; Secretary Knox and the second man were in the limousine's rear seat. And that night, just before eight o'clock, a Georgetown resident out walking a dog and passing in front of that second man's fourteen-room house at 1647 Thirtieth Street would have noticed another limousine, this one bearing diplomatic license plates, pull into the driveway and park. For Lord Lothian, the British ambassador, was joining Secretary Knox and that other man for dinner.

That other man, the owner of the Georgetown mansion, was Colonel William J. Donovan, World War I hero, a behind-the-scenes power in the Republican party, and a New York–based lawyer with limitless contacts abroad. As a result of his conversation with Secretary Knox that afternoon in the privacy of the deck of the *Sequoia*, he was about to take on one more role: chief of the clandestine arm of the Roosevelt administration. He was going to Britain, and Lothian had come to supply him with letters of introduction.

Among the people who might have witnessed the Knox–Donovan–Lothian encounters, someone must have been suspicious, because as Donovan boarded the *Lisbon Clipper* in the Baltimore waterfront the next morning, reporters were on hand, asking him why he was leaving. He gave them a canned story. He was heading for Britain, he stated, to investigate fifth column activities. A fifth column, one of the reporters queried, in Britain? Saying no more, Donovan went aboard the *Clipper*.

Once in London, Donovan checked into Claridge's, as he usually did, indicating that he was present on legal matters that were purely private. After a rest, he went by ordinary taxi to 52 Broadway, a grimy, nondescript office building opposite the St. James's tube station; all that gave a hint of the building's significance were the guards outside, wearing blue uniforms with brass buttons. Inside, however, everything was different. In an office in the building's interior, Donovan closeted himself with Colonel Stewart Menzies. Menzies was of the uppermost of the British upper classes; his parents had been friends of King Edward VII; Menzies also was head of the current Majesty's Secret Intelligence Service.

With his background, Colonel Menzies might have seemed like the last person to share secrets with a Yank. Donovan, however, was no ordinary Yank: Through Knox, he was an emissary of the president of the United States, and the British were desperate for the president's goodwill. So in that nondescript building at 52 Broadway, Donovan learned a great deal: about the existence of ULTRA, the cryptographical system the British used to break the German military codes; about Prime Minister Churchill's private army, financed out of the king's own secret funds and trained in the arts of propaganda, sabotage, and murder; and about the British Ministry for Economic Warfare.

Donovan later visited Winston Churchill, going to Whitehall and descending the staircase that led to the prime minister's war rooms. Wearing his famous boilersuit, Churchill greeted him eagerly. They dined together, toting their own trays of food in the underground mess. Churchill assured Donovan of Britain's complete cooperation.

Donovan's popularity was based on more than his social graces. The "object of Bill Donovan's mission," Admiral John H. Godfrey, the director of Britain's naval intelligence, wrote in his memoirs— Godfrey, like Colonel Menzies, was for Donovan a principal channel into Britain—"was to discover if we were worth supporting." Great Britain, in Donovan's judgment, *was* worth supporting, as Donovan, upon his return to Washington, reported to Roosevelt. However, he recommended something else as well to the president. America, Donovan believed, should develop a new, and centralized, intelligence agency. Based on what Donovan had seen in Great Britain, this central intelligence agency would gather information, engage in sabotage, and carry out various forms of economic warfare.

■ ■ ■

Donovan dealt regularly with Arthur Purvis, who handled war supplies, Arthur Satler for shipping, Noel F. Hall on economic warfare, and David Bowes-Lyon, the queen's brother, who did propaganda.

All of these Britishers operated outside the confines of their own embassy in Washington. Of course, he was in touch with William Stephenson, the dapper little Canadian who ostensibly was the British passport control officer in New York and actually was charged with bringing the United States into the war by any means possible. Donovan, in fact, consulted with Lord Lothian, and Lothian cultivated Donovan.

For Donovan represented power. He was a Republican and, back in the mid-1930s, he had supported Frank Knox for the GOP presidential nomination. In his Beekman Place duplex, he had hosted political dinners for Knox. Knox lost out in 1936 to Governor Alf Landon of Kansas; undeterred, Donovan from behind the convention scene engineered the vice-presidential nod for Knox. So Knox, now secretary of the navy, owed Donovan; and Roosevelt, grateful to a Republican for having joined a Democratic administration as navy secretary, owed Knox.

Donovan's power base tapped into deeper sources still. In the early 1930s, a small group of men met monthly at 34 East Sixty-second Street, in an apartment "with an unlisted telephone number and no apparent occupant." Members of the group dubbed themselves The Room. Dedicated to the proposition that only an Anglo-American entente could contain the forces of worldwide revolution, The Room included Kermit Roosevelt, the son of Theodore Roosevelt; David Bruce, son-in-law of Andrew Mellon; Nelson Doubleday, of publishing fame; Winthrop Aldrich, the New York banker and grandfather of a generation of Rockefellers; and "Wild Bill" Donovan.

The intelligence services of the regular military saw Donovan as an enemy: He stepped on their turf. Given his power base, however, Donovan soon had what he wanted, a centralized intelligence agency. And Roosevelt soon had what he wanted, an agency for clandestine action.

■ ■ ■

The creation of the CIA, of course, lay in the future. For the moment, the issue confronting the White House was how America could best prop up the British Isles.

Generally speaking, the president knew he could count on public support for that aid; for what was happening in Europe, an English official wrote, "fitted easily into the traditional pattern of the Western. The bad men, tough, ominous, ruthless, and brutal, had ridden into town, terrorizing the innocent bystanders and shooting down those who were slow on the draw. Only one man, Mr. Sheriff Churchill, stood between the bad men and victory. The Sheriff's courage was high but his stock of ammunition was low. Would the worthy citizens in the next town refuse to send the 50 bullets that might give the Sheriff a chance of shooting back successfully? You did not have to wait for next week's thrilling installment to test audience reaction." The English writer, Philip Goodhart, a parliamentary secretary, was referring to the proposition that America should supply fifty overaged destroyers to Britain.

The real question was how the administration in Washington could reconcile the transfer of destroyers with the neutrality laws. Here the Century Club, and its principal agent, Dean Acheson, came into play.

"It has been suggested that fresh legislative authority is required to permit the executive branch of the government to release these old destroyers for sale to Great Britain. We should like to place on record our own legal opinion that this is not the case." So began a letter signed by Dean Acheson and three other attorneys, published in *The New York Times* on August 11, 1940.

The letter was long, going on for three and a half columns, and in all probability most of the *Times* readers scarcely bothered to wade through it; in a press conference, Roosevelt himself confessed that he had only skimmed the piece. But the sheer density of the letter was precisely the point. Acheson had shown it around, to Stimson, Frankfurter, and Knox, as well as the leaders of the Century Club, and after several drafts he had produced what amounted to mountainlike consensus. The point of the letter was that if the transfer of American destroyers would serve the nation's defense—*and* if the British were willing to give their Caribbean bases in exchange—the deal would violate no law.

On August 17, 1940, *The New York Times* reported that Roosevelt denied rumors America and Britain would trade destroyers for bases. On August 21, 1940, the *Times* announced the bases-for-destroyers deal.

■ ■ ■

"Hello, good people, how are you?"

Seated in the low-backed chair aboard his private train car, F. D. R. was returning to Washington on September 3, 1940, from the Tennessee border, where he had just dedicated the Chicamauga Dam. He invited reporters to gather around for an informal press conference.

"This is the first train press conference since Germany moved into Denmark," one of the journalists commented.

"I guess that's right," the president responded.

"We had a big talk with you at that time about . . . Greenland," said another.

"You are learning geography," Roosevelt teased. "There was another press conference where we talked about the Celebes Islands." Everyone chuckled.

"We were clear to the Cocos before we knew," still another reporter added, and they all laughed again.

Then the president turned serious: "I have something for you for your own information. . . . In twenty minutes there is going to the Congress the following message. . . . It . . . is probably the most important thing that has come for American defense since the Louisiana Purchase. . . . 'I transmit here for the information of the Congress,' " Roosevelt read aloud, " 'notes exchanged between the British ambassador at Washington and the Secretary of State . . . under which this government has acquired the right to lease naval and air bases in Newfoundland, and in the islands of Bermuda, the Bahamas, Jamaica, St. Lucia—' "

"What is the last one?" a reporter asked.

"St. Lucia," Roosevelt answered.

"How do you spell it?"

"S-t. L-u-c-i-a . . .," Roosevelt spelled. "Now I am not fooling on those. These are real places." The reporters guffawed. "Trinidad and Antigua, and in British Guiana," the president continued. ". . . The right to bases in Newfoundland and Bermuda are gifts—generously given and gladly received. . . . The other bases mentioned have been acquired in exchange for fifty of our overage destroyers."

As Roosevelt's train crossed through the northern Virginia countryside, passing the famous Civil War battle sites at Fredericksburg, Manassas, and Bull Run, the president was dealing with the press, and through the press with the American people, in his customary manner. Here was a radical step—bases for destroyers—and a step that in all but name revealed the creation of the Anglo-American alliance. In the creation of that alliance, furthermore, F. D. R. had not consulted Congress. He had only informed it. Invoking the Louisiana Purchase, and wrapping himself in the mantle of Thomas Jefferson he clothed an assertion of power in the garb of the American tradition.

■ ■ ■

General George C. Marshall, chief of staff of the army, and Admiral Harold Stark, chief of naval operations, both sobersided, straitlaced officers of integrity and caution, had argued strongly against sending the destroyers to Britain. Britain, to them, was on the verge of defeat; arming Britain would be tantamount to arming Germany. Donovan, however, convinced Roosevelt that Britain would hang on. The bases-for-destroyers deal symbolized not the collapse of the Atlantic community but rather the turning point in World War II. With the destroyers deal, America was starting to roll back the German conquests.

Rollback certainly was what the Century Club advocated next; rollback in the Atlantic and rollback in the Pacific.

■ ■ ■

The morning of July 27, 1940, in Tokyo had been hot and sultry; as the nation's highest admirals and generals convened in the palace for a "liaison conference" with the emperor, the armpits of their khaki uniforms were stained with sweat. Yet the weather was only one reason for the sweat. Despite all the swagger, these men were desperate. The economy was in shambles, the China war was just a drain on resources, manpower, and morale—in China, the army was resorting more and more to the use of germ warfare—and on the home front, the government was having to use every known device—uinformity of dress, spy scares, mountains of words in the newspapers about Japan's "just cause"—to stifle domestic dissent. The government could not go backward from the China war; to do so would be to show weakness and invite revolution. But the government could not go forward, either—not as long as China kept getting aid from abroad.

Seizing the agenda at the liaison conference in Tokyo, General Tojo Hideki, the new and hard-hitting army chief of staff, presented the group with a plan entitled, "Main Japanese Policy Principles for Coping with the Situation Which Has Developed in the World." The plan called for new steps to cut off Western aid via Indochina and Burma to Chiang Kai-shek; stronger ties between Japan and Germany; and a Japanese thrust, economic if possible but military if necessary, toward Southeast Asia and the Dutch East Indies. "Positive arrangements," the plan stated, "will be undertaken to include the English, French, Dutch, and Portuguese [Macao] islands of the Orient within the substance of the New Order."

Admiral Yamamoto Isoroku, who as a young man had lost two fingers in the Russo-Japanese war and now was the navy's chief of staff, protested. What about the United States, he asked? Expansion into the European territories, he argued, would lead inevitably to war with the United States; and in a war across the Pacific, the United States inevitably would win.

The conference flared with debate. The army accused the navy of cowardice; the navy accused the army of stupidity.

The liaison conference ended with a compromise. On August 1, 1940, Tokyo announced its intention of creating a "Co-Prosperity Sphere in Great East Asia"—Japanese dominion over Korea, Manchuria, China, and eventually Southeast Asia.

■　■　■

On both sides of the Pacific, action begot reaction. On July 26, 1940, President Roosevelt, as Congress had allowed him to do, restricted export licenses for heavy melting scrap steel (this amounted to about 20 percent of U.S. scrap exports to Japan), tetraethyl lead, lubricating oil, and aviation gasoline.

Although much U.S. oil and gasoline did continue to flow to Japan, Tokyo on July 27 threatened curbs on rubber and tin from Malaya and the Indies; Japanese newspapers on August 5, 1940, told of demands placed by the Tokyo government on the French colonial regime in Hanoi.

On the same day, August 5, 1940, the Senate Military Affairs Committee reported favorably on the selective service bill, America's first peacetime draft; and President Roosevelt asked Congress for stricter spy laws, laws that would control "subversive activities, seditious act, and those things which might slow up or break down our common defense program." Two days later, a former American steamship now flying the Panamanian flag reached Manila: On board were sixty-four American-made airplanes and 1,000 tons of munitions originally routed for Rangoon; from Rangoon they would have been slipped into China via the Burma Road. Because of the closing of the road, the skipper was going to store the cargo in Manila for the time being. The Japanese consulate in Manila filed a protest.

The next day, August 8, 1940, news reports indicated an impending Japanese assault on Indochina. Eighteen Japanese troop ships and convoying warships had headed southward from Taiwan; a flotilla of Japanese troops were massing near Lungchow, in China's Kwangsi Province, just above Indochina.

August 13, 1940: Writing in The New York Times, Harold Callender, a reporter traveling with other correspondents on Pan American's inaugural flight from San Francisco to Australia, filed a story from Pearl Harbor. He listed the vessels he had seen: "ten battleships; two aircraft carriers; 15 cruisers; about 50 destroyers; and many submarines, some painted blue, some black." All in all, Callender wrote—in a piece certain to be read by the Japanese— "one gets the impression that [military] preparations are going forward rapidly."

August 18, 1940, a Sunday: Reporters on the platform of the train station in Ogdensburg, New York, close to the Canadian border, received a press handout. The president's train had pulled into the station, and he was in his private car, conferring with Prime Minister Mackenzie King; War Secretary Stimson was also present. The United States and Canada, the handout said, had agreed on the creation of a Joint Defense Board; it would be coordinating efforts in the Atlantic and the Pacific.

In Independence Square the same day, William C. Bullitt, formerly the ambassador to France, addressed an audience of 4,000 sweltering Philadelphians. He was standing on a flag-draped platform. "America is in danger," he proclaimed; he had cleared the speech with Roosevelt. "It is my conviction . . . that the United States is in as great peril today as was France a year ago. And I believe that, unless we act now, decisively, to meet the threat, we shall be too late. . . . Why are we sleeping, Americans? When are we going to wake up? When are we going to tell our government that we want to defend our homes and our children and our liberties, whatever the cost in money or blood? . . . When are we going to tell them that we want to know what are our duties, not what are our privileges? When are we going to say to them that we don't want to hear any longer about what we can get from our country, but we do want to hear what we can give to our country?" These words, reworked for President John F. Kennedy's inaugural address, became, "And so, my fellow Americans, ask not what your country can do for you; ask what you can do for your country." As Bullitt spoke, young John F. Kennedy had just published a book, *Why England Slept*; Henry R. Luce had written the foreword.

August 22, 1940: Cabling *The New York Times* from Canberra, Harold Callender reported an exchange with Robert G. Menzies, the Australian prime minister. "Will the creation of a joint United States–Canadian defense board," the Australian leader asked the assembled Americans, "have any bearing on American relations with Australia and New Zealand?" A flotilla of U.S. vessels had just reached Australia; Menzies, therefore, one of the journalists replied, had only to think about the presence of American warships in the Sydney harbor. A member of the press was acting as a government spokesman.

August 23, 1940: If Japan pursued its present course, the State Department warned, pushing ever farther—that is, into Southeast Asia—the "time of reckoning" would come.

August 25, 1940: At a clambake near his retirement home in Newport, Rhode Island, Admiral Harry E. Yarnell spoke to a group of other naval officers, urging more aid to both Britain and China. He spoke again two days later, proposing that the United States use Singapore as a naval base. A foreign office spokesman in Tokyo termed Yarnell's statement "unbelievable."

August 27, 1940: In Batavia (now Djakarta), the capital of the Netherlands, or Dutch, East Indies, the touring American reporters inspected the naval yard, machine shops, repair facilities, seaport, and airfield—the Netherlands East Indies had received U.S.-made Curtiss pursuit planes and Glenn Martin bombers. Cabled Callender: "An interesting features of [the naval air patrols] is the fact that the Netherlands patrol area overlaps the area [north of Borneo] covered by the United States Navy seaplanes based on Manila." That overlap symbolized "what the Netherlands would like to think are our common interests in the Pacific." The Americans' visit to Batavia just happened to coincide with the visit of a Japanese trade delegation, sent to win lower tariffs on Japanese goods. *Yomiuri*, a Japanese newspaper, charged that the arrival of the U.S. correspondents constituted a "large-scale anti-Japanese demonstration" and that the new Pan American air route was further evidence of the U.S. encirclement of Japan.

September 2, 1940: The British, Dutch, and American military attachés in Singapore denied press reports that they had been holding joint staff talks; actually, they had, with an American present as an observer. The "traveler cannot help observing," Callender wired to the *Times*, "that in the air journey from Honolulu to New Zealand and thence via Australia and the Netherlands Indies to Singapore he passes vast series of actual or potential air and naval bases, strung along United States, British, and Netherlands territories. The last of this series [Singapore] was seen today in a drive along a winding road through rubber trees. [In a clearing, an] Indian Army band in turbans was playing Scotch bagpipes . . . while Indian troops under British officers lay flat on the ground in a long row behind automatic guns. . . . Later, while planes soared overhead, we walked beside [a] dry dock capable of holding a dreadnought, beside one of the biggest floating docks in the world, and through the new and spacious and multiplying barracks and machine shops designed to accommodate a large fleet. . . . The buildings, of concrete, are bright and new. The houses of the officers on the hills above the Straits are commodious bungalows with dark tile roofs, wide verandas, and windows suiting the climate." The Japanese scarcely could miss the point: The headline over the article read, "NEW DEFENSES RISE AT SINGAPORE."

September 3, 1940: *Asahi*, the Tokyo daily, declared: "Japan must take measures to prevent French colonies in the South Seas from falling under British control." New Caledonia and the New Hebrides were important to Japan, *Asahi* went on, because "when the increasing radius of aircraft is considered, Japan must extend its vision farther and farther into the Pacific."

September 5, 1940: Secretary of State Hull said that a Japanese invasion of Indochina would have an "unfortunate effect" on U.S. public opinion. Frank Knox said that the United States was building three new naval bases in Alaska.

September 8, 1940: *Kokumin*, the right-wing Japanese newspaper, saw United States–British collaboration as a "menace" to Japan's plans for a "Greater East Asia."

September 11, 1940: Returning to the United States from his Pacific junket, Harold Callender summarized his impressions. "Everywhere [from Honolulu to Hong Kong]," his *Times* story went, ". . . the scenes were similar—barbed-wire barriers, machine-gun posts, new airfields equipped with the latest bombers, expanding mobile armies, swift naval vessels patrolling the coasts. The Manila base maintains constant aerial patrols, just as Surabaja [the port on the eastern end of Java], Batavia, and Singapore do. At Manila, they are called 'neutrality patrols,' but that is the only difference."

September 13, 1940: *Kokumin* termed recent American policy "an undisguised challenge to Japan."

September 14, 1940: President Roosevelt extended the licensing scheme to cover airplane engines and parts to Japan.

September 20, 1940: Japan gave the French authorities in Hanoi two days to accept a long string of demands. Observers in Shanghai believed Japan was ready "to shoot the works."

September 21, 1940: Lord Lothian visited Cordell Hull in the State Department. According to press reports—that neither the British nor the Americans denied—they discussed the joint use of

Singapore, of the base at Newcastle on the eastern coast of Australia, and of Gilbert and Ellice, and Phoenix, and Friendly, British islands in the Pacific.

September 24, 1940: The administration in Washington forbade all American sales of iron and scrap steel to Japan.

September 29, 1940: Lord Lothian invited Major James McHugh, the U.S. Marine officer attached to the Chiangs in Chungking and now stationed at Quantico, up to the embassy for lunch. Lothian had a proposal for McHugh—that the United States base its Pacific fleet at Singapore. Nothing came of the proposal; War Secretary Stimson did note, however, that by controlling Singapore and "at the same time, cutting off all American commerce with Japan, we should eventually reduce that country to comparative impotency." Roosevelt kept the fleet at Pearl Harbor. There, he believed, it would suffice as a deterrent.

■   ■   ■

The explosion came in the last week of September 1940. Protected by tanks and planes, Japanese troops landed in Indochina, capturing Haiphong and Hanoi and seizing the French coastal batteries at Doson. The Japanese now controlled the rail lines into China—and were in a position to help themselves to the rice of the Mekong Delta.

■   ■   ■

"Hitler and Mussolini have pulled another surprise," William Shirer wrote in his diary for September 27, 1940. Count Galeazzo Ciano, the Italian foreign minister, had come to Berlin; but Shirer thought Ciano's purpose was to bring Spain into the war. "I came to my senses this morning," Shirer went on, "when I noticed the school children who had marched to the Wilhelmstrasse to cheer—waving Japanese flags." Then he received a telephone call: At 1:15 that afternoon, journalists and diplomats were to assemble promptly in the Hall of Ambassadors at the Reich Chancellery; there they would hear an important announcement.

As the foreigners took their places, they saw at the head of the room two shiny, long mahogany tables pushed end to end. Microphones stood along the tables, and behind three writing pads, officials were scratching with their pens. One official was Foreign Minister von Ribbentrop, sallow-faced, blank-eyed, and wearing a double-breasted suit. The second was black-haired and pudgy, wearing a Fascist uniform with gold epaulets and ribbons that seemed to cover his chest—Ciano. The third, a small man in morning clothes, was Kurusu Saburo, the Japanese ambassador to Germany. Then the pens stopped scratching. Adolf Hitler entered the chamber. He strode to the high-backed leather chair placed exactly behind the center of the two tables and sat. He clasped his hands in triumph.

The three diplomats, von Ribbentrop, Ciano, and Kurusu, had just signed the Tripartite, or Axis, Pact. The document was brief:

> Article I: Japan recognizes and respects the leadership of Germany and Italy in the establishment of a new order in Europe.
> Article II: Germany and Italy recognize and respect the leadership of Japan in the establishment of a new order in Greater East Asia.
> Article III: Japan, Germany, and Italy agree to cooperate in their efforts on the aforesaid lines. They further agree to assist one another with all political, economic, and military means when one of the three Contracting Parties is attacked by a power at present not involved in the European war or in the Sino-Japanese conflict. . . .

American newspapers printed maps, with arrows that emanated from the three Axis partners and aimed at the United States. But the concluding words of the agreement read:

> The treaty, of course, does not pursue any aggressive aims against America. Its exclusive purpose is rather to bring the elements pressing for America's entry into the war to their senses by conclusively demonstrating to them that if they enter the present struggle they will have to deal automatically with the three Great Powers [Germany, Italy, and Japan] as adversaries.

In Washington the reaction was mild. The Axis Pact, an official commented, only ratified the existing state of affairs.

CHAPTER
18

NO FOREIGN WARS

"I have said this before, but I shall say it again and again and again: Your boys are not going to be sent into any foreign wars!" With these words, spoken to a tumultuous crowd in the Boston Garden, Roosevelt brought the presidential campaign of 1940 to a close. This is what he said in public. In private, chatting with his speechwriter, Robert Sherwood, Roosevelt added a qualification: "If we're attacked," the president said, "it's no longer a foreign war."

From the spring of 1940 onward, the upcoming presidential election dominated American politics. Questions about the election commanded national attention. Who would capture the Republican nomination? Answer: a bulky man with a broad face, tousled hair, and a countrified air that belied his meteoric rise in the New York–based utilities industry, Wendell Willkie. Would a Democrat other than Roosevelt—Burton Wheeler from Montana, perhaps, or Postmaster General James Farley, or Joseph P. Kennedy, make a serious run for the Democratic nomination? Answer: no. Would Roosevelt run for an unprecedented third term? Answer, at the last moment in which he could file: yes.

The campaign itself started in September 1940, but it started slowly. Roosevelt's strategy was to look presidential, staying in the White House as long as possible; Willkie's challenge was to flush F. D. R. into the open. And little that Willkie tried was working. He portrayed himself as an internationalist, like Roosevelt—and

Republican bosses grumbled that he was merely a "me, too" candidate. He used the third-term issue to intimate that Roosevelt was a would-be dictator—and with German bombers over Britain and Japanese troops penetrating Vietnam, the public found the third-term issue boring. He attacked Roosevelt on the ground that unemployment was still high—and a war boom was on, with workers flocking into the airplane factories of the Far West, the steel mills and auto firms of the Midwest, the shipyards of the Northeast, and the textile plants of the South.

Then, late in September 1940, Willkie found his issue. "If [Roosevelt's] promise to keep our boys out of foreign wars is no better than his promise to balance the budget," Willkie cried out in a voice gone so hoarse that it sounded gravelly, "they're already almost on the transports."

Suddenly the public was listening, so Willkie stepped up the attack. Roosevelt was a warmonger, Willkie declared; Roosevelt had entered into a secret alliance with Britain and the Commonwealth. The charge hit home, especially since Congress passed, and the president signed, the Selective Service Act. Isolationists started flocking to Willkie and, according to the Gallup Poll, Roosevelt's lead was vanishing. Democratic politicians were taking fright in every region of the country and, as with one voice, they begged the president to come out of the White House, to come out and fight, to come out and answer the charges.

Roosevelt, at last, came out.

In Philadelphia, on the night of October 23, 1940, he roared out that "I am an old campaigner and I love a good fight!" A huge crowd roared back. He was in wonderful form, reporters agreed. By turns he was "intimate, ironic, bitter, sly, sarcastic, indignant, solemn." And he answered Willkie's charge: "I give to you and to the people of this country this most solemn assurance," he said. "There is no secret treaty, no secret obligation, no secret understanding, in any shape or form, direct or indirect, with any other government. . . ."

In New York, in Madison Square Garden five nights later, Roosevelt countercharged that the Republicans were "playing politics with national defense." He mentioned three Republicans by name: "Martin, Barton, and Fish." Congressman Joseph W. Martin of Massachusetts was the Republican national chairman; Bruce Barton was a U.S. representative from Manhattan; Hamilton Fish was a congressman from Roosevelt's own district, around Dutchess County, New York; all three were die-hard isolationists. Roosevelt's speechwriters had hit on the device of lumping three names together and, listening to him in the Garden, wondered if Roosevelt would pick up on the rhythm. He did. "Martin, Barton, and Fish!" Repeating the phrase several times, he swung his forefinger back and forth, in cadence. The crowd caught on, soon chanting the names along with him.

In Boston, in the train yard and seated in the low-backed armchair of his private car, Roosevelt looked up; Harry Hopkins was handing him a telegram. Voters, the cable said, *still* were unsure, still were afraid that, once reelected, Roosevelt would betray his promise about no foreign wars. Turning to Sherwood, who was seated nearby, Roosevelt demanded, "How often do they expect me to say it? It's in the Democratic platform and I've repeated it a hundred times."

"Evidently," Sherwood said, "you've got to say it again—and again—and again."

Thus a phrase was born. Speaking soon to his Boston audience, Roosevelt recited the by-then famous litany, "Martin, Barton, and Fish"; and addressing himself through the battery of microphones to the "mothers and fathers" of America, he reiterated his promise to stay out of the wars overseas. It was the last time he made that promise.

■ ■ ■

Most of the leaves had fallen around the Hyde Park estate and the presidential flag above the Roosevelt mansion stirred in the crisp autumnal breeze. The date was November 5, 1940: election day. As dusk fell, friends and members of the family started gathering inside, groups of them clustering around radios that were scattered throughout the house. Roosevelt himself sat at the mahogany table in the family dining room; new tickers chattered nearby. A handful of freshly sharpened pencils lay on the table. Roosevelt was making initial marks on tally sheets spread out before him.

At first, a biographer wrote, "the President was calm and businesslike. The early returns were mixed. Morgenthau, nervous and fussy, bustled in and out of the room. Suddenly Mike Reilly, the President's bodyguard, noticed that Roosevelt had broken into a heavy sweat. Something in the returns had upset him. It was the first time Reilly had ever seen him lose his nerve.

" 'Mike,' Roosevelt said suddenly, 'I don't want to see anybody in here.'

" 'Including your family, Mr. President?'

" 'I said anybody. . . .'

"Reilly left the room to tell Mrs. Roosevelt and to intercept Morgenthau's next trip back to the dining room. Inside, Roosevelt sat before his charts. His coat was off; his tie hung low. . . . The news tickers clattered feverishly."

The results were slow to arrive. The earliest figures were from Dutchess County, home of Roosevelt and of Fish of "Martin, Barton, and Fish." There, as he expected, he was losing; Roosevelt had never carried his own neighborhood. Then the tickers told of New York City with its boroughsful of Italian-Americans, African-Americans, Irish-Americans, and Jewish-Americans, all of whom had benefited from the programs of the Roosevelt New Deal—only the Jews were solid for Roosevelt.

In the end he took New York State by a mere 225,000 votes, a margin too narrow for comfort. New Jersey came in; in Jersey the Democrats and the Republicans were running neck and neck, the cities going Democratic, the suburbs and the counties going Republican. The upper New England states, as expected, were falling in with Willkie. The ticker tapes then started to tell of the Midwestern states: Willkie was carrying Indiana and Michigan. Cincinnati was Willkie's; six of the farm states clearly were going for Willkie. As he filled in his boxes, Roosevelt could see the pattern plainly: Using the 1936 landslide as the standard of comparison, he was slipping with every major group of Americans, except for the Jewish community.

But then, glacially at first and with a force that gathered only slowly, the numbers in the boxes on the charts began to shift. Massachusetts, Illinois, and Pennsylvania, and then New Jersey, and Ohio as a whole, all of the states with huge Eastern European populations and all of them critical in the electoral college count, came in, and they were for Roosevelt. Now the South was reporting in. Georgia was safe. Byrnes had done the job in South Carolina. North Carolina and Virginia were solidly Democratic.

Roosevelt called out to Mike Reilly, and the dining room door opened. Morgenthau could bustle in again and the president was smiling; from all around the house others approached with fresh reports of victory.

No one had heard from the West Coast yet, but the electoral vote was swinging decisively to Roosevelt. In the end the electoral count was 449 to 82.

Residents of the village of Hyde Park came out of their houses. They were carrying torches, and they formed a parade that progressed to the Roosevelt estate.

Reporters gathered around the portico. Their flashbulbs were popping.

The front door opened.

Helped by his sons, the president appeared.

"I will still be the same Franklin Roosevelt you have always known," he said.

■　■　■

Even before the election, Roosevelt made sure that America's motion picture industry churned out the propaganda he wanted. James Roosevelt, his oldest son, was president of Globe Productions, and produced *Pastor Hall*, a film that dramatized the courage of Martin Niemöller, the World War I U-boat captain who turned preacher and pacifist in the face of the Nazis. *Pastor Hall* did poorly at the box office. The president himself asked Nicholas Schenck, chairman of Loew's, which controlled MGM, to make a defense and foreign policy movie called *Eyes of the Navy*. Wondering about profits, Schenck was reluctant to proceed. Roosevelt, however, offered Schenck a deal he could hardly refuse: Schenck's brother, Joseph, president of Twentieth Century Fox, stood convicted of income tax evasion, but Roosevelt (along with James, to whom Joseph Schenck had lent $50,000) urged Attorney General Robert H. Jackson to let the brother off with a fine. *Eyes of the Navy* reached neighborhood theaters in mid-October, just in time for the presidential election.

Shortly before the election, furthermore, and on Roosevelt's behalf, William Knudsen, the blue-eyed Danish immigrant who had fought his way up to the top of the General Motors Company and who now, at the head of the Office of Production Management, was America's economic czar, did what czars do: He went on an inspection tour. Knudsen's tour, however, was scarcely through Potemkin villages. Followed by a retinue of officials and reporters, he visited the Curtiss-Wright airplane plant in Paterson, New Jersey, looking over a new airplane motor that gave bombers radii of 6,000 miles; and he checked out the United Aircraft Corporation's plant at East Hartford, Connecticut, boasting to the press that here was the "fastest pursuit plane in the world." Such aircraft production, dramatized by the Knudsen visits, was but a part of the 50,000 military airplane production program that Roosevelt had requested of Congress.

Only three days after the election, then, the White House announced an American–British–Australian agreement: Bases in both Australia and Singapore would be available for use by the U.S. Pacific fleet.

Shortly after the election, President Roosevelt wrote a friend in a confidential letter: "For practical purposes, there is going on a world conflict, in which there are aligned on one side Japan, Germany, and Italy, and on the other side China, Great Britain, and the United States."

■　■　■

Late one afternoon, nine days after the U.S. election, Prime Minister Churchill emerged from his warren of offices deep beneath Whitehall, popping into a limousine that was to whisk him to Chequers, the prime minister's official country residence; Churchill was looking forward to a weekend outside the city. But just before the car took off, a security official handed him a sealed yellow box. The box contained "Enigma" messages. Churchill opened it—and the car had barely reached Kensington Gardens before Churchill was yelling at the driver, "Back! Back to Downing Street!" The "Enigma" transcripts had revealed a massive German air raid that night on a North Country city famed for its tire industry, its Rolls Royce and Vickers airplane engine plants, and its cathedral. The city's name was Coventry.

At 7:11 P.M., November 14, 1940, sirens screamed into the Coventry night; within moments the bombs began their downward flight. They were incendiary bombs and they seemed to be falling everywhere—"on tenement gutters, and on warehouse roofs; lodging drain-pipes and window ledges; on pavements and in doorways; on the chancel roof of . . . St. Michael's Cathedral. They burned with a sizzling blue-white glare; above them, chandelier flares came dripping beautifully down, like Chinese lanterns, bathing the streets, the factories, the slate roofs in a white glow purer than moonlight. . . . Everywhere . . . were alien sights . . . drifting barrage balloons bobbing like giant whales at roof-top level . . . a kitten patting . . . at charred scraps of paper floating across a garden . . . a length of streetcar track sailing 20 clear yards like a monstrous rocket, clean over a three-story house . . . a knee-high river of boiling butter from a dairy . . . coursing down a street." From 6,000 feet over the city, a German pilot could make out the smell of burning buildings; from nine miles away, in Leamington Spa, just after dawn, an English fireman could see slates from rooftops fly up in the air. Six weeks before the end of 1940, with the city gutted, the world acquired a new word of war: to devastate a city with bombs from the air now was *koventrieren*, to "coventrate."

In Washington, a small man with a Canadian accent had a secret talk with Roosevelt. He was William Stephenson, code-named "Intrepid," World War I hero, Canadian radio pioneer, industrialist, self-taught intelligence expert, ally of Churchill, head of the innocuous-sounding British Security Organization, with its main office in Rockefeller Center, and, most important, coordinator of all British intelligence operations in the United States of America.

What did "intelligence" mean? Information-gathering, of course. But also, by hook or by crook, bringing America into the war. Hence Stephenson's confidential chat with Roosevelt. Stephenson's revelation was extraordinary: The "Enigma" transcripts that Churchill read in his limousine on his way out of Whitehall, Stephenson said, had specified the name of Coventry. Yet Churchill had wired no warning. Had he done so, the Germans would have realized that the British had broken their codes.

Roosevelt must have seemed shocked. "War is forcing us more and more to play God," he said, at least in one account. "I don't know what I should have done. . . ."

■ ■ ■

Raising a glass of *mao-t'ai*, the strong Chinese wine, Sir Archibald Clark Kerr, Great Britain's ambassador to China, made a welcome announcement. Speaking to hundreds of Chinese officials who had come for the banquet, he said that, with the backing of the United States, Great Britain had decided to reopen the Burma Road. T. J. Tcheng, China's vice-minister of foreign affairs, returned the toast: ". . . wine will be waiting for you when you reach Kunming."

The British and the Chinese exchanged toasts in mid-October 1940. As they were lifting their cups, coolies in Lashio, at the Chinese–Burmese border, were lifting cargoes—lock nuts for lathes, rolls of adhesive plaster, flashlights, tins of high-octane gasoline, rifle barrels, barrels of kerosene, bales of raw cotton, even airplane wings—onto trucks that had come up the Burma Road. The trucks numbered about 2,000 and they had been built in America; loaded at last, the trucks lined up in the darkness and departed for China. According to *Time*, thousands of coolies cheered.

The cheering soon stopped. By late October, Japanese airplanes had started bombing the Burma Road, strafing trucks, attacking bridges, taking lives, causing delays. But the trucks—paid for out of America's loan to T. V. Soong and to China—kept moving; bridges went back up; living laborers replaced the dead; and the Burma Road proved to be like the later Ho Chi Minh Trail, with the goods ever flowing.

Why had the British reopened the Burma Road? Helping China meant hurting Japan, Germany's partner; helping China meant diverting the Japanese from Singapore and Australia; helping China—and this point Lord Lothian had hammered home to London—meant conveying to the American people Great Britain's determination to keep on with the fight. Helping China was a way of drawing America into the war.

■ ■ ■

"For several months," Ambassador Joseph Crew reported from Tokyo on November 10, 1940, "squads of men and schoolgirls have been working in the big plaza opposite to the [Imperial] Palace, leveling it off, setting up decorative poles, laying out an enormous number of flowers, and finally building a big pavilion and rows of seats in front of it for about 50,000 people. The [50,000] were the only people, all specially invited, who could witness the ceremony, because no one was allowed on the roofs or in the windows of the big office buildings in Marunouchi, which would have afforded observation spots for many more thousands. No one may look down upon the Emperor, and I noticed how completely vacant those roofs and windows were." During the ceremony itself—the Commemoration of the 2,600th anniversary of the founding of Japan—Grew had to speak to the emperor directly; the experience, he wrote, was "an ordeal." He had "to walk sedately in front of all the guests in the pavilion and then in front of 50,000 people below in complete silence, face the Emperor, bow, get out spectacles and manuscript, read, bow, replace manuscript and spectacles, bow again, turn backwards, and pace solemnly back to my place."

To this point, Emperor Hirohito sat on his throne with a wholly blank expression. But when Grew spoke—Grew's text called for peace and international cooperation—the emperor nodded with vigor. In fact, Grew reported to Washington, "Arsené-Henry, the French ambassador, came to see me the next day . . . to tell me that he had watched the Emperor's face and was convinced that his nods of approval were given to impress the government . . . with his own desire for peace."

The emperor's nods produced nothing. The Japanese government—meaning the foreign office, the army, and the navy—had already decided on three things that would necessitate military action: (1) a vast reinforcement of Anglo-American armed strength in East Asia, including the Philippines; (2) Anglo-American cooperation "to exert pressure upon Japan," including the United States' use of Britain's strategic bases; and (3) an all-out embargo by America and others on their exports to Japan, "thus rendering Japan unable to acquire essential materials." Each of these things was beginning to happen.

In Indochina, accordingly, the Japanese army was sending agents into the south: They were to explore, survey, and make studies of the French naval base at Cam Ranh Bay. The Japanese now were extending their influence toward Saigon.

■ ■ ■

In mid-October 1940, British intelligence picked up the following intercept:

Fuhrer's Headquarters,

12 October 1940

1. The Fuhrer has decided that from now on until the spring, preparations for landing in England will be maintained purely as a military and political threat. . . .
2. All measures concerning the relaxing of the state of readiness for attack must be regulated from the following viewpoints:
A. The English must retain the impression that from now on we are preparing to land on a large scale. . . .

—(s) Keitel,
C.–inC. Armed Forces

The Germans, in short, were feinting toward Britain while readying an attack upon Russia.

■ ■ ■

America, too, was readying itself for war.

General George C. Marshall went to Senator James F. Byrnes with a problem. The best way to improve the army, Marshall believed, was by granting quick promotions to young officers of great ability; but Kentucky's Andrew May, chairman of the House Military Affairs Committee, had pigeonholed the needed legislation. Finding Byrnes in a corridor of the Senate Office Building, Marshall asked for help. Byrnes nodded—and soon attached the amendment Marshall wanted to an appropriations bill, which bypassed the military affairs committees.

Marshall got what he wanted; Dwight D. Eisenhower, Mark Clark, and George Patton shot up through the ranks. Byrnes, too, got what he wanted: South Carolina acquired a new training camp at Spartanburg, the expansion of Camp Jackson into a full-fledged fort at Columbia, federal funding for a new airport in Lexington County (the training site for Jimmy Doolittle's 1942 bombing raid on Tokyo), a major expansion of the navy yard at Charleston, antiaircraft and naval defense batteries at Myrtle Beach, and orders for tents, uniforms, and other cotton goods at textile mills throughout the state.

Dean Acheson, the lawyer, entered the government. He had been there before, in the Treasury Department, but he had a falling-out with Roosevelt. Now he was back all full of praise for the president. "You say that the President has done nothing for seven years to improve our defense," Acheson wrote to an old friend in New York. "I say that the fact we have a first-rate Navy . . . greatly increased and in fighting trim, is due to him alone." Acheson became the assistant secretary of state for economic affairs. His charge was to use his energy and his intelligence to hone economics as an instrument of war.

Douglas MacArthur, chief of staff of the Philippine army, had a vision; and Theodore White, who had voyaged to Manila, recorded that vision. MacArthur, White found, was a "spectacle. His hand trembled; his voice sometimes squeaked, but he could not talk sitting down. He paced, and roared, and pointed and pounded, and stabbed with his cigar, and spoke with an intelligence and a magniloquence and a force that overwhelmed. . . . This was a year before Pearl Harbor, but he insisted war was coming. . . . He, himself, was building the new Philippine Army for [President] Manuel Quezon, and if he had enough time, he could make it into a fighting force. . . ." In particular, MacArthur wanted air power, more and more of it, fighters and transport planes and bombers, bombers that could reach Japan. All this White put into his dispatches to New York—and he added that, of all the generals, French, Dutch, British, and American, he had interviewed in Southeast Asia, MacArthur was the best.

MacArthur invited White again to the penthouse balcony that overlooked Manila Bay. The interview took place late in an autumn afternoon. MacArthur was dressed, White remembered, "in an old West Point bathrobe of blue and gray wool which displayed the Army "A" on its back; his skinny shanks protruded as he paced, and occasionally he puffed on a corncob pipe. We rejoiced together that we alone understood the Japanese peril to America, the Japanese threat. . . ." In the end, MacArthur got his way. So impressive was the Philippine buildup in 1941 that Major General Lewis H. Brereton, MacArthur's new air commander, feared that the Japanese might decide on a preemptive strike.

■ ■ ■

Without question tensions were rising.

In the middle of November 1940, Japan flooded southern Vietnam with agents. Pan American Airlines applied to the Civil Aeronautics Board for an air link to Singapore. Japan opened its own South Seas Airlines, routed to Palau in the Pacific-mandated islands.

On Thanksgiving Day, 1940, Hungary joined the Axis (Romania and Slovakia followed suit the next day). China accepted what it termed "full alignment" with Britain and America against the Axis. The U.S. government announced the sale of twenty-six B-17 bombers, equipped with Wright Cyclone engines and built by the Consolidated Aircraft Corporation at San Diego, to Great Britain. The British government acknowledged the truth of reports that Australians and New Zealanders were fighting alongside the Greeks against the Italians; the U.S. government said that the extent of its own involvement in Greece was a secret.

Two reports came out of Asia. The Soviet Union was stepping up its aid to China; the United States was opening a consulate in

Vladivostok. The circle around Japan had tightened by two more notches.

At the very end of November 1940, a Japanese "study team" went to Saigon. It was blunt about its mission: It was on the lookout for a base from which it could bomb Singapore and threaten the passage to the United States of rubber and tin from Malaya through the South China Sea.

The bars in Singapore suddenly were crowded with Australian pilots; U.S. bombers were appearing on Singapore runways. Admiral Stark, the chief of Naval Operations, urged the military strengthening of Guam.

On December 7, 1940, exactly one year before Pearl Harbor, President Roosevelt promised aid—money and airplanes—to Greece.

■ ■ ■

The next day, Sunday, December 8, 1940, the Morgenthaus and the Soongs had lunch at the White House. They had gone there, we can infer, on a most special mission. Claire Chennault had returned from China, bearing a memorandum from Chiang Kai-shek, a document in which Chiang had requested 500 new airplanes for China. The idea, as Chennault explained it to Morgenthau, was to "burn out the industrial heart of the [Japanese] Empire with fire-bomb attacks on the teeming bamboo ant heaps of Honshu and Kyushu."

From the Morgenthau diary, December 8, 1940: "After lunch at the White House and, in the presence of Mrs. Morgenthau and Mrs. Soong I said that I had read General Chiang Kai-shek's memorandum in which he asked for 500 planes. . . . So I said, 'Well, his asking for 500 planes is like asking for 500 stars.' I then said that we might get him planes by 1942, but what did he think of the idea of some long-range bombers with the understanding that they were to be used to bomb Tokyo and other Japanese cities? Well, to say he [Soong] was enthusiastic is putting it mildly. He said, 'This would give us a chance to hit back!' . . . I . . . intimated that it was the President's idea . . . because he has mentioned to me that it would be a nice thing if the Chinese would bomb Japan. I told him that if we let American planes be flown to Canada, I did not see why these bombers could not be flown to China via Hawaii and the Philippines. . . . I told T. V. Soong that Cordell Hull has brought up the question himself of the advisability and feasibility of bombing Japan from China. . . ."

Wasting no time, Soong hit the lobbying trail again. He invited Joseph Alsop, the journalist and Roosevelt kin, to dinner; Alsop had to decline, but instead had Soong plus sidekick Rajchman to lunch. Soong did get Edward R. Stettinius, Jr., up to the stone mansion for drinks—in letters of thanks, Stettinius expressed gratitude for Soong's autographed photograph, for a copy of the *Tanaka Memorial*, and for the "attractive picture."

Even as Soong worked, Pacific affairs grew worse. On December 10, 1940—amid reports of Japanese troop concentrations in the Spratly Islands—President Roosevelt put iron ore, pig iron, and ferrous alloys on the licensing list. He had already banned scrap exports to Japan; now he also restricted the sale of iron and steel manufactures. Five days before Christmas, 1940, the president also granted "full powers" to a four-person defense board: The board consisted of Secretaries Stimson and Knox, Sidney Hill for labor, and William Knudsen as director; on the same day, Germany, Italy, and Japan established a Joint War Board. It was aimed, they said, against America.

"I have good news for you," Secretary Morgenthau said. On December 20, 1940, he had summoned T. V. Soong to the Treasury. "Yesterday morning I had the chance to deliver . . . your memorandum to the President. He was simply delighted, particularly . . . about the bombers. Yesterday after Cabinet I asked for a chance, and the President had Hull, Stimson, and Knox stay, and we all had your map out [Soong had provided a chart of airfields in unoccupied China; some were no more than 650 miles from Japan] and the President gave it his approval. I said, 'Should we work it out and come back?' and he said that was not necessary. He said, '. . . [Y]ou work out a program.' "

Henry Morgenthau's residence at 2201 R Street, just off Massachusetts Avenue in the Embassy Row sector, was three stories high and made of yellowish brick; with its narrow windows and classical pediments, it could have been the fortress of a rich prince conspiring against somebody or other in the Italian Renaissance. Indeed, the meeting held there on the afternoon of December 21, 1940, took place in considerable secrecy.

Soong and Chennault were present, and their purpose was to work out what Roosevelt had called "a program." The president, Morgenthau told them, was "seriously considering trying to make some four-engine bombers available to the Chinese in order that they might bomb Japan. . . ." Chennault stuck in a caveat: The B-17s, he maintained, would require American crews, mechanics, bombardiers, pilots. Not to worry, Morgenthau retorted. The U.S. Army was already willing to release fliers from active duty. Morgenthau himself had a question. Could the B-17s carry incendiary bombs? The Japanese cities, after all, were made of paper and wood. The B-17s, Chennault replied, could do the job.

At a follow-up session at Woodley the next day—Stimson, Knox, and General Marshall were present—Morgenthau went "over the whole question of bombers for China." Now Marshall raised questions. Could America spare the bombers? Should they not be sent to England instead? After considerable discussion, Stimson brought Marshall around. Marshall "is going," Morgenthau wrote in his diary, "to work out a plan for China."

■　■　■

In a late December scene in Berlin, Adolf Hitler and Erich Räder, Germany's top admiral, met in bitter confrontation. Everywhere he looked, Räder expostulated, he saw "glaring proof of the United States' unneutrality." Räder trotted out the facts. The bases-for-destroyers deal was blatantly anti-German. The "Pan American Safety Zone," a line of "neutrality" Roosevelt had drawn around the Western Hemisphere, where Britain had colonies, benefited Great Britain alone. United States warships were trailing Axis merchant vessels in transatlantic waters and the U.S. ships, Räder's cryptographers had shown, were helping the British track German blockade-runners. Furious, Räder demanded authority to strike back, to start sinking American ships.

Hitler put him off. Sinking American ships was precisely what brought the United States into the 1914–1918 war and, besides, as

Hitler knew, Germany now possessed fewer than sixty submarines. He begged Räder for time: Wait until 1942, he requested; by then Germany might have more U-boats. Frustrated, Räder stormed out of the Chancellery.

■   ■   ■

On the evening of December 29, 1940, Arthur Prettyman, the president's valet, wheeled Roosevelt into the stuffy little diplomatic reception room of the White House; F. D. R. was wearing a bow tie and his pince-nez. Prettyman directed the wheelchair to a spot just behind a plain desk; the desk supported a battery of network microphones. A small group of persons had been waiting in the room: Sara Roosevelt, the president's mother; Secretary of State Cordell Hull; a few other cabinet members; speechwriters Samuel Rosenman and Robert Sherwood; Clark Gable and his wife, Carole Lombard, both of them ardent Roosevelt supporters. Gable wore a pin-striped gray suit; Lombard was decked out in black, with a black hat and veil, and their presence was supposed to lend glamor to Roosevelt's talk.

In this, his end-of-the-year fireside chat, Roosevelt had a surprise for the American nation. In a press conference eight days before, he had hinted at the surprise. Suppose your neighbor's house "catches fire," the president had said. You lend him your "garden hose." You don't ask the cost. All you want is the "hose back" when the fire is out.

Roosevelt now was able to say what he meant. Glancing down at his text, he spoke into the microphones.

"Never before since Jamestown and Plymouth Rock," he said to his fellow Americans, "has our American civilization been in such danger as now. . . . The Nazi masters of Europe have made it clear that they intend not only to dominate all life and thought in their own country, but also to enslave the whole of Europe and then use the resources of Europe to dominate the rest of the world. . . . The experience of the past two years has proven beyond doubt that no nation can appease the Nazis. No man can tame a tiger into a kitten by stroking it. . . . There will be no 'bottlenecks' in our determination to aid Great Britain. No dictator, no combination of dictators, will weaken that determination. . . ." Roosevelt's climactic words ring down through history: "We must be the great arsenal of democracy. For us this is an emergency as serious as war itself. . . ."

In this famous fireside chat, Franklin D. Roosevelt was bringing his next step to the attention of the American public. He wanted to put in place a program of aid for Britain—the program would be called lend-lease. Lend-lease was a virtual declaration of war.

PART V

·

1941

CHAPTER
19

ENTANGLING ALLIANCES

The beginning of 1941 brought cold air but sunny skies to Washington, perfect weather for the inauguration; the ceremony was set for January 20, at noon. An hour and a half beforehand, Roosevelt and his family set forth from the White House, riding in state to St. John's, the eighteenth-century buff-colored Episcopal church that faced the White House through the bare trees of Lafayette Park. Roosevelt used this church because he could enter its side door without having to confront steps. Once in his cushioned pew, Roosevelt watched as his old headmaster from Groton, the Reverend Endicott Peabody, ascended to the pulpit.

Peabody preached from the Twentieth Psalm: ". . . Some put their trust in chariots, and some in horses; but we will remember the name of the Lord our God." As he spoke, the stained glass windows of the little colonial church transformed the pale light of winter into streams of red and turquoise. Roosevelt lowered himself to his knees. An earlier president, too, James Madison, had knelt in this church in time of war, and ordinary Americans had prayed alongside. Now the galleries were full of Secret Service men, their hands quiet on pistols in their pockets. After the benediction, the Roosevelts rode to the Capitol.

As flags slapped and bands played, a great crowd, many with wool stockings and extra sweaters and toting thermos bottles and blankets as if at a football game, crowded into the Mall. High above them, the inaugural platform gleamed with fresh white paint. Henry Wallace, the new vice-president, took his oath. The Marine Band played "Hail to the Chief." Then Roosevelt inched forward. The crowd in the Mall grew silent. Chief Justice Charles Evans Hughes, frail and bent now but with a voice as stern as ever, recited the president's oath. Roosevelt repeated it: "I, Franklin Delano Roosevelt, do solemnly swear that I will faithfully execute the office of the president of the United States and will, to the best of my ability, preserve, protect, and defend the Constitution of the United States."

Hughes's tone was firm. "So help you God?"

"So help me God."

The chill of the wind in his face, Roosevelt turned toward the crowd. His inaugural address was his shortest ever, only sixteen minutes long, and his climactic words were blunt. "We do not retreat," he averred. "Democracy is not dying."

Few present would have disagreed. Riding on horseback below the stand, General George C. Marshall led the parade; behind him came a seemingly endless column of "soldiers, sailors, Marines, Coast Guardsmen, big guns, little guns, bayonets, trucks, horses, flags, brass bands, nurses and ambulances . . . and squadrons of airplanes roaring overhead." Never, certainly not in their memories, reporters agreed, had the government staged so impressive a display of military might. One correspondent in particular was filled with foreboding. He was something of a history buff and from his reading, only Lincoln's inauguration, in the spring of 1861, had seemed more ominous; the correspondent was Bruce Catton.

Now, eighty years later, America again was preparing itself for war. Those preparations were myriad.

■ ■ ■

American cryptographers were tracking Japan, and Germany, too, carefully, with listening posts scattered around the world. Decoding was far from perfect, of course: MAGIC (code name for a code-cracking system developed the year before) applied to Japan's diplomatic codes alone. Still, U.S. naval intelligence was reading the ciphers of the Japanese naval attachés and a special code of the Japanese admirals. And from each deciphering only one conclusion was possible: In Europe and Asia alike the war was going to spread. Germany was going to go east. Japan was going to go south. And America was going to get ready.

Certainly the bureaucracy was getting ready; and Dean Acheson, the lawyer who had gone into the State Department as assistant secretary for economic affairs, left an account of what "getting ready" meant. It meant using dollars to win the war. The "two most beckoning salients at the time for a Washington warrior," Acheson wrote—he definitely considered himself a Washington warrior— "were those of economic warfare and economic aid. Economic warfare was then very much in favor and fashion due to the efforts of two young people at the British Embassy, Miss Mary Craig McGeachy, a Canadian, and Noel Hall, an English don serving as British Minister for War Trade. One gathered that their activities were more stirring than James Bond's of a later day and their ministry [Economic Warfare] potent enough to strangle Hitler's Europe. Everyone in Washington 'wanted in' on economic warfare"—and just about everyone got in.

Economic warfare abroad, however, meant economic change at home: Change meant control, centralized government control of the nation's economy; and the principal controller was to be the new commerce secretary, the head of the Reconstruction Finance Corporation, and the power behind Roosevelt's throne all rolled into one, Jesse Jones of Texas. A news magazine photograph taken early in 1941 at a Jesse Jones press conference was revealing: Reporters were almost as numerous as at a Roosevelt press conference; T. V. Soong sat at the right hand of Jesse Jones; Jones himself, his double-breasted suit jacket unbuttoned, lolled back in his leather chair, one foot propped up on the corner of his desk. Jones could afford to look relaxed. So great was his power that with a hint or a gesture alone, he could make or break members of boards of directors in the construction industry practically anywhere in the nation. Now, early in 1941, he was using his power for the sake of what he considered the national defense.

Defense, for Jesse Jones, required three things. First, manage-

ment had to convert civilian production into military production—
turn plowshares into swords. Second, labor had to put the lid on
strikes—to subordinate individual interest to the collective interest.
Third, contractors had to spread the wealth, to put defense plants
where there had been no defense plants, in places like Fort Worth,
Dallas, and Houston. What was good for America was good for
Texas and what was good for Texas was good for the developer
named Jesse Jones.

The country as a whole was cranking up. Factories from New
England and New Jersey, through the smokestack belt of the Midwestern states, down to Texas and out to Los Angeles and Seattle,
were churning out guns and planes and trucks and squarish cars
called Jeeps as never before in the history of the republic. Young
men by the thousands were learning to march in formation and to
load their rifles and to make their cots. Artists, after a decade of
unemployment, were finding new leases on life as poster-propagan-
dists, portraying an America full of villainous saboteurs, and gorgeous female traitors under, or in, nearly every bed. Movie
directors and magazine editors were whipping up support for action
abroad; *Time* made Prime Minister Winston S. Churchill its man of
the year. And from the recesses of the White House, President
Franklin D. Roosevelt was cementing America's alliance—an alliance partly covert but nonetheless real—with Britain and the
Commonwealth.

In his farewell address to the American nation, President George
Washington counseled his fellow citizens against "entangling alli-
ances"; and President Woodrow Wilson in the time of World War
I described the United States consistently as only an "Associated
Power." For more than a century American presidents, reflecting
the will of the nation, saw foreign alliances as anathema. But in
January 1941, President Franklin D. Roosevelt changed all that.

■   ■   ■

Late in January 1941, Great Britain's new ambassador reached the
shores of America. The old ambassador, Lord Lothian, a Christian
Scientist, had died of uremic poisoning. The new ambassador, foreign secretary under Prime Minister Neville Chamberlain, a scion

of the British aristocracy, and the owner of vast estates in Yorkshire, was Edward Frederick Lindley Wood, Viscount Halifax.

Taller always it seemed than anyone else around him, Halifax possessed a long and shrewd face that made him look at once religious and crafty; his nickname was "Lord Holy-Fox." Ambassador Joseph P. Kennedy had been less subtle: After one particularly exasperating meeting with Halifax in the Foreign Office, he had come out screaming about "Halifax and all that God stuff!" Halifax had little of Lord Lothian's charm, a fact well known to the government in London. Harold Laski, a professor at the London School of Economics and a great chum of Justice Felix Frankfurter, paved the way for Halifax. "There is something of the genuine saint" about Halifax, Laski wrote to the *Washington Post*. It "is this quality that made so vivid an appeal to Mr. Gandhi." Midway through January 1941, Lord and Lady Halifax boarded the battleship HMS *King George V*, and set off from Liverpool to America.

Fast, powerful, riding low in the water, and accompanied by a convoy of destroyers, the huge battleship seethed across the gray of the Atlantic. Close to Boston the convoy dropped off and the *King George V* plowed on alone. In the cold mist of the morning of January 24, 1941, it entered the mouth of the Chesapeake Bay. Wrote Halifax: "We made way up to Chesapeake Bay all the morning, but except that it was smooth we might have been in mid-Atlantic, for the fog prevented us seeing any land. . . . We anchored about two o'clock and for some time nothing seemed to happen except that it poured with rain." Suddenly, however, the ship received electrifying news. In an unprecedented step, the American president was coming to greet the British ambassador.

Back in Washington and just after lunchtime, a five-car presidential motorcade sped out of the White House, raced through intersections to New York Avenue, hurtled onto U.S. 50—now a hodgepodge of condominiums and fast food restaurants but then, running through piney woods and swamps, designated the "Defense Highway"—and twisted along slippery curves until it reached the Academy pier at Annapolis.

The rain had turned to a downpour. Halifax, aboard the *King George V*, could see nothing but the wet. The captain and he decided that, nevertheless, they would "receive the President with all the honors due to a Sovereign."

Accompanying the president, Navy Secretary Frank Knox, Chief of Naval Operations Admiral Harold Stark, White House Secretary Edwin "Pa" Watson, and eight Secret Servicemen got out of their limousines at dockside. Roosevelt was helped into a launch and then the party boarded the presidential yacht *Potomac*, waiting at anchor in the basin of the Severn. Officers and midshipmen snapped to attention; the executive flag broke out from the foremast; and, as pipers played traditional tunes, the president was hoisted over the side. The *Potomac* raised anchor, and in the midst of the squall, put out in the direction of the *King George V*.

Halifax now could see the yacht materializing out of the mist and starting to circle the battleship. The *King George V* boomed out a twenty-one–gun salute. A launch left the yacht for the side of the battleship and returned bearing Lord and Lady Halifax, just in time for tea.

Frank Knox and "Pa" Watson met them in the companionway, taking them straight to the dining saloon. Roosevelt was seated behind a table. In just one moment, Halifax wrote in his diary, "he had put us completely at our ease, and we were chattering away as if we had known each other all our lives. Nothing could have been more friendly, and he said that he regarded this as dispensing with any formal business of presentation of credentials. Much talk over tea—quite easy and intimate, and at times pleasantly indiscreet."

After tea, they kept on talking, discussing "everything under the sun, and I liked him very much. He spoke a great deal about his experiences in Europe at the end of the last war and about various common friends. Finally, he told me that he hoped that I should find myself free to ring up the White House at any time and ask to see him, and be prepared myself to be called by him at any time."

Night came and the reporters who had clustered along the Annapolis quay—word had gotten around the Washington press corps that something very big was up—were shivering in the blackness. Then a beam cut through the dark—swinging back and forth in the night, the *Potomac*'s light was searching out the pier.

As the presidential yacht pulled alongside, reporters could see into the saloon, where Roosevelt and his aristocratic guests were still seated at dinner. *Time* described the scene: "The saloon was warm and brightly lit; there was a bowl of pink roses on the table; President Roosevelt was talking animatedly and laughing while Lord Halifax listened. Photographers mobbed Lord and Lady Halifax when they appeared on deck, got their pictures as the ambassador apologized for keeping them waiting in the rain. He read a brief statement to reporters, who were standing on the cold, windswept pier: "Lady Halifax and I are very glad to be here . . . and now the President has done my country the great honor of coming to greet us on arrival. . . . I have come here, as a member of the War Cabinet serving as His Majesty's ambassador, to make known to the government and people of the United States . . . in what ways, if they are willing, they can best give us the help we need. . . ." Then, slipping into the president's limousine, Lord and Lady Halifax sped to the British Embassy in Washington; out in the night, the *King George V* was streaking back to sea.

The president, the U.S. Constitution declares, "shall have the Power, by and with the Advice and Consent of the Senate, to make Treaties, provided two thirds of the Senators present concur. . . ." The arrival of Lord Halifax led to what amounted to a treaty. But Roosevelt never submitted this treaty to the Senate for "Advice and Consent." The treaty was probably the most important in America's history; it also was a secret treaty, in effect an alliance with the Commonwealth and with Britain.

This alliance also further linked America and Canada. From the U.S. State Department, Jay Pierrepont Moffat became ambassador to Ottawa, ensconcing himself in 100 Wellington Street, the sumptuous chateau-style building that directly faced the center of Canada's Parliament. From the Canadian Department of External Affairs, Leighton McCarthy, a tall, white-haired businessman and lawyer, became minister to Washington, taking up his own residence in this high-windowed gray structure at 1745 Massachusetts Avenue. Between them, Moffat and McCarthy negotiated a defense highway from the forty-eight states to Alaska, landing fields for use by air units of both countries, expanded trade for munitions, and joint air patrols 1,000 miles out to sea.

The alliance even provided the foundation of ANZUS, the later

Australia–New Zealand–United States treaty. Australia's pudgy little prime minister, Robert G. Menzies, paid a protracted visit to Washington where, escorted around at night by his emissary, the dashing Richard Casey, he curried American favors: Australia, Menzies announced, would allow U.S. naval vessels to put in at its ports as they passed from Hawaii and Asia.

Most important, the de facto alliance found overt expression in a law passed by Congress. "Give us the tools and we will finish the job," Churchill lisped over the radio, and Congress, passing the Lend-Lease Act (patriotically numbered H.R. 1776), gave the tools. The measure was short but to the point. As a recent historian pointed out, everything in the law came to the word "any."

The law, which passed through Congress in March 1941, started with the term "defense article": "Defense article" meant "any weapon, munitions, aircraft, vessel, or boat." "Any law to the contrary," the act went on, the president could authorize the head of "any . . . department or agency" to manufacturer "any defense article . . . the President deems vital," to "Sell, . . . exchange, lease, lend, or otherwise dispose of . . . any defense article to any friendly government," to "communicate to any such government any defense information pertaining to any defense article furnished to such government. . . ." In short, President Roosevelt could produce anything he wanted, use it any way he wanted, share intelligence with anyone he wanted, and therefore unleash any kind of clandestine operation he wanted.

In his first inaugural address, President Franklin D. Roosevelt asked Congress for broad executive powers, and in the first hundred days he did acquire new powers: to close and open the banks; to print greenbacks and to buy silver; to set farm prices and to suspend antitrust laws; to create public works and to provide unemployment relief; to regulate the stock market and to establish social security. After the Japanese assault on Shanghai in August 1937, he received more powers still: to spend $17 million on the army and the navy; to use the Reconstruction Finance Corporation for an expansion of plant; to commandeer factories in the interest of defense; to direct the distribution of raw materials; to place embargoes on the sale of American goods to foreign countries. In peacetime, President

Franklin D. Roosevelt already enjoyed greater powers than President Woodrow Wilson had in wartime. Then came lend-lease: Now, without the expressed approval of Congress, Roosevelt could enter into any war he wanted.

■ ■ ■

TO BE KEPT UNDER LOCK AND KEY
It is requested that special care be taken to
ensure the secrecy of this document.

So stated the cover page of the American–British–Canadian (ABC) Agreement, the secret treaty, delivered to President Roosevelt on March 27, 1941. Dressed in mufti and meeting secretly in the Public Health Building on Constitution Avenue, military officers of the three countries had negotiated the agreement. In America, only Roosevelt and his secretaries of state, war, and navy, along with the negotiators and the chiefs of staff, were to have knowledge of this document. The conclusion read thus:

"12. The strategic concept includes the following as the principal offensive policies against the Axis Powers:—

(a) Application of economic pressure by naval, land, and air forces and all other means, including the control of commodities at their source by diplomatic and financial measures.

(b) A sustained air offensive against German military power, supplemented by air offensive against other regions under enemy control which contribute to that power.

(c) The early elimination of Italy as an active partner in the Axis.

(d) The employment of the air, land, and naval forces of the Associated Powers [President Wilson's old term for the United States and others who fought alongside Great Britain], at every opportunity, in raids and minor offensives against Axis military strength.

(e) The support of neutrals, and of Allies of the United Kingdom, Associates of the United States, and populations in Axis-occupied territory in resistance to the Axis Powers.

(f) The building up of the necessary forces for an eventual offensive against Germany.

(g) The capture of positions from which to launch the eventual offensive."

No wonder the secrecy was important! Here, drawn up in the first three months of 1941, was an Allied plan for war.

■　■　■

The president's men now swung into action. They were closing the vise on the Axis.

Harry Hopkins, Roosevelt's aide, took off for London. Ostensibly, he was to serve as interim ambassador, holding the fort until John G. Winant, the former governor of New Hampshire, could win Senate confirmation. (The previous ambassador, Joseph P. Kennedy, had resigned.) Actually, Hopkins's job was to get to know Churchill, to prepare for a late summer summit meeting between the prime minister and the president.

William J. Donovan, international lawyer and international spy, was in the Near East, visiting Egypt, Palestine, Greece, Bulgaria, and Yugoslavia, trying to build up a Balkan front against the Reich. Cooperative Balkan countries, Donovan intimated, would be eligible for American aid.

Harold Stark, admiral and chief of naval operations, was positioning his forces for oceanic war. Following the curve of the globe, his air patrols were flying as far up as Iceland and his destroyers were escorting convoys as far as Liverpool. These convoys, to Admiral Erich Räder, head of the Germany navy, presented a direct threat of war. He begged Hitler to strengthen Germany's Atlantic forces, and Hitler, in a limited way, consented—he unleashed the *Bismarck*.

American power was also reaching across the Pacific. Bit by bit, the ring around Japan was tightening inexorably.

The navy's premier Japan-basher, Admiral Harry E. Yarnell—Yarnell had commanded the USS *Augusta* in the Shanghai harbor in the summer of 1937—came out of retirement. His assignment, given him by Navy Secretary Frank Knox, was to give recruiting speeches to college seniors. The speeches were pointedly hostile toward Japan.

The administration in Washington slapped another embargo on

Japan. This one restricted sales of copper, brass, and bronze, zinc, nickel, and potash; and a host of semimanufactured products.

And late in March 1941, a flotilla of American ships, two cruisers and five destroyers, steamed into the Sydney harbor. As the vessels came into view, half a million jostling and crowding Australians elbowed their way to the waterfront. From office windows above them, confetti and streamers looped to the ground. The Aussies greeted the Yanks, in some instances, with open arms. The visit also had its practical effects: more trade; better air links; new facilities for communication by radio. As with America and Britain and America and Canada, America and Australia were pulling together in the face of the mutual enemy, Japan.

■ ■ ■

War by money and war by ships were both in the offing. So was war by long-range bombers. Early in winter, General Henry H. "Hap" Arnold, head of the U.S. Army Air Corps, popped into the White House, where he had been invited to join a small group for dinner. He turned out to be the first to arrive, but Roosevelt was waiting for him anyway, seated already next to a tray of drinks. Throwing his head back and flashing his famous smile, Roosevelt extended his greetings. "Good evening, Hap," the president said. "How about my mixing you an old-fashioned?" Arnold hardly ever touched liquor, for once he had a drinking problem. In those bad old days he had been hooked on old-fashioneds; now, obviously, somebody had been checking up on him and reporting to Roosevelt. "Thanks, Mr. President," Arnold answered. "I haven't had one for about twenty years, but I assure you I will enjoy this one with you, tremendously."

Arnold soon found out what Roosevelt wanted. "Hap" Arnold was a visionary, an aging flyboy who ate and breathed the idea of American bombers cruising the globe. As an organizer, however, he was hopeless—and Roosevelt wanted him to team up with one superb organizer, a balding Wall Street lawyer who was assistant secretary of war and Henry L. Stimson's protégé, Robert A. Lovett. The team of Arnold and Lovett went right to work. Operating out of adjacent offices in the Munitions Building, they set out to produce the greatest bomber force the world had ever seen.

Bomber production, of course, was still limited; and a host of competitors, the British, the Canadians, and the Chinese, not to mention the U.S. Army Air Corps, lined up to lay claim to each bomber that came off an assembly line at, say, Willow Run, Michigan, or Long Beach, California. No one could get enough bombers, even with the official goal now at 50,000 a year, and for the U.S. Army brass, China's needs were low on the list of priorities. But if pilots based in China "could get even six or seven bombing trips into Japan," General George C. Marshall conceded, "they could cause considerable trouble there."

. . .

The plan to bomb Japan was moving forward. Early in January 1941, a short, graying, mild-looking White House economist named Lauchlin Currie set off on the long air trek to China. Currie had never flown before and his idea of excitement, rumor had it, was to dictate technical papers while lying on a sofa with his eyes closed. But he went. He went because he was loyal. He went because Roosevelt needed someone, not the feisty Chennault, not the oily Soong, not the hyperactive Morgenthau, but rather someone who was sober, subservient, and shrewd. Currie fit the bill, and he was to produce an independent assessment of China. Was the idea of basing bombers in China, Roosevelt wanted to know from Currie, truly feasible? Currie's conclusion: It was.

On his return to Washington in March 1941, Currie found himself cast in the role of an old China hand, an advocate in the court of Roosevelt for the cause of Chinese airpower. Playing out that role to which he had been assigned, he persuaded Roosevelt to extend lend-lease aid to China. Lend-lease would finance an American air force for China. It also would enrich T. V. Soong beyond imagination.

. . .

The Japanese were watching.

> The main object of CURRIE's mission was to ascertain the things required by Chungking . . . to continue as a belligerent. . . . The U.S. . . . may, after studying CURRIE's findings, advance a much larger loan than is at present contemplated. Already, sev-

eral dozens of experts have arrived on the scene [in China].
Apparently . . . the U.S. has recognized the necessity for
strengthening the Chinese Army, through additional training and
arms. . . .

So went a Japanese radiocast, sent from Manchuria to Tokyo on
February 16, 1941, and decrypted soon in Washington. Japanese
coding machines were chattering away; and through the MAGIC
intercepts, we can reconstruct much of the world as the Japanese
saw it early in 1941.

From Japan's legation in Ottawa, to Tokyo: "We have already
transferred the codebooks to the official residence." Diplomatic
apartments were insecure, vulnerable to burglary by American,
British, and Canadian agents.

From Japan's consulate in New Orleans, to Tokyo: "Secretary of
the Navy Knox flew here from Pensacola. While there he inspected
the new shipbuilding yards and met naval reserve aviators. . . . He
. . . expressed the view that this country would become involved
in the war within two or three months." America was dangerous
and America was coming.

From the Japanese consulate in Vancouver, to Tokyo: "This office
is at present employing a spy (an Irishman with Communist party
affiliations). . . . We intend to send this man . . . to Prince Rupert
and Yukon, inasmuch as progress of the United States–Canada joint
defense plans and the question of air connection with Alaska deserve
our attention." The very idea of an American airbase in the Aleutian
Islands of Alaska had the Japanese spooked; the base was called
Dutch Harbor.

From the Japanese Embassy in Mexico City, to Tokyo: "Mexico's
seizure of Axis ships, the Mexican–American air agreement, and the
refusal of Bolivia to supply Japan with tungsten [indicates] that the
United States [is] exerting its economic influence against Japan in
Latin America." The United States was closing the eastern littoral
of the Pacific Basin to most Japanese interests.

From the Japanese consulate in Sydney, to Tokyo:

. . . United States naval observers have been ordered to various
countries. . . . Their number is a secret but about 25 officers

have been dispatched, especially to the Dutch East Indies, and they are under the direct command of the United States Navy Department and form a special observation post. It is said that they will be permitted to use special shortwave wireless sets of the British Navy in order to keep in touch with Australia, Singapore, and other points.

The ABC powers were expanding to become the ABCD powers, the D standing for the Dutch East Indies.

From the Japanese consulate in Batavia, to Tokyo: ". . . the Netherlands Indian officials are practicing censorship of all letters. Letters marked 'in case of' addressed to people who are supposed to have diplomatic immunity . . . are in no case excepted. None will escape. . . ." As the Japanese had once interfered with official American mail in Manchuria, so the Dutch were now interfering with official Japanese mail in the Indies; tit for tat.

From the Japanese consulate in Batavia, again, to Tokyo, snippets of a dialogue between a Japanese named Isizawa and a Dutchman named Hofstraaten, assistant to the director of economic affairs:

> Isizawa: "Lately Australian and Netherlands newspapers have been reporting rumors of an impending crisis between Japan and the United States. . . . I am at a loss to understand . . . the real meaning of these reports."
>
> Hofstraaten: "We cannot view the situation . . . optimistically. . . . Japan has placed soldiers in French Indochina. . . . It is hard to believe that her power will not be extended south of French Indochina and that it will not . . . become a threat to [Singapore] and the Dutch East Indies. . . . England and America cannot be expected to remain blind spectators. . . . By the time Japan begins directly to threaten Singapore, her supply lines . . . will be cut off and, moreover, the United States will stop all her exports to . . . Japan. You may be sure that the Dutch East Indies, too, know which side of the bread their butter is on. . . . When all this happens it will not take long for resources-poor Japan to collapse."

As night follows day, the Dutch, the British, the Australians, and the Americans were all moving against Imperial Japan.

■ ■ ■

Imperial Japan, too, was on the move. Foreign Minister Matsuoka Yosuke was working out a neutrality treaty with Russia. The Japanese navy was feverishly fortifying the Marianas, the Carolines, and the Marshalls, those sticky, stinking Pacific islands with drooping palm trees and tin-roofed stores that Japan had received as mandates from the League of Nations: By international treaty, Japan had promised to refrain from fortifying these islands, and aside from dredging harbors and building seaplane ramps, Japan had complied; with the U.S. naval buildup of 1939, however, and then with a great rush in early 1941, the Japanese started to turn these islands into little forts. Surrounding Guam and menacing Wake, these islands now threatened to cut America's Pacific lifeline.

The Japanese navy, furthermore—as MAGIC suggested—was putting together plans for an assault on the Indies. And Ambassador Grew sent a message from Tokyo to Washington: A "member of the [American Embassy] was told . . . from many quarters, including a Japanese one," Grew cabled on January 27, 1941, "that a surprise mass attack on Pearl Harbor was planned by the Japanese military forces."

■ ■ ■

A similar message reached the State Department. This one was sent to Secretary Hull by Haan Kilsoo, a Korean.

Haan was a shadowy figure. In U.S. Army intelligence files, his name turned up first in Honolulu. There he warned a colonel named George Patton about a putative Japanese invasion of the islands. He turned up again in Washington, this time as head of the Sino-Korean People's League, with headquarters at 101 D Street, N.E. As the China lobby had hooked up with the British, the Korea lobby had hooked up with the Chinese.

Haan, nevertheless, may have heard something. In his memorandum to Hull, sent on March 25, 1941, he predicted that the Japanese would conquer the Philippines, try to close the Panama Canal, and attack Hawaii.

■ ■ ■

Just as Haan submitted this warning, the Balkans boiled over. Back in January 1941, William J. Donovan had discovered that Prince Paul, the Yugoslav regent, was planning to join the Axis: German agents had been thick in Belgrade and they had smothered the prince with promises. Donovan, therefore, crossed the Danube to see General Dušan Simović, head of the Yugoslav air force. This air force, Churchill was to write, was "a clandestine center of opposition to German penetration into the Balkans and to the inertia of the Yugoslav government." As head of that opposition, General Simović engineered a coup: On March 27, 1941, he overthrew the Yugoslav government, forcing Prince Paul into exile and aligning the country with Britain and America.

Why had Simović done it? Rumor had it that Donovan promised him money. Donovan's papers, to be sure, mention no such promise; but then Donovan's papers contain many obvious gaps. But whatever is exact cause—*Time* referred to "Mr. Donovan's War"— to Hitler the Belgrade coup was a threat, a pretext, or both. German forces had already been concentrating in the Balkans, in Romania and in Bulgaria. Then, at the beginning of April 1941, a new blow fell. Stalin, German intelligence revealed, was on the verge of signing a mutual defense pact with General Simović. Hitler ordered his columns into Yugoslavia and the war was on again.

■   ■   ■

President Roosevelt was exhausted; the pace of his work had become unrelenting. On one day alone in the middle of March 1941, he (1) read Lauchlin Currie's report on the trip out to China; (2) conferred with William Donovan, just back from the Balkans; (3) talked with William Bullitt on plans for a home defense; (4) listened to Harold Smith, director of the budget, explain how to control inflation; (5) chatted with Frank Knox about problems of naval efficiency; (6) discussed new issues of labor unrest with William Knudsen; and then went over all these matters and more with Harry Hopkins, now returned from Great Britain. Besides, F. D. R. had a head cold that had hung on for weeks.

So, on March 19, 1941, the president rounded up Hopkins, Harold Ickes, Attorney General Robert Jackson, Rear Admiral Ross G.

McIntyre, the presidential physician, and White House secretaries "Pa" Watson and Steve Early, and set off by train for Florida. Jesse Jones went along for the ride but headed straight back to Washington. The rest of the party boarded the *Potomac*, all gleaming and shining, and readied for a Caribbean cruise. They nearly failed to return.

Less than 200 yards from where the *Potomac* was docked, a swastika flew in the breeze. Soon after the war's outbreak, a British cruiser had chased the *Arauca*, a German freighter, into the harbor at Port Everglades, Florida. Interned by U.S. authorities, the *Arauca* had sported a swastika, albeit a small one. Now, with the arrival of Roosevelt, the captain broke out the large one. And as a black servant passed out drinks on the Potomac's rear deck, forty-four interned German seamen, crowding up to the rail of their boat, were able to peer down almost directly on the president of the United States as he sat, sipped a cocktail, and chatted calmly.

As the *Potomac*, armed now fore and aft with .50-caliber machine guns and escorted by two U.S. Navy destroyers, cast off and steered out toward the sea, it ran into rain. The rain grew stronger and the sea ran higher. By March 26, the storm was so violent that, as Ickes and Jackson looked out from their cabin, waves were breaking out of sight over their porthole. If the yacht capsized, Ickes wrote later, "there wasn't a chance for a single one of us." The next night, too, was bad. But then the storm subsided, the sea turned smooth, and the sun came out. For two more glorious days, Roosevelt fished, sorted his stamps, and worked on his tan.

On March 30, 1941, he returned to the White House. He was rested. And he was ready.

WASHINGTON GOES
TO WAR

The bureaucracy, too, was ready. Then as now, readiness in bureaucracy above all else meant expansion: expansion in paperwork, expansion in people, expansion in places of work. By the spring of 1941, typewriters in Washington were clattering away day and night, clerical workers, officers and enlisted men, and, naturally, lobbyists were pouring into the capital—the 1940 census revealed that Washington was the nation's fastest growing city—and the silhouettes of dozens of cranes jutted up on the skyline.

Contractors around Washington had never seen such a boom. The Reconstruction Finance Corporation got palatial new quarters. The Office of Production Management got the old Social Security Building and the Social Security Administration got new offices out on the edge of Washington. The capital as a whole got the new Washington National Airport. And the military—dissatisfied with its two main structures on Constitution Avenue plus twenty-three other buildings scattered around northern Virginia, southern Maryland, and the District of Columbia—got Congress to approve an American colossus. This monster building, David Brinkley would remember, "was to rise . . . on a site near Arlington National Cemetery, and to have three times the floor space of the Empire State Building. It would hold the War Department in a mammoth, five-sided agglomeration of concrete corridors and offices a mile in circumference, filled with the military secretariat, officers and enlisted men and civilian clerks and all their desks, file cabinets, cafeterias, mimeograph machines and mechanical typewriters that, in time, would turn out notices to families that their sons, brothers, and fathers had been killed in battle."

The building would be called the Pentagon. Washington was going to war.

■ ■ ■

Certainly Charles Lindbergh thought so.

"Personally, I do not believe that England is in a position to win the war. If she does not win, or unless our aid is used in negotiating a better peace than could otherwise be obtained, we will be responsible for futilely prolonging the war and adding to the bloodshed and devastation of Europe, particularly among the democracies." This was Charles Lindbergh testifying before Congress on January 23, 1941, and speaking out against the lend-lease bill. Lindbergh had gone to Washington as the premier representative of a new antiwar coalition, America First. Embracing such figures as Kathleen Norris, the novelist, and Burton K. Wheeler, the Democratic senator (and Roosevelt-hater) from Montana, America First was the isolationists' best and last answer to the interventionists. Unfortunately, for its own sake at least, Lindbergh was the most prominent spokesman the group could offer; and just as unfortunately, the group let Lindbergh be Lindbergh.

On April 23, 1941, they turned him loose on a mass meeting at the Manhattan Center in New York City. "England," Lindbergh declared, "is largely responsible for the mess we are being dragged into."

The martyrdom, self-imposed perhaps, of Charles A. Lindbergh had begun. Two days after the speech, after Stephen Early of the president's staff had planted questions with the White House press corps, one reporter started. Had the president, he asked, opening a press conference, read Lindbergh's speech? Roosevelt said that he had. Another correspondent spoke up. Why had Lindbergh, a reserve officer in the U.S. Army Air Corps, not been called into active service?

In "answer to this question," the Associated Press reported, "Mr. Roosevelt said that during the Civil War . . . both sides let certain people go. That is, they were deliberately not called into service. The people [in the North] thus ignored were Vallandighams [so-called after Clement L. Vallandigham of Ohio]. The president explained that the Vallandighams were people who from 1863 urged immediate peace, arguing that the North could not win the War between the States. There were also many appeasers at Valley Forge, he went on, who urged George Washington to quit, arguing that the British could not be defeated. He urged that the newsmen read what Thomas Paine wrote at that time on the subject of quitting.

" 'Are you still talking about Colonel Lindbergh?' a reporter asked.

"A simple and emphatic affirmative was the answer," said the Associated Press.

"These are the times that try men's souls," Thomas Paine wrote on December 19, 1776. "The summer soldier and the sunshine patriot will, in this crisis, shrink from the service of his country. . . ." And Senator Clement L. Vallandigham of Ohio had been arrested for treason. So headlines around the country proclaimed: "PRESIDENT CALLS LINDY A TRAITOR!"

Then Lindbergh fell into Roosevelt's trap. Responding to the goad, the flyer resigned his commission. Editorialized *The New York Times*: "Mr. Lindbergh [has] shocked those who believed him to be a loyal American. . . ."

Lindbergh kept giving speeches, although with less and less credibility. His journal entry of May 1, 1941, shows why. "The pressure for war is high and mounting," he wrote. "The people are opposed to it, but the administration seems to have 'the bit in its teeth' and [is] hell-bent on its way to war. Most of the Jewish interests in the country are behind war, and they control a huge part of our press and radio and most of our motion pictures. There are also the 'intellectuals' and the 'Anglophiles' and the British agents who are allowed free rein, the international financial interest. . . ." Such rantings—Henry Luce, for example, was neither Jewish nor an intellectual nor an Anglophile—became standard stuff in Lindbergh's speeches, and his audiences drifted away.

The America First movement was shot through with fallacies and contradictions. Its diatribes against the Eastern urban interests belonged to a bygone era and its hatreds seemed directed more against Roosevelt than against any particular war. But the group's greatest mistake lay in its very name. For who, America First or President Roosevelt, stood more for America? As in the press conference in which he denounced Lindbergh, Roosevelt had only to invoke the ghosts of Lincoln and Washington to convey the impression that he, not Lindbergh, put America first.

Besides, events were on the president's side. The Germans were on the march.

■   ■   ■

Kicking up towering clouds of dust, General Erwin Rommel, hero of the Battle of France and commander of Germany's Afrika Korps, went swirling into the Libyan desert. He arrived in Tripoli in the wintertime—the British had been on the brink of driving Germany's allies, the Italians, out of North Africa altogether—and took a look around. The desert, he realized, was made just for him—for there, he wrote, "speed is the only thing that matters."

So, despite orders from Berlin to go easy, Rommel's panzers early in April 1941 "exploded over Cyrenaica [the hump of Libya that lay east of the Gulf of Sidra] like a bomb-burst . . . hurled in every direction, confusing the enemy, and seizing at a whirlwind pace the main focal points." Close to the Libyan–Egyptian border, however, Rommel's columns came to a halt. There, by the ocean, stood the ancient fortress of Tobruk; and there, inside the fortress, four brigades of Australians had retreated and regrouped. They were ready to have a go at Rommel, and a mere siege was no damper on their spirits.

Simultaneously, German forces were sweeping down through the Balkans. Yugoslavia fell early in April; next came Greece, during Easter week, 1941. Finally came Crete. Luftwaffe bombers reached Crete, that long, barren, mountainous island southeast of Greece, in the middle of May; there the British had no air cover. Shortly after dawn on May 20, 1941, an observer in Crete looked up. Overhead, in the lightening sky, masses of bombers were approaching, and they were flying so close together that their wing tips seemed to touch; some of these planes trailed gliders. Looking like "young vultures following the parent bird from the roost," the gliders descended. Then, from transport planes even higher above, specks appeared, specks that were white, specks that grew larger, specks that were parachutes floating to earth and bearing members of the Hitler Youth, the elite of the German army.

Crete fell—and as it did so, many thought the Third Reich unstoppable. But not quite. A map carried in the April 18, 1941, issue of *U.S. News* depicted, in cartoon fashion, a column of freighters loaded with airplanes and stretching all the way from New York to Suez and the Red Sea. America was using the Atlantic to help the British in Egypt—and to keep Germany away from the Persian Gulf.

Into the Atlantic Ocean streaked the world's greatest battleship and the pride of the German navy, the *Bismarck*. The British were losing 350,000 tons of shipping a month; but with the U.S. convoys, the Reich's navy needed more firepower. Accompanied by the cruiser *Prinz Eugen,* the *Bismarck* moved out of Kiel at the start of the last week of May 1941.

When Churchill first learned of the move, he became, in the words of Anthony Eden, the foreign secretary, "nervy and unreasonable." One can see why. The Bismarck had harder armor, bigger guns, and greater speed than any other ship afloat. What was worse, after a British reconnaissance plane spotted it off the coast of Norway, the *Bismarck* disappeared, obscuring itself in the fogs and mists of the North Atlantic.

It was sighted again at dawn on May 24, silhouetted against the gray of an icecap. Esmond Knight, an actor doing service aboard the *Prince of Wales*—two British battleships, the *Prince of Wales* and the *Hood,* had gone out in search of the *Bismarck*—described the scene. After "minutes of staring at the blank distance," he wrote, "suddenly—and one could scarcely believe one's eyes—there appeared the top masts of two ships! Again that phrase was shouted by the first man who could find his voice—'enemy in sight!' " Knight watched, transfixed, as the German warships moved forward. "There they were," he continued, "in deep, dark silhouette on the horizon—*Bismarck* and *Prinz Eugen,* steaming in smokeless line ahead, unperturbed and sinister. 'Ye gods!—what a size!' I heard someone mutter." Just before 6:00 A.M. the fire order flashed on. "Almost immediately after there were great orange flashes and huge clouds of black smoke belching from the fo'ard turrets of the *Hood* as she fired her first salvo." The *Prince of Wales,* too, let loose. "Two more moments of unendurable ecstacy, then that pulverizing, crashing roar, which for a second seemed to knock one senseless— we had opened fire! We were blinded by a dense sheet of flame which rose before us, mixed with clouds of black, bitter-smelling smoke."

The smoke cleared—and the German ships were still standing on the horizon. Then the *Bismarck* positioned itself to fire. At first, Lieutenant Knight remembered, everything seemed motionless, the *Bismarck* looming dark with its back to the icecap. Only a moment later, however, the great ship erupted with "brilliant flashes and . . . jet black smoke. . . ."

Shells from the *Hood* might have been unable to reach the *Bismarck* but shells from the *Bismarck* certainly were able to reach the *Hood.* As Lieutenant Knight watched aghast, it took only one missile from the *Bismarck* to strike the *Hood,* enter the magazine, and produce a "great shouting explosion. . . ." Enormous "reaching tongues of pale-red flame shot into the air, while dense clouds of whitish-yellow smoke burst upwards, gigantic pieces of brightly burning debris being hurled hundreds of feet in the air. I just did not believe what I saw—*Hood* had literally been blown to pieces." Of the 1,400 men aboard the *Hood,* three survived.

As the *Bismarck* then took aim at the *Prince of Wales,* the latter quickly drew out of range. Lieutenant Knight, however, was no longer a witness. An explosion on his own ship had left him blind.

But the *Bismarck* had received a hit. The blow was only minor, a rupture in one of the fuel tanks, yet enough to make the ship start to trail oil. Her range thus reduced, the *Bismarck* made for the French port of Saint-Nazaire for repairs. The crew expected to be back at sea soon.

In crossing down the Atlantic, however, Admiral Gunther Lutjens made a critical error of judgment. He radioed Berlin a long account of his victory at sea and then, incredibly, continued to broadcast messages.

As his radio waves went forth, the huge receivers atop the Admiralty in London were turning, listening, fixing the *Bismarck's* approximate position; getting the word, British cruisers and also the *Arc Royal,* an aircraft carrier, began to close in. They only lacked the *Bismarck's* exact location.

Then, on the morning of May 26, 1941, a British seaplane 700 miles off France came to a break in the clouds. The seaplane was a twin-engined Catalina, built in San Diego, and the British pilot was accompanied by an American intelligence observer. As the American peered down toward the water, he cried out, "What the devil's that? Looks like a battleship." The dark form down there was a battleship. It was the *Bismarck.*

Shortly before nightfall, fifteen biplanes went up from the flight deck of HMS *Arc Royal.* They approached the *Bismarck* in the fast-gathering darkness—and its fifty-six antiaircraft guns blazed away, scoring hit after hit on the obsolete British aircraft. Yet obsolescence had its advantage. The planes were covered with canvas; and although the shells from below tore countless holes, they caused little real damage.

So torpedoes were fired. One torpedo only bounced off the armor on the side of the ship; another hit home. This second torpedo crashed into the side of the engine room, jamming the steering system. Now the rudders were stuck, and the *Bismarck* could turn only to the right, away from Saint-Nazaire and toward the oncoming British flotilla. The *Bismarck* still could return fire, but it had lost the ability to maneuver.

It survived the night. By dawn, though, more and more of the British ships were finding the target. One shell destroyed a forward turret on the *Bismarck*; another demolished the fire control machinery. With the *Bismarck* now ablaze, the *King George V,* the battleship that had borne Lord Halifax to America, came up to the scene, four miles away, two miles, and then at nearly point-blank range. Shells were pouring onto the *Bismarck.*

Just after 10:00 A.M., Lieutenant Commander Gerhard Junack, chief turbine engineer and one of the few who would survive, made his way to the deck of the *Bismarck*. "There was no electric light," he wrote, "only the red glow from numerous fires; smoke fumes billowed everywhere; crushed doors littered the deck, and men were running here and there, apparently aimlessly. It seemed highly unlikely that one would survive."

Junack and about one hundred others were able to clamber into lifeboats. "Hardly were we free of the ship," he went on, "when it keeled over to port, rolling the deck-rail under and bringing the bilge-keel out of the water. A pause—then *Bismarck* turned keel-up, slowly, the bows rose in the air, and, stern first, *Bismarck* slid to the bottom."

The *Prinz Eugen* made it to France. But, reinforced with lend-lease aid, the Royal Air Force was well within range; and the Royal Navy, similarly reinforced, was squeezing Germany's oil supply to a trickle.

■ ■ ■

Pedestrians in mid-Manhattan saw the headlines in the kiosks but they had no idea there was a link between the sinking of the *Bismarck* and the workings of an office high above them, right in Rockefeller Center. Up in that office, William Stephenson's British Security Coordination team had been relaying intelligence passed along from the U.S. Navy and Coast Guard straight to the Admiralty in London. If intelligence gathering is a form of war, then the United States had been in the thick of the war.

Dealing with the Washington press corps, to be sure, President Roosevelt denied America's belligerency. "Yes, America also had patrols in the Atlantic, but those patrols," Roosevelt told reporters, "were like a band of scouts sent ahead of a wagon train to locate the Indians. . . ." Roosevelt was shading the truth. In April and May 1941, he ordered a flotilla out of the Pacific and into the Atlantic, extended America's "defense zone" so far across the Atlantic Ocean that it included Greenland, the Azores, and much of the Cape Verde Islands, and put out so many sweeps and cruises in the Atlantic that the American flag was flapping steadily in the face of Germany's navy.

Roosevelt hoped—so Lord Halifax cabled London after lunch on

May 2, 1941, with the president—that the U.S. patrols in the Atlantic would lead to gunfire, started by Germany.

F. D. R. intimated the same thing to two advisers. To Harold Ickes he said: "I am not willing to fire the first shot." To Henry Morgenthau he said, "I am willing to be pushed into the situation."

■ ■ ■

Nomura Kichisaburo, Japan's new ambassador to the United States, was "tall, robust, in fine health, with an open face," wrote Secretary of State Cordell Hull. "He spoke a certain—sometimes an uncertain—amount of English. His outstanding characteristic was solemnity, but he was much given to a mirthless chuckle and to bowing. I credit Nomura with having been honestly sincere in trying to avoid war between his country and mine." Like Joseph C. Grew, his counterpart in Tokyo, Nomura had tried to avert the slide into war. Each of their governments, furthermore, wanted peace. But each wanted peace only on its own terms.

■ ■ ■

On the Japanese side:

Matsuoka Yosuke, Japan's crew-cut and incessantly talkative foreign minister, did his best to undermine the Hull–Nomura talks. On May 9, 1941, he sent the ambassador an inflammatory cable: "Should matters [the American buildup vis-à-vis Japan] continue unchecked, Japan will be forced to live up to her obligations under the Japan–Germany–Italy Tripartite Pact. It has already been made clear that Japan has every intention of living up to her promises." Nomura withheld those words from Hull. Hull, through MAGIC, read them anyway.

In the Sengoku district of Tokyo, workers had been busy erecting buildings—about fifty structures in all, including refineries, warehouses, and research labs—and, planting trees all around, produced a complex that, Japanese-style, looked like a "barracks area with little ponds and greenery." Here Japan's nascent atomic bomb project, authorized by the Japanese government in April 1941, was housed. Did the American government know about the project? Possibly. In his 1956 book, *Atomic Quest*, Arthur H. Compton, a physicist and a leader of America's Manhattan project, wrote that in 1940 at least, Japanese research was "running parallel to ours."

A State Department official later described Foreign Minister Matsuoka as "loose talking, always in a state of excited confusion, deceiving, and unstable. . . ." Perhaps so. Nevertheless he kept his promise to stick by the Axis. "It seems that the Netherlands East Indies, following the suggestion of Great Britain," Matsuoka told the Imperial Liaison Conference at the end of May 1941, "intend to prevent rubber . . . from being shipped to Germany." Wanting to ensure the flow of goods to the Reich—and to secure its own imports from the Indies—Matsuoka wanted Japan to move to the south.

American intelligence was aware of Matsuoka's position. Admiral Walter Anderson, the director of naval intelligence, warned that Japan "will strike soon."

■   ■   ■

On the American side:

In the spring of 1941, Henry Luce, the magazine magnate, along with his new wife, Clare Booth Luce, flew to Chungking. Luce had already used his power to create the United China Relief, a New York–based fund-raising organization that would send millions of dollars to China, Chiang Kai-shek, and T. V. Soong; the board of directors included Wendell Willkie, Thomas W. Lamont, the banker, and David O. Selznick, producer of *Gone with the Wind*.

Luce then went to China, wanting to gather firsthand impressions with which he could whip up American feeling against Japan still further. Theodore White, the *Time* reporter, went out to the Chungking airport in shorts and a sun helmet to meet the Luces. Tall and "majestic"—White's word—Luce bowled him over. Although he had not spoken Chinese since he was a missionary brat in Shantung Province, Luce found that the language came back immediately.

Luce was merciless with his hosts. "Conversation with Luce," White remarked, "was like conversation with a vacuum cleaner. He could strip almost anyone clean of all they knew in a first conversation, leaving them exhausted; and the next morning he would have more questions; and more questions at the end of the day." With all this information, Luce intended to persuade America that "England's fate and China's were her own." No restraint, White commented, stopped Luce from "using his magazines to spread the message. . . ."

The message was that China deserved all the help America could deliver; help meant aid through the lend-lease program; and the lend-lease program meant monies channeled through a corporation called China Defense Supplies and *set up by order of the president*. Situated at 1601 V Street in Washington—the beige-brick building now is called The Roosevelt, and serves as a retirement home for the indigent—the corporation's staff included a familiar cast of characters: Claire Chennault; Harry B. Price, the China missionary; and Ludwig Rajchman, the Polish physician and behind-the-scenes political operator. T. V. Soong was the director; Thomas "Tommy the Cork" Corcoran, White House adviser and Felix Frankfurter protégé, was the principal attorney. China Defense Supplies, however, was more than a conduit for money. To use a term made fashionable a decade later by the China lobbyists themselves, China Defense Supplies was a "front."

By federal law, American pilots and mechanics who fought with foreign belligerents could lose their U.S. citizenship—but, as authorized by the signature of the president of the United States, China Defense Supplies, chartered in Delaware, could hire the pilots and the mechanics. *Then* they could go off to China.

So they did. Hired on the promise of $500 for each Japanese airplane they shot down, a considerable sum back then—the funding was to come from the coffers of lend-lease—airmen from around America converged on San Francisco. Led by Claire Chennault, they would comprise the American Volunteer Group, or the Flying Tigers.

These Flying Tigers were hotheads, soldiers of fortune, adventurers, and, like Chennault himself, highly individualistic. Behind them and supporting them, however, was something that was anything but individualistic: a massive, organized, systematic effort on the part of the U.S. government to prepare for the bombing of Japan. The evidence? On April 22, 1941, at 1409 L Street in Washington, the Steering Committee of the Export Control Commodity Division of the U.S. Department of Commerce—only a government could come up with such a title—held a meeting. At that meeting a Mr. Morse said that he, a Colonel Burr, and a Mr. Ballif "had been checking on what the Army and the Navy were doing in the way of locating bombing objectives [in Japan)."

In a subsequent meeting at the same address, Colonel Burr, who had gone to New York, made two points: (1) a "Mr. Ford from Chicago, who is very familiar with Japanese industry . . . has agreed to take an active part in the work of locating Japanese plants; and (2) *Life* Magazine [a Luce publication] is ready to supply 10,000 photographs of Japan and . . . World Wide Photos also has a large pictorial library. . . ." A follow-up Commerce Department document stated: "The objective is to determine how the United States can effect the maximum economic injury to Japan at a minimum cost to itself."

Japan was aware of the threat. On "the 28th [of May 1941], PA [probably a Japanese intelligence agent] handed a member of my staff"—this was a MAGIC transcription of a cable from Tokyo to Nanking, Shanghai, Peking, and Canton—"a strictly secret note which read as follows: 'A part of the $50,000,000 export loan by the United States to China [out of lend-lease] is to be used in purchasing 800 airplanes from the United States. These planes, it appears, are of two types, including the Boeing B-17. The United States will under this arrangement send pilots and mechanics to manage the planes. . . .' In this connection, XYZ [another agent] reports that a Boeing can leave a given base in China, fly to Tokyo, raid the city for two hours, and then fly back to China."

CHAPTER
21

BARBAROSSA

Summertime, Noel Coward remarked after visiting the White House early in June 1941, "always seems to catch Washington unawares, to break over it like an awesome seventh wave, flooding it with sudden, sweltering discontent. There is air-conditioning, of course, and there are iced-drinks and sun-blinds and electric fans, but even those fail to dispel, for me at any rate, a feel that . . . we are all about to frizzle, curl up, and die." The heat—added to the pressures of office—was bothering Roosevelt, too, probably more than ever.

One correspondent thought the president looked quite ill. His "hands, gesturing for emphasis, lighting one cigarette after another, and flicking the ashes off his wrinkled seersucker suit, shook rather badly," Louis Adamic noted after a session at the White House. "The rings under his eyes were very dark and deep. The sharpest feeling he projected on that hot afternoon . . . was one of tense concern crossed with resentment against men like [Colonel Lindbergh] who had obstructed his efforts to prepare the country psychologically and militarily."

Yet not even heat and sickness could stop those efforts; the president used every trick available to gather political support. The president was making a pitch for the allegiance of Polish Americans.

With Roosevelt's blessing, Lord Halifax, the British ambassador, hit the lobbying trail, journeying to the West, selling Britain's cause to Kiwanis and Rotary clubs, and doing his best to pretend that he was not a snob. And Director J. Edgar Hoover, in consultation with the White House, stepped up FBI wiretappings and mail openings, going so far as to gather information on "the attitude of congressional groups toward the President's international relations or foreign policy"; Hoover was spying on Congress.

Harold Ickes, behind the scenes but ever on the telephone, used Fight for Freedom, a spin-off of the Century Club and indeed of the interventionist lobby, as a de facto propaganda agency for Roosevelt. Speaking for Roosevelt, Harold Ickes again lashed out in public at Lindbergh, branding him anti-Semitic. Wendell Willkie, after a conference in the Oval Office, called Lindbergh "un-American."

The administration also was launching a secret war. At the end of May 1941, Frank Knox wrote to Felix Frankfurter, who had been a one-man employment agency of the Roosevelt New Deal; "frankly and privately," Knox complained, he was disappointed "that the administration is not making better use of Bill Donovan's services." Back-room negotiations took place—the army and the navy were deeply suspicious of Donovan—and in the end Knox's letter paid off. On July 6, 1941, *The New York Times* carried a headline, "COL. DONOVAN, WHO STUDIES NAZI ESPIONAGE, IS SLATED FOR A BIG POST." That big post, the *Times* reported four days later, would be that of "Coordinator of Information," or COI, the functions of which were "without precedent in government's operations."

On July 11, Roosevelt signed an order that established the COI; and in an official announcement, the White House stated that "Mr. Donovan will collect and assemble information and data bearing on national security. . . ." But what the White House did *not* say was even more significant. "Mr. Donovan may from time to time be requested by the President to undertake activities helpful in the securing of defense information not available to the government through existing departments and agencies." Press Secretary Stephen Early had drafted these words but, perhaps on instructions from the Oval Office, had withheld them. The public thus was unable to read of the COI's true purpose: Bypassing the regular services, it was to engage in clandestine activities and "covert offensive operations." Donovan set up shop in the Apex Building.

Standing at the juncture of Constitution and Pennsylvania avenues, the Apex Building looks dowdy now and lacks the sparkle of its glamorous neighbor nearby, the East Wing of the National Gallery. In the summer of 1941, however, Donovan's building was still under construction, and visitors had to make their way "through crowds of sculptors, masons, and general laborers helping the master sculptor Michael Lantz create [a] great frieze of heroic figures. . . ." Upstairs in Donovan's office, things seemed equally chaotic. Donovan was more an idea man than an organizer; but he was also an empire builder par excellence, and he soon made clear that the COI would consist of far more than a bunch of owlish professors studying, scribbling, and presenting reports. The Coordinator of Information, as one of Donovan's aides put it, was going to be involved in "actual warfare."

Warfare, for Donovan, meant three things. It meant propaganda: At 270 Madison Avenue in New York, editors, broadcasters, radio technicians, and linguists began to fill the airwaves with Donovan's anti-Axis slant on the news. It meant economic warfare: With Atherton Richards, a pineapple executive from Honolulu, as special assistant, COI launched studies of how best to disrupt the oil and steel reserves of Germany and Japan. It meant sabotage: Working with British Security Coordination, the COI used a secluded camp by a lakeside near Toronto to train the aspiring James Bonds of the ABC secret alliance.

That alliance was gaining adherents—we could almost call it the ABCFR alliance, for America was drawing ever closer to France, Vichy France, and Russia. In June 1941, Robert Murphy, the U.S. diplomat who had been with the embassy in Paris, negotiated a deal with General Maxime Weygand, Vichy's North African commander; America would unfreeze French funds and allow Vichy to buy consumer items in the States; Weygand would get goodies with which he could obtain Arab assistance against the Germans.

And on the evening of June 26, 1941, Ambassador Constantine Oumansky of the USSR slipped into the State Department to tell Undersecretary Sumner Welles that Germany had invaded Russia. Welles as always was frigid and aloof; Oumansky, dapper in a white suit, white shirt, and white shoes, was trying to overcome a reputation for duplicity and sliminess. And as they emerged from Welles's office, both men wore the forced smiles that accompany diplomatic marriages of convenience. Oumansky, nonetheless, had won a victory. He came out of the State Department building with an American vow to extend lend-lease aid to the Soviets.

In June 1941, the major elements of America's overall strategy in World War II were already in place: the ties with China and Great Britain; thoughts of an operation in North Africa; and also what Winston S. Churchill would call the "grand alliance" among America, Britain, and Russia. And Hitler had just made his last roll of the dice.

• • •

Winter hung on late in Russia in 1941, at least in Moscow and Leningrad; snow was on the ground even on May Day, and the chilly fogs were still rolling in from the shores of the Baltic well into June. Even the summer carried the promise of winter again, for late June was unseasonably cool. Despite these omens, however, Hitler plunged ahead.

Operation Barbarossa, the führer's scheme for the defeat of Russia, started off in grand style. From a series of points along the borders of Poland and East Prussia, a massive force of 3 million German soldiers, riding everything they could climb onto from panzers and armored cars to motorcycles, horses, and bicycles, swarmed into the Soviet Union in what proved to be history's largest military assault. The attack went swimmingly, in some cases literally, as soldiers forded streams in Lithuania, Belorussia, and the Ukraine. Engineers threw up pontoon bridges as fast as they could, and then the infantry was able to cover as many as thirty miles a day. The panzers pushed even faster: By sundown on the first day of the invasion, German armored units had reached more than fifty miles into the vastness of the Soviet Union.

The advance was so swift and so sudden—Stalin and the Soviet government had ignored reports that assault was pending—that at one point a German motorcycle unit startled a group of Soviet recruits who were just learning to march. The pace was exhausting. But as in the great triumph the year before in the Low Countries and France, General Heinz Guderian stood high in the turret of his tank and urged his forces ever onward.

By July 10, thousands of Russian troops were dead or prisoners of war and German armored units were approaching Smolensk, more than 300 miles into the Soviet Union. A photograph taken at the time showed members of a panzer team, some squatting and some standing in a field just beside their tank. One soldier was pointing the way on a map; another was beaming with confidence.

Even General Franz Halder, the German chief of staff and a man by nature cautious, was ready to celebrate. "It is probably no overstatement," he wrote in his diary, "to say that the Russian campaign has been won in the space of two weeks."

Unfortunately, from Halder's point of view, Russia was a third-world country, and the farther the German columns penetrated the countryside, the worse the roads—when roads even existed—became; maps were proving almost useless. Russia, furthermore, spread east "like an enormous funnel." The Germans had begun their advance in three coordinated columns, but the farther they ranged ahead, the farther apart they had to spread; and the farther apart they spread, the more the Russians were able to form guerilla bands in the fields and marshes between.

And those guerrillas were fighting unfairly, or so, at least, ran the German lament. The Russians were breaking the rules, and using "Asiatic tricks." They "would lie on the ground pretending to be dead, then leap and shoot Germans who passed over them. Or they would wave white flags of surrender, then fire at those coming to capture them." The German troops heard such tales all up and down the Russian front. In response, many of them murdered Russians who were genuinely trying to surrender or who were already prisoners. Atrocities raged back and forth. "Our ranks got thinner every day," recalled Colonel Dietrich von Choltitz, who headed a regiment in the Ukraine. "Numberless cemeteries full of our dead appeared along our route."

General Guderian continued to flail onward; and east of Smolensk, he even found occasion to chuckle. On the ground along the route his advance guards had planted hand-painted signposts that read, "To Moscow." Moscow was his destination: He could capture

Moscow, he believed. Then he could destroy the Red Army—just as he had captured Paris and then destroyed the French army.

But Hitler got into the act.

Late in July, he ordered one of the three German columns north toward Leningrad and another, Guderian's, down into the Ukraine.

Guderian was disgusted.

"This meant that my panzer group would be advancing in a south-westerly direction," he wrote, "that is to say, toward Germany."

Hitler was giving up the idea of capturing Moscow.

But the Germans had already been sinking toward a stalemate, a point being trumpeted in the major U.S. newspapers. Headlines alone told the story. July 21, 1941: "RUSSIANS REPORT NAZI DRIVES HALTED IN FOUR SECTORS WITH HEAVY LOSSES" (*The New York Times*). July 29, 1941: "NAZI DRIVE BROKEN, RED ARMY ON OFFEN-SIVE, RUSSIANS SAY" (*Washington Post*). The headlines exaggerated, for the German drive was by no means broken yet; but the blitz-krieg had slowed to a crawl.

The U.S. legation in Vichy commented on the Soviets' surprising strength; and the American embassy in Rome stated that, in the judgment of the Italians, Russia was starting to look like a "second China." Officials in Washington were taking note: General Marshall believed that inferior lubricating oil was wearing out the German tanks; Henry L. Stimson estimated that the Germans had received half a million to a million casualties; Adolf Berle, Jr., on the last day of July 1941, held that the German invasion of Russia was "already a failure."

Henry Morgenthau spoke for the president. Now, he declared, was the "time to get Hitler."

■ ■ ■

That time, indeed, had come.

Henry L. Stimson, early in June 1941, made a bit of history: He opened, conducted, and closed a press conference in nine minutes flat. Despite the heat, the electric fan in the War Department's council room was turned off so Stimson, aged seventy-three, could hear the reporters' questions. "I have one piece of news for you, . . ." he stated. "Beginning on June 7, the U.S. Army will train 8,000

British pilots a year in U.S. flying schools. The first group [of 550 Britons] will arrive early next week."

New Yorkers that week were treated to a rare sight: A new battleship, the USS *North Carolina*, came out of the Brooklyn Navy Yard and onto the East River. Like its sister ship, the USS *Washington* down at Philadelphia, the *North Carolina* was even faster, bigger, better armed, and designed with greater firepower than the *Bismarck*. Both battleships would soon be at sea.

Out in the Atlantic, British shipping losses fell five times from April to July 1941. Simultaneously, with Germany's campaign in Russia soaking up just about all the oil Romania could drill, the German navy's oil quota was shrinking drastically.

And then, relieving the British garrison, U.S. Marines poured ashore in Iceland. The move was not quite an invasion—reluctantly but induced by the promise of aid, the Icelandic government had invited America to take over the country's defense. The move, however, was of great strategic importance. A force in Iceland could help guard the convoys and also provide a transfer point for ferrying airplanes from North America to Britain. Still another reason existed for the occupation: German airplanes had been scouting over Reykjavik, the capital, and F. D. R. feared that Iceland would become another Crete. Roosevelt, as Henry Morgenthau put it, was "getting [to Iceland] first."

Roosevelt already had written to Churchill: "I believe the outcome of this struggle is going to be decided in the Atlantic, and unless Hitler can win there he cannot win anywhere in the world." And Iceland was the key to control of the Atlantic.

■ ■ ■

In the Pacific the options were narrowing fast.

Henry B. Claggett, a U.S. brigadier general and commander of the Philippine air force, followed Lauchlin Currie, heading up a mission to China; Claggett's trip had the official and publicized blessing of the U.S. government. In his report, submitted in July to the White House, Claggett urged more planes for China, both to help defend the cities there and to provide a force for bombing Japan.

Owen Lattimore, a lean and bespectacled professor at Johns Hopkins University, also flew to Chungking. Designated a "political adviser," he arrived on July 19, 1941. He had impeccable credentials: He was academe's foremost expert on Asia; Lauchlin Currie had recommended him to Roosevelt; and Admiral Harry E. Yarnell, who had known him in China, had written an enthusiastic letter of recommendation. As Roosevelt's personal liaison with Chiang Kai-shek, Dr. Lattimore symbolized America's de facto alliance with China by his presence in Chungking. Henry Luce's *Time* called Lattimore the "advance guard in the Battle of the Pacific."

Daniel Arnstein also went to China. Arnstein was diametrically different from Lattimore: He was a ham-fisted, loud-mouthed slum kid from the stockyard district of Chicago who had risen to control New York's second largest fleet of taxies. *The New Yorker* described him thus: "Built like a heavy tank, Arnstein . . . is always at least partially in training. . . . His suits, which cost $125 and which he orders a half-dozen at a time, are all double-breasted. He almost never buttons the coat except when he's getting ready to punch somebody, a situation which comes up frequently. While the object of his attention is removing his own coat, Arnstein quickly buttons his. This gives him a slight edge of time. He is a firm believer in the efficacy of the first punch. His shirts and noisy ties are by Sulka. His trousers are always pressed to a sharp edge. That Arnstein has a valet is a circumstance which occasionally strikes him as slightly incongruous. 'Imagine a goddamn hoodlum like me with a dresser,' he says in mock astonishment to his friends."

Yet this "goddamn hoodlum" had his uses. Harry Hopkins had known him in New York—as Hopkins had known just about everyone who counted in New York, from Virginia Gildersleeve, the dean of Barnard, to Arnstein—and had brought him to Roosevelt's attention. Arnstein knew transport, and on Roosevelt's behalf he went out to survey the requirements of the Burma Road. And what he found fit right into Roosevelt's plans—the Burma Road needed more trucks, and soon was scheduled to get them.

Douglas MacArthur, already out in Asia, won a political victory. He already had been badgering Washington for guns, bullets, food, ships, bombers, and, above all, a clear-cut link with the military might of the United States. He got part of it. On July 26, 1941, President Roosevelt decreed MacArthur "commanding general, United States Army Forces in the Far East." The Filipino and the American armies were now united—and MacArthur had a promise from Washington for bombers.

And Claire Chennault was on a roll. He, his buddy, T. V. Soong, and their newfound ally and courtier in the White House, Lauchlin Currie, had sold their cause to the president: Roosevelt now fully sanctioned the idea of basing bombers in China. So meeting in the chandeliered lobby of the Mark Hopkins Hotel, high atop Nob Hill in San Francisco, Chennault and his Flying Tiger volunteers proceeded to the Embarcadero and onto a Dutch freighter, the *Jaegersfontane*. The volunteers carried false passports, masquerading as clerks or students, bankers, and even musicians. Accompanied by two U.S. cruisers, the Dutch ship swung down to Australia and then, picked up by another cruiser out of the Dutch East Indies, to Singapore. The flyers then went by train to Rangoon, in British Burma, awaiting transit to China.

■ ■ ■

Japanese intelligence knew all about them. As we can see through the MAGIC intercepts, the sense in Tokyo was one of mounting alarm.

June 6, 1941:

> . . . American aviators are to be utilized in the transportation of bombers to China, the assembly of airplanes, and a study of actual fighting. . . . It seems that about one-third of those sent are to take part in the war.

July 5, 1941:

> According to information . . . 10 Boeing B-17 types and 18 heavy bombers . . . and 220 trucks . . . will reach Rangoon sometime between July 15 and 20 on board a steamship belonging to the Ford Company. The bombers are to be sent into the interior as they are. The trucks will be assembled in Rangoon and will leave

that city toward the end of July or about the middle of August after being loaded with freight.

July 16, 1941:

QUO TAI-CHI [China's ambassador to Great Britain] held in a conversation with the British, American, and Soviet ministers and it is being widely rumored that a military alliance is imminent. . . . The United States asked Chungking to lend her an airport near the coast in case Japan advances southward. Chungking gladly agreed but as yet the exact spot has not been determined.

July 16, 1941:

The United States will send men to improve the Burma Road. . . . [T]he American ambassador [John Winant in London] declared that it is the policy of the United States to continue its policy of assisting Soviet Russia just as prior to the outbreak of the war between Germany and Russia. . . .

Seeing America similarly assisting China, the government in Tokyo now stepped up the pace. Japan furthered its atomic bomb research at Konan, an industrial complex in resource-rich Korea. Admiral Yamamoto Isoroku drew up preliminary plans for an aircraft carrier attack on Pearl Harbor. And, to break what it saw as the deadly encirclement, the Imperial Liaison Conference decided that now, at all costs, the military had to move south. So after the government sent an ultimatum to the Vichy authorities, Japanese troops moved into southern Vietnam, on July 24, 1941.

And, as MAGIC revealed to Washington, Tokyo had still more in mind. Once in control of Saigon, an intercept of July 19 indicated, Japanese forces would "launch therefrom a rapid attack" on Singapore and on the Indies.

■   ■   ■

Washington responded with vehemence. On July 26, 1941, President Roosevelt froze Japanese funds in the United States and issued an executive order that limited American oil shipments to Japan. That order—the point needs emphasis—placed an embargo on high-grade aircraft oil only. From the time the executive order was issued, however, no U.S. oil flowed to Japan.

Why not? Why the disparity between what Roosevelt said and what happened?

A *U.S. News* photograph, taken the week Roosevelt signed the order, shows two men seated on a bench in Lafayette Square and involved intensely in conversation. On the right, wearing a dark suit and, despite the heat, a gray fedora, one of them had white hair and a Roman nose. He was old now and no longer openly active in government—during World War I, he had served as chairman of the War Industries Board, thus running the nation's economy—but he was still fabulously rich and a major contributor to Democratic political campaigns. Several southerners, including especially Senator James F. Byrnes from the man's native South Carolina, had been his protégés; he had made campaign contributions to sixty or more members of Congress. When he spoke, even from the bench in Lafayette Square, people listened. He was Bernard Baruch.

Born in 1870 in Camden, South Carolina, Baruch as a boy migrated with his family to Manhattan; there, starting as a clerk on the stock exchange, he made one of his era's great fortunes. He turned his fortune into influence—contributing lavishly to congressional campaigns and hosting countless figures of prominence at his plantation near Georgetown, South Carolina. In 1941 he held no official position in the government; his influence, nonetheless, remained great.

On the left in the photograph, wearing a silk necktie and a light-colored summer-weight suit, was a younger man, expensively groomed and with a British Guardsman–style moustache. He was the assistant secretary of state for economic affairs, Dean Acheson.

We can only guess at what they were saying. *U.S. News*, whose editor, David Lawrence, had incomparable sources in the Roosevelt administration, ran the photograph right under a headline that went:

OUR CHANCES OF VICTORY IN ECONOMIC WARFARE;
Freezing of Funds, Export Licensing Potent Weapons
in Hands of U.S.;
Vulnerability of Japan to restrictions on needed
basic raw materials.

And with influential persons all around the country just then demanding a total embargo against Japan, it seems reasonable to assume that Baruch was advising Acheson on what course to follow.

What did happen next was that Acheson in the State Department, Morgenthau in the Treasury Department, and Stimson in the War Department agreed among themselves to prevent Japan from getting hold of export licenses for oil. When the Japanese applied for such licenses, the relevant departments would simply stall. Thus the embargo on oil to Japan was de facto—and complete.

All this and the fact that Roosevelt acquiesced in the State–Treasury–War Department de facto embargo emerges from documents of the time. Why would Roosevelt agree to a complete embargo on oil? One theory holds that Roosevelt, a busy man, simply rubber-stamped what the bureaucrats were already doing. Perhaps. But given Roosevelt's strength of character, the vast power he had striven to accumulate, and his long-honed skill at using others as hatchetmen, makes another theory equally plausible: that Roosevelt had signaled Acheson, possibly through Baruch, that the president actually wanted a total embargo.

Roosevelt's way would have been the classic way of political leaders who want others to do their dirty work for them. Roosevelt, after all, knew full well where a total embargo would lead. "[T]o cut off oil altogether at this time [to Japan]," the president had said on July 19, 1941, "would probably precipitate an outbreak of war in the Pacific and endanger British communications with Australia and New Zealand." And one more detail: Ambassador Nomura Kichisaburo reported to Tokyo a conversation held in the Oval Office.

> The president said that if Japan attempted to seize oil supplies by force in the Netherlands East Indies, the Dutch would, without a doubt, resist, the British would immediately come to their

assistance, war would then result between Japan, the British, and the Dutch, and, in view of our own policy of assisting Great Britain, an exceedingly serious situation would immediately result.

· · ·

By the end of July and the beginning of August 1941, Washington was soggy, sweltering, and broiling. The heat, *Time* wrote, was melting the tar on Massachusetts Avenue. Anyone who could flee the capital did so, and Roosevelt was no exception. Soon, the papers announced, he would leave on vacation. He was going to take the yacht *Potomac* for a cruise off the coast of New England.

Late on Sunday morning, August 3, the executive flag came down from over the White House and, accompanied by three aides, Roosevelt rode up to Union Station. Leaving Washington at 11:00 A.M., the presidential train streaked northward—soldiers with fixed bayonets stood guard at every bridgehead—and at 8:15 P.M. it reached New London, Connecticut. The station stood at the edge of the harbor; and as a crowd watched from around Nathan Hale's old schoolhouse and the Congregational church up the hill, Roosevelt transferred to the yacht. In the last glow of the sunset, the *Potomac* slipped down the Thames River and into the ocean beyond. After dropping anchor off Point Judith, by the mouth of Rhode Island Sound, the vessel proceeded at dawn to South Dartmouth, Massachusetts, where Roosevelt entertained members of the Norwegian and Danish royal families-in-exile; their presence aboard the *Potomac* made all the New England papers. Late in the afternoon, the *Potomac* took off again, putting in at Martha's Vineyard.

The Vineyard Sound was full of American warships—the cruisers *Augusta* and *Tuscaloosa*, and the destroyers *Madison*, *Moffett*, *Sampson*, *Winslow*, and *McDougal*. Aboard the cruisers were General George C. Marshall, Admiral Harold R. Stark, General Henry H. Arnold, and Admiral Ernest J. King, commander in chief of the U.S. Atlantic Fleet.

The American press, however, saw little of these men. It did not see Roosevelt being moved to the *Augusta*, Harry Yarnell's old cruiser from the Shanghai harbor. It did not see the departure of

Prime Minister Churchill from Ten Downing Street, or his own train ride to the north, or his arrival at Scapa Flow in the Orkneys. It did not see the nearly simultaneous departure of U. S. and British flotillas, the one from Martha's Vineyard, the other from the islands above Scotland.

The press did not see the secret rendezvous point. That point was in Placentia Bay, just off a fishing village called Argentia in southeastern Newfoundland.

CHAPTER
22

ARGENTIA

At the end of July 1941, in Tokyo, Hirohito and his ministers met ceaselessly in the Imperial Palace. Outside the open windows they could hear power shovels at work; even on the imperial grounds themselves, laborers were digging up trees to make pits for antiaircraft guns. The emperor and his ministers were frightened. America was building up the Burma Road, sending pilots and flight crews to Rangoon, shutting down Japan's precious reserves of oil. Each day, 28,000 gallons of petroleum seeped away. Something, clearly, had to give.

Prince Konoye had an idea. Konoye, the foppish aristocrat, had been in and out of power as prime minister—now he was in—and, as often before, he felt trapped between his military's intransigence and the Americans' hostility. But now, early in August, he popped up with an idea that he thought might resolve the crisis. He would put his kimono aside, don a business suit, hop aboard a Pacific steamer, make the trip to Washington, and there have a heart-to-heart talk with President Franklin D. Roosevelt. The proposal went to Joseph C. Grew on August 18, 1941—Konoye had dismissed Foreign Minister Matsuoka as too belligerent, so the new foreign minister, Admiral Toyoda Teijiro, made the presentation—and the American ambassador was impressed. "For a Prime Minister of Japan thus to shatter all precedent and tradition," Grew wrote in his diary, "in this land of subservience to precedent and tradition, and to wish to come hat in hand, so to speak, to meet the President of the United States on American soil, is a gauge of the determination of the [Japanese] government to undo the vast harm already accomplished in alienating our powerful and progressively angry country. . . . Prince Konoye's [ship] is ready, waiting to take him to Honolulu or Alaska or any other place designated by the President, and his staff of the highest military, naval, civil officers is chosen and rarin' to go."

So the offer of a Japanese-American summit meeting reached Washington. But Cordell Hull, the good gray secretary of state, even grayer from a throat ailment—he had just returned via the C&O from taking the cure at White Sulphur Springs—found the idea absurd. "I estimated right at the outset," he wrote in his memoirs, "that there was not one chance of success in twenty or one in fifty or one in a hundred. Japan's past and present records, her unconcealed ambitions, the opportunity for aggrandizement lying before her while embroiled Europe demanded a large part of our attention, and the basic divergence between our outlooks on international relations, were all against the possibility of such an accord."

Roosevelt agreed.

Following the MAGIC transcripts, he assumed that the Japanese to a person were bent upon war. He had no way of knowing that, behind the scenes, General Tojo Hideki, the minister of war, had lent his support, albeit with a time limit, to Konoye's proposal. But Roosevelt also manifested no interest at all in finding out what Konoye really had on his mind. Roosevelt failed even to reply to Konoye's offer. "The Emperor," reported an attendant in Tokyo, "was very sad."

■　■　■

He had good reason to be sad. The American players were all in place.

Brigadier General John Magruder of the United States Army flew to Chungking. He headed an official American advisory mission to China.

Averell Harriman entered the government. The only son of Edward Harriman, who had been a railroad magnate and one of the richest men in the world, Averell Harriman had grown up in a family that "more closely resembled a medieval duchy than an American household." A graduate of Groton and Yale, not to mention of a series of stone pile residences along Manhattan's Fifth Avenue, the son was an aristocrat to the tips of his toes, tall, lean, cool, somewhat plodding, aloof. He was also intense and busy, and a Democrat, and throughout much of 1941, he chafed over being left out of things, over being unable to offer official service to his country, or at least to those of his fellow countrymen who lived in Georgetown.

Roosevelt, being Roosevelt, had teased Harriman, playing him along, dangling vague offers. Then suddenly, in August 1941, F. D. R. ended Harriman's misery. He made Harriman, the consummate capitalist, chief of the U.S. lend-lease mission in Moscow. The joke was on both Harriman and Stalin. Harriman nonetheless flew off, first to Great Britain and then to the Soviet Union; his job was to make sure that the Russians got their aid and that they used it well.

Assistant Secretary of War Robert A. Lovett, the balding, fawn-eared, Yale graduate who was on the periphery of Harriman's circle, was slick, and by August 1941, he had moved himself into a critical new role. He was now coordinator between the air commands of the army and the navy.

Undersecretary of State Sumner Welles carved out his own empire. Carving, for Welles, was no problem. Hull, his nominal boss, grave, saintly, and ill, had become almost an absentee secretary, uninterested in paperwork and more than content to leave the administration to that rigid, frigid, and gay scion of New England, Sumner Welles. Welles, a columnist said, looked "like a man with a bit of bad fish caught in his moustache." But Welles was also a doer, and on behalf of his mentor, the man he knew as Frank Roosevelt, he managed to bring almost all the twenty republics of Latin America into a de facto alliance with America: Almost all the resources of Latin America were now available to the United States; very few of them to Japan.

Henry L. Stimson kept an appointment book that read like the schedule of the fast train to New York. His closet aides—Robert

Lovett, Undersecretary of War Robert Patterson, and Assistant Secretary of War John J. McCloy—were made in his own image. They were New York lawyers, hard-working bureaucrats, and patriots dedicated to winning the war. Lovett was handling air matters; Patterson was in charge of procurement; McCloy supervised lend-lease. The Stimson team presided over an army that, through the draft, had grown to a million and a half officers and men. That army was still at peace; its secretary and his lawyers were not. Seeing themselves already at war, they were purchasing weapons, developing bases, and deciding who, overseas, should get just how many long-range bombers.

Even the men in the black robes, the justices of the United States Supreme Court, were playing their parts. By venerable tradition, the justices, like Victorian children, were to be seen but not heard—save when they were rendering judicial opinions. But in the summer of 1941, the Court tossed that tradition aside—and the fact that seven of the nine justices had been appointed by Roosevelt was hardly a coincidence.

Justice Byrnes—the former senator from South Carolina—was an ardent supporter of lend-lease; Justice Frankfurter, of the Minersville flag-salute case, had played a part in making Donovan head of the COI. But more: Justice Frank Murphy, the former attorney general, spoke to the international convention of the Knights of Columbus, in Atlantic City, and warned against the putative threat from the Nazis. Justice Stanley Reed addressed a Freedom Bell rally at Bridgeport, Connecticut, and declared that "force must be met by force." Justice Hugo Black—reviled once as a member of the Ku Klux Klan and then the Court's most ardent supporter of the First Amendment—accepted an honorary doctorate from his alma mater, the University of Alabama. Said Black, adorned in his robes: "More than peace, we love freedom. That we shall spare no effort to preserve—peaceably if we can, forcibly if we must."

These people were only bit players. The main actors were staging their drama in Placentia Bay. The curtain on this larger drama opened at 9:00 A.M., precisely, on Saturday, August 9, 1941.

■ ■ ■

With Canadian destroyers providing a gigantic shield in the Atlantic, a British battleship, the *Prince of Wales*, pushed its way through the dark waters off the coast of Newfoundland, approaching the mouth of Placentia Bay. A fog came up and, from the deck of the USS *Augusta*, already at anchor, the British ship was nearly invisible. Suddenly the fog lifted. And out there, surrounded by dozens of naval ships, all American, all flying the Stars and Stripes, and all with their decks crammed with cheering and waving sailors, the *Prince of Wales* popped into view. A formation of U.S. patrol planes roared overhead. Down by the railing of the great deck below them, a figure appeared. He was short and pudgy, like a bulldog, and dressed in a naval uniform, and he was peering out toward the *Augusta*.

On the deck of the *Augusta*, another figure was peering back. He was sitting in a wheelchair.

The first man was Winston S. Churchill. The second was Franklin D. Roosevelt.

■ ■ ■

"How are you, Harry?"

Harry was Harry Hopkins. He had flown to London, and from there to Moscow to get a firsthand impression of the war taking place between the Germans and the Soviets in Russia. Deep in the Kremlin, the Soviets put on a grand show for Harry Hopkins, referred to in the American press as "Hurry Upkins": long dinners with plenty of caviar and vodka; inside information about Russia's defenses; a frank conversation with Joseph Stalin. The Germans were strong, Stalin acknowledged; but the snows were about to fall and after the first of October, Stalin said, the Germans would be unable to launch a new offensive.

Stalin went even further: During the bleak midwinter, the German battle line would stretch "probably not more than 100 kilometers away from where it is now." Hopkins was impressed: The Soviets were capable of effecting at least a stalemate. That impression in mind, Hopkins flew back to Britain, to Scapa Flow, and from there had set sail with Winston S. Churchill for Placentia Bay in Newfoundland. A special launch took Hopkins from the *Prince of Wales* to the *Augusta*, where Roosevelt welcomed him back.

"Are you all right?" Roosevelt asked. "You look a little tired."

Exhausted and ailing, Hopkins waved the concern aside. All Hopkins said was, "The Russians are confident." They had good reason to be confident: German military production was only one-fourth of what it had been in 1918.

At 11:00 A.M., Churchill followed Hopkins to the *Augusta*. Dressed in navy blue—as prime minister, Churchill had the right to wear the nautical uniform of the warden of the Cinque Ports— and surrounded by the military chiefs of Britannia, resplendent in their ribbons, braids, and buttons, he lowered his corpulent body down into the admiral's barge. The barge set off.

Churchill could hardly miss the contrast between the *Augusta* and the ship he had just left. "The *Prince of Wales* was camouflaged," wrote a British journalist; "her guns protruded from their turrets like rigid pythons. The American ships were uncamouflaged and shone in peacetime gray. We had been in action, and our brass was either painted or tarnished and our decks were not what they would have been in other days. The American ships were spotless. We admired the beautiful steps of their pinnaces, the gleaming brass, the pine-white woodwork, as those craft lay tossing in our grim shadow."

Dressed in a Palm Beach suit, Roosevelt stood waiting under an awning, supporting himself on the arm of his son Elliott. The chiefs of staff and a few top advisers were nearby; they were standing at attention, and down by the railing a U.S. Marine band was striking up "God Save the King." Winston Churchill had just stepped out on deck. He "was unmistakable," Elliott Roosevelt wrote: "short, rotund, . . . florid . . . —not an especially prepossessing figure at an instant's glance, yet a man whose calm, confident power required but a moment to make itself evident. . . ."

The band played the "Star-Spangled Banner" and Churchill stepped forward. Facing Roosevelt and making a formal bow, he presented the president with a letter of salutation from King George VI. Then Churchill and Roosevelt shook hands, officers and advisers introduced themselves to their counterparts, Churchill lit up a cigar,

Roosevelt inserted a cigarette in his long black holder, and the two leaders, Churchill walking and Roosevelt in his wheelchair, went off for a tour of the ship. The Argentia Conference had started.

Roosevelt gave a dinner for Churchill that night aboard the *Augusta*, the two men and the military brass gathering at a table in the captain's cabin. As the silver glowed and the candles flickered, the host and his guests enjoyed an all-American meal. The first course consisted of "almonds, vegetable puree, and hors d'oeuvres"—this from a copy of the menu, autographed by the president and preserved in the Roosevelt Library. White-jacketed waiters then served broiled chicken as the entrée, along with "buttered sweet peas, spinach omelet, candied sweet potatoes, mushroom gravy, hot rolls, and currant jelly." Then came crackers and cheese; dessert was chocolate ice cream and cookies.

Following standing orders of the U.S. Navy, the *Augusta* served no spirits. No matter: Churchill's conversation was wine enough for his dinner mates. He must have been impressive indeed. After coffee, he "rared back in his chair," Elliott Roosevelt wrote, ". . . slewed his cigar around from cheek to cheek, and always at a jaunty angle, his hands slashed the air expressively, his eyes flashed. He held the floor that evening and he talked. Nor were the rest of us silent because we were bored. He held us enthralled even when we were inclined to disagree with him." Even President Roosevelt was quiet, listening intently.

■   ■   ■

Sunday morning witnessed a famous event, one celebrated in photographs, newsreels, and then histories. The sky itself was remarkably clear, especially for the Newfoundland coast: "[a] really lovely morning," one of the Britons wrote in his diary, "just like a summer's day on the west of Scotland." The breeze was warm, the hills around Argentia were green, and the waters of Placentia Bay had taken on a "beautiful shimmering gray look." Leaving its anchorage, the destroyer USS *McDougal* drew even with the *Augusta*'s main deck. The president, hatless and dressed in a double-breasted blue suit, stood by the railing. Then, clutching a cane and helped along by Elliott, he moved onto a gangway and crossed to the *McDougal*.

The *McDougal* proceeded to the side of the *Prince of Wales*. And Roosevelt walked again.

This time, as a British band played the two national anthems, Roosevelt stood stark still, positioned at the end of the deck of the prime minister's battleship. Then he started. He was determined to make his way the entire length of the battleship to his chair of honor on the quarterdeck. Never since being afflicted by polio had he attempted a walk of this length. Churchill, wearing the double-breasted blues of the Royal Yacht Squadron, stood on the quarterdeck, watching. Air Vice Marshall W. M. Pool stood beside him. Many "of us in England had thought that the President was unable to walk at all . . . ," Pool wrote. "One got the impression of great courage and strength of character as he slowly approached the assembled company. It was obvious to everybody that he was making a tremendous effort and that he was [intent on] walking along that deck even if it killed him."

He made it—all the way from the deck of the *Augusta* to the deck of the *McDougal*, then to the deck of the *Prince of Wales*, then to the front of that great battleship for divine services in the worship of God.

As a renowned photograph shows, Roosevelt and Churchill sat side by side under the sunshine on the open deck, each with a hymn book in hand as together they faced the pulpit. Sailors, British and American, lined both sides of the quarterdeck; General George C. Marshall stood directly behind Churchill; Harry Hopkins, frail and sick-looking in his overcoat, stood behind Marshall. As the two chaplains, one American and one British, stepped forward, the congregation opened its hymnals.

None "who took part in it will forget the spectacle presented that sunlit morning on the crowded quarterdeck," Churchill wrote, "—the symbolism of the Union Jack and the Stars and Stripes draped side by side on the pulpit; the American and British chaplains sharing in the reading of the prayers; the highest naval, military, and air officers of Britain and the United States grouped together behind the President and me; the close-packed ranks of British and American sailors, completely intermingled, sharing the same books and joining fervently together in the prayers familiar to both." Churchill himself had selected the hymns: "For Those in Peril on the Sea"; "Onward, Christian Soldiers"; "O God, Our Help in Ages Past." This Sunday morning service was the keystone of the Argentia Conference. If "nothing else had happened while we were here, that would have cemented us," Roosevelt told his son. " 'Onward, Christian Soldiers'. We *are*, and we *will* go on, with God's help."

Back on the *Augusta* that night, Roosevelt gave another dinner for Churchill, but this time without the brass and the braid; only civilian advisers were present, and Elliott Roosevelt. "You sensed," Elliott wrote of this second dinner, "that two men accustomed to leadership had sparred, had felt each other out, and were now readying themselves for outright challenge. . . . Churchill still arrogated the conversational lead, still dominated the after-dinner hours. But the difference was beginning to be felt."

Conflict, Elliott Roosevelt wrote, soon erupted. "Father started it all by bringing up imperial preference. 'Of course,' he remarked, with a sly sort of assurance, 'of course, after the war, one of the preconditions of any lasting peace will have to be the greatest possible freedom of trade.'

"He paused. The P.M.'s head was lowered; he was watching Father steadily, from under one eyebrow.

" 'No artificial barriers,' Father pursued. 'As few favored economic agreements as possible. Opportunities for expansion. Markets open for healthy competition.' His eye wandered innocently around the room. . . .

"Churchill's neck reddened and he crouched forward. 'Mr. President, England does not propose for a moment to lose its favored position among the British Dominions. . . .'

" 'You see,' said Father slowly, 'it is along in here somewhere that there is likely to be some disagreement between you, Winston, and me. I am firmly of the belief that if we are to arrive at a stable world peace it must involve the development of backward countries. Backward peoples. . . . I can't believe that we can fight a war against fascist slavery, and at the same time not work to free people all over the world from a backward colonial policy.'

"Around the room, all of us were leaning forward attentively.

Hopkins was grinning. Commander Thompson, Churchill's aide, was looking glum and alarmed. The P.M. himself was beginning to look apoplectic. Roosevelt ignored the danger signals.

" 'The peace,' he concluded, 'cannot include any continued despotism. The structure of the peace demands and will get equality of peoples.' With that said, he allowed Churchill hurriedly to change the subject."

Elliott Roosevelt may have exaggerated but the leitmotiv of the Argentia Conference was clear to all present: America was going to be making the rules.

■ ■ ■

Roosevelt's whereabouts, so far, had remained a secret. "The mysterious absence of the President and the Chief of Staff and the Chief of Naval Operations still continues and speculation is very rife," Henry L. Stimson, in Washington, wrote in his diary on August 7; the secretary of war himself had no idea that a summit conference was taking place at Argentia. The press, to be sure, was getting suspicious, for word had come in from London that Churchill, too, had disappeared. Headlines were trumpeting a virtual certainty: Roosevelt and Churchill were meeting somewhere. But where? No one knew yet.

■ ■ ■

Monday morning saw Churchill back aboard the *Augusta*. The discussion turned to Japan. To Churchill, Hitler's Germany was public enemy number one, so he tried to pin Roosevelt to an Atlantic First strategy. Roosevelt agreed in principle, and he even promised to have Secretary Hull keep talking with Japan's Ambassador Nomura. Still, Roosevelt's attitude worried Churchill. If Japan expanded further—this from Sumner Welles's record of the conversation—"various steps would have to be taken by the United States notwithstanding the President's realization that the taking of such further measures might result in war between the United States and Japan."

■ ■ ■

On Monday evening, after dinner again aboard the *Augusta*, Churchill apparently exploded in anger, according to Elliott Roosevelt. Pacing up and down in the cabin and waving a "stubby forefinger," he burst out: "Mr. President, I believe you are trying to do away with the British Empire. Every idea you entertain about the structure of the post-war world demonstrates it."

To all this tension between Churchill and Roosevelt, granted, we have but one eyewitness—Elliott Roosevelt. And he may have dramatized, even invented. In general terms, nonetheless, what he wrote makes sense. In 1932, following America's great tariff hike, Britain and the Commonwealth created an imperial preference system, giving preferred treatment to each other's goods—and discriminating against American goods. Furious, Washington for the next decade railed against the system. And now, at Argentia, with Churchill clearly the supplicant, Roosevelt, being Roosevelt, could hardly have resisted the temptation to raise the issue.

■ ■ ■

"The President of the United States of America and the Prime Minister, Mr. Churchill, . . . deem it right to make known certain common principles . . . on which they base their hopes for a better future for the world."

Thus began the preamble of the Atlantic Charter, signed by Roosevelt and Churchill the morning of Tuesday, August 12, 1941.

"First, their countries seek no aggrandizement, territorial or other.

"Second, they desire to see no territorial changes that do not accord with the freely expressed wishes of the peoples concerned.

"Third, they . . . wish to see the sovereign rights and self-government restored to those who have been forcibly deprived of them.

"Fourth, they will endeavor . . . to further the enjoyment by all states, great or small, victor or vanquished, of access, on equal terms, to the trade and to the raw materials of the world which are needed for . . . prosperity.

"Fifth, they desire to bring about the fullest collaboration between all nations in the economic field. . . .

"Sixth, after the final destruction of the Nazi tyranny, they hope to see established a peace which will afford . . . assurance that all the men in all the lands may live out their lives in freedom from fear and want.

"Seventh, such a peace should enable all men to traverse the high seas and oceans without hindrance.

"Eighth, they believe that all the nations of the world . . . must come to the abandonment of the use of force. . . ."

Having agreed to these sentiments, Roosevelt and Churchill lunched together again on Tuesday; after lunch they went to the *Augusta*'s quarterdeck to say their formal farewells. Churchill was holding two copies, illuminated and on heavy cardboard, of Longfellow's poem, "Sail On, O Ship of State." In a letter of January 20, 1941, to Churchill, Roosevelt had copied the poem:

> Sail on, Oh Ship of State!
> Sail on, Oh Union strong and great.
> Humanity with all its fears
> With all the hopes of future years
> Is hanging breathless on thy fate.

The president and the prime minister signed both copies, each keeping one, and they swapped their autographed portraits. The U.S. Marine band played "God Save the King"; and Churchill, for the last time, stepped down to his launch.

At 4:45 P.M., the gangway of the *Prince of Wales*, one of the British newsmen recorded, "came in; the anchors came up. The battleship began to vibrate. On the stroke of five she turned and passed slowly from the bay." As the ship started up, Churchill went to the railing. Hunched and stubby, his body, uniformed, formed a silhouette against the light on the bay and the mist on the distant hillside. As he stood there watching, the *Augusta* grew smaller and smaller, and then the clouds closed in and a drizzle descended, and he could see the *Augusta* no more. He went to his cabin.

What did the Argentia Conference portend?

In one sense, very little indeed. Roosevelt made no promises not already made, revealed no plans not already known, made no statements not already professed. The Atlantic Charter was long on generalities, short on specifics, and to anyone who read it with eyes even half open, scarcely a shock.

In another sense, however, the Argentia Conference was of monumental significance, for Roosevelt, in private, was candid. "The President," Churchill later told the British Cabinet, ". . . said he would wage war, but not declare it [and] that he would become more and more provocative. . . ." "Everything," F. D. R. had said, "was being done to force an 'incident' that could lead to war." For the time was coming when F. D. R. could force an incident and get away with it: Japan's shortages were growing; Germany was losing the Atlantic; and Hitler's armies, as Hopkins reported to Roosevelt, were fast approaching stalemate in Russia.

■   ■   ■

Based in the Panama Canal Zone, General Frank Maxwell "Andy" Andrews—Andrews as in Andrews Air Force Base just outside Washington—was running the Caribbean. A West Point graduate, Andrews also had been one of the early hell-raising pilots. Back in the days before instrument flying, he had taken a biplane one soggy day to the army–navy game in Philadelphia, only to find no cloud openings through which he could coast for a landing. Furthermore, his radio sender had iced over, leaving him no way to report to the ground. So he just cruised in circles over Philadelphia listening to the broadcast of the game—and to news bulletins about his probable death—and then he landed outside the city. Andrews also broke three long-distance records set by Lindbergh—a point with undoubted appeal to Roosevelt.

Fifty-seven years old in August 1941, General Andrews was still trim, and he was Roosevelt's man. His responsibilities were substantial: arming Puerto Rico and the Canal Zone; developing U.S. airfields in British Guiana, St. Lucia, Antigua, and the Bahamas; and turning Trinidad into a main operating base for patrols, air pursuits, and long-range bombardments. In Trinidad, Andrews had a covey of B-17s, bombers capable of sweeping any invader, German or Japanese, from the Canal Zone, the old Spanish Main, the mouths of the Amazon, and the hump of Brazil.

Out in the Pacific, furthermore, on an atoll huddled inside a coral ring, a detachment of white-clad U.S. sailors went through a time-honored ceremony; this was just at the time of the Argentia Conference. Bugles blared, a flag ran up a pole, and sentries went on watch. The island was Midway; and the navy was setting to work furiously, sculpting out a harbor for use in time of war.

Midway's skipper was only a commander. The island's importance to the United States, however, in *Time*'s words, "was far out of proportion to the three stripes on its commander's shoulder boards. From Midway's dredged-out central lagoon (landing place for Pan Am clippers) the largest Navy seaplane tenders can mother a fleet of patrol bombers, ranging as far north as Japan itself." Lest anyone miss the point, *Time* carried a little map. From Midway to Tokyo, the diagram showed, was 2,625 nautical miles. If they could cross over to bases in China, the B-17s would be able to cover the distance.

Even farther out in the Pacific, Hubertus J. van Mook, appointed by Holland's Queen Wilhelmina as cabinet minister in Batavia, was using U.S. aid to strengthen the Indies. Hubertus van Mook was a big man, blond and burly, forty-six years old; he had studied economics at Stanford University. There, under the palm fronds and the red tile roofs, he had picked up American slang, and plenty of contacts. Back in the Indies he kept up those ties: Among his closest friends in 1941 was U.S. Consul General Walter A. Foote. Under van Mook's leadership, the Indies were facing Japan with an Anglo–Dutch–American defense line that, running from the Malay Peninsula and Singapore to Bali and the Celebes, covered nearly one-seventh of the earth's circumference.

■　■　■

Colonel Chennault and his crews of rowdies had reached the capital of Burma. Of his purpose in being there Chennault left no doubt at all.

On August 8, 1941, still in Burma, Chennault wrote the following epistle to Madame Chiang Kai-shek:

Excellency:—
Information received recently is that 24 bombers have been allotted to China for early delivery and that this number will be

increased to 66 by subsequent shipments. . . . In this connection the following plan is proposed.

1. Organization of a second American Volunteer Group to employ the medium speed, long range bomber.

2. Assignment of the high speed, short range bombers to a Chinese group.

The principal objective of the Second Volunteer Group to be Japanese factories and shipping at sea. . . .

Wearing mosquito boots, tropical shorts, and a shirt, Chennault had rendezvoused with the first group of his flyers on the docks of Rangoon. Despite scarcities of mechanics, parts, and planes— because of the great competition back in Washington for bombers, Chennault still did not have his promised twenty-four B-17s—the pilots went into training right away.

Back in Washington, on September 12, 1941, Henry L. Stimson, renowned throughout the capital for his aloofness, coolness, and imperturbability, practically shed tears of joy. He was in the White House, addressing the cabinet. He had just received wonderful news, he said: Nine B-17s had just arrived in Manila. Those bombers, he asserted, "completely changed the strategy of the Pacific and lets American power into the Islands in a way which it has not been able to do for twenty years." The president, Stimson wrote in his diary, "was impressed."

■ ■ ■

In Tokyo, Prince Konoye, the premier, was worried. His proposal for a summit with Roosevelt was dead and the hard-liners in the military were making a powerful argument: The only concession America would have accepted anyway was Japan's withdrawal from China, and that was unthinkable. With American economic sanctions in place and with American B-17s en route to the Pacific, Japan had only one choice. Japan had to strike—and to strike first.

Doubters existed in both the army and the navy, but by August 1941, the twin specters of oil starvation and firebombing had left the opposition in silence. By August 16, therefore, the navy was ready to present Konoye's cabinet with plans for "the naval aspects of the occupation of the Philippines, Malaya, the Netherlands East

Indies, Burma, and the South Pacific islands." And to keep America at bay until Japan could fortify these new possessions, the navy put its last touches on Admiral Yamamoto's Plan Z.

Training exercises for Plan Z were already under way. At the Saeki Air Base in Kyushu, the southernmost of Japan's four main islands, navy pilots were practicing carrier takeoffs and landings. At the nearby Tominaka Air Base, other pilots were working out the tactics of night attacks. At Kagoshima Bay, also in the south, more pilots still were learning to zoom over rooftops and chimneys, cut back on their speed, drop to low altitudes, and release torpedoes when their airplanes were nearly skimming the surface of the water. And at Mitsukue Bay, far to the north on Shikoku Island, young ensigns were exploring the details of how to steer midget submarines into a harbor shaped like Pearl.

Then, early in September, the navy's top brass gathered at the War College in Meguro, the Tokyo suburb, to try to solve an urgent fleet problem. Convening around a tabletop, three teams, representing the fleet that would go south, the fleet that would go east, and the American forces based in Hawaii, started moving miniature pieces around on a board. The southbound force encountered few problems, striking successfully at Manila, Hong Kong, Singapore, and Batavia. The eastbound flotilla, Yamamoto's flotilla, however, ran into trouble. One of the admirals at the table, Takahashi Ibo, had moved tiny mock U.S. naval patrol planes out of Pearl Harbor and, on the big chart of the Pacific, up toward Midway.

There they crossed the path of the oncoming carriers. Yamamoto's fleet on the table had been detected.

■ ■ ■

President Roosevelt had an incident to report.

He had gone by train to Hyde Park, for his mother died in September; and in his time of mourning he spent several days in seclusion. But on September 11, he went on the air for one of his fireside chats, and talked about a naval episode concerning the USS *Greer*.

Painted two tones of gray, the *Greer* was an old destroyer, of World War I vintage, and it had gone out from Boston and then Argentia on a mail run to Reykjavik. Nearing Iceland on September

4, 1941, *Greer* received word from a British patrol plane that a German submarine lay in its path. Under orders to track and locate any U-boats in the area, the *Greer* spent several hours on the search. It finally found the submarine and informed the British of the vessel's whereabouts. With the U-boat submerged, a Royal Air Force plane passed overhead and dropped depth charges. The U-boat responded by firing two torpedoes at the *Greer*.

Successfully dodging them, the *Greer* fired back with its own depth-charge attack. Then twilight came, and the submarine made its escape.

Wearing a black armband and seated beside a poster that said, "Keep 'Em Flying," the president spoke on the radio. Some 60 million Americans were listening. He said nothing about the sequence of events that had led the U-boat to fire. He framed the issue differently: "[I]t is now clear that Hitler has begun his campaign to control the seas by ruthless force," Roosevelt told his audience. ". . . There has now come a time when you and I must see the cold inexorable necessity of saying to these inhuman, unrestrained seekers of world conquest: 'You shall go no further' . . . When you see a rattlesnake poised to strike, you do not wait until he has struck before you crush him. . . ."

Driving through LaFollette, Tennessee, an impoverished Tennessee town near the Norris Dam, Samuel Rosenman, the Texas-born presidential speechwriter, was listening to Roosevelt on his car radio. "The atmosphere was quiet and peaceful down there . . . on that still September night," Roseman remembered. "It seemed so far away from the world of conflict and destruction, . . . that the bold, resolute—almost belligerent—tones of the President seemed a little like a voice coming from another planet."

"Let this warning be clear," that voice went on. "From now on, if German or Italian vessels of war enter the waters the protection of which is necessary for American defense, they do so at their own peril."

As in the later Gulf of Tonkin incident, a U.S. president had glossed over the facts of who had fired upon whom, and when. After his fireside chat, moreover, this president, Roosevelt, ordered the American navy to search for the German U-boat that had tried to torpedo the *Greer*. If found, the submarine was to be "eliminated"; American vessels were to "shoot on sight."

In London, Churchill was jubilant. "Hitler will have to choose between losing the Battle of the Atlantic," the prime minister wrote, "or coming into frequent collision with United States ships." In Berlin, Admiral Eric Räder warned the führer to expect offensive acts "at every encounter." "There is," Räder stated, "no longer any difference between British and American ships." In America, Senator C. Wayland Brooks, a Republican from Chicago, said: "You cannot shoot your way a little bit into war any more than you can go a little bit over Niagara Falls."

CHAPTER
23

A SECRET MAP

At lunchtime that day, President Roosevelt ate, as usual, from a tray placed on his desk; and between spoonfuls of cottage cheese, he put pencil to legal pad, revising and rerevising the speech he was scheduled to give that night. Dinner was late at the White House on the evening of October 27, 1941, and the president lingered with his guests, for he knew the dramatic value of keeping his other audience waiting. But eventually, with the help of Secret Service agents, he slipped away, put on a raincoat and a fedora, and had himself driven to the Mayflower Hotel.

The occasion there was the annual Navy Day dinner, and for Washingtonians it was *the* black tie event of the season. As limousines pulled up to the Connecticut Avenue entrance, their passengers dodging the rain as they scurried inside, just about anyone who was anyone seemed to be present: the navy brass, of course, but also General George C. Marshall and his wife, most of the cabinet members and their wives, and the Supreme Court justices and *their* wives. Notables chatted in the long corridor that led past the reception desk; dinner was served under the chandeliers in the ballroom. Patricia Grady, society reporter for the *Washington Post*, gushed. The "rustling of emerald velvet curtains behind the speakers' table . . . ," she wrote, "made Washington officialdom and society desert their after-dinner coffee to ask each other, 'Do you suppose he's coming, after all?' "

He came.

He arrived in tuxedo and black tie, and after the Marine Corps band had played "Hail to the Chief," he took a chair at the dais. For a few moments he chatted with his neighbors. Then William P. Donovan, toastmaster for the evening, rose to introduce the president. Roosevelt moved to the lectern. In the ballroom before him, American flags hung from every wall; from second-tier boxes miniature lifesavers labeled "U.S. Navy" were suspended. Roosevelt let his audience hush. Then he began, speaking into the microphones of all the national networks.

He promised that convoys for Britain were going to get through no matter what, and the guests in their formal wear clapped and cheered. Then he produced a shock.

"Hitler," Roosevelt stated, "has often protested that his plans for conquest do not extend across the Atlantic Ocean. I have in my possession a secret map, made in Germany by Hitler's government—by planners of the new world order. . . . It is a map of South America and a part of Central America as Hitler proposes to reorganize it."

As one could see from the map, Roosevelt continued, Hitler planned to reduce fourteen Latin American republics to "five vassal states . . . bringing the whole continent under [Nazi] domination."

This plot, Roosevelt held, threatened "our great lifeline, the Panama Canal." Hitler also, Roosevelt added, was scheming to have Nazism replace all the religions of the world, and the new Bible would be entitled *Mein Kampf*.

Then the president concluded: "[T]he map makes clear, my friends," he said, "the Nazi design, not only against South America but against the United States as well."

Certain reporters apparently smelled a rat. At a White House press conference the next morning, a journalist asked if he could see a copy of the map. Roosevelt refused permission. The map, he declared, "has on it certain manuscript notations, which if they were reproduced would in all probability disclose where the map came from." Disclosure, he appended, would also "dry up the source of future information."

But, another newsman pointed out, Berlin had already denounced the map as a forgery. How did the president respond to that charge?

Roosevelt tried to change the subject.

The reporter persisted: "Let me pursue my question. . . . What would you say to the charge of the suspicion that the map was—had been foisted on you in some way? That it was also a forgery or a fake of some sort?"

The map had come, Roosevelt stated at last, from "a source which is undoubtedly reliable. There is no question about that!"

. . .

There, publicly and in 1941, the suspicions about the authenticity of the secret map died away. But what was the truth? H. Montgomery Hyde, a former British intelligence agent, mentioned the map in a book called *Room 3603*; someone, Hyde claimed, had stolen the map from a German courier, and that courier had "met with an accident." And, in the 1976 bestseller, *A Man Called Intrepid*, author William Stevenson repeated Hyde's account, but added that the name of the German courier was Gottfried Sandstede. This Sandstede did die, but only later, on the Russian front in 1944, and not, as Hyde implied, in 1941.

Then, in 1985, in *The Wilson Quarterly*, a scholarly journal, two researchers, John F. Bratzel and Leslie B. Rout, Jr., exploded a bomb: They published the truth about Roosevelt's secret map. The map unquestionably existed; it is preserved in the holdings of the Roosevelt Library at Hyde Park, New York. It looks, furthermore, approximately the way Roosevelt described it in his address of October 27, 1941. It shows the continent of South America reduced to five countries: Brazil; Argentina, expanded to the north and possessing a corridor to the Pacific; Chile, even more elongated than before and, with the exception of the Argentinean corridor, occupying almost all the Pacific littoral; the three Guianas—Dutch, British, and French—united and granted to Vichy France; and "New Spain," meaning Venezuela, Colombia, Panama, and the Panama Canal Zone. The Falkland Islands went to Argentina. Lines on the map connect all the major cities; the map's title, translated from the German, is "Air Traffic Grid of the United States of South America's Main Lines."

As Roosevelt said in his press conference, furthermore, the map does show "manuscript notations." However, those notations, in German, only deal with the production, storage, and shipment of gas and oil. They say nothing that would have revealed "where the map came from."

So where *did* the map come from? How did it get into Roosevelt's hands? Was it authentic?

In March 1941, Lieutenant Colonel M. A. Devine, the U.S. military attaché in Argentina, sent one of his reports to Washington. On a wall of the headquarters of the Nazi party in Buenos Aires, he cabled, stood a huge map of Latin America. Colonel Devine may have seen the map. In any case, according to his report, the map in Buenos Aires gave the Falkland Islands, Uruguay, Paraguay, and part of Bolivia to Argentina; the rest of Bolivia plus French and Dutch Guiana to Brazil; British Guiana to Venezuela; Panama and the Canal Zone to Colombia; and Ecuador, split up, to Peru and Colombia.

The point of this map would have been unmistakable: If certain Latin American countries—Venezuela, Colombia, Peru, Brazil, and Argentina—supported German war aims, Germany would support those countries' traditional territorial aims. Certain Argentineans, at least, must have been interested. "At the appropriate time," Colonel Devine informed the U.S. War Department, "I had an opportunity of asking the assistant chief from military intelligence in the Argentine government if he had seen the map, and he replied in the affirmative, voicing no objection to the contemplated territorial adjustments."

So Roosevelt's map may have come, originally, from Buenos Aires, possibly from Nazi headquarters there. But even so, the map described by Colonel Devine differed from the map in Roosevelt's possession. Colonel Devine's showed nothing of the Guianas going to Vichy or of Chile elongated and pointed like a dagger toward Central and North America.

We do know how Roosevelt's version got to the White House. James R. Murphy, later a Washington lawyer but in 1941 a special assistant to William Donovan, the COI, hand-carried the map to 1600 Pennsylvania Avenue.

But how did Donovan get the map?

Did he invent it?

Did he doctor it?

Did he get it from the British?

Did the British purloin it from Buenos Aires and doctor it themselves?

Did they invent it?

No one knows; or, at least, no one dead or alive has ever told. Four points, nonetheless, are clear. First, no original version of Roosevelt's secret map has ever turned up. Second, in a September 5, 1941, memorandum to the secretary and undersecretary of state, Adolf Berle, Jr., warned that British intelligence was "manufacturing documents detailing Nazi conspiracies in South America." "I think," Berle stated, "we have to be a little on our guard against false scares." Third, on October 21, 1941, Donovan told Roosevelt that the British had made the map available. And fourth, Roosevelt's revelation of the map coincided with his fight to have Congress repeal the neutrality acts altogether.

By late October 1941, the president wanted to arm merchant ships and to have them protected by U.S. destroyers all the way to Great Britain and indeed to the Soviet Union, through Archangel, in northern Russia; but to do so he needed enabling legislation. He even had a new incident to bolster his case: On October 17, 1941, and thus about a month after F. D. R.'s shoot-on-sight order, the USS *Kearny*, a destroyer, had tracked and depth-charged a German submarine; the U-boat had retaliated, firing a torpedo that damaged the *Kearny* and killed eleven American seamen. Even so, the neutrality repeal bill had passed through the Senate Foreign Relations Committee, on October 25, by a margin of only thirteen to ten; and the floor fight in the House of Representatives promised to be close. Roosevelt needed ammunition—and Donovan sent it over.

Did Roosevelt lie about the map? If not, then *either* he was somebody's—Britain's or Donovan's—dupe, which is hard to imagine, *or*, wishing to distance himself from dirty deeds, he asked no questions. But Roosevelt himself may have resolved this dilemma. On May 14, 1942, he said to Treasury Secretary Henry Morgenthau: "I may have one policy for Europe and one diametrically opposite for North and South America. I may be entirely inconsistent, and furthermore, I am perfectly willing to mislead and tell untruths if it will help us win the war. . . ."

• • •

Roosevelt did get his total neutrality repeal, but barely—even after a U-boat off Ireland, on October 31, 1941, sank the destroyer USS *Reuben James*, with the loss of 115 American lives. The vote in both houses of Congress was close: the Senate as a whole by 50 to 37; the House of Representatives, on November 13, 1941, by 212 to 194. And a joke went around the corridors on Capitol Hill. A pilot and three foreigners—a German, a Greek, and an Englishman—were together aboard a faltering aircraft. The wings were icing badly, and when the pilot informed his passengers that he was losing altitude, the German saluted, said "Heil Hitler," and parachuted out. But the airplane was still in trouble, and, turning around, the pilot this time said that the load was too heavy. So the Englishman saluted, said "There'll always be an England," and threw the Greek out.

Question: What, for Roosevelt, was going wrong? Answer: his very success.

Images of unmistakable triumph and victory were already reaching the public eye. Leafing through the magazines and old newspapers is revealing. In the *New York Daily News*: a photograph of 114 cargo ships, all bound for Great Britain and all seeming to steam at once through the Verrazano Narrows. In *Time*: a photograph of antiaircraft guns in London and the caption, "Hot-bath and telephone services . . . nearly normal." In *U.S. News*: a photograph of an American-made bomber landing in Britain. In *Time*: a picture of a Russian village burning but also one of German units bogged down in snow and sleet. In *U.S. News*: a portrait of Colonel Donovan and an accompanying article about his plans, under way, for sabotage in Axis-conquered lands. In *Time*: in Long Island's Camp Upton, a photograph, taken through a barbed-wire fence, of a War Department "concentration camp"—empty for the moment but ready for occupancy by "enemy aliens." In the *St. Louis Post-Dispatch*: a cartoon of Hitler pacing before three looming figures in shrouds, one labeled "Failure to Smash Britain," the second "Failure of

Atlantic Blockade," and the third "Failure to Blitz Russia." And in *Time* again: a World Wide photograph of Hitler addressing troops near the Russian front and saying, "By the skin of our teeth we have escaped destruction."

At least he had escaped so far. But his war machine ran on oil, and even if his columns took the oil fields of the Caucasus, Germany had no tankers with which to transport the oil back to Europe, or to the ships in the Atlantic.

Hitler's problems at home, furthermore, had only magnified. As the nights grew longer, so did the attacks from the British Royal Air Force. On one night alone, 400 British aircraft bombed Mannheim, a half dozen other targets, and Berlin itself, in a raid more devastating than anything the Germans had been able to throw at Great Britain. A British naval force simultaneously sank an Italian convoy of seven ships crossing the Mediterranean to supply the desert forces of General Rommel.

And then there was Russia: The "cruel Russian winter fell equally on the opposing armies," a British historian has written, "but it was unequally felt. Stalin's troops were well-clad, skilled in winter warfare [they had, after all, gone through the Finnish campaign], with skis and equipment adapted to sub-zero temperatures; they were also fighting close to their industrial base. Not so Hitler's armies. . . . The retreating Russians had methodically wrecked the water towers, bridges, and railroad installations as well as the rolling stock. In consequence, the supply of [German] food, equipment, and ammunition to the entire eastern front suddenly choked to a halt. Instead of 17 supply trains a day, each [German] army on the Leningrad front was lucky to get one; instead of 18, Guderian's Second Panzer Army was getting only three."

The same British historian quoted one of the Germans who ended up on the eastern front: "In wave after wave of densely packed soldiers, the enemy offensive rolled across the snowscape toward us. Our machine guns hammered away at them without letup; you could not hear yourself speak. Like a dark and somber carpet a layer of dead and dying stretched across the snow in front of us, but still the masses of humanity came at us, closer and closer, seemingly inexhaustible. . . ." A German officer had used the key word: the Russian "offensive." And Hitler, at last, issued orders allowing German naval vessels to open fire on American ships.

■ ■ ■

The U.S. press reported a coup in Panama. Washington was acutely concerned about that country because, in 1940, Arnulfo Arias, a young politician who resembled and acted like Errol Flynn, won the presidency. He had also been Panama's envoy to Italy and, once in office back home, he gave vent to Fascist ideas and anti–United States feelings. Arias, the U.S. Embassy reported, "referred to the desirability of improving the nation's racial strains by selected immigration" and scorned "as biologically without justification the 'demagogic concept' that 'all men are born free and equal.' "

But Arias's days were numbered. In the third week of October 1941, only days before Roosevelt made his "secret map" speech, the second-ranking officer in the Panamanian National Guard approached U.S. Ambassador Edwin C. Wilson: Would Washington, Wilson was asked, look with favor on a coup? Under the Good Neighbor policy, the administration in Washington had promised to refrain from military intervention in countries like Panama. So all Wilson could say was that the United States would not stand in opposition—and the coup went ahead. The coup, said Henry Stimson, was "a great relief to us, because Arias had been very troublesome and very pro-Nazi." Added Adolf Berle, Jr., "I don't like revolutions on principle," but this one was "probably all to the good."

Had the United States instigated the coup? Perhaps not: "I state clearly and categorically for the record that the United States government has had no connection, direct or indirect," declared Secretary of State Hull, "with the recent governmental changes in Panama." Still, the coup was good for America: Arias had forbidden the arming of merchant ships under Panamanian registry, but the new government lifted the ban. The Panama Canal was safe again.

The coup against Arias, in fact, symbolized the progress the United States had made toward hemispheric solidarity: Mexico, Uruguay, and Brazil had agreed to allow U.S. bases on their soil (each, of course, demanding foreign aid in return); Brazil had forbidden the export of strategic materials to the Axis countries; and, in return for the promise of lend-lease funds, Bolivia, Cuba, the Dominican Republic, Haiti, Nicaragua, and Paraguay had become America's de facto allies. And to make sure it all stuck together, thirty-two-year-old Nelson Rockefeller, designated the coordinator of inter-American relations, put together a $100 million project of hospitals, housing, sanitation, water systems, transportation, and communications facilities, a veritable New Deal all over again, for Latin American countries—no matter how vicious their internal regimes—who were cooperative.

All this, by early November 1941, was plain to the attentive American public. Indeed, Roosevelt's efforts to secure a victory over the Axis powers had almost peaked too soon. So, with Congress manifestly losing interest in the war, Roosevelt had to regain the initiative. He found a new rationale for war, shifting his emphasis from freedom of the seas to freedom of the hemisphere—hence the secret map—but even *that* was barely enough. He needed a new incident.

■ ■ ■

Across the Pacific Ocean, Singapore had become a new hub of action. Location alone made Singapore important, for this port city, actually an island ninety miles above the equator, sat at the end of the Malay Peninsula; and with a rearming America clamoring for goods, Singapore had burgeoned as the world's greatest emporium for rubber and tin. Almost everything about Singapore bespoke this role: the train cars full of raw rubber and tin as they rolled in from the plantations to the north; the streets of Singapore as they led to the edge of the water, affording views of brown-sailed junks in Keppel Harbor; the conveyor belts of coolies as they loaded the freighters; the passenger liners at docks in the outer roads; the British air and naval base as it bristled and, supposedly, protected; and, facing the sea as the main street turned around the waterfront, the Raffles Hotel.

The Raffles Hotel was the very symbol of Singapore. Named for Sir Thomas Stamford Raffles, the British bureaucrat-buccaneer of the early 1800s, the hotel had been an imperial watering hole for nearly a century. Situated beside the greens and courts of the Singapore Cricket Club, the hotel, ornate and rambling, was flanked by its own lawns and palms; couples—whites only—could dance in the roofed-over veranda. Some people still danced. But now, in the autumn of 1941, the lobby was taken over by white and khaki uniforms, naval and military, and the insignia on those uniforms were American, Dutch, and British.

Formal talks among the Americans, Dutch, and British (the ABD powers) had begun in Singapore back in April 1941. Their intent, even then, was offensive. "Our object," stated the ABD Agreement of April 27, 1941, "is to defeat Germany and her allies, and hence in the Far East to maintain the position of the Associated Powers against Japanese attack, in order to sustain a long-term economic pressure against Japan until we are in a position to take the offensive."

A later ABD memorandum, stamped "Top Secret" and sent from Singapore on September 19 to General MacArthur in Manila, spelled out the meaning of "take the offensive." The document, preserved in the MacArthur Archives in Norfolk, Virginia, called on the ABD forces to:

. . . Create "subversive organizations in the China coast ports, and in French Indo-China. These must commence operation as soon as possible concentrating on propaganda, terrorism, and sabotage of Japanese communications and military installations. . . .

". . . Develop subversive organizations in Thailand. . . . Assassination of individual Japanese should also be considered.

". . . Reinforce the American garrison of the Philippines, particularly in air forces and submarines: and spread propaganda to emphasize our strength, the increasing weakness of Japan, and the fact that Hitler has no longer any hope of winning the war.

". . . Prepare to defeat Japan without suffering grievous loss ourselves. . . . We must base mobile forces as near to Japan as is practicable. To the north, within air range of her vitals, is Russia with air and submarine bases in the Vladivostok area. To the west there is China where air bases are already being prepared and stocked. . . . To the south there is Luzon in the Philippine Islands, within easy air range of Hainan, Formosa, and Canton, and extreme range of southern Japan. . . . [D]evelopment of further air bases is proceeding. . . . The American Pacific fleet is superior to the Japanese fleet and is especially strong in aircraft carriers."

The point of these various missions—the ABD memorandum lumped them together under the rubric "204 Mission"—was two-fold. First, the ABD powers intended to confine Japan "as nearly as possible to the defense of her main islands." Second, they proposed to "cut Japan off from all sea communications with China and the outside world by intensive action in the air and waters around Japan, and to destroy by air attack her war industries."

Two months before the Pearl Harbor attack, that is, the United States of America was party to a secret international agreement to firebomb Japan. Did the Japanese know? Or did they at least suspect, beyond a reasonable doubt?

■ ■ ■

The MAGIC intercepts were full of their fears. Pounding away on their cipher machines, Japanese agents reported such matters as the American shipment of airplanes and oil to Vladivostok, the inspection by a Soviet air mission of B-19 heavy bombers in Los Angeles, a British offer to the United States of use of the Singapore base, the arrival of Australian troops at Singapore (intended to "throw fears into the hearts of the Japanese"), and the American plans, starting in September 1941, to build fourteen new air bases in China.

Overt sources reinforced the covert sources. On October 31, 1941, *U.S. News* carried a two-page relief map, a view of the rim of the globe with Japan at the center, and with arrows, plus flying times, of bomber lanes to Tokyo: from Singapore, thirteen hours; from Dutch Harbor in Alaska, ten and three-quarters hours; from Chungking, eight hours; from Cavite in the Philippines, seven and a half hours; from Hong Kong, seven and a quarter hours; from Guam, recently fortified, six and a quarter hours; and from Vladivostok—should the Soviets give permission—one and three-quarters hours. These arrows and bombers in tiny outlines were colored red, as was a circle drawn around Honshu, the main island of Japan. Tokyo itself was marked with a red bull's-eye.

And behind the scenes in London and Washington, still more was going on. Churchill promised Roosevelt that Britain would send the *Prince of Wales* around Africa and Asia to Singapore. Roosevelt himself decided, on October 16, 1941, to step up plans for sending bombers to the Philippines. In this accelerated scheme, thirty bombers were to go by December 1, 1941; thirty more by January 1, 1942; and sixty-five by February 1, 1942. In this speeded-up arrangement, American air units in the Philippines were to have at their disposal, by March 1, 1942, 165 long-range bombers.

Then, on November 7, 1941, as Stimson recorded in his diary, Roosevelt raised the question in the cabinet of "whether the people would back us up in case we struck at Japan." The war secretary made no mention of the cabinet's response. He did say, however, that he was sure Roosevelt had "the big bombers in mind."

■   ■   ■

Toward evening on October 17, 1941, General and War Minister Tojo Hideki received an urgent telephone call. An official from the Imperial Palace was on the line: Tojo was to come at once for an audience with the emperor. Tojo set off right away, and in the press room of the War Ministry, questions began to buzz. Why had Tojo been summoned? Was he going to receive a reprimand? After all, he had been adamant about the need to keep troops in China. Or was he going to be made . . . ? No one knew. But the reporters were alert.

A news photograph, taken that night of October 17, 1941, showed Tojo, probably as he was leaving the War Ministry: His high uniform collar was buttoned and he had removed his military hat, holding it in his white-gloved right hand. He was almost wholly bald, and everything about his narrow-boned face—the plain horn-rimmed glasses, the sparse moustache, the press of his lips—suggested tightness. He had good reason to be tight. His visit to the palace should have taken no more than ten minutes, but he did not return to the War Ministry for more than an hour. When he did get back, he explained to colleagues that he had been consulting the gods at the Yasakuni Shrine, Japan's memorial to those lost in war. For General Tojo was now the prime minister of Japan.

Newsboys scurried through Tokyo's streets that night, lugging warm papers and shrilling "Extra! Extra!" Announcing the advent of Tojo, headlines spoke of the fall of Prime Minister Prince Konoye. People peered at the news in the dim light of the lampposts, then trudged on. The press in America raised alarms. Tojo, said *Time*, in its issue of November 3, 1941, "might be the raging snickersnee that the Japanese Army has been crying for. . . ." Secretary Hull did advise Roosevelt that Tojo was a moderate; but U.S. Army intelligence portrayed Tojo to General Marshall as "anti-foreign and highly nationalistic."

The truth about Tojo was more complicated than any of these estimates. Tojo's course was to prepare for war while pursuing peace or, as Ambassador Nomura put it, trying to wear two pairs of shoes at the same time. He had no intention of dishonoring the Japanese troops who had lost their lives in China, so any premature withdrawal from China was out of the question.

In a marathon meeting with the highest brass—the conference took place on November 1 and went on for seventeen straight hours—Tojo took up two conceivable schemes for staying at peace with America, Proposals A and B. Proposal A would be a promise to America that eventually, in two or five to twenty-five years, depending on (unspecified) circumstances, Japan could withdraw from China and, thereafter, from Indochina. Proposal B—to be proffered if the Americans rejected Proposal A—would trade peace in Southeast Asia (and would include a Japanese pullback from southern Vietnam) for Japanese access to the oil of the Indies. Neither proposal was popular with Tojo's ministers. The argument became so bitter, in fact, that the new cabinet nearly broke apart; and with regard to Proposal A, Tojo just gave up.

That left Proposal B—the putative deal over Southeast Asia. But one of the generals in the cabinet told Tojo to his face that Proposal B was only academic, that America had already decided on war and was preparing for it with a vengeance. Tojo largely agreed, but he was prepared to do just about anything—save withdraw from China. So at the end of the long meeting of November 1, 1941, and with his face gray from exhaustion, Prime Minister Tojo authorized what he believed he was compelled to authorize: The diplomats in Washington would lay Proposal B before the American government; the military in Japan would iron out the details of the Pearl Harbor attack.

On November 5, 1941, aboard the flagship *Nagato* in Saeki Bay, Admiral Yamamoto Isoroku received the following order:

> 1. In the interest of self-defense and survival, the Empire is due to open hostilities with the United States, Britain, and Holland in the first ten days of December. Preparations are to be completed for the various operations involved.
> 2. The commander in chief of the Combined Fleet [Yamamoto] is to carry out preparations for the operations under his command [the Pearl Harbor assault].

■ ■ ■

The warnings abounded.

On November 3, 1941, Ambassador Joseph Grew cabled Washington from Tokyo, stating that the Japanese had no intention of yielding in the face of American pressure. Washington, he cautioned, should underestimate neither Japan's "capacity to rush headlong into a suicidal struggle with the United States" nor her "obvious preparations to implement a program of war if her peace program fails." "Armed conflict," Grew predicted, "may come with dangerous and dramatic suddenness."

On September 24, 1941, a radio message, coded, went out from Tokyo to Honolulu:

> Strictly Secret
> Henceforth, we would like to have you make reports concerning vessels along the following lines insofar as possible.
> 1. The waters (of Pearl Harbor) are to be divided roughly into five sub-areas. . . . Area A. Waters between Ford Island and the Arsenal. Area B. Waters adjacent to the Island south and west of Ford Island. . . . Area C. East Loch. Area D. Middle Loch. Area E. West Loch and the communicating water routes.
> 2. With regard to warships and carriers, we would like to have you report on those at anchor, . . . tied up at wharves, buoys, and in docks. (Designate types and classes briefly. If

possible we would like to have you make mention of the fact
when there are two or more vessels alongside the same wharf.)

A supplemental radiogram, sent back from Honolulu on September
29, 1941, stated that the "following codes will be used hereafter to
designate the location of vessels . . . 1. Repair dock in Navy Yard
. . .; KS. 2. Navy dock in Navy Yard (the Ten Ten Pier); KT.
3. Moorings in the vicinity of Ford Island; FV. 4. Alongside Ford
Island; FG. . . ."

The "you" in question in the first radiogram was Nagao Kita, a
Japanese spy who had reached Honolulu on March 14, 1941, and
who had integrated himself into the city's Japanese colony. Kita may
not have realized it, but the messages he received and sent were
reaching the Washington desk of Colonel Rufus S. Bratton, chief of
the Far Eastern Section of U.S. Army Intelligence. Bratton found
the messages worrying: "Tokyo," he wrote in a memorandum he
sent upstairs, "directs special reports on ships in Pearl Harbor,
which is divided into five areas for the purpose of showing exact
locations." The brass paid little attention to this warning. Bratton,
nonetheless, was persistent. Buying himself a National Geographic
map of the Pacific and mounting it on a board on his wall, he
started placing pins in any location that, according to the MAGIC
intercepts, was likely as a site of attack. He stuck one of his pins
in Pearl Harbor.

■   ■   ■

Another Pearl Harbor warning came from Haan Kilsoo. Haan was
the Korean agent-lobbyist who had settled in Washington, struck
up an alliance there with the China lobby, and, back in the springtime, already passed one cautionary note to the State Department.
Now, on October 28, 1941, he repeated his message. Korean
sources inside Japan had let him know, he claimed, that the Japanese were planning to bomb Pearl Harbor.

In his high-ceilinged office in what is now the Old Executive
Office Building, a State Department official read Haan's new warning. "In evaluating information given by Mr. Haan," the official
wrote in a memorandum to the secretary of state, "we must take

into account the fact that Haan is a Korean, a bitter enemy of Japan, and a man who would like to see war between the United States and Japan. At the same time, the Koreans do have certain contacts in Japan, as do the Chinese, which enable them to get some information which no Americans or Europeans seem able to get. Mr. Haan has from time to time furnished our military intelligence with information which proved authentic and also of value. We cannot dismiss Haan or information given by him as being mere chaff, froth, or whole-cloth invention."

The memorandum recommended that the Roosevelt administration take Haan Kilsoo's Pearl Harbor warning with a high degree of seriousness. The author of the memorandum was the former professor, then number-three person in the U.S. State Department, and long-time intimate of Secretary of War Stimson, Stanley K. Hornbeck.

THE AMERICAN
ULTIMATUM

By the time of Roosevelt's reelection, the Atlantic seaboard had taken on the look of a war zone. All the great ports were jammed with freighters taking on crates; and on some of the ships, fighters and bombers, missing their wings but still too large for the holds, stood fully in view on the decks. Most of those planes were bound for Britain, but some were en route to Russia, and a few were destined for Asia—for the bombing of Japan.

Completing its mid-November 1941 run from Honolulu and the Pacific, the Pan American clipper put down through the Golden Gate, where the promontories bristled with guns, and pulled up to its berth at San Francisco's Embarcadero. After the passenger door had opened, a small and compact Japanese emerged, wearing a homburg and a Chesterfield coat. He was Dr. Kurusu Saburo, special envoy from the government in Tokyo; and in his possession he had a copy of Premier Tojo's peace overture to America, Proposal B.

Kurusu spoke English passably well, for he had served in the consular service in Chicago and there had married an American woman, Alice Little. Back in the States now, he gave a press conference, standing on the seaplane pier with Nob Hill in the background. "The people of Japan and the United States should take peace for granted . . . ," he said. "I fully realize the difficulty of my task, making a tight scrum [an aide hastily explained to the American reporters that "scrum" was a term from British rugby], I wish I could break through the line and make a touchdown."

"There are many people," he added, "who want to bring our two countries into war for their own advantage."

"Do you mean Germany and Italy?" a reporter called out.

Appearing not to hear, Kurusu turned, strode away, and boarded a plane for Los Angeles.

Was Kurusu awed by what he saw from the air in California, on a route designed for him by the U.S. government? He should have been. As his airplane coursed southward, down the San Joaquin valley with its seemingly infinite farmlands and oil derricks, he was seeing visible proof of the might of the United States of America. And when his plane put down at the Hollywood–Burbank airport, he had to have seen the huge Vega and Lockheed plants nearby, covering nearly 400 acres in the yellow-brown terrain. Standing in the fields just outside the factories, furthermore, were hundreds of military airplanes, in various stages of completion, fighters and seaplanes, and bombers that, even from Hawaii and Singapore, could reach across the ocean to Japan. From southern California, Kurusu flew via TWA to Albuquerque—onto a huge new U.S. Army air field—and from there to LaGuardia Field and down over Baltimore: From Baltimore, factories, including the giant Martin airplane plant, stretched in a continuous line through the dark piney woods all the way to Washington.

At Washington's new airport, straight south of the White House on the Potomac's south bank, one American official alone, Joseph Ballantine, was on hand to welcome Kurusu. Kurusu spoke no more of touchdowns. "Finishing my long and strenuous trip . . . ," he said, "I still feel I have a . . . chance for the success of my mission. . . ."

■   ■   ■

That chance was slim to none.

Although Dr. Kurusu could hardly have known it, Colonel Donovan in the Apex Building had had his underlings locate uranium sources in China: Deposits in Hunan and Kiangsi provinces were to be controlled by America and not by Japan. And on November 17, Ralph Cory, a former U.S. consular official who had served in Peking, Seoul, Tokyo, and Nagasaki, and who now worked under Donovan, proposed COI-sponsored sabotage in the Japanese colony of Korea. Wrote Cory: "Sabotage activities directed at military, industrial, and communications objectives would effectively hamper the movement of Japanese military personnel and material and would prove to be most helpful in inspiring Koreans to undertake such activities themselves." Among the Korean sites Cory targeted for sabotage was Konan, where the Japanese were working away feverishly at their atomic bomb research.

Dr. Kurusu also had no way of knowing that U.S. intelligence had read a message from Tokyo to the embassy in Washington: "[W]e have decided," the Japanese Foreign Office stated, "to gamble once more on the continuance of the parleys [referring to Kurusu's joining Nomura for the talks with Hull], but this is our last effort. . . ." Nor would Dr. Kurusu have known of the memorandum submitted by Admiral Stark and General Marshall to President Roosevelt on November 5, 1941: "At the present time," the memo said, "the United States Fleet in the Pacific is inferior to the Japanese Fleet and cannot undertake an unlimited strategic offensive in the Western Pacific. . . . [But] the U.S. Army air forces will have reached . . . projected strength by February or March, 1942. The potency of this threat will have then increased to a point where it might well be a deciding factor in deterring Japan in operations in the areas south and west of the Pacific." Stark and Marshall recommended going to war against Japan only if Japan struck first, at the Philippines, Singapore, or the Indies. But they *did* suggest "[t]hat aid to the American Volunteer Group be continued and accelerated. . . ."

Dr. Kurusu, however, would certainly have read press clippings kept in the yellowstone Japanese embassy on Massachusetts Avenue. In its edition of November 21, 1941, *U.S. News* held that "plans for a short war have been made . . . (in Washington)." *Time*, on November 17, carried a cover story about Reuben Harris, the San Diego–based builder of the new B-24s, the so-called Liberators. The biggest bombers yet, and with a range of at least 5,200 miles, these giants already, said *Time*, were being ferried "to the Dutch in the Netherlands East Indies."

And Kurusu could scarcely have missed Arthur Krock's article in the November 19, 1941, *New York Times* and the headline, "NEW AIR POWER GIVES [PHILIPPINE] ISLANDS OFFENSIVE STRENGTH, CHANGING STRATEGY IN PACIFIC." Indeed, the *Times* piece may have been aimed at Kurusu.

. . .

Inside the War Department Building in Washington, a press conference extraordinaire had taken place. On the morning of Saturday, November 14, 1941—three weeks and one day before the Pearl Harbor attack—General George C. Marshall called the leading Washington correspondents into his office and, while pledging them to secrecy, said: "We are preparing an offensive war against Japan."

"For two months," Marshall explained, "we have been moving troops and planes into the Philippines, and the movements are continuing. MacArthur has been unloading at night, no one has been allowed to approach the docks or other key points. How he has done it, I don't know, but so far there hasn't been a leak. We have also been sending our Flying Fortresses, via Hawaii, Midway, Wake, New Britain [a Pacific island just east of New Guinea], and Port Darwin, Australia. We now have thirty-five Flying Fortresses in the Philippines—the greatest concentration of bomber strength in the world. The Japs think we have only a few. We are sending more as rapidly as we can get them and train crews. . . ."

This quotation comes straight from a *Newsweek* transcript, preserved in the archives of the Marshall Foundation in Lexington, Virginia. In an interoffice memo marked "restricted," Robert Sherrod, a reporter with *Time*, recorded essentially the same words. And on September 21, 1949, Marshall himself wrote Hanson Baldwin, military correspondent of *The New York Times*, saying that the above quotation, and what is to follow below, were "correct."

The "trip to the main Japanese centers and back is just a little bit too far for the B-17's," General Marshall went on. The Washington press corps must have been scribbling away frantically. "But they could fly from the Philippines, drop their loads, and continue to Vladivostok. At present we have no arrangement with the Russians, but if we get into war out there, we would expect to have an arrangement. Japanese cities are very vulnerable—and so are their naval bases. When we get the B-24's out there [the Liberators] they will be able to fly higher than any pursuit plane the Japanese have, and if the weather were suitable for precision bombing, would be able to play havoc with Japanese naval bases. We expect the Japanese navy to appreciate this factor, when they learn about it. Also, we might add, where bases are securely held, [we can] bomb from China. Indochina, of course, would be within easy reach. In addition to our bases in the Philippines, we have established fuel depots at Port Darwin and Rabaul [in New Britain], on the routes used by the Flying Fortresses and we are making arrangements at the Dutch airfields in the East Indies. We can also operate from Singapore. For shorter range we have medium bombers, including the old Martins, dive-bombers, and pursuit squadrons. *Our aim is to blanket the whole area with air power.*" (Emphasis added.)

"*Our own fleet, meanwhile,*" Marshall said, "*Will remain out of range of Japanese air power, at Hawaii.*" (Emphasis added.) "If you look at the globe, you will see that this is probably the only area in the world, except perhaps the eastern Mediterranean, which lends itself to this treatment. The navy has sent more submarines to Manila, but will keep most of its surface craft at greater distance."

The general had almost finished. "We believe we have in the Philippines sufficient troops to make an attack by the Japanese extremely hazardous," Marshall opined, "and by December 15, we will feel secure there. . . . The ships carrying . . . troops and supplies [to the Philippines] have been sent in convoys escorted by the navy. The shipping shortage has been a problem, but with the reinforcements en route—including special units from Panama—or scheduled to leave within a few days, we will be in very good shape by December 10. Our first interest in the Philippines is the defense of the airfields from which will radiate our striking power."

Marshall closed the press conference with a note of caution: The papers were, to be sure, to print nothing of what he had said. His message, rather, was "from the White House or the State Department directly to Japanese officials—presumably Kurusu." Confidentiality, Marshall repeated, was critical. If the Japanese "fanatics" got wind of what he had just told the press, they would "demand war immediately." But if no leaks occurred, Dr. Kurusu could go back home and "say to the Cabinet: 'Look here. These people really mean to bomb our cities, and they have equipment with which to do it. We'd better go slow.' " Thus, General Marshall finished, "war might be averted"—if the press just kept quiet.

Questions, however, arise. If General Marshall was so insistent on secrecy, why did he talk to the press at all? He was, after all, no fool. A possible answer: Various U.S. newspapers and magazines had been sniffing down the trail, putting together, and publishing, bits and pieces of the American military buildup against Japan. But why should Marshall have confirmed those suspicions? That George C. Marshall, dutiful staff officer that he was and always had been, would have made his remarks to the press without the prior approval of his commander in chief, President Franklin D. Roosevelt, is virtually inconceivable. Marshall simply *had* to have been carrying out presidential wishes. And when Roosevelt himself, in his own dealings with the press, wanted to keep a secret, he turned reporters away with quips or looks, or even implicit threats. Roosevelt, of course, did speak off the record; but he always did so with the intent of being able later to use reporters to his own advantage.

Conclusion?

Acting as Roosevelt's representative, General Marshall spoke to the press, quite likely in the full knowledge that *somebody* would leak his remarks.

"The changed condition [in the Far East and the Philippines]," Arthur Krock wrote in his *New York Times* article of November 19, 1941, ". . . is the consequence of two developments. . . . One is the naval alliance [of the United States] with Great Britain, joining for all practical purposes the fleets of the two nations in the Pacific. The other is the coming of age of aircraft in battle. . . . And there are two other lesser factors responsible for the change—prepared air positions in Alaska, making possible a pincer attack by air on Japan, and the extension of the Lend-Lease program to the Soviet, which opens up terminal and service points in Siberia for American fighting planes that have flown from Manila. . . . If the American commanders [of the Philippines] decided to 'defend' by attacking, there are enough bombing planes, and of sufficient strength, to drop bombs on Japan, land in Siberia, refuel, and rebomb and repeat the enterprise on a return trip to Manila."

Arthur Krock was a reporter-columnist of great importance with *The New York Times*; and the *Times* was the most authoritative newspaper in America. So why had the administration leaked the word to Krock?

Roosevelt may have wanted peace—his campaign speeches of 1940 might have been perfectly sincere—but he wanted something else still more: a return to the status quo ante, and, in the case of the Pacific, Japan's evacuation of China. But Japan gave no indication at all that it intended to evacuate China. Roosevelt, therefore, must have decided to force the issue. How? He did so in the time-honored way of statesmen. He issued, or he had Marshall issue, an ultimatum.

Roosevelt's ultimatum was not a technical one. He operated as always by indirection and, in any case, the issuance of a formal challenge would have made the United States seem the perpetrator of war. F. D. R.'s ultimatum, rather, was de facto, extended through a high-ranking bureaucrat and broadcast through the medium of the press. Why through the press rather than private diplomatic channels? With its attendant publicity, an announcement on the bulletin board of the American press made the ultimatum irrevocable. And why an ultimatum at all? Why the implicit threat that if Japan failed to stay out of Southeast Asia or get out of China, or both, the United States would firebomb Tokyo?

One answer seems reasonable. The time had come, the Roosevelt administration had decided, to impose a solution on the Far Eastern problem.

In his remarks to the Washington press corps, then, was General Marshall also trying to lure Japan into an attack on Pearl Harbor? His words—"Our own fleet, meanwhile, will remain out of range of Japanese air power at Hawaii"—reflecting as they did an assumption of Japanese inferiority, seem almost a taunt. They did not appear directly in the press. Arthur Krock, however, thought them significant enough to repeat them in paraphrase: "This new establishment in the [Philippine] islands would release the United States Fleet in the Pacific for heavy operations in conjunction with the British Fleet," he wrote. "That would create a naval force outnumbering the Japanese and capable of making an attack of its own."

The implication was clear. Japan's only salvation lay in taking out the United States Pacific fleet, wherever it lay.

■   ■   ■

Events now took on the quality of sleepwalking.

Thanksgiving, by presidential proclamation, came early in 1941, on November 21. In New York the Thanksgiving Day parade ended, as was customary, on the Thirty-fourth Street side of Macy's, near Seventh Avenue; and Dinah Shore sang "A Merry American Christmas" from a wooden grandstand. In all the U.S. military ships, training camps and forts, and far-flung outposts around the world, save in Iceland, American servicemen and women sat down to turkey dinners—the press highlighted this point.

In Washington the weather had turned so warm that people strolled through Lafayette Park without hats or coats. President and Mrs. Roosevelt, along with their son James and his wife, partook of dinner in the White House. According to the *Washington Post*, ever the gossip rag for the nation's capital, the Roosevelts dined from among "little clams with saltines, clear chicken consomme with whole wheat wafers, curled celery, stuffed olives, roast turkey with giblet gravy and chestnut dressing, cranberry sauce, sausage, cauliflower, beans, casserole of sweet potatoes with marshmallows, dinner rolls, green salad, cheese straws, pumpkin pie, ice cream with caramel sauce, and coffee," all thoroughly American, thoroughly traditional. One thing alone was untraditional about the president's Thanksgiving. Since going to the White House he had spent every Thanksgiving, except that of 1937, in Warm Springs, Georgia. This time he had elected to stay in Washington. Roosevelt was waiting.

Accompanied by Ambassador Nomura—a big man for a Japanese who wore his hair in an iron-gray crew cut—Dr. Kurusu had started to make almost daily treks to the State Department. Somber-looking in their dark suits, the two men would trudge along the marble corridors, enter the secretary's office at the corner of the building, sit in the leather armchairs that faced his desk, and go around and around in their diplomatic discussions without making any progress. Through what they gleaned from the press as well as through their espionage networks, the Japanese perceived America as tightening the encirclement to the vanishing point; through his reading of the MAGIC intercepts, Secretary Hull saw the Japanese as intending to attack Southeast Asia no matter what; so he had rejected even Proposal B. Dr. Kurusu kept talking but he, too, was waiting.

From down Pennsylvania Avenue in the Treasury Department, a midranking official named Harry Dexter White staged an intervention. White was a chunkily built economist from Harvard and very much the activist, believing Hull an old fuddy-duddy incapable of boldness. Apparently trying to break the Pacific deadlock, White banged out a long memorandum he entitled "An Approach to the Problem of Eliminating Tension with Japan and Helping Defeat of Germany." With bold strokes of his typewriter, White would have had the United States "withdraw the bulk of [its] naval forces from the Pacific . . . sign a 20-year non-aggression pact with Japan . . . promote a final settlement of the Manchurian question . . . [and] give up all extra-territorial rights in China. . . ." White also would have had Japan withdraw from China—but that was the joker in the deck. Japan was *not* going to withdraw from China and America was *not* going to withdraw from the Pacific; and that was that. White's memo went nowhere; and in his own corner office, Treasury Secretary Henry Morgenthau, Jr., was waiting.

Then Secretary of State Hull roused himself for a time. Bringing his Far Eastern advisers into his high-ceilinged office for a working Thanksgiving weekend, he covered his desk with various peace plans and from them culled what he termed a modus vivendi, a way of living together. The idea was that Japan and America might take one step together—and see if that one step might lead to a second. For example, Japan might withdraw from southern to northern Vietnam; America, on a month-to-month basis, would grant Japan access to low-grade petroleum products; and representatives from Japan and America would meet in Manila to discuss the future of China.

Would this proposal fly? Lord Halifax, whom Hull consulted, thought it might. But Churchill in London saw the idea as appeasement; and the *Prince of Wales*, in any case, was just then refueling in Capetown. And in Chungking, Chiang Kai-shek, who had been in touch with T. V. Soong, expressed outrage. Screaming "occidental treachery," he practically accused Hull of selling China down the river, a charge as potent on the American scene in 1941 as it was to be a decade later, during the Korean War and the rampage of Senator Joseph McCarthy. So Hull gave it up, deciding on the morning of Wednesday, November 26, 1941, to "kick the whole thing over"; in his conversation later that day with envoys Kurusu and Nomura, he withheld mention of any modus vivendi.

The day before Hull kicked it over, he, along with Stimson, Marshall, Knox, and Stark, had met with the president in the Oval Office. For an account of that meeting we have Henry Stimson's diary: "Then at 12 o'clock we (viz., General Marshall and I) went to the White House, where we were until nearly half past one. . . . There the President . . . brought up entirely the relations with the Japanese. He brought up the event that we were likely to be attacked perhaps (as soon as) next Monday, for the Japanese are notorious for making an attack without warning, and the question was what we should do. *The question was how we should maneuver them into the position of firing the first shot without allowing too much danger to ourselves* [emphasis added]."

One "problem troubled us very much." This was Stimson, testifying to an array of representatives and senators, seated before him in joint committee five years later. "If you know that your enemy is going to strike you, it is usually not wise to wait until he gets the jump on you by taking the initiative. In spite of the risk involved, however, in letting the Japanese fire the first shot, we realized that in order to have the full support of the American people it was desirable to make sure that the Japanese be the ones to do this so that there should remain no doubt in anyone's mind as to who were the aggressors."

The White House meeting to which Stimson referred took place on November 25. Two days later—one day, that is, after Hull had given up on the modus vivendi, the administration received a jolt:

A Japanese fleet, intelligence reports showed, was moving southward from Shanghai toward Singapore and the Indies. Now Secretary of War Stimson, too, was waiting.

■   ■   ■

Envoys Kurusu and Nomura received instructions from Tokyo to
keep the talks with Hull going until December 7, 1941. That meant
ten days to go.

November 28: As MAGIC showed, the Foreign Ministry in Tokyo
advised the consulates throughout America to take down their portraits of the emperor. Japan's espionage network in Honolulu
received these words: "Report upon the entrance or departure of
capital ships and the length of time they remain at anchor, from
the time of entry into the port until the departure."

November 29: "Say very secretly to [the Germans] that there is
an extreme danger that war may suddenly break out between the
Anglo-Saxon nations and Japan through some clash of arms," Tokyo
instructed its embassy in Berlin, in words read by the MAGIC
cryptographers, "and add the time of the breaking out of this war
may come quicker than anyone drams." "We have been receiving
reports from you on ship movements," Tokyo radioed its Honolulu
consulate, "but in future you will also report even when there are
no movements."

November 30: As MAGIC picked up, Tokyo ordered the destruction of all code machines aboard, save the one in the Washington
embassy.

December 1, 1941: Intercepted by MAGIC, coded messages
about ship moorings and movements at Pearl Harbor flashed out of
Honolulu toward Tokyo.

December 2: "In view of the present situation," came the
response from Tokyo,

> the presence in port of warships, airplane carriers, and cruisers
> is of utmost importance [emphasis added]. . . . Hereafter, to the
> utmost of your ability, let me know day by day. Wire me in
> each case whether there are any observation balloons above
> Pearl Harbor or if there are any indications that they will be

sent up. Also advise me whether or not the warships are provided with antimine nets.

Thus November passed into December. Each of these messages, along with the other MAGIC intercepts, was circulated to the secretary of the navy, the secretary of state, and the president of the United States.

One other person had access to similar messages—the coordinator of information, Colonel William J. Donovan. As Donovan's papers reveal, he had offered a $1 million bribe to Hans Thomsen, the blond and charming German chargé in Washington, trying to induce Thomsen to defect. Thomsen had refused. Yet he did do Donovan another favor, in return for what is unclear: He passed word to the COI that the Japanese were going to attack Pearl Harbor.

The account of Anthony Cave Brown, Donovan's biographer and author of *C: The Secret Life of Sir Stewart Menzies, Spymaster to Winston Churchill*, goes thus: "The sense was widespread that America had been led by a new Machiavelli. Yet nothing was proved even when, in 1980, Donovan's own papers were discovered, unedited and untouched since 1946 when they were consigned to a room under the ice-skating rink at Rockefeller Center in New York City. The file on Dr. Hans Thomsen, the German chargé d'affaires in Washington, the man to whom Donovan offered $1 million if he would desert his post and attempt the overthrow of Hitler, did show that Thomsen had warned that the Japanese intended to attack the United States at Pearl Harbor, and that he had passed that intelligence to Donovan." It is hard to believe that Donovan would not have told Roosevelt—Donovan was in the Oval Office several times in November and in early December, 1941.

CHAPTER
25

THIS WAS PEARL

They were often admitted to be "the ablest men in the nation and they were very up in the Defense Effort and the best was none too good for them," wrote Bruce Catton, later the famous historian of the American Civil War but, in 1941, a member of the Washington press corps; he was reporting on a dinner in Washington. "If, collectively," he went on, "they were neither as beautiful nor as terrible as any army with banners, individually they were very impressive. Their faces had that indefinable but unmistakable gloss which comes to faces that are photographed a great deal (good food, right living, and the proper kind of publicity can do much for a man) and if the North Lounge of the Carlton had been set aside for the party it was only fitting and proper."

These sleek men, about two dozen of them, including Donald Nelson, the host, William Knudsen, Floyd Odlum, Edward Stettinius, Jr., and Frank Knox, represented that intermingling of the high and the mighty, of the public and the private, that in our own time we call the military–industrial complex. Supposedly they were gathered together to honor Henry Wallace, the vice-president. Actually, they had met to hear Frank Knox. Bruce Catton called them the "War Lords of Washington." The evening was that of Thursday, December 4, 1941.

The paneled walls of the Carlton Hotel, Catton continued, "were lost in a haze of dim lights and cigar smoke. . . . After a time the men got around the long table for dinner. Dim light on the high

384

walls, ruddy faces over white shirt fronts, deft waiters serving from silver dishes, a sharp-visaged *maître* hovering unobtrusively in the background, a hum of talk dotted with occasional bursts of masculine laughter. . . . And finally the plates were taken away and the cigars were lighted, and Nelson got up to enfold the diners in the soft arms of after-dinner talk." Wallace spoke, and so did Knudsen and Stettinius. Then Frank Knox rose. He looked serious.

"I feel that I can speak very frankly, within these four walls," said the secretary of the navy. "I want you to know that our situation tonight is very serious—more serious, probably, than most of us realize. We are very close to war. War may begin in the Pacific at any moment. Literally, at any moment. It may even be beginning tonight, while we're sitting here, for all we know. We are that close to it."

Knox paused. Then he resumed.

"But I want you to know that no matter what happens, the United States Navy is ready! Every man is at his post, every ship is at its station. The navy is ready. Whatever happens, the navy is not going to be caught napping. . . ."

■   ■   ■

Only that morning, the *Chicago Daily Tribune* and the *Washington Times-Herald*, the *Tribune*'s subsidiary, had stunned the capital with a "scoop": "F.D.R.'S WAR PLANS!" the *Tribune*'s banner headline screamed. "A confidential report prepared by the joint Army and Navy high command by direction of President Roosevelt," the front-page article, datelined December 3, stated, "calls for American expeditionary forces aggregating 5,000,000 men for a final . . . offensive against Germany and her satellites." One "of the few existing copies of this astounding document . . . ," Colonel Robert McCormick's flagship newspaper stated, "became available to the *Tribune* today."

This plan, the *Tribune* alleged, "is a blueprint for total war on a scale unprecedented in at least two oceans and three continents, Europe, Africa, and Asia. . . . July 1, 1943, is fixed as the date for the beginning of the final supreme effort by American land forces to defeat the mighty German Army in Europe. In the meantime,

however, increasingly active participation is prescribed for the
United States, to consist of a gradual encirclement of Germany by
the establishment of military bases, an American air offensive
against Germany from bases in the British Isles and in the Near
East, and possible action by American expeditionary forces in Africa
and the Near East. . . . Against Japan the report recommends eventual 'strategic methods' consisting of a strong defense of Siberia
. . . ; a strong defense of Malaysia, an economic offensive through
blockade, a reduction of Japanese military power by air raids, and
a Chinese offensive against Japanese forces of occupation. . . . [T]he
report . . . calls for . . . strong naval offensives in the eastern Atlantic and the central and western Pacific Ocean. . . . The surface and
sub-surface vessels of the Axis must be swept from the seas, particularly in the Atlantic waters. . . . Overwhelming air supremacy must
be accomplished. . . . The economic and industrial life of Germany
must be rendered ineffective. . . . Popular support of the war effort
by the peoples of the Axis powers must be weakened, and their
confidence shattered by subversive activities, propaganda, depriva-
tion, and the destruction wrought."

According to the *Tribune*, the secret report also scorned the idea
that Roosevelt's main goal was the overthrow of Hitler. "It is
believed," the *Tribune* purported to quote, that "the overthrow of
the Nazi regime by action of the German people is unlikely in the
near future, and will not occur until Germany is upon the point of
military defeat. Even though a new regime were to be established,
it is not at all certain that such a regime would agree to peace terms
acceptable to the United States."

And on the same day that Donald Nelson and his fellow captains
of industry were dining amid the sumptuousness of the Carlton
Hotel, only a mile or so away, up on Capital Hill, all hell was
breaking loose. Waving a copy of the *Tribune*'s article from the well
of the House, Representative George H. Tinkham, a Republican
from Massachusetts, charged that Roosevelt had "betrayed the
American Republic"; Henry L. Stimson shot back from the War
Department, accusing the *Tribune* the next day of lacking "loyalty
and patriotism." Some members of Congress called for the president's impeachment; just about all of them were agape.

But was the *Tribune's* charge correct? Did F. D. R.'s war plan exist?

Yes.

On September 25, 1941, the Joint Board of the U.S. Army and Navy submitted a report to the White House, stating as America's military objectives the following points: (1) "preservation of . . . the integrity . . . of the Western Hemisphere"; (2) "prevention of the disruption of the British Empire"; (3) "prevention of further extension of Japanese territorial dominion"; (4) "eventual establishment in Europe and Asia of balances of power which will most nearly ensure political stability in those regions and the future security of the United States; and, so far as practicable, the establishment of regimes favorable to economic freedom and individual liberty."

To carry out these objectives, the Joint Board's report, the Victory Plan, called for 215 U.S. divisions, 2,500 naval vessels, and bombers with a "4,000 miles radius of action." Departing from the British strategic principle of encirclement, the Victory Plan declared that "we must prepare to fight Germany by actually coming to grips with and defeating her ground forces and definitely breaking her will to combat." As the wording of the Victory Plan makes clear, the Roosevelt administration had shifted from deterring the enemy to launching offensive war.

Even though Roosevelt did not formally approve the Victory Plan until the evening of December 7, 1941, evidence assembled in the postwar period shows that General Marshall and Admiral Stark, following Roosevelt's instructions, had produced a plan from which the *Tribune* quoted almost verbatim.

Who leaked the plan was, and is, unclear. American actions in the week before the Pearl Harbor attack, nonetheless, only confirmed the *Tribune's* allegations. A detachment of forty-six U.S. mechanics and trucking experts, *The New York Times* reported, was on its way to improve the workings of the Burma Road. New U.S. bombers reached Singapore—as had the *Prince of Wales* and another British battleship. The United States gained access to new bases in Australia. American tanks, lighter but faster than any German models, were now in the Libyan desert, doing battle against the columns of General Rommel. The United States acquired a major air base in Freetown, Liberia, allowing transport planes to reach Suez more easily.

Secretary Knox gave a press conference, on December 2, 1941, in which he stated that the U.S. Navy now had all but beaten the German submarine force in the Atlantic Ocean. And good news, for Washington, came in from the Russian front: Because of the cold, the lack of fuel, and the poor quality of available gasoline mixtures, Germany's mechanized divisions had come to a near standstill. The snowy birch forests were littered with the dark hulks of broken-down German tanks.

So Adolf Hitler was reaching the end. From 1939 onward, he sought diligently to avoid provoking America. But now his world had shattered; now he knew that war with the United States was inevitable.

■   ■   ■

Just as the *Chicago Tribune* was hitting the stands, a message of significance reached the Capitol. Out in Cheltenham, Maryland, a huge navy radio tower picked up a news broadcast from Tokyo. The broadcast included a weather report, and used the expression, "east wind, rain." Military Intelligence in Washington already had received from Elliot Thorpe, the U.S. Army attaché in the Dutch East Indies, a coded message to the effect that if a broadcast from Tokyo contained those words, the Japanese were going to attack the Hawaiian Islands. A transcript of these words then reached the Navy Building on Constitution Avenue.

At this point we enter a realm of confusion. During and after the war congressional investigations devoted tens of thousands of words to the question of what happened to the "winds" message after it reached the Navy Department. But to this question we have no definitive answer. The best we can say is that *somebody* received it.

■   ■   ■

Two days later, in Oahu, George W. Bicknell, a lieutenant colonel with army intelligence, received a telephone call from an acquaintance who was with the FBI; Robert L. Shivers, the agent, wanted to show him something "of great importance." Driving down frond-

lined Kamehameha Avenue, Bicknell reached the Dillingham Building in the center of Honolulu. In the FBI office there, Shivers
revealed the transcript of a telephone call between a Mrs. Moto-
kazu, whose husband was a Honolulu dentist, and the *Yomiuri
Shimbun*, the Tokyo newspaper. The conversation had taken place
the evening before and would have cost more than $200.

It went like this:

"(From Japan): Hello, is this Mori?"

"(From Honolulu): Hello, this is Mori."

"I am sorry to have troubled you. Thank you very much."

"Not at all."

"I received your telegram and was able to grasp the essential
points. I would like to have your impressions on the conditions you
are observing at present. Are airplanes flying daily?"

"Yes, lots of them fly around."

"Are they big planes?"

"Yes, they are quite big. . . ."

"What about searchlights?"

"Well, not much to talk about."

"Do they put searchlights on when planes fly about at night?"

"No. . . ."

"What is the climate there now?"

"These last few days have been very cold with occasional rainfall,
a phenomenon very rare in Hawaii. Today the wind is blowing very
strongly, a very unusual climate. . . ."

"Do you know anything about the United States fleet?"

"No, I don't know anything about the fleet. Since we try to avoid
talking about such matters, we do not know much about the fleet.
At any rate the fleet here seems small. . . ."

Something, obviously, was going on. It was 5:30 P.M., Hawaiian
time, December 5, 1941; rushing back to his car, Colonel Bicknell
headed out into the rush-hour traffic to report what he had been
shown to General Walter Short at Fort Shaftner.

■ ■ ■

"The rules do not apply here. The Navy Yard has been directed to
give you highest priority—anything you ask for within reason—with-

out paperwork of *any* kind. Of this you can rest absolutely assured; the president himself has directed it."

Unfolding a secret telegram, Commander Harry Slocum, an officer in the U.S. Asiatic Fleet headquarters on the Manila waterfront, ordered Kemp Tolley, then a young navy lieutenant, to take over and equip a motor-powered windjammer, the USS *Lanikai,* and to take it out to sea for a two-week cruise. The date was December 4, 1941; Tolley was to be ready to go within forty-eight hours.

On the morning of December 6, 1941, Tolley reported for last-minute orders. He received a sealed envelope—he was to open it only when he reached the open seas. Sailing toward the mouth of Manila Bay late that afternoon, he dropped anchor inside the entrance, waiting until sunrise to thread his way through the mine fields already laid. Topside, he wrote, "I watched the hundreds of lights twinkling in the clear air over the great fortress of Corregidor, 'The Rock', bulging huge and black nearby."

Underway again in the morning, Tolley checked his orders: He was to proceed, slowly, down the South China Sea toward Singapore. Under new orders, soon picked up on the radio, however, he changed course, making his way now toward the Indies. Why the change of orders? Tolley thought he knew. In a book published three decades later, *Cruise of the Lanikai,* he expressed the conviction that President Roosevelt had ordered the *Lanikai* directly into the path of the oncoming Japanese fleet.

The *Lanikai* had embarked on a suicide mission; when it was sunk, Roosevelt would have precisely the kind of incident he wanted with Japan. But then the *Lanikai* became irrelevant.

■　■　■

Clocks in Washington read 7:30 A.M., December 7, 1941; Colonel Rufus S. Bratton, in charge of Japanese affairs with U.S. Army intelligence, was at his desk in the Munitions Building. As the sun shone through the windows, he busied himself, reading the MAGIC intercepts that had come in overnight. By 9:00 A.M., he had received two more intercepts. One of these two was later called the "one o'clock message." "Will the [Japanese] ambassador please submit to the United States government (if possible to the secretary of state) our reply [indicating that further negotiations were fruitless] at 1 P.M. on the 7th, your time."

Stunned, Colonel Bratton said to a colleague, Colonel Thomas J. Betts, that "I tried to figure *where it would be dawn* when it was one o'clock in Washington. Then, without looking at a time-date chart of the Pacific, I guessed it would be about 2 A.M. the next day—or Monday—in Manila and 3 A.M. in Tokyo, but it would be *just about sunrise,* or 7:30 A.M., in Hawaii."

Bratton raced upstairs to the office of the chief of staff, General George C. Marshall. Marshall was not present. Calling the general's quarters at Fort Myer, Bratton learned that Marshall had gone out for his customary Sunday morning ride.

Ten o'clock had come. Conferring with generals Sherman Miles and Leonard T. Gerow, Bratton later testified, "we believed there was important significance in the time of delivery of the reply, 1 P.M., an indication that some military action would be undertaken by the Japanese at that time. We thought it probable that the Japanese line of action would be into Thailand but that it might be into any one or more of a number of areas. General Miles urged that the Philippines, Hawaii, Panama, and the West Coast be informed immediately. . . ."

At about 10:15 A.M., General Marshall returned to his Fort Myer lodging for a shower. Bratton reached him by telephone ten minutes later, saying that intelligence had received a "most important message" which Marshall should see at once.

Tearing out of Fort Myer in his stepson's red sportscar, Marshall raced through the Arlington National Cemetery and hurtled across the Potomac via the Memorial Bridge; at the other end of the bridge, a khaki-colored army sedan met him, whisking him past the Lincoln Memorial to the Munitions Building.

In the adjoining building, the navy also had sprung into action. Lieutenant Commander Alwin D. Kramer, a Japanese-language officer, had received the "one o'clock message," sent over from the army; working on a navigator's plotting circle, he too surmised that the Japanese were about to strike, somewhere. He reached Admiral Stark, who telephoned the White House—only to be told that the president was unavailable. Roosevelt was having his sinuses drained.

General Marshall was reading the same message. Picking up a pencil, he scrawled out his own message: "The Japanese are presenting at 1 P.M. Eastern Standard Time today what amounts to an ultimatum. Also they are under orders to destroy their code machine immediately. Just what significance the hour set may have we do not know, but be on alert accordingly." These words were to go to Panama, the West Coast, the Philippines, and Pearl Harbor. They did so, by Western Union. They arrived too late.

■ ■ ■

Just about every American of a certain age remembers precisely what he or she was doing when the news came through. Certainly no one would remember it better than the U.S. personnel stationed at Pearl Harbor on the morning of December 7, 1941. Indeed, no one in Hawaii could have been more shocked than Admiral Husband E. Kimmel, commander in chief of the U.S. Pacific Fleet. On the evening of December 6, 1941, in fact, he attended a dinner party that was as uneventful as the next day was eventful. Kimmel and his wife dined with several other naval couples at the Halekulani Hotel, an old establishment whose atmosphere was stuffy, conservative, and relaxing. The affair was so dull that two of the wives just walked away, heading for the bar.

Kimmel did not mind the dullness, for he had reached the point of bone-deep tiredness. Razor sharp and driving, he had been pushing himself and his staff to the limit, trying hard to assess the likely course of events. Intelligence reports had been disturbing. Any day now, Washington had been saying, Japan and America could be going to war: The Japanese, MAGIC had revealed, had been burning their codes and sending carriers into the Pacific. But into where in the Pacific? No one in Washington knew, or seemed to know.

As became clear later, Washington did know that at 1:00 P.M., Eastern Standard Time, December 7, 1941, the Japanese embassy on Massachusetts Avenue was going to destroy its code machine—but General Marshall notified Lieutenant General Walter Short at Oahu's Fort Shafter by commercial telegraph alone. And Washington had received word from Elliott R. Thorpe, the U.S. Army attaché in the Indies, that Dutch intelligence, having broken the Japanese naval code, was predicting the Pearl Harbor attack—but no one in Washington had passed the word to Kimmel.

Washington had even picked up Tokyo's December 2 request for information about observation balloons above Pearl Harbor and the location of warships around Ford Island. And Washington had recorded the response of the Japanese consulate in Honolulu to Tokyo. That response was dated December 6, 1941. It read:

> . . . At the present time there are no signs of barrage balloon equipment. In addition, it is difficult to imagine that they actually have any. However, even though they have actually made preparations, because they control the air over the water and land runways of the airports in the vicinity of Pearl Harbor, . . . there are limits to the balloon defense of Pearl Harbor. I imagine that in all probability there is considerable opportunity left to take advantage for a surprise attack against these places. . . .

And a *second* wireless message from Honolulu to Tokyo, *also* chronicled in MAGIC and *also* sent out on December 6, stated:

> . . . The following ships were observed at anchor on the 6th: 9 battleships, 3 light cruisers, 3 submarine tenders, 17 destroyers, and, in addition, there were 4 light cruisers, 2 destroyers lying at docks (the heavy cruisers and airplane carriers have all left). . . . It appears that no air reconnaissance is being conducted by the fleet air arm.

The U.S. Defense Department released the MAGIC transcripts in 1977; they were published by the U.S. Government Printing Office. Many of the intercepts were decoded and translated within the day of their receipt, and forwarded immediately to the secretaries of state, war, and navy, and to the president. In the volume that reprints the first of the above dispatches—the request for information from Tokyo—is a notation stating that this particular dispatch "was not translated until December 30, 1941." But with regard to the Honolulu responses, no such notations exist.

Kimmel apparently knew none of this. He must have heard that

on December 6, President Roosevelt had sent an appeal for peace—
on a gray, or virtually open, code—to the emperor of Japan. Admiral
Kimmel's chief concern, however, was with the safety of his base;
and since intelligence reports had the Japanese moving down into
Southeast Asia, he had dismissed his aides. Shortly after nightfall,
he had his chauffeur drive him and his wife to the Halekulani Hotel.
While Kimmel's party dined on the terrace near the big majagua
tree, the driver stayed in the staff car outside, slapping mosquitoes.
As he said to a passerby, it wasn't the bugs that were getting to
him. It was the boredom.

■ ■ ■

At that very moment, cruising along under the cover of darkness,
the flotilla of Japanese aircraft carriers was about 500 nautical miles
northwest of Hawaii, racing full throttle toward the island of Oahu.
In charge of the task force, Rear Admiral Nagumo Chuichi, although
maintaining radio silence himself, received welcome news from
Tokyo: With the exception of the heavy cruisers and the carriers,
the American fleet was riding at anchor, all snug and lined up in
the watery basin of Pearl Harbor.

■ ■ ■

Soon after three that morning and just a few miles south of Oahu,
the cloud cover parted and the moon started to glint. Scanning the
swells, Ensign R. C. McCloy, deck officer aboard the *Condor*, a
minesweeper returning to Pearl Harbor after its nightly rounds,
fixed his binoculars upon a peculiar object. At first he thought the
object, some fifty yards off port bow, might be a mine. Then he
changed his mind. The object looked more like a periscope. Sending
word to the USS *Ward*, a destroyer on patrol nearby, he reported
that the periscope, or whatever it was, seemed to be following the
Condor. The *Ward* drew close by, but found nothing. At 04:35, the
submarine net at the mouth of the harbor swung open, admitting
the *Condor*. McCloy checked again. Sure enough, the object was
coming in right through the gap.

■ ■ ■

Dawn was now about an hour away; and aboard the Japanese aircraft carriers pilots were up and about, eating traditional red beans and rice, checking their mock-ups of Pearl Harbor, buckling on their flight helmets, and filing out along the decks toward their bombers. Around his neck, Fuchida Mitsuo, designated as the lead pilot, slung a white sash, a gift from the crew; then he hoisted himself up into his cockpit. Just after six in the morning, he gunned his motor. Taxiing down the carrier's runway, amidst roars of applause, he took off. The ship was short and his bomber dipped almost to the tops of the waves. Gradually, however, he straightened out, rose, turned, and soared up toward the clouds.

He glanced far off to the east. There he saw the first orange streaks of the sun.

∎ ∎ ∎

At the U.S. Army's Opana radar station, by Kahuku Point on the northern tip of Oahu, the servicemen on duty were ready for breakfast. Even for a Sunday morning, their watch had been desultory. During that 04:00 to 07:00 shift, even on weekends, spotters usually would have noticed a dozen or more airplanes on the screen and would have occupied themselves by identifying the aircraft and plotting out the probable routes. On this morning, December 7, 1941, however, they had seen scarcely a thing. Just before seven, to be sure, the screen had flickered—two small aircraft were coming in from the north—but it had shown nothing else. The clock in the radar room pointed to seven, and most of the men left for the mess hall.

Two army privates, George Elliott, Jr., and Joseph Lockard, stayed behind. Elliott was at the controls of the radar. Noticing a sudden formation on the oscilloscope, he motioned for Lockard to come have a look. The two young men peered at the screen. So many blips were showing up that, for a moment, they thought the machine must be broken. Broken it was not. Elliott and Lockard were looking at airplanes, they quickly realized; about fifty planes in some kind of formation. Scurrying to the plotting board, Elliott calculated that the airplanes were 132 miles away.

At this point the clock showed two minutes past seven. Elliott turned back toward Lockard, saying that they ought to call the army telephone exchange at Fort Shafter. Lockard hesitated: The switchboard down there, he thought, might be closed for the weekend. Elliott, however, persisted, and Lockard finally consented.

By this point, as the screen showed, the airplanes had drawn twenty-five miles closer. Elliott worked the telephone, trying to persuade the switchboard operator at Shafter to get in touch with someone, anyone, who might be on duty. After several minutes, a Lieutenant Tyler came on the line.

By now, the airplanes were about ninety miles from Oahu. Tyler, obviously, had just gotten out of bed.

Elliott spoke to Tyler, trying to get through, trying to describe the situation. Lockard got on the phone, saying that the blips were the biggest radar sightings he had ever seen. Did Tyler, Lockard asked, know what was going on?

Tyler did his best. He had just been listening to some Hawaiian music on the radio, and he was remembering how, once, some pilot had told him that that station was supposed to play Hawaiian music as a beam for B-17s that would be flying in from the mainland. So all those blips on the radar screen must be B-17s, the Flying Fortresses, Tyler guessed. Anyway, he said as he hung up, "Don't worry about it."

■ ■ ■

Just as Tyler was speaking, Fuchida Mitsuo, in the lead Japanese bomber, also was tuning in to the Hawaiian music station. The radio's beam, in fact, enabled him to calibrate his airplane's position. Only thirty-five miles off Oahu now, he adjusted his course ever so slightly—and the armada of airplanes behind him did the same.

The clouds below him were thick. Would they be, Fuchida wondered, all the way to Pearl Harbor? Could bombing be accurate in such weather? The closer he flew toward Oahu, the more convinced he became that his mission was bound to fail.

Then the Honolulu radio station, the radio station with all the Hawaiian music, broke in with a bulletin. Fuchida's English was poor. He was able, nonetheless, to make out a few phrases: ". . . partly cloudy . . . mostly over the mountains . . . ceiling 3,500 feet . . .

visibility good. . . ." Fuchida glanced down again. The clouds were beginning to thin and to reveal a white line of surf washing against the jagged green of the shore. Fuchida's bomber droned onward. Now he could make out the fronds of the palm trees and the pink of the roof tiles and then, far off to his left, he saw the shimmering blue-gray of his target, Pearl Harbor. Down there before him were the hulks of the great battleships, strung out in parallel rows. Even from his cockpit, Fuchida could tell which ship was which: *Tennessee, West Virginia, Arizona*.

Yet he was still in agony. Had the Americans caught on to what was happening? Were they alerted, awake, waiting for his plane? Were they tracking him in their sights, readying themselves to fire, even now, even as he was beginning his descent toward the glinting and silvery water of the Hawaiian harbor called Pearl?

■ ■ ■

In the harbor below, the ceremony of the morning was about to start. The ritual never changed. At 07:55, a blue prep flag would ascend the pole on the signal tower atop the navy's huge watering tank; then every U.S. naval vessel in the harbor would raise the Stars and Stripes; and, finally, bands aboard the larger ships would strike up the national anthem.

At six or seven minutes before eight in the morning, therefore, boatswains and buglers approached their appointed stations. The blue prep flags rose to the top of its mast, and then it came down again. Throughout the harbor other flags began to flutter in the clear air of the morning. Musicians put reeds and mouthpieces to their lips. Then, aboard the battleship *Arizona*, one of the brass players noticed some specks in the sky.

Others, too, noticed those specks, and realized that they were airplanes, somebody's airplanes, nosing straight down toward the harbor. A quartermaster aboard the destroyer *Helm* gave the approaching aircraft a wave. A pharmacist's mate on the battleship *California* heard someone say that maybe the Russians had a carrier nearby—the oncoming airplanes seemed to have red markings. A signalman on the *Helena* started to trace the paths of the airplanes through his binoculars. Something about the way they were gliding perked his interest; it seemed so familiar.

It was familiar, all right. All too familiar. Four years before, that signalman had been on duty in Shanghai, serving aboard the U.S.S. *Augusta*; in Shanghai, he had witnessed the Japanese attacks against the skyline of the city. He had noted then the way the Japanese pilots had dropped their bombs—as they approached their targets they would glide, glide, glide, then dive. These planes, too, these planes with the red markings painted on the sides of their fuselages, these planes too were gliding, gliding, gliding over the very docks of Pearl Harbor; and now they were diving.

EPILOGUE

S o we turn at last to questions.

Did the United States enter the war just because of Pearl Harbor? No. America was in a naval war with Germany from the middle of 1941 on and in an economic war with Japan from even earlier; and America's plans to firebomb Japan no later than early 1942 were an open secret.

Did Roosevelt have advance knowledge of the Pearl Harbor attack? Possibly. The following are hard facts:

• Early in 1941, Ambassador Joseph C. Grew warned the State Department by cable that a Pearl Harbor attack was impending.

• Twice in 1941, once in March and once in October, Haan Kilsoo, the Korean agent-lobbyist, passed the same warning along to the State Department.

• In October 1941, the State Department's Stanley K. Hornbeck urged the administration to take Haan's warning seriously.

• On December 6, 1941, MAGIC cryptanalysts picked up Tokyo's request for the specific location of ships in Pearl Harbor.

• On the same day, MAGIC overheard the response from Japanese agents in Honolulu—the response that listed the battleships' locations.

• William Donovan, coordinator of information, had advance warning of the attack.

• Donovan did visit Roosevelt frequently.

The question of F. D. R.'s own knowledge, therefore, is open.

Did the United States provoke Germany into its declaration of war and Japan into its Pearl Harbor attack? Yes.

• Despite the neutrality acts, the United States had *not* been neutral. It was giving support to the Chinese, the British, the Soviets, and others from well before Pearl Harbor.

• Speaking in public, President Roosevelt had invoked the word "victory"; and the Axis powers could scarcely have missed the leak of the Victory Plan.

• By mid-1941, U.S. war production was soon to be outpacing those of Germany and Japan. [Published figures alone are revealing. In World War I, America spent $13 billion on the military. Such spending plummeted after that, and in 1938 was just over $1 billion. Then the curve turned upward, higher and higher: 1939, $3.3 billion; 1940, $8.8 billion; 1941, with lend-lease, *another* $7 billion. At this time, in March 1941, the Commerce Department estimated that Japan was spending $1.7 billion and Germany $23 billion for warfare. But then, in July, Budget Director H. D. Smith predicted that U.S. war spending would rise by $1 billion a month (so that in two months, the United States would equal Japan's *annual* military spending); and in September, the Office of Production Management projected an armaments program of $66 billion a year, more than twice that of Japan and Germany together. (*The New York Times,* March 9, March 23, and July 6, 1941.)]

• Chennault's American Volunteer Group, the embargoes against Japan, the buildup of the Burma Road, the "shoot at sight" order, lend-lease, the de facto ultimatum to Japan, and the sailing of the Lanikai were all provocative acts. And the Japanese certainly knew it.

At the later Tokyo War Crime Trial, General Tojo Hideki stated: "To adopt a policy of patience and perseverance under such impediment [the American pressure] was tantamount to self-annihilation of our nation. Rather than await extinction, it was better to face death by breaking through the encircling ring and find a way for existence." Here was no mere deterrence; here was deterrence that amounted to provocation.

Was the provocation deliberate? Three times, twice to Lord Halifax and once to Prime Minister Churchill, Roosevelt intimated that he was trying to force "an incident" that would lead America more deeply into the fray. He may have hated war, but he presided over policies that came to be indistinguishable from incitements to war.

■   ■   ■

The real question is not *whether* Roosevelt provoked a war but rather *why* he did. We must start with some negatives.

Roosevelt did *not* enter the war to save the Jews, the Chinese, or the British: His administration blocked substantial immigration of refugees from the holocaust; F. D. R. long resisted breaking off trade relations with the Reich; and the massive U.S. buildup in the Atlantic and the Pacific came about *after*, as the White House saw it, the Chinese, the British, and the Russians could stalemate the enemy. Furthermore, Roosevelt did *not* enter the war to save democracy: He consorted with all manner of characters, Nicaragua's Somoza, Spain's Franco, France's Pétain, China's Chiang, and Russia's Stalin, all of them knaves and none of them democrats.

And Roosevelt did *not* lead us to war because of a clear and present danger to the security of the United States. With the decline of Britain's power in China, with the fall of France in 1940, and with atomic bomb programs in Germany and Japan, the world must have seemed turned upside down. *By early 1941, however, and increasingly so in the course of the year, any danger, real or imaginary, to America was receding.*

America's own atomic bomb program, the Manhattan Project, was rushing ahead and could have continued without America actually fighting; Roosevelt, through foreign aid or bribes—whichever term one prefers—had safeguarded the Americas against Axis penetration (despite F. D. R.'s lurid portrayals of one Latin domino knocking over another); the Japanese were mired down in China; the Germans were bogging down in Russia and, simultaneously, slipping behind in the war of the Atlantic; and America was surging forth with the development of the most stupendous military machine in the history of the world.

Safe from invasion and even embarked on the road to victory, Roosevelt's America could have stopped. It could have accepted a stalemate. But, like the caissons of World War I, America just kept rolling along.

Why?

In part, surely, because in his drive for reelection in 1940, Roosevelt had the good sense, politically, to speak out of both sides of his mouth, promising peace while preparing for war. In part, just as surely, because the war preparations took on a life of their own, with promises of promotions, contracts, and federal spending. But in part, also, because President Franklin D. Roosevelt and a gathering coalition of interventionists around him—lobbyists, journalists, bureaucrats, ministers, and lawyers—saw themselves, and America, as engaged in a titanic struggle for the right to make the rules for the world.

■ ■ ■

We must examine the context.

To many Americans, as to Franklin D. Roosevelt himself, the world into which he was born, the world of the 1880s and the 1890s, had seemed to be a golden age. America was making money; Great Britain was ruling the seas; and, aside from squabbles on the periphery of one European empire or another, and the Spanish-American War, just about everyone seemed to be enjoying the peace.

The age, however, was more gilded than golden: The siege of Peking was like a thunderclap in a clear summer sky, partly because it was a harbinger of revolution and partly because its immediate aftermath was to illuminate Japan's imperial quest. With Russia crushed in the 1904–1905 war, Japan emerged, for Americans, as Pacific public enemy number one. Three presidents—Theodore Roosevelt, Taft, and Wilson—used treaties to restrain Japan. Japan erupted anyway—while the great powers of Europe were preoccupied with their civil war of 1914–1918, Japan placed its twenty-one demands on China.

For President Wilson Europe was of greater concern than Asia. Ever since its unification under Bismarck in the early 1870s, Germany, with its huge population, wealth, and might, had stood like a colossus over the center of Europe, fulfilling Great Britain's ancient nightmare—that of a rival power with the potential of dominating the resources of the Eurasian landmass.

Hoping to restore the balance in Europe—a balance that really meant Anglo-Saxon dominance—Wilson led America into World War I. Then he dictated, or largely dictated, the terms of the peace: rule by law; national self-determination; and a Germany shrunken but intact. For Wilson, the world was to operate by American rules; making the world "safe for democracy," his most famous utterance, was the necessary first step.

Far from repudiating Wilson's ideas, the next administration, that of Republican President Warren G. Harding, applied them to Asia. During World War I, the United States became the world's principal creditor; during the Washington Conference on the Limitation of Armaments of the early 1920s, Secretary of State Charles Evans Hughes used America's new wealth to good advantage, trading access to Wall Street for adherence to Wilsonian principles. Japan and America retained suspicions of each other; but as long as the great American money machine kept pumping out the greenbacks, Japan stuck by the Washington Conference system.

Until 1929. Then, with the stock market crash, the well went dry. Bereft of funds, the Japanese turned to the Asian mainland—and the Germans turned to Hitler—and, with America's Smoot-Hawley tariff, Britain and the Commonwealth turned to the imperial preference system. Even the Commonwealth was launching a trade war against America! As the new president, Franklin D. Roosevelt had as his overriding task that of leading the world back to stability.

He had to deal, of course, with the economic emergency at home. Even in 1933, however, he was safeguarding the flanks. Refraining from military intervention in Cuba, financing a huge steel plant in Brazil, tolerating the corruption and brutality of Anastasio Somoza in Nicaragua, pressuring oil companies into accepting, with what the companies deemed negligible compensation, Mexico's expropriations of their wells—all these the signs of the Good Neighbor policy—Roosevelt cemented much of the Western Hemisphere into an anti-Axis bloc.

F. D. R. also moved, early on, to contain Japan. He pressured

European bankers to shut off their loans to Tokyo; he persuaded Congress to grant China a $50 million credit for wheat, cotton, and airplanes; and, spending $238 million as "public works," he inaugurated a shipbuilding program that included two new aircraft carriers for use in the Pacific. Trying to box in Japan diplomatically, furthermore, F. D. R. in 1933 recognized the government of the Soviet Union. (Many of Roosevelt's political opponents, staunch anti-Communist Republican isolationists like Idaho's Senator William E. Borah, accepted the recognition of Russia, just as long as Russia and Japan were enemies: Borah's isolationism pertained to Europe, not to Asia.) Roosevelt for a time tried to steer a middle course: Japan was America's third-best customer. In 1937, with the *Panay* incident, he had the choice of withdrawing from Asia or running an arms race with Japan. He chose the latter course. One step then led to another until the Japanese saw fit to bomb Pearl Harbor.

■　■　■

But, once again, why did America enter the war?

Less than a decade after the Pearl Harbor attack, Theodore White, the journalist who had covered the war in China, was posted in Europe, now an observer of the Marshall Plan. The Marshall Plan, White wrote, "exposed me to the effect of legend on politics— or how myths controlled action. In my dispatches, I described . . . the memory of the Century of England, or the myth of the Golden Yesterday.

"The Golden Yesterday was a period of history which . . . . stretched from the last minuet of the Congress of Vienna in 1814, when the autocrats buried the memory of Napoleon, to the last waltz in London in 1914 [with the outbreak of World War I]. In that explorers' century, the entire globe was made one. Europe made it one—and England led Europe. . . . The stability of the pound, and the globe-girdling authority of the British Navy as it brought the heathen to accounting, set up a rhythm of economic progress never before matched. . . .

"This rhythm—memory or image—was the closest thing to doctrine in the Marshall Plan. . . . What guided [American officials] was the image of a world that educated Americans had learned about from teachers, from historians, from grandparents. They meant to restore it—though shorn of the grossness, the abuse, the extortions, and inhumanities of the 19th century." The vision of the Marshall Planners was that of America in England's place—only, of course, better.

President Franklin D. Roosevelt and those around him had the same vision in the months and years before Pearl Harbor. The Roosevelt administration, you sense, wanted to return to the status quo ante, to the world before the Great Depression, before the Great War, before the Russian Revolution, above all, to the world as it existed before the rise of Germany and Japan. Only with Germany and Japan removed from international affairs—indeed, only with America in Britain's place—would the golden age return.

But did it return? Or was the golden age simply a matter of American pride?

The poets of ancient Greece told the story of Sisyphus: Arrogant enough to assume a great burden, Sisyphus found himself condemned forever and ever to keep on assuming that burden. And so it was with America, for at least half a century after the entry into World War II. As the British had learned the century before in India—a lesson Americans were unwilling to learn then—and as the Japanese were learning, to their rue, in China, one extension of power only leads to another. America defeated Japan and Germany. But a new challenge arose, that of Russia and China; and the United States found itself with forces at point after point along the great arc of the globe that swept from the shores of the Baltic to the Sea of Japan. And other points along that arc were Korea, Vietnam, and Iraq.

NOTES

Prologue

ix–x. Based on *The New York Times* and the *Washington Post*, December 9, 1941.

x–xii. The scene and the Roosevelt speech from the *Washington Post*, December 9, 1941.

Chapter 1

3–6. Based on Peter Fleming, *The Siege at Peking*, pp. 60–66.

7. Yamamoto quotation from John Deane Potter, *Yamamoto: The Man Who Menaced America*, pp. 12–13.

8. T. R. quotation in Paul A. Varg, *The Making of a Myth: The U.S. and China, 1897–1912*, p. 83.

8. "Japanese mail was always . . . ," Herbert Croly, *Willard Straight*, p. 210; Straight's comment quoted in Akira Iriye, *Pacific Estrangement, 1847–1911*, p. 179.

8. The *Examiner*, quoted in Roger Daniels, *The Politics of Prejudice: The Anti-Japanese Movement in California and the Struggle for Japanese Exclusion*, pp. 70–71.

9. *Mainichi Shimbun* quoted in Robert A. Hart, *The Great White Fleet: Its Voyage Around the World, 1907–1908*, p. 32.

Chapter 2

10. F. D. R. quoted in Frank Freidel, *Franklin D. Roosevelt: The Apprenticeship*, 1957.

12. "Lansing moved up . . .": Ray Stannard Baker, *Woodrow Wilson: Life and Letters*, Vol. 5, p. 187; "economic campaign . . .": John W. Coogan, *The End of Neutrality: The U.S., Britain and Maritime Rights*, p. 193; counterblockade of Germany: Walter Karp, *The Politics of War*, p. 311.

14–15. On Hughes's speech: John Chalmers Vinson, *The Parchment Peace*, p. 123.

15. "intensely dramatic moment . . .": Merlo J. Pusey, *Charles Evans Hughes*, pp. 466–470.

16–17. ". . . the Japanese empire": quoted in Isaac Don Levine, *Mitchell: Pioneer of Air Power*, pp. 336–338.

17–18. The wedding scene: Emily Hahn, *The Soong Sisters*, pp. 139–143.

18. Quotations from *loc. cit.*

18–19. ". . . the cause of war": quoted in William L. Neuman, *America Encounters Japan: From Perry to MacArthur*, p. 177.

19–20. Weihaiwei description: *The Times*, September 29, 1930.

21. ". . . swords of ice": quoted in Elting E. Morison, *Turmoil and Tradition: A Study of the Life and Times of Henry L. Stimson*, p. 332.

21–22. ". . . of the Appalachians. . . .": W. B. Courtney, "Blueprint for Empire," *Collier's*, April 22, 1936.

22. ". . . no results": Carl Crow, "How Japan Slams the Door," *Saturday Evening Post*, May 7, 1936.

23. On Manchurian cities: Edgar Snow, "Japan Digs In," *Saturday Evening Post*, January 4, 1936.

23. On Japanese railways: Edgar Snow, "The Japanese Juggernaut Rolls On," *Saturday Evening Post*, May 9, 1936.

23–24. On secret agents: Edgar Snow, "The Coming Conflict in the Orient," *Saturday Evening Post*, June 6, 1936.

24. On the Chinese secret societies: Carl Glick and Hong Sheng-hua, *Swords of Silence: Chinese Secret Societies, Past and Present*, pp. 55–57.

25–26. Description of Hyde Park: Henry L. Stimson Diary, Vol. 25, pp. 92–96.

26. The two conversations with Roosevelt: *Ibid.*, Vol. 27, pp. 32–33; *ibid.*, Vol. 28, pp. 69–78.

27. Passage from Grew's diary: quoted in Waldo H. Heinrichs, Jr., *American Ambassador: Joseph C. Grew and the Development of the United States Diplomatic Tradition*, p. 326.

28. ". . . improve the world.": quoted in Arthur J. Marder, *Old Friends, New Enemies: The Royal Navy and the Imperial Japanese Navy*, pp. 23–25.

28–29. Chiang Kai-shek's description: quoted in Robert Payne, *Chiang Kai-shek*, pp. 199–219.

30. Willard Price description: quoted in Edward Behr, *Hirohito: Behind the Myth*, pp. 158–159.

30. On the Marco Polo Bridge incident: David J. Lu, *From the Marco Polo Bridge to Pearl Harbor*, p. 16.

31. Palace Hotel scene: *Shanghai Times*, August 15, 1937; Vicki Baum, *Shanghai, '37*, p. 409.

32–33. The Reischauer death, *The New York Times*, September 12, 1937.

Chapter 3

34–35. Carlson's description: Evans Fordyce Carlson, *Twin Stars of China*, pp. 1–2.

35. ". . . bosom of the family": Franklin D. Roosevelt Library, President's Secretary's File (P.S.F.)

36. ". . . at the pier.": *The New York Times*, August 21, 1937.

36. Yarnell's message: F. D. R. Library, P.S.F., Box 37.

37–38. Carlson's letter: F. D. R. Library, P.S.F.

38. McGinnis's report: *The New York Times,* August 19, 1937; Abend, *The New York Times,* August 20, 1937.

38–39. The White House meeting: *Washington Post,* August 17, 1937.

39. Hull's announcement: *The New York Times,* August 17, 1937.

40. Carlson's report: F. D. R. Library, President's Personal File (P.P.F.), Boxes 4929–4969.

41. Carlson's report: *ibid.*

41–42. F. D. R.'s western trip: James MacGregor Burns, *Roosevelt: the Lion and the Fox,* p. 317.

42. Bombing outside Shanghai: *The New York Times,* August 27, 1937; F. D. R. "seething": Harold Ickes, *Secret Diary,* p. 213.

42. McCormick description: based on Fred Friendly, *Minnesota Rag,* pp. 66–68.

42–43. For the speech and description, *The New York Times,* October 6, 1937.

43. F. D. R. and Grace Tully: Burns, *op. cit.,* p. 318.

43. Hyde Park press conference: *The New York Times,* October 7, 1937.

44. The Japanese reaction: F. D. R. Library: P.S.F., Box 30.

44. Mustard gas: *The New York Times,* October 9 and 11, 1937.

44–45. The October 13, 23, and 25, 1937, paragraphs: *The New York Times,* October 29, 1937.

45. The October 27, 1937, incident: *ibid;* the journalist's account in Dick Wilson, *When Tigers Fight,* p. 35.

47. Carlson to the White House: F. D. R. Library, P.P.F, Boxes 4929–4969.

Chapter 4

48. Shanghai scene: *Collier's,* November 10, 1937.

48. Battle description: Carlson, *ibid.*

48. ". . . act independently.": *The New York Times,* November 29, 1937; Gauss's protest, *The New York Times,* November 30, 1937.

49. Japanese in Shanghai: *The New York Times,* December 4, 1937; also *All About Shanghai,* p. 38.

49. The Suhu attack: *The New York Times,* December 6, 1937.

50. Dr. Blaber's report: *The New York Times,* December 2, 1937; the Hong Kong incident: *The New York Times,* December 12, 1937; the pipeline: *Time,* December 6, 1937.

50–51. Burma Road scene: Wanda Cornelius and Thayne Short, *Ding Hao: America's Air War in China, 1937–1945,* pp. 9, 10, 26.

51–53. Morgenthau: Joseph Alsop and Robert Kintner, "Henny Penny: Farmer at the Treasury," *Saturday Evening Post,* April 1, 1939. Morgenthau's intelligence network; *ibid.;* ". . . Chinese silver": John Morton Blum, *From the Morgenthau Diaries,* Vol. I, p. 479.

53. Quotation from Arthur N. Young, *China and the Helping Hand, 1937–1945,* p. 32.

53. Cable: F. D. R. Library, Official File, Boxes 1–2.

53–54. Roosevelt's comments: Blum, *op. cit.*, pp. 483–484.

54. Chennault on the runway: Cornelius and Short, *op. cit.*, pp. 84–86.

55. ". . . princess to me": quoted in Martha Byrd, *Chennault: Giving Wings to the Tiger*, p. 68.

55. Nanking scene: Cornelius and Short, *op. cit.*, p. 70.

55. Chennault diary: quoted in Byrd, *op. cit.*, p. 82.

Chapter 5

56–65. The chapter is based on: Dr. Essen M. Gale, "The Yangtze Patrol," *U.S. Naval Institute Proceedings*, March 1955; Manny T. Koginos, *The Panay Incident: Prelude to War*; Hamilton Darby Perry, *The Panay Incident: Prelude to Pearl Harbor*; Kemp Tolley, *Yangtze Patrol: The U.S. Navy in China*; F. D. R. Library, "Report of the Commanding Officer of the *Panay*"; Library of Congress, Manuscript Division, Harry E. Yarnell Papers, Box 13, "China Incident, Shanghai, China."

65–66. Hallett Abend account: *The New York Times*, December 18, 1937.

66. The Stimson letter: *The New York Times*, December 22, 1937.

66–67. F. D. R. to Ickes: Harold Ickes, *op. cit.*, pp. 272–275.

67. Norman Alley's flight: *The New York Times*, December 29 and 30, 1937.

67–68. The *Panay* newsreel: Movietone News Archive, University of South Carolina.

68. Movie theater scene: *The New York Times*, December 31, 1937.

68–69. The Ingersoll mission: Royal E. Ingersoll, Columbia University Oral History, pp. 70–71; Marder, *op. cit.*, p. 71.

Chapter 6

73–74. Roosevelt scene: drawn from James MacGregor Burns, *Roosevelt: The Soldier of Freedom*, pp. 61–63, and from the displays at Hyde Park.

74. F. D. R.'s style: Burns, *Soldier of Freedom*, p. 62.

74–75. The "munitions boom . . .": *The New York Times*, January 1, 1938.

75–76. Hugh Byas in Tokyo: Hugh Byas, *Government by Assassination*, pp. 17–18.

76. Hirohito: *The New York Times*, January 12, 1938; "annihilation": *ibid.*

77–78. Magee's account: *Reader's Digest*, "The Sack of Nanking," October 1938.

78–79. Atrocity accounts: quoted in Dick Wilson, *When Tigers Fight: The Story of the Sino-Japanese War*, pp. 74, 95, 96.

79. "By the middle of January . . .": H. J. Timperly, ed., *What War Means: The Japanese Terror in China, A Documentary Record*, pp. 35–36.

80–81. The *Tanaka Memorial*: William Fitch Morton, *Tanaka Giichi and Japan's China Policy*, pp. 205–214.

81. Guerrillas in China: *The New York Times*, January 13, 1938; Japanese air attacks in China, *The New York Times*, January 27, 1938.

82. Japanese "fishermen": *The New York Times*, January 22, 1938.
82. Japanese relations with Westerners: Irvine Anderson, *The Standard Vacuum Company and United States East Asia Policy, 1933–1941*, p. 110; slapping of Allison: *The New York Times*, January 28, 1938.
82–83. Nelson T. Johnson's cable: quoted in Michael Schaller, *The U.S. Crusade in China, 1938–1945*, p. 18.
83. The Yarnell cable: quoted in Stephen E. Pelz, *Race to Pearl Harbor: The Failure of the Second London Naval Conference and the Onset of World War II*, p. 199.
83–84. "Yarnell makes a lot of sense . . .": *loc. cit.;* "Now . . . a significant piece . . .": Drew Pearson and Robert S. Allen, "Washington Daily Merry-Go-Round," *Washington Herald*, November 26, 1938.
84. Leahy description: *Davenport* (Iowa) *Democrat*, May 10, 1938; "mystery fleet . . .": *New York World Telegram*, April 19, 1938.
85. The bill passed: quoted in the *Washington Star*, March 24, 1938.
85. The 1938 version of ORANGE: quoted in Louis Morton, "War Plan ORANGE: Evolution of a Strategy," *World Politics*, January 1959, pp. 247–248.

Chapter 7

87. The Hitler quotation: John Toland, *Adolf Hitler*, Vol. I, pp. 475–478.
87. The Ickes quotation: Harold Ickes, *op. cit.*, p. 321.
88. "We crossed the river . . .": W. H. Auden and Christopher Isherwood, *Journey to a War*, pp. 64–65.
88. "Madame now began . . .": *ibid.*, p. 65.
89. Isherwood's description: *ibid.*, p. 66.
90. Japanese vulnerability: *ibid.*, p. 70.
90–91. Carlson's report: U.S. Marine Corps Archives, Evans F. Carlson Papers, "Observations of the Sino-Japanese Armies During the Battle of Tai-er-chwang," Personal Papers, Box 1B45, folder P.C.; "It was nearing nine . . .": Evans Carlson, *Twin Stars*, p. 145.
91. "Everything seemed to be going . . ." : description and quotation from John Hunter Boyle, *China and Japan at War, 1937–1945*, pp. 138–139.
91. Springtime description: Auden and Isherwood, *op. cit.*, p. 252.
91–93. McClure's rendezvous: Munroe Scott, *McClure: The China Years*, pp. 239–242.
93–94. Dulles quotation: Henry L. Stimson Diary, April 26, 1938; trip to Woodley, *ibid.*, April 26, 1938.
94. Hornbeck description: Richard Dean Burns, "Stanley K. Hornbeck: The Diplomacy of the Open Door," in Richard Dean Burns and Edward M. Bennett, eds., *Diplomats in Crisis: United States-Chinese-Japanese Relations, 1919–1961*.
94. Hornbeck's answers: Stimson Diary, Vol. 28, p. 139.
95. Japanese tactics: Jack Belden, *Still Time To Die*, pp. 44–45.
96. The refugee columns: Dick Wilson, *op. cit.*, p. 98.
96. McClure's recollection: Monroe, *op. cit.*, p. 242.

96. Departure for Hsüchow: Dick Wilson, *op. cit.*, p. 106; the entry into the city: *ibid.*, p. 107.
97. Late in February . . .: *The New York Times*, February 22, 1938; early in March: *The New York Times*, March 4, 1938.
97. Early in April . . .: *The New York Times*, April 4, 1938.
97–98. In June, 1938 . . .: *The New York Times*, June 7, 1938.
99. Description of Hull: Dean Acheson, *Present at the Creation*, pp. 30–31.
99. "You must realize . . .": quoted in Ted Morgan, *FDR: A Biography*, p. 371.
100. For an account of the meeting; Jonathan G. Utley, *Going to War with Japan, 1937–1941*, p. 36; also: *United States Foreign Relations: Japan*, Vol. II, pp. 201–202.

Chapter 8

101. Scene based on *Toronto Globe and Mail*, August 19, 1938.
102–103. F. D. R.'s promise: F. D. R. Library, Speech File. TS.
104. Changkufeng scene: Alvin D. Coox, *Nomonhan: Japan Against Russia, 1939*, Vol. I, pp. 120–142.
105–106. Shooting of the airplane: William M. Leahy, *The Dragon's Wing: The China National Aviation Corporation and the Development of Commercial Aviation in China*, pp. 118–121.
107. The trail to Trippe: *The New York Times*, April 4, 1940; military use of planes: Leary, *op. cit.*, p. 128.
109. Rotunda scene: *Time*, October 9, 1938.
109. On Pittman: Betty Glad, *Key Pittman: The Tragedy of a Senate Insider*, pp. 252–259.
110–111. On the Japanese allegations: John McCook Roots, *Chou: An Informal Biography of China's Legendary Chou En-lai*, pp. 86–88.
112. Grew's mood: Waldo H. Heinrichs, *American Ambassador*, p. 260.
112. F. D. R.'s second inauguration: James MacGregor Burns, *Roosevelt: The Lion and the Fox*, p. 291.
113. F. D. R.'s southern tour: Ted Morgan, *F.D.R.*, pp. 495–496.
113. F. D. R.'s comment to Ickes: Ickes, *op. cit.*, p. 311.
114. Morgenthau's plea: quoted in Blum, *op. cit.*, p. 249.

Chapter 9

115. Konoye's speech: Heinrichs, *American Ambassador*, p. 262; *U.S. Foreign Relations, Japan*, Vol. I, pp. 473–481.
116. Arita quoted in: Akira Iriye, *Second World War*, pp. 68–69.
117. The Japanese armada: *The New York Times*, October 13, 1938.
117. Canton scene: Edna Lee Booker, *News Is My Job: A Correspondent in War-torn China*, pp. 323–326.
118. The foreigners' report: Dick Wilson, *op. cit.*, p. 122.

119–120. Japanese gas warfare: Peter Williams and David Wallace, *Unit 731: Japan's Secret Biological Warfare in World War II*, pp. 1–91.

120. Hornbeck and Hull: Robert K. Wolthuis, *United States Foreign Policy Toward the Netherland Indies, 1937–1945*, pp. 44–45.

120. Carlson's epistle: *Twin Stars*, p. 295.

121. "In mid-September . . .": *The New York Times*, September 1, 1938.

121–122. Edgar Snow's commentary: Edgar Snow, "The Sun Also Sets," *Saturday Evening Post*, June 4, 1938.

122. Hull's note: Wolthuis, *op. cit.*, p. 43.

122–123. Morgenthau's memo: Blum, *op. cit.*, pp. 58–63.

123–124. Morgenthau's deal: Hoover Institution, Arthur Young Papers, Chen to Kung, November 17, 1938; Japanese response to Morgenthau: *The New York Times*, December 27, 1938.

124–125. Yardley's arrival: Herbert O. Yardley, *The Chinese Black Chamber: An Adventure in Espionage*, pp. 7–17.

126. MacArthur's office: D. Clayton James, *The Years of MacArthur*, Vol. I, p. 1.

126. "on the flank of Japan's . . .": quoted in William Manchester, *American Caesar: Douglas MacArthur, 1880–1964*, p. 182.

127. "Kunming . . .": quoted in Byrd, *op. cit.*, pp. 93–95.

128. Down the Burma Road: James McHugh Papers, Cornell University, letter from General Holcomb to McHugh, July 19, 1938.

128–129. Ambassador Johnson with F. D. R.: quoted in Russell D. Buhite, *Nelson T. Johnson and American Policy Toward China, 1925–1941*, p. 140.

Chapter 10

133–136. White House scene: F. D. R. Library, "Conference with the Senate Military Affairs Committee in the White House, January 31, 1939," P.P.F.

136. F. D. R. press conference: F. D. R. Library, President's Press Conferences. T.

139–139. Naval air scene: Lt. Stephen Jurika, Jr., "Pilots, Man Your Planes," *Saturday Evening Post*, January 21, 1939.

140. Japan scene: *The New York Times*, January 31, 1939.

140. The slogans: Leonard Mosley, *Hirohito: Emperor of Japan*, p. 191.

141. The Bullitt and Churchill quotations: Robert Dallek, *Franklin D. Roosevelt and American Foreign Policy, 1932–1945*, p. 182.

141–142. Scene in the Commons: Simon Newman, *March, 1939: The British Guarantee to Poland*, p. 6.

143. Japan's Pacific thrust: quoted in Herbert Feis, *The Road to Pearl Harbor: The Coming of War Between the United States and Japan*, p. 18.

Chapter 11

143–144. Adapted from Alan S. Wheelock, "False Dawn, the New York World's Fair and the Onset of World War II," a paper presented to the Siena College Conference on World War II, 1989.

145. Theodore White: Theodore H. White and Anna Lee Jacoby, *Thunder Out of China*, p. 8.

145–146. Yardley in Chungking: Yardley, *op. cit.*, p. 44.

146. Yardley checked his calendar: *ibid.*, p. 54.

147–148. White on bombing: Theodore H. White, *In Search of History*, pp. 80–83.

148. Yardley's observation: Yardley, *op. cit.*, p. 93.

148–149. Annapolis scene: based on Roger Dingman, "Farewell to Friendship: The U.S.S. *Astoria*'s Visit to Japan, April, 1939," *Diplomatic History*, Spring 1986.

149–150. Grew's protest: *Foreign Relations of the United States*, Vol. I, *Japan*, pp. 643–645.

150–153. *Astoria* in Japan: Dingman, *op. cit.*, pp. 133–138; also Heinrichs, *American Ambassador*, p. 281, and *The New York Times*, May 27, 1939.

153. A. L. Patterson: *The New York Times*, April 16, 1939.

153. *Asahi-Shimbun*: *The New York Times*, April 18, 1939.

154. Lindbergh scene: based on Morgan, *op. cit.*, p. 507.

154. Isherwood on Tientsin: quoted in Edward Behr, *The Last Emperor*, pp. 155–156.

Chapter 12

157–159. Based on *The New York Times* and the *Washington Post*, June 8, 1939; also Benjamin P. Rhodes, "The British Royal Visit of 1939 and the 'Psychological Approach' to the United States," *Diplomatic History*, 1978.

159–160. Conclusion of the visit: John H. Wheeler-Bennett, *King George VI: His Life and Reign*, p. 389.

160. Untermeyer: American Jewish Archives (Cincinnati), Samuel Dickstein Collection, Box 7, Folder 7; Judd: Paul A. Varg, *Missionaries, Chinese and Diplomats*, and Oberlin College Archives, Shansi Collection; Barkley: University of Kentucky Archives, Alben W. Barkley Collection, General File, 1937–1940 (XII); Morgenthau: F. D. R. Library, Morgenthau Diary, Book 205.

160–161. Quotation from *China Weekly Review*: F. D. R. Library, P.S.F.

161. Question to Chamberlain: *The Times*, June 23, 1939; Davis episode in Tientsin: *The New York Times*, July 3, 1939.

162. Tokyo mob: *The New York Times*, June 16, 1939.

162. The Chamberlain letter: quoted in Peter Lowe, *Great Britain and the Origins of the Pacific War: A Study of British Policy in East Asia, 1937–1941*, p. 79.

163. His Majesty's Government: *ibid.*, p. 89; In plain language: Donald Cameron Watt, *How War Came: The Immediate Origins of the Second World War*, p. 359.

163–164. Fegan's letter: F. D. R. Library, P.S.F., Fegan to Roosevelt, June 3, 1939.

164. The Ickes quotation: Harold C. Ickes, *Secret Diary*, Vol. II, p. 653; the Roosevelt memorandum: F. D. R. Library, P.S.F., Roosevelt to Frank Murphy, July 1, 1939.

164. Notice of treaty abrogation: *The New York Times*, July 27, 1939.

165. Madame's letter: Cornell University Archives, McHugh Papers, letter of July 28, 1939.

165. The Confederation of Chinese Patriotic Associations: F. D. R. Library, Chinese Embassy, Washington, to Secretary Hull, August 12, 1939; the Japanese reaction: *The New York Times*, July 27, 1939; Anderson's memo: F. D. R. Library, P.S.F., Navy: memorandum of August 25, 1939.

166–167. The Inner Asian conflict and the judgment of the Tokyo War Crimes Trial: Alvin D. Coox, *Nomonhan: Japan Against Russia, 1939*, Vol. II, p. 1078.

167. London on September 3, 1939: *Time*, September 4, 1939.

168. Vincent Massey and the king: Donald Creighton, *The Forked Road: Canada, 1939–1957*, p. 2.

168–169. F. D. R.'s phone call from Bullitt: *The New York Times*, September 2, 1939.

169. The press conference: *Time*, September 11, 1939.

169–170. The Japanese reaction: Herbert Feis, *The Road to Pearl Harbor*, pp. 34–37.

Chapter 13

171. Invasion of Poland: based on William L. Shirer, *The Rise and Fall of the Third Reich*, p. 827.

171–172. Biddle's journey entry: Philip V. Cannistaro, Edward D. Wynot, Jr., and Theodore P. Kovaleff, eds., *Poland and the Coming of the Second World War*, p. 95.

172. F. D. R. letter to Churchill: quoted in Francis L. Loewenheim, Harold G. Langley, and Manfred Jonas, eds., *Roosevelt and Churchill*, p. 89.

173–174. The Sachs scene: from Richard Rhodes, *The Making of the Atomic Bomb*, p. 313.

174. F. D. R.–Sachs conversation: quoted in *ibid.*, p. 314.

174–175. General Yasuda: adapted from Robert K. Wilcox, *Japan's Secret War*, pp. 51–53.

175–179. The espionage scenes: drawn from Ladislas Farago, *The Broken Seal: The Story of "Operation Magic" and the Pearl Harbor Disaster*, pp. 141–195.

179. Marquand in Japan: Millicent Bell, *Marquand: An American Life*, p. 207.

179–180. Fictional protagonist: John P. Marquand, *Your Turn, Mr. Moto*, p. 27.

180. Vulnerable: W. G. Beasley, *Japanese Imperialism, 1894–1945*, p. 27; also Michael Barnhart, *Japan Prepares for Total War: The Search for Economic Security*, pp. 148–157.

180. Grew in America: quoted in Heinrichs, *American Ambassador*, pp. 289–290.

181–182. Grew's speech: *Foreign Relations of the United States*, Vol II, *Japan*, pp. 19–29.

182. Praise for Grew: Heinrichs, *American Ambassador*, p. 293.

183. The Japanese response to Grew: *Time*, November 20, 1939, and *The New York Times*, November 3, 1939.

183. Nomura: *The New York Times*, October 21, 1939

183. The attaché's report: *U.S. Intelligence Reports*, Japan, Reel 15, No. 1073.

183–184. Kung's question: *Time*, October 31, 1939.

184. Berle and F. D. R.: David G. Haglund, *Latin America and the Transformation of U.S. Strategic Thought, 1936–1940*, pp. 143–144.

184. "dead silence": F. D. R. Library, A. A. Berle, Jr., Diary, Box 211, September 21 and 22, 1939.

185. Description of Byrnes: *Time*, September 25, 1939.

185–186. F. D. R.'s address, *Newsweek*, October 2, 1939.

186. F. D. R. and Tweedsmuir: quoted in Dallek, *op. cit.*, pp. 202–203.

186. Lindbergh: *Time*, September 25, 1939.

186–187. America's isolationists: David Brinkley, *Washington Goes to War*, p. 28.

187. Senator Johnson: *Newsweek*, October 3, 1939.

188. Senator Connally: *Newsweek*, October 16, 1939.

189. The isolationists' mistake: *Newsweek*, October 30, 1939.

189. On Dorothy Thompson: Ted Morgan, *F.D.R.; A Biography*, p. 507.

190. The signing ceremony: *The New York Times*, November 3, 1939.

193. The U.S. protest: *The New York Times*, December 20, 1939.

Chapter 14

197. Oval Office scene: drawn from Richard Collier, *1940: The World in Flames*, p. 1.

198. *Lusitania* memorandum: F. D. R. Library, Naval MSS collection.

199. Hans Thomsen: quoted in Saul Friedländer, *Prelude to Downfall, Hitler and the United States, 1939–1941*, p. 81; "awful Nazis," quoted in Brinkley, *op. cit.*, p. 37.

199–200. Kennedy scene: Michael Beschloss, *Kennedy and Roosevelt: The Uneasy Alliance*, pp. 199–200.

200. Shirer passage: Shirer, *op. cit.*, p. 213.

201. The king: *The Times*, January 2, 1940.

201. The Scandinavian offensive: John Colville, *The Fringes of Power: Downing Street Diaries*, Vol I, *1939–October, 1941*, p. 71.

203–204. The early China lobby: Warren I. Cohen, *The Chinese Connection: Roger S. Greene, Thomas W. Lamont, and George E. Sokolsky, and American-East Asian Relations*; Donald J. Friedman, *The Road from Isolation: The Campaign of the American Committee for Non-Participation in Japanese Aggression, 1938–1941*.

204. Lothian: J. R. M. Butler, *Lord Lothian (Philip Kerr), 1882–1940*, p. 279.

205–206. China description: Hallett Abend, *Japan Unmasked*, pp. 49–51.

206. As if to taunt Japan . . .: *The New York Times*, March 25, 1940.

207. Wang Ching-wei: John Hunter Boyle, *China and Japan at War, 1937–1945: The Politics of Collaboration*, pp. 293–294.

207–208. On the currency: Arthur N. Young, *China and the Helping Hand, 1937–1945*, pp. 159–160.

208–209. Horinouchi's statement: *Newsweek*, February 5, 1940.

209. "yen bloc": *ibid.*

209–210. The Japanese threats: *Foreign Relations of the United States, Japan*, Vol. II, p. 281; also Feis, *op. cit.*, p. 52.

210. Bullitt's pledge: *The New York Times*, March 30, 1940.

211. Did Kennedy actually say . . .: Charles A. Lindbergh, *The Wartime Journals*, p. 420.

211–212. And Bullitt . . .: D. C. Watt, *op. cit.*, pp. 129–130; also Will Brownell and Richard Billings, *So Close to Greatness: A Biography of William C. Bullitt*, p. 273, and David Irving, *Hitler's War*, p. 33.

212–213. British task force: Martin Gilbert, *Winston S. Churchill*, Vol. VI; *Finest Hour; 1939–1945*, p. 97.

Chapter 15

214. Moffat: Nancy Harvison Hooker, ed., *The Moffat Papers: Selections from the Diplomatic Journals of Jay Pierrepont Moffat, 1919–1943*, p. 304.

215. The Norwegian invasion: Florence Jaffray Harriman, *Mission to the North*, p. 151.

217. Minister Harriman: *ibid.*, p. 182.

217–218. Leo Amery's speech: quoted in Gilbert, *op. cit.*, p. 292.

218. Churchill's speech: quoted in *ibid.*, p. 346.

218–219. Randolph Churchill: quoted in *ibid.*, p. 358.

219. Colville's corroboration: Colville, *op. cit.*, p. 144.

219. "You can put it this way . . .": quoted in Joseph P. Lash, *Roosevelt and Churchill, 1939–1941; The Partnership that Saved the West*, p. 121; also *The New York Times*, April 15, 1940.

219–220. The squeeze on Japan: Yoji Akashi, *The Nanyang Chinese National Salvation Movement, 1937–1941*, p. 24.

220. Yasuda and Suzuki: Wilcox, *op. cit.*, pp. 51–52.

220. Japan's naval buildup: Hiroyuki Agawa, *The Reluctant Admiral*, p. 193.

220–221. Arita's press conference: James William Morley, ed., *The Fateful Choice: Japan's Advance into Southeast Asia, 1939–1941*,

221. Grew: Heinrichs, *American Ambassador*, pp. 302–307.

221. Japanese in China: *The New York Times*, April 1 and April 2, 1940, p. 136–137.

221. "dreadfully morose": quoted in Heinrichs, *American Ambassador*, p. 303.

222. "security patrol": *The New York Times*, April 27, 1940.

222–223. Grattan's article: C. Hartley Grattan, "An Australian-American Axis?" *Harper's Magazine*, May 1940.

223. Civil Aeronautics Board: *The New York Times*, June 13, 1940.

224. The Taussig testimony: *The New York Times*, May 2, 1940.

224–225. F. D. R.'s reflections: quoted in Joseph P. Lash, *op. cit.*, p. 126.

Chapter 16

227. Late in the hot, steamy . . .: Telford Taylor, *The March of Conquest: The German Victories in Western Europe, 1940*, p. vii.
231. Halder: quoted in Robert Leckie, *Delivered from Evil*, p. 166.
232. "Ramsay witnessed a . . .": Walter Lord, *The Miracle of Dunkirk*, p. 47.
232. The flotilla: *ibid.*, p. 161.
233. Churchill's famous speech: *The Times*, June 2, 1940.
233–235. Rommel's letters: quoted in B. H. Liddell Hart, ed., *The Rommel Papers*, pp. 44–67.
235. Robert Murphy: Robert Murphy, *Diplomat Among Warriors*, p. 55.
236. On Lippmann: Ronald Steel, *Walter Lippmann and the American Century*, p. xv.
236–237. Lothian and Lippmann, *ibid.*, pp. 384–386.
237. "the diffusion within . . .": quoted in Robert Justin Goldstein, *Political Repression in Modern America*, p. 240.
237. Fifth columnists: *The New York Times*, May 25, 1940.
237–238. The Smith Act: quoted in Don R. Pember, "The Smith Act as a Restraint on the Press," *Journalism Monographs*, May 1969, p. 7.
238–239. The *Gobitis* case: Irving Dilliard, "The Flag-Salute Cases," in John A. Garraty, ed., *Quarrels That Have Shaped the Constitution*, pp. 222–242.
239. Byrnes on Lindbergh: *The New York Times*, May 23, 1940.
239–240. F. D. R. and wiretapping: F. D. R. Library, Morgenthau Diary, May 20, 1940.
240. Memorandum to Jackson: quoted in Joseph P. Lash, *op. cit.*, p. 139.
240–241. Roosevelt went further: quoted in Robert Dallek, *op. cit.*, p. 225.
241. Whose mail?: quoted in *ibid.*, pp. 225–226.
241. "If I should die tomorrow": quoted in Lash, *op. cit.*, p. 141.
241–242. The interventionist lobby: Mark Lincoln Chadwin, *The Hawks of World War II*, pp. 32–42.
243. The University of Virginia commencement: *The New York Times* and *Washington Post*, June 11, 1940.
243–244. F. D. R.'s guests: Haglund, *op. cit.*, pp. 208–209.
244–245. Sherwood and MacLeish: Allan M. Winkler, *The Politics of War Information, 1942–1945*, p. 15.
245–246. F. D. R.'s remaking of the government: Bruce Catton, *The War Lords of Washington*, p. 7.
247. Arita on the radio: *The New York Times*, May 19, 1940.
247. *Nichi-Nichi: The New York Times*, June 30, 1940; Government House in Hanoi: Feis, *op. cit.*, p. 66.
247–248. Reports to Hitler: David Irving, *op. cit.*, pp. 136, 137, 145.
248. On Oumansky: Cordell Hull, *The Memoirs*, Vol. I, p. 743.

Chapter 17

249. "the grave of British hopes . . .": quoted in Leonard Mosley, *The Battle of Britain*, pp. 18–19.

250. Germany's effort: based on David Irving, *op. cit.*, p. 152.

251. The London bombing: Leonard Mosley, *Battle of Britain*, p. 110.

252. Description of Murrow: A. M. Sperber, *Murrow: His Life and Times*, pp. 170–171.

252–254. The Murrow broadcasts: Edward Bliss, Jr., ed., *In Search of Light: The Broadcasts of Edward R. Murrow, 1938–1961*, pp. 48–56.

254. Archibald MacLeish: quoted in Michael S. Sherry, *The Rise of American Air Power*, p. 94.

254–255. Hopkins with Roosevelt: Robert E. Sherwood, *Roosevelt and Hopkins*, p. 11.

255–257. The Century Club: Chadwin, *op. cit.*, pp. 43–73; on Council on Foreign Relations, Shoup and mminter, p. 130.

258. "Think of it": *Life*, March 24, 1941.

259. Jones description: *Current Biography*, 1940.

259–260. On Soong's connections: *Life*, op. cit; Library of Congress, Corcoran Papers.

260. Rajchman: *McCall's*, September 1941; also *Washington Times-Herald*, February 17, 1941.

261. Japanese cable: National Archives.

262–263. Donovan passage: Richard Dunlop, *Donovan: America's Master Spy*, pp. 203–218; Anthony Cave Brown, *The Last Hero: Wild Bill Donovan*, pp. 147–167; and Thomas F. Troy, *Donovan and the C.I.A.*, pp. 23–43.

263. Quotation on Godfrey: Dunlop, *op. cit.*, p. 211.

264. On Stephenson: Troy, *op. cit.*, pp. 34–36.

264. Donovan's career: Dunlop, *op. cit.*, pp. 190–191.

264. "The Room": Anthony Cave Brown, *"C"; The Secret Life of Sir Menzies, Spymaster to Winston Churchill*, p. 123.

265. "pattern of the Western . . .": Philip Goodhart, *Fifty Ships That Saved the World: The Foundation of the Anglo-American Alliance*, p. 148.

266. The press conference: quoted in *ibid.*, pp. 180–181.

267. The liaison conference: *Diplomats in Crisis*, p. 275; germ warfare: Williams and Wallace, *Unit 731*, pp. 65–66.

268. Tojo: David Bergamini, *Japan's Imperial Conspiracy*, pp. 754–756.

268–269. Pacific action and reaction: *The New York Times*, July 28, August 6, and August 8, 1940.

270. On Bullitt: *The New York Times*, July 5, 1940; also Brownell and Billings, *op. cit.*, pp. 268–269.

270. The news reports: *The New York Times*, August 24 and 28, 1940.

270. Joint staff talks: W. David McIntyre, *The Rise and Fall of the Singapore Base*, p. 173.

270–271. Callender report: *The New York Times*, September 2, 1940.

272. The Japanese scarcely could have missed . . .: *The New York Times*, September 3, 1940.

272. *Asahi: The New York Times*, September 4, 1940.

272–273. News reports: *The New York Times*, September 6, 9, 14, and 22, 1940.

273. Stimson, F. D. R., and deterrence: William L. Langer and S. Everett Gleason, *The Undeclared War, 1940–1941*, p. 42.

273. Axis announcement: William Shirer, *Berlin Diary*, pp. 395–396.

274. Axis text: *Foreign Relations of the United States*, Vol. II, *Japan*, pp. 165–166.

274. "The treaty, of course . . .": quoted in Friedländer. *op. cit.*, p. 138; the Washington reaction: *The New York Times*, September 28, 1940.

Chapter 18

275–276. Start of the campaign. Burns, *op. cit.*, p. 449.

276. Willkie found his issue: quotation from *ibid.*, p. 443.

276. "most solemn assurance . . .": quoted in *ibid.*, p. 447.

277. Sherwood: Quoted in *ibid.*, p. 448; "anxiety psychosis": quoted in James V. Compton, *The Swastika and the Eagle: Hitler, the United States, and the Origins of World War II*, p. 85.

277–279. Hyde Park scene: Burns, *op. cit.*, pp. 451–452.

279–280. The movies: Clayton R. Koppes and Gregory D. Black, *Hollywood Goes to War: How Profits and Propaganda Shaped World War II*, pp. 30–35.

280. The Knudsen tour: *The New York Times*, October 17, 1940.

280. "For practical purposes . . .": F. D. R. Library, F. D. R. to Francis B. Sayer, December 31, 1940.

280–281. Churchill and Enigma messages: Richard Collier, *op. cit.*, p. 208.

281–282. Coventry: *Ibid.*, pp. 212–213.

282. "War is forcing us . . .": quoted in William Stevenson, *A Man Called Intrepid*, pp. 165–166.

282. ". . . wine will be waiting . . .": *Time*, October 28, 1940; "coolies cheered": *Time*, October 28, 1940.

282–283. Why had the British . . .: Peter Lowe, *Great Britain and the Origins of the Pacific War: A Study of British Policy in East Asia, 1937–1941*, pp. 167–175.

283. Grew: quoted in Leonard Mosley, *Hirohito*, pp. 200–201.

283. "Arsené-Henry . . .": quoted in *ibid.*, p. 202.

283–284. The Japanese decision: Marder, *op. cit.*, pp. 134–135; Morley, *op. cit.*, pp. 218–219.

284. Keitel's order: Brown, *op. cit.*, pp. 304–305.

284–285. Marshall and Byrnes: James F. Byrnes, *All in a Lifetime*, p. 144.

285. Acheson's letter: quoted in David S. McClellan and David Acheson, *Among Friends: Personal Letters of Dean Acheson*, p. 40.

285–286. White on MacArthur: Theodore White, *In Search of History*, pp. 108–109.

286. Brereton: Forrest C. Pogue, *George C. Marshall: Ordeal and Hope, 1939–1942*, p. 187.

286. The British government: *The New York Times*, November 25, 1940.

286–287. Two reports: *The New York Times*, November 29, 1940.

287. The bars in Singapore: Byrd, *op. cit.*, p. 107; December 7: F. D. R. Library, Morgenthau Diary, Book 342, pp. 4–7.

287. Chennault: quoted in Michael S. Sherry, *The Rise of American Airpower*, p. 102.

287–288. From the Morgenthau diary, F. D. R. Library, Morgenthau Diary, Book 342a, pp. 2–4.

288. Wasting no time: Library of Congress, Manuscript Division, Joseph and Stewart Alsop Papers, Container No. 2, Folder: June–December, 1940; University of Virginia Library, Stettinius Papers, Box 661, Folder: S—Soong, T. V.

288. Joint War Board: *The New York Times*, December 11, 1940.

288. "I have good news . . .": F. D. R. Library, Morgenthau Diary, Book 342a, p. 18.

288–289. Scene in Morgenthau's house: *ibid.*, pp. 24–25.

289. Scene at Woodley: *ibid.*, p. 27.

289–290. Hitler and Räder: Irving, *op. cit.*, p. 190.

290–291. F. D. R.'s fireside chat: *The New York Times* and *Washington Post*, December 30, 1940.

Chapter 19

295–296. St. John's Church: *Washington Post*, January 21, 1941.

296. Few present . . .: *Baltimore Sun*, January 21, 1941.

296–297. Tracking Japan: Farago, *op. cit.*, p. 163.

297. Acheson: Dean Acheson, *op. cit.*, p. 46.

299. Laski on Halifax: *Washington Post*, January 11, 1941.

299. Halifax diary: Borthwick Institute of Historical Research, University of York, diary entry of January 21, 1941.

299–300. Halifax aboard battleship: The Earl of Birkenhead, *Halifax; The Life of Lord Halifax*, p. 473.

300. "everything under the sun . . .": Halifax diary, January 24, 1941.

301. Pierside at Annapolis: *Time*, February 3, 1941.

302. De facto alliance: Geoffrey Perrett, *Days of Sadness, Years of Triumph*, p. 75.

303–304. The secret alliance: Naval Historical Center, Washington Navy Yard, Strategic Plans Division, Series VII, Box 117.

304. Stark: Compton, *op. cit.*, pp. 161–162; Yarnell: Naval Historical Center, Yarnell papers.

305. American flotilla: Raymond A. Esthus, *From Emnity to Alliance: U.S.–Australian Relations, 1931–1941*, p. 103.

305–306. F. D. R. and Arnold: quoted in Henry H. Arnold, *Global Mission*, p. 194.

306. But if pilots based in China . . .: Michael S. Sherry, *op. cit.*, p. 102.

306. Currie description: *Current Biography*, 1941.

306–307. Japanese observation of Currie: National Archives, "Collection of Japanese Diplomatic Messages," Record Group 457, Folder 018, February 16, 1941.

307–308. The Japanese messages: U.S. Department of Defense, *The "MAGIC" Background of Pearl Harbor*, Vol. I, pp. 35, 84, 85, 95, 102, 142, 205, 208.

309. Island fortification: Thomas Wilds, "How Japan Fortified the Mandated Pacific Islands," *United States Naval Institute Proceedings*, April 1955.
309. Grew's cable: *ibid.*, p. 5; Haan's message: Hoover Institution Archives, Stanley Hornbeck papers.
310. Donovan in the Balkans: Brown, *The Last Hero*, p. 156; Winston S. Churchill, *The Grand Alliance*, p. 140. "Mr. Donovan's War": *Time*, March 31, 1941; German intelligence: Irving, *op. cit.*, p. 223.
310–311. F. D. R.'s cruise: William K. Klingaman, *1941*, pp. 247–248.

Chapter 20

312. The bureaucracy, too . . .: based on David Brinkley, *Washington Goes to War*, p. 72.
313. Lindbergh's testimony: *The New York Times*, January 24, 1941.
313. "On April 23 . . ." *The New York Times*, April 24, 1941.
313. The martyrdom . . .: Leonard Mosley, *Lindbergh: A Biography*, p. 281.
314. "Mr. Lindbergh has shocked . . .": *The New York Times*, April 29, 1941.
314. Lindbergh's journal entry: *The Wartime Journals of Charles A. Lindbergh*, p. 481.
315. Africa scene: Ronald Lewin, *The Life and Death of the Afrika Korps*, p. 43; "exploded over . . .": Basil Liddell-Hart, ed., *Rommel Papers*, p. 109.
315–316. Crete: Laird Archer, *Balkan Journal*, pp. 165–166.
316. When Churchill first . . .: Anthony Eden, *Memoirs: The Reckoning*, p. 283.
316–318. *Bismarck* quotations: Barrie Pitt, ed., *The Battle of the Atlantic*, pp. 47–48.
318. Then, on the morning . . .: quoted in Klingaman, *op. cit.*, p. 205.
319. "There was no electric . . .": Pitt, *op. cit.*, p. 49.
319. Pedestrians in mid-Manhattan . . .: Stevenson, *op. cit.*, p. 269; "Yes, America also had patrols . . .": *The New York Times*, April 26, 1941.
319. F. D. R.'s naval expansion: Waldo Heinrichs, *Threshold of War*, pp. 46–47.
319–320. F. D. R. to Halifax: *ibid.*, p. 78; F. D. R. to Ickes and Morgenthau: Morgan, *op. cit.*, p. 589; Nomura: quoted in Herbert Feis, *The Road to Pearl Harbor*, p. 172.
320. Matsuoka's cable: U.S. Defense Department, *op. cit.*, p. 66; Sengoku district: Wilcox, *op. cit.*, p. 58.
321. "loose talking . . .": Feis, *op. cit.*, pp. 80–81; Matsuoka's statement: quoted in Nobutaka Ike, *Japan's Decision for War: Records of the 1941 Policy Conference*, pp. 43–44; "will strike soon": quoted in Heinrichs, *Threshold*, p. 52.
321. Tall and "majestic": quoted in W. A. Swanberg, *Luce and His Empire*, p. 184.
322. "No restraint . . .": White, *In Search of History*, pp. 126–127.
322. China Defense Supplies: National Archives, Thomas Corcoran papers; Princeton University Archives, Whiting Willauer papers, recorded tape, December 1, 1960, p. 2; Hoover Institution, T. V. Soong Papers, R. W. Bonneville to General S. M. Chu, May 19, 1941.

322–323. April 22, 1941, meeting: National Archives, F.E.A./Administrator of Export Control, Box 698, Entry 88.

323. Loan to China: National Archives, War Department transcript.

Chapter 21

324. Summertime, Noel Coward: quoted in Klingaman, *op. cit.*, p. 482; "hands gesturing . . .": Louis Adamic, *Dinner at the White House*, p. 15.

324–325. Paderewski: Adam Zamoyski, *Paderewski*, pp. 238–239; J. Edgar Hoover: Robert Dallek, *Franklin D. Roosevelt and American Foreign Policy*, pp. 289–290; Ickes: Chadwin, *op. cit.*, pp. 202–203; Lingbergh "un-American": Mosley, *Lindbergh*, pp. 292–302.

325. "frankly and privately": quoted in Troy, *op. cit.*, p. 57.

325–326. The Apex Building: Brown, *The Last Hero*, p. 169; "actual warfare": Troy, *op. cit.*, p. 74.

326. lakeside near Toronto: Stevenson, *op. cit.*, p. 202; Murphy and Weygand: Robert Murphy, *Diplomat Among Warriors*, pp. 99–100.

328. Franz Halder: quoted in Nicholas Bethell, *Russia Besieged*, p. 70; "enormous funnel": *ibid.*, p. 71; "Asiatic tricks": *ibid.*, p. 72. "Our ranks got thinner . . .": *ibid.*, p. 73.

329. "This meant that my . . .": quoted in *ibid.*, p. 75.

329. U.S. legation in Vichy: Heinrichs, *Threshold*, p. 138; "time to get Hitler": *loc. cit.*

329–330. Stimson's announcement: *Time*, July 7, 1941; British shipping losses: W. N. Medlicott, *The Economic Blockade*, Vol. I, pp. 44–63.

330. Getting to Iceland: F. D. R. Library, Morgenthau Diary, June 4, 1941; F. D. R. to Churchill: quoted in Warren F. Kimbal, ed., *Churchill and Roosevelt: A Complete Correspondence*, p. 184.

331. Lattimore: F. D. R. Library, P.S.F.: China: Lattimore, letter of May 2, 1941.

331. Arnstein: *The New Yorker*, January 17, 1942; MacArthur: D. Clayton James, *The Years of MacArthur*, Vol. I, p. 590.

332. Chennault: Sherry, *op. cit.*, p. 103.

332–333. Japanese intelligence: National Archives: "Japanese Diplomatic Messages."

333. Konan: Wilcox, *op. cit.*, p. 64; Yamamoto: Agawa, *The Reluctant Admiral*, pp. 223–227; "launch therefrom a rapid attack": quoted in Heinrichs, *Threshold*, p. 123.

335. "OUR CHANCES OF VICTORY . . .": *U.S. News*, August 1, 1941.

335. All this . . . emerges . . .: Irvine H. Anderson, Jr., "The 1941 *De Facto* Embargo on Oil to Japan: A Bureaucratic Reflex," *Pacific Historical Review*, May 1975.

335. "To cut off oil . . .": *ibid.*, p. 219; "The President said . . .": quoted in *Pearl Harbor Hearings*, Vol. 12, p. 9.

336. Late on Sunday . . .: drawn from Theodore Wilson, *The First Summit: Roosevelt and Churchill at Placentia Bay, 1941*, p. 68.

Chapter 22

338–339. "For a Prime Minister of Japan . . .": quoted in Mosley, *Hirohito*, pp. 210–211.

339. "was very sad": quoted in *ibid.*, p. 212.

339–340. Averell Harriman: Isaacson and Thomas, *The Wise Men*, p. 46.

340. "like a man with a bit . . .": quoted in *Time*, August 11, 1941.

341. Hugo Black: *U.S. News*, September 5, 1941.

343. "Are you all right . . .": Wilson, *op. cit.*, p. 83.

343. "The *Prince of Wales* . . .": H. V. Morton, *Atlantic Meeting*, pp. 95–96. For discussion of F.D.R.'s knowledge of the German-Russian stalemate, see Bruce M. Russett, *No Clear and Present Danger*, pp. 24–29.

343. Elliott Roosevelt's account: Elliott Roosevelt, *As He Saw It*, p. 69.

344. "really lovely morning . . .": Wilson, *op. cit.*, p. 108.

345. Many "of us . . .": *ibid.*, p. 109.

345–346. "the symbolism of the Union Jack . . .": Churchill, *op. cit.*, p. 431.

346. Back on the *Augusta* . . .: Elliott Roosevelt, *op. cit.*, p. 33.

347. "change the subject": ibid., pp. 35–37.

347. "various steps would have to be taken . . .": *United States Foreign Relations*, Vol. I, *Japan, 1941*, p. 358.

348. "Mr. President . . .": Elliott Roosevelt, *op. cit.*, p. 41.

348. F. D. R. and Imperial Preferences: Warren F. Kimball, "Lend-Lease and the Open Door: The Temptation of British Opulence, 1937–1942," *Political Science Quarterly*, June 1971.

348–349. Churchill's statement to cabinet: Public Record Office, CAB65, 84(41); British War Cabinet Minutes, August 19, 1941.

351. From Midway to Tokyo: *Time*, August 11, 1941.

351–352. Chennault's letter to Madame: Hoover Institution, Claire Chennault's papers.

352. "was impressed": Stimson diary, September 12, 1941.

352. "the naval aspects . . .": quoted in Ike, *op. cit.*, pp. 121–124; training exercises, Farago, *op. cit.*, p. 216.

354. Rosenman: Samuel Rosenman, *Roosevelt*, p. 292.

355. "shoot on sight": *U.S. News*, September 12, 1941; "Hitler will have . . .": Churchill, *op. cit.*, p. 517.

355. Räder: quoted in Compton, *op. cit.*, p. 168.

Chapter 23

356. At lunchtime . . .: *Washington Post*, October 28, 1941.

356. Navy Day dinner: *Washington Post*, October 28, 1941.

357. Certain reporters: John F. Bratzel and Leslie B. Tour, Jr., "F.D.R. and the 'Secret Map'," *The Wilson Quarterly*, New Year's 1985, p. 168.

358–361. Secret map: Based on *ibid.* At the Wilhelmstrasse, the German Foreign Office, officials apparently searched for the map, but in vain. Frieldänder, *op. cit.*, p. 302.

361. Joke quoted in Dallek, *op. cit.*, p. 292.
361–362. News items: *Time*, September 29, 1941; *Time*, October 27, 1941; *U.S. News*, October 24, 1941; *Time*, November 10, 1941; *U.S. News*, October 3, 1941; *U.S. News*, September 26, 1941.
362. Hitler and oil: Irving, *op. cit.*, pp. 339–340.
362. "cruel Russian winter . . .": *ibid.*, p. 347.
362. "in wave after wave . . .": quoted in *ibid.*, p. 351.
363. On the Arias coup: George Black, *The Good Neighbor*, p. 74.
363. Had the U.S. . . .: quoted in *Current History*, December 1941, p. 356.
364. Roosevelt had bought the hemisphere: Gerald K. Haines, "Under the Eagle's Wing: The Franklin Roosevelt Administration Forges an American Hemisphere," *Diplomatic History*, Fall 1977.
365. "Our object . . .": quoted in Maurice Matloff and Edwin M. Snell, *Strategic Planning for Coalition Warfare, 1941–1942*, p. 65.
365–366. The MacArthur document: MacArthur Archives, MacArthur Personal File, Box 1, Folder: "The Problem of Defeating Japan; Review of the Situation."
366. The MAGIC intercepts: U.S. Defense Department, *op. cit.*, pp. 165, 169, 174, 393.
368. Newsboys scurried: *Time*, November 3, 1941; ". . . highly nationalistic": Alvin D. Coox, *Tojo*, p. 100.
368. Proposals A and B: *ibid.*, p. 104.
368. That left Proposal B . . .: *ibid.*, p. 111.
369. Yamamoto's order: quoted in Agawa, op. cit., p. 237.
369. Grew's warning: quoted in Heinrichs, *American Ambassador*, p. 355.
369–370. MAGIC intercepts: U.S. Defense Department, *op. cit.*, pp. 189–190.
370. Japanese spy: Farago, *op. cit.*, pp. 230–233; Bratton, *ibid.*, p. 232.
370–371. Hornbeck's memo: Hoover Institution, Stanley K. Hornbeck papers, Box 197, Folder: "Kilsoo Haan."
371. In the week before Pearl Harbor, Hornbeck wondered if war really was imminent. Japan faced great shortages, he knew, and so might not dare fight. But *if* Japan fought, he seemed to fear, the nation might well hit Pearl Harbor.

Chapter 24

372–373. Kurusu: *Time*, November 24, 1941.
373. "Finishing my long . . .": *ibid.*
374. Sabotaging Japan: John King Fairbanks, *Chinabound: A Fifty Year Memoir*, p. 181; U.S. Army War College, Donovan Papers, Cory to Larson, November 17, 1941.
374. The bombing of Japan: Stimson diary, November 6, 1941.
374. Kurusu's trip: *U.S. News*, November 21, 1941 and *Time*, November 17, 1941.
375. "For two months . . .": Sherry, *op. cit.*, pp. 108–109; also National Archives, Records of the War Department Staff Records, Office of Chief of Staff, November 26, 1941, in Chief of Staff Project Decimal File, 1941–1943 (Philippines).

375. Baldwin's letter: George C. Marshall Foundation; Hanson Baldwin Papers, Box 8, Folder 20.

375–376. Marshall statements: quoted in Sherry, *op. cit.*, p. 109.

376. "Our own fleet . . .:" *The New York Times*, November 19, 1941.

379–380. The dinner: *Washington Post*, November 22, 1941.

380. The White memorandum: Princeton University Archives, Harry D. White papers, Box 6, Folder 16.

381. Churchill: Heinrichs, *Threshold*, p. 210; Utley, op. cit., pp. 173–175.

382. November 28: Brown, *The Last Hero*, p. 198; November 29: *loc. cit.*; November 30: *Pearl Harbor Attack*, Vol. 14, p. 1409.

382. November 30: Brown, *Last Hero*, p. 199.

383. Donovan's knowledge: Brown, *"C,"*, pp. 383 and 385; Brown, *Last Hero*, pp. 187–188: Donovan's presence in Oval Office, University of Virginia Archives, Edwin Watson Papers, Presidential Appointment Calendar.

Chapter 25

384. Scene in the Carlton: Bruce Catton, *The War Lords of Washington*, p. 3.

385. Knox's statement: *ibid.*, p. 9.

385–386. *Chicago Tribune*: *Chicago Tribune*, December 4, 1941.

387. Joint Board's report: Matloff and Snell, *op. cit.*, p. 60.

387. On the leak: Tracy Barrett Kittredge, "A Military Danger: The Revelation of Secret Strategic Plans," *United States Naval Institute Proceedings*, July 1945.

388–389. The taped conversation: A. A. Hoehling, *The Week Before Pearl Harbor*, pp. 123–128.

390. On the Kemp Tolley affair: Kemp Tolley, *Cruise of the Lanikai: Incitement to War;* also Kemp Tolley, "The Strange Mission of the Lanikai," *American Heritage*, October 1973.

390–391. On Colonel Bratton: Hoehling, *op. cit.*, pp. 164, 166, 170, 175, 179.

391–392. What was known in Washington: Elliott R. Thorpe, *East Wind Rain, The Intimate Account of an Intelligence Officer in the Pacific, 1939–1949*, pp. 52–53; *The "MAGIC" Background*, Vol. IV, pp. 113, 154–155.

392–398. Based on Walter Lord, *Day of Infamy;* Gordon Prange, *At Dawn We Slept;* Blake Clark, *Remember Pearl Harbor;* Mitsuo Fuchida, "I Led the Air Attack on Pearl Harbor," *United States Naval Institute Proceedings*, September 1953; and the *Honolulu Advertiser*, December 8, 1941.

Epilogue

399. Lack of clear and present danger: spelled out at length in Bruce M. Russett, *No Clear and Present Danger: A Skeptical View of the U.S. Entry into World War II.*

400. "To adopt a policy . . .": Langer and Gleason, *op. cit.*, p. 852.

404–405. White: *In Search of History*, pp. 286–287.

BIBLIOGRAPHY

Primary Sources

Dean Acheson Papers: Yale University Library and the Harry S Truman Library.

Administrator of Export Control Papers, National Archives.

Joseph and Stewart Alsop Papers, Library of Congress, Manuscript Division.

Frank Andrews Papers, Library of Congress, Manuscript Division.

Henry H. Arnold Papers, Library of Congress, Manuscript Division.

Hanson Baldwin Papers, University of Kentucky Library.

Hugh Byas Papers, Yale University Library.

James F. Byrnes Papers, Clemson University Library.

Evans F. Carlson Papers, Franklin D. Roosevelt Library and the U.S. Marine Corps Museum Archives.

Claire Chennault Papers, Hoover Institution.

Council on Foreign Relations, *War–Peace Studies*, Northwestern University Library.

U.S. Congress, Joint Committee on the Investigation of the Pearl Harbor Attack, *Pearl Harbor Attack*.

Thomas Corcoran Papers, Library of Congress, Manuscript Division.

U.S. Department of Defense, *The "MAGIC" Background of Pearl Harbor*.

Samuel Dickstein Papers, Jewish Archives, Hebrew Union College.

William Donovan Papers, U.S. Army War College.

Herbert Feis Papers, Library of Congress, Manuscript Division.

Foreign Relations of the United States, Japan: 1931–1941, Volumes I and II.

Lord Halifax Papers, York University.

Thomas Hart Papers, Center for Naval History.

Harry Hopkins Papers, Franklin D. Roosevelt Library.

Stanley K. Hornbeck Papers, Hoover Institution.

Cordell Hull Papers, Library of Congress, Manuscript Division.

Nobutaka Ike, ed., *Japan's Decision for War: Records of the 1941 Policy Conferences* (Stanford: 1967).

Royal Ingersoll, Columbia University Oral History.

David Irving, ed., *Breach of Security: The German Secret Intelligence File on Events Leading to the Second World War* (London: 1968).

Nelson T. Johnson Papers, Library of Congress, Manuscript Division.
George F. Kennan, ed., *From Prague after Munich: Diplomatic Papers, 1938–1940* (Princeton: 1968).
Owen Lattimore Papers, Franklin D. Roosevelt Library.
William Leahy Papers, Library of Congress, Manuscript Division.
Douglas MacArthur Papers, MacArthur Library.
James McHugh Papers, Cornell University Archives.
David S. McLellan and David Acheson, *Among Friends: Personal Letters of Dean Acheson* (New York: 1980).
Milton Miles Papers, Center for Naval History.
William Mitchell Papers, Library of Congress, Manuscript Division.
Henry Morgenthau, Jr., Papers, Franklin D. Roosevelt Library.
James William Morley, ed., *The China Quagmire: Japan's Expansion on the Asian Continent, 1933–1941* (New York: 1983).
———, ed., *The Fateful Choice: Japan's Advance into Southeast Asia, 1939–1941* (New York: 1980).
———, ed., *Japan's Foreign Policy, 1868–1941: A Research Guide* (New York: 1974).
Robert D. Ogg Oral History Interview, National Archives.
Franklin D. Roosevelt Papers, Franklin D. Roosevelt Library.
Marion Turner Sheehan, ed., *The World at Home: Selections from the Writings of Anne O'Hare McCormick* (New York: 1956).
Carl Spaatz Papers, Library of Congress, Manuscript Division.
Joseph W. Stilwell Papers, Hoover Institution.
Henry L. Stimson Diary, Yale University Library.
T. V. Soong Papers, Hoover Institution.
U.S. Military Intelligence Reports (Frederick, Maryland): *China, 1911–1941; Germany, 1919–1941; Japan, 1918–1941; Mexico, 1919–1941; Soviet Union, 1919–1941*.
Arthur Vandenburg Papers, University of Michigan Library.
Vichy Intercepts, National Archives.
Edwin Watson Papers, University of Virginia Library.
Harry D. White Papers, Princeton University Library.
Whiting Willauer Papers, Princeton University Library.
Harry Yarnell Papers, Library of Congress, Manuscript Division and Center for Naval History.
Arthur N. Young Papers, Hoover Institution.
Public Records Office, London: Halifax and Churchill Reports.

Secondary Sources

Patrick Abbazia, *Mr. Roosevelt's Navy: The Private War of the Atlantic Fleet, 1939–1942* (Annapolis: 1975).
Hallett Abend, *Japan Unmasked* (London: 1941).
Dean Acheson, *Present at the Creation: My Years in the State Department* (New York: 1969).

Louis Adamic, *Dinner at the White House* (New York: 1946).

Frederick Adams, *Economic Diplomacy: The Export-Import Bank and American Foreign Policy, 1934–39* (Columbia, Missouri: 1976).

———, "The Road to Pearl Harbor: A Reexamination of American Far Eastern Policy, July, 1937–December, 1938," *Journal of American History,* June 1971.

Henry H. Adams, *Harry Hopkins: A Biography* (New York: 1977).

———, *Witness to Power: The Life of Fleet Admiral William D. Leahy* (Annapolis: 1985).

Selig Adler, *The Isolationist Impulse: Its Twentieth-Century Reaction* (New York: 1957).

———, *The Uncertain Giant* (New York: 1965).

Hiroyuki Agawa, *The Reluctant Admiral: Yamamoto and the Imperial Navy* (New York: 1979).

Yoji Akashi, *The Nanyang Chinese National Salvation Movement, 1937–1941* (Lawrence, Kansas: 1970).

Robert Hayden Alcorn, *No Bugle for Spies* (New York: 1962).

Joseph Alsop and Robert Kintner, *American White Paper* (New York: 1940).

Irvine H. Anderson, Jr., "The 1941 *De Facto* Embargo on Oil to Japan: A Bureaucratic Reflex," *Pacific Historical Review,* May 1975.

———, *The Standard-Vacuum Oil Company and United States East Asian Policy, 1933–1941* (Princeton: 1975).

Henry H. Arnold, *Global Mission* (New York: 1949).

Raymond Aron, *The Century of Total War* (Garden City, New York: 1954).

———, *The Imperial Republic: The United States and the World, 1945–1973* (Cambridge, Massachusetts: 1975).

W. H. Auden and Christopher Isherwood, *Journey to a War* (London: 1954).

M. A. Aziz, *Japan's Colonialism and Indonesia* (The Hague: 1955).

Thomas A. Bailey and Paul B. Ryan, *Hitler vs. Roosevelt: The Undeclared Naval War* (New York: 1979).

Noel Barber, *A Sinister Twilight: The Fall of Singapore, 1942* (Boston: 1968).

Michael A. Barnhart, *Japan Prepares for Total War: The Search for Economic Security, 1919–1941* (Ithaca: 1987).

Bruce R. Bartlett, *Cover-Up: The Politics of Pearl Harbor, 1941–1946* (New Rochelle, New York: 1978).

Vicki Baum, *Shanghai, '37* (New York: 1940).

John Baylis, *Anglo-American Defense Relations, 1939–1984,* 2nd ed. (London: 1984).

Carleton Beals, *The Coming Struggle for Latin America* (New York: 1938).

W. G. Beasley, *Japanese Imperialism, 1894–1945* (Oxford: 1987).

Jack Belden, *Still Time to Die* (New York: 1945).

Millicent Bell, *Marquand: An American Life* (Boston: 1979).

Roger J. Bell, *Unequal Allies: Australian-American Relations and the Pacific War* (Melbourne: 1977).

Edward M. Bennett, *Franklin D. Roosevelt and the Search for Security: American-Soviet Relations, 1933–1939* (Wilmington, Delaware: 1985).

Abraham Ben-Zvi, *The Illusion of Deterrence: The Roosevelt Presidency and the Origins of the Pacific War* (Boulder: 1987).

Barton Bernstein, "Roosevelt, Truman and the Atomic Bomb, 1941–1945: A Reinterpretation," *Political Science Quarterly*, 1975.

David B. Bergamini, *Japan's Imperial Conspiracy* (New York: 1971).

Beatrice B. Burle and Travis B. Jacobs, eds., *Navigating the Rapids, 1918–1971; From the Papers of Adolf A. Berle* (New York: 1973).

The Earl of Birkenhead, *Halifax: The Life of Lord Halifax* (London: 1965).

Jim Bishop, *FDR's Last Year* (New York: 1974).

George Black, *The Good Neighbor* (New York: 1988).

Gregory D. Black and Clayton R. Koppes, *Hollywood Goes to War: How Politics, Profits, and Propaganda Shaped World War II* (New York: 1987).

Clay Blar, *Silent Victory: the U.S. Submarine War Against Japan* (Philadelphia: 1975).

William H. Blanchard, *Aggression American Style* (Santa Monica: 1978).

Edward Bliss, Jr., *In Search of Light: The Broadcasts of Edward R. Murrow, 1938–1961* (New York: 1974).

John Morton Blum, *From the Morgenthau Diaries*, two vols. (Boston: 1965).

Edna Lee Booker, *Flight from China* (New York: 1945).

———, *News Is My Job: A Correspondent in War-Torn China* (New York: 1941).

Dorothy Bord, "Notes on Roosevelt's 'Quarantine' Speech," *Political Science Quarterly*, 1957.

———, *The United States and the Far Eastern Crisis of 1933–1938* (Cambridge, Massachusetts: 1964).

——— and Shumpei Okamoto, eds., *Pearl Harbor as History: Japanese-American Relations, 1931–1941* (New York: 1973).

Paul Boyer, *By the Bomb's Early Light: American Thought and Culture at the Dawn of the Atomic Age* (New York: 1985).

John Hunter Boyle, *China and Japan at War, 1937–1945: The Politics of Collaboration* (Stanford: 1972).

J. M. Braga, *Hong Kong and Macao* (Hong Kong: 1960).

John F. Bratzel and Leslie B. Rout, Jr., "FDR and the 'Secret Map'," *The Wilson Quarterly*, 1985.

William B. Breuer, *The Secret War with Germany* (New York: 1988).

David Brinkley, *Washington Goes to War* (New York: 1988).

Anthony Cave Brown, *"C"; The Secret Life of Sir Stewart Menzies, Spymaster to Winston Churchill* (New York: 1987).

———, *The Last Hero; Wild Bill Donovan* (New York: 1982).

Courtney Browne, *Tojo: The Last Banzai* (New York: 1967).

Will Brownell and Richard Billings, *So Close to Greatness: A Biography of William C. Bullitt* (New York: 1987).

Lester H. Brune, *The Origins of American National Security Policy: Sea Power, Air Power and Foreign Policy, 1900–1941* (Manhattan, Kansas: 1981).

Pearl S. Buck, "Chinese War Lords," *The Saturday Evening Post*, April 22, 1933.

Thomas H. Buckley, *The United States and the Washington Conference, 1921–1922* (Knoxville: 1970).

Russell D. Buhite, *Nelson T. Johnson and American Policy Toward China, 1925–1941* (East Lansing: 1968).

Orville H. Bullitt, ed., *For the President Personal and Secret: Correspondence Between Franklin D. Roosevelt and William C. Bullitt* (Boston: 1972).

Gerald E. Bunker, *The Peace Conspiracy: Wang Ching-wei and the China War, 1973–1941* (Cambridge, Massachusetts: 1972).

William A. M. Burden, *The Struggle for Airways in Latin America* (New York: 1943).

Charles B. Burdick, *Germany's Military Strategy and Spain in World War II* (Syracuse: 1968).

James MacGregor Burns, *Roosevelt: The Lion and the Fox* (New York: 1956).

———, *Roosevelt: The Soldier of Freedom* (New York: 1970).

Richard Dean Burns, "Inspection of the Mandates, 1919–1941," *Pacific Historical Review*, 1968.

——— and Edward M. Bennett, eds., *Diplomats in Crisis: United States-Chinese-Japanese Relations, 1919–1941* (Santa Barbarba: 1974).

J. R. M. Butler, *Lord Lothian (Philip Kerr), 1902–1940* (London: 1960).

Robert J. C. Butow, *The John Doe Associates: Backdoor Diplomacy for Peace, 1941* (Stanford: 1974).

———, *Tojo and the Coming of the War* (Princeton: 1961).

Hugh Byas, *Government by Assassination* (New York: 1942).

Martha Byrd, *Chennault: Giving Wings to the Tiger* (Tuscaloosa: 1987).

James F. Byrnes, *All in One Lifetime* (New York: 1958).

———, *Speaking Frankly* (New York: 1947).

Philip V. Cannistaro, Edward D. Wynot, and Theodore Kovaleff, eds., *Poland and the Second World War; The Diplomatic Papers of A. J. Drexel Biddle, Jr., 1937–1939* (Columbus: 1976).

Mary Tarpley Campfield, "Oberlin in China, 1881–1951," Ph.D. diss., University of Virginia, 1974.

Evans Fordyce Carlson, *Twin Stars of China* (New York: 1941).

William Carr, *Poland to Pearl Harbor: The Making of the Second World War* (London: 1985).

William Casey, *The Secret War Against Hitler* (New York: 1988).

Bruce Catton, *The War Lords of Washington* (New York: 1948).

James Chace and Caleb Carr, *America Invulnerable: The Quest for Absolute Security from 1812 to Star Wars* (New York: 1988).

Mark Lincoln Chadwin, *The Hawks of World War II* (Chapel Hill: 1968).

Eugene Keith Chamberlain, "The Japanese Scare at Magdalena Bay," *Pacific Historical Review*, 1955.

Hsi-Sheng Ch'i, *Nationalist China at War: Military Defeats and Political Collapse, 1937–45* (Ann Arbor: 1982).

Alan Clar, *Barbarossa: The Russian-German Conflict, 1941–1945* (New York: 1965).

Blake Clark, *Remember Pearl Harbor* (Honolulu: 1942).

Ronald W. Clark, *Einstein: The Life and the Times* (New York: 1971).

Ronald Clark, *The Man Who Broke Purple* (Boston: 1977).

Nicholas R. Clifford, *Retreat From China: British Policy in the Far East, 1937–1941* (Seattle: 1967).

Howard F. Cline, *The United States and Mexico* (Cambridge, Massachusetts: 1961).

Thomas M. Ciffey, *HAP: The Story of the U.S. Air Force and the Man Who Built It, Gen. Henry H. "Hap" Arnold* (New York: 1982).

Warren I. Cohen, *The Chinese Connection: Roger S. Greene, Thomas W. Lamont, George E. Sokolsky and American-East Asian Relations* (New York: 1978).

———, *New Frontiers in American-East Asian Relations* (1983).

Wayne S. Cole, *America First; The Battle Against Intervention, 1940–1941* (Madison: 1953).

———, *Charles A. Lindbergh and the Battle Against American Intervention in World War II* (New York: 1974).

———, *Roosevelt and the Isolationists, 1932–1945* (Lincoln: 1983).

———, *Senator Gerald P. Nye and American Foreign Relations* (Minneapolis: 1962).

———, *1940; The World in Flames* (London: 1979).

———, *The Road to Pearl Harbor* (New York: 1983).

John Colville, *The Fringes of Power; Downing Street Diaries*, Vol. I, *1939–October, 1941* (London: 1985).

James V. Compton, *The Swastika and the Eagle: Hitler, the United States, and the Origins of World War II* (New York: 1967).

Stetson Conn, Rose C. Engelman, and Byron Fairchild, *The Western Hemisphere: Guarding the United States and Its Outposts* (Washington: 1964).

Stetson Conn and Byron Fairchild, *The Western Hemisphere: The Framework of Hemispheric Defense* (Washington: 1960).

Robert H. Connery, *The Navy and the Industrial Mobilization in World War II* (Princeton: 1951).

Hilary Conroy, "Japan's War in China: An Ideological Somersault," *Pacific Historical Review*, 1952.

———, "The Strange Diplomacy of Admiral Nomura," *Proceedings of the American Philosophical Society*, 1970.

Joseph J. Corn, *The Winged Gospel: America's Romance with Aviation, 1900–1950* (New York: 1983).

Wanda Cornelius and Thayne Short, *Ding Hai: America's Air War in China, 1937–1945* (Gretna, Louisiana: 1980).

John Costello, *The Pacific War, 1941–1945* (New York: 1982).

Frank Costigliola, *Awkward Dominion: American Political, Economic, and Cultural Relations with Europe, 1919–1933* (Ithaca: 1984).

Alvin D. Cox, *Nomonhan: Japan Against Russia, 1939*, 2 vols. (Stanford: 1985).

———, *Tojo* (New York: 1975).

———, and Hilary Conroy, eds., *China and Japan: A Search for Balance Since World War I* (Santa Barbara: 1978).

Donald Creighton, *The Forked Road: Canada, 1939–1957* (Toronto: 1976).

Herbert Croly, *Willard Straight* (New York: 1924).

James B. Crowley, *Japan's Quest for Autonomy* (Princeton: 1966).

Robert Dallek, *Franklin D. Roosevelt and American Foreign Policy, 1932–1945* (New York: 1979).

Roger Daniels, *The Politics of Prejudice: The Anti-Japanese Movement in California and the Struggle for Japanese Exclusion* (Gloucester, Massachusetts: 1966).

Raymond H. Dawson, *The Decision to Aid Russia, 1941; Foreign Policy and Domestic Politics* (Chapel Hill: 1959).

Roberta A. Dayer, *Bankers and Diplomats in China, 1917–1925* (London: 1981).

———, "The British War Debts and the Anglo-Japanese Alliance, 1920–1923," *Pacific Historical Review*, 1976.

William Paul Deary, " 'Short of War': Events and Decisions Culminating in the United States Naval Escort of British and Allied Convoys in the Atlantic and in the Undeclared Naval War with Germany, 1939–1941," M.A. thesis, George Washington University, 1970.

Sander A. Diamond, *The Nazi Movement in the United States, 1924–1941* (Ithaca: 1974).

Bernard F. Dick, *The Star-Spangled Screen: The American World War II Film* (Lexington, Kentucky: 1985).

Roger Dingman, "Farewell to Friendship: The U.S.S. *Astoria*'s Visit to Japan, April, 1939," *Diplomatic History*, 1986.

———, *Power in the Pacific: The Origins of Naval Arms Limitation, 1914–1922* (Chicago: 1976).

Robert A. Divine, *The Illusion of Neutrality* (Chicago: 1962).

———, *The Reluctant Belligerent: American Entry into World War II* (New York: 1965).

———, *Roosevelt and World War II* (Baltimore: 1969).

Justus Doenecks, *When the Wicked Rise* (Lewisburg, Pennsylvania: 1984).

J. W. Dower, *War Without Mercy: Race and Power in the Pacific War* (New York: 1986).

Richard Dunlop, *Donovan: America's Master Spy* (Chicago: 1982).

John Erickson, *The Road to Stalingrad: Stalin's War with Germany* (London: 1974).

Raymond A. Esthus, *From Enmity to Friendship: U.S.-Australian Relations, 1931–1941*, (Seattle: 1964).

———, "President Roosevelt's Commitment to Intervene in a Pacific War," *Mississippi Valley Historical Review*, 1963.

John K. Fairbank, *China Perceived: Images and Policies in Chinese-American Relations* (New York: 1974).

———, *The United States and China*, 4th ed. (Cambridge, Massachusetts: 1983).

Jonathan Foster Fanton, "Robert A. Lovell: The War Years," Ph.D. diss. Yale University, 1978.

Ladislas Farago, *The Broken Seal; The Story of "Operation Magic" and the Pearl Harbor Disaster* (New York: 1967).

T. R. Fehrenbach, *F.D.R.'s Undeclared War, 1939–1941* (New York: 1967)).

Henry L. Feingold, *The Politics of Rescue: The Roosevelt Administration and the Holocaust, 1938–1941* (New Brunswick, New Jersey: 1970).

Herbert Feis, *The Road to Pearl Harbor: The Coming of War Between the United States and Japan* (Princeton: 1950).

Robert H. Ferrell, *American Diplomacy in the Great Depression* (New Haven: 1957).

———, "The Mukden Incident: September 18–19, 1931," *Journal of Modern History*, 1955.

Peter Fleming, *The Siege at Peking* (London: 1959).

Roger Franklin, *The Defender: The Story of General Dynamics* (New York: 1986).

Frank Freidel, *Franklin D. Roosevelt: The Apprenticeship* (Boston: 1952).

———, *Franklin D. Roosevelt: Launching the New Deal* (Boston: 1973).

Saul Friedländer, *Prelude to Downfall: Hitler and the United States, 1939–1941* (New York: 1967).

Donald J. Friedman, *The Road from Isolation: The Campaign of the American Committee for Non-Participation in Japanese Aggression, 1938–1941* (Cambridge, Massachusetts: 1968).

Theodore Friend, *Between Two Empires: The Ordeal of the Philippines, 1929–1946* (New Haven: 1966).

Fred Friendly, *Minnesota Rag* (New York: 1981).

Michael G. Fry, *Illusions of Security: North Atlantic Diplomacy, 1918–22* (Toronto: 1972).

Alton Frye, *Nazi Germany and the American Hemisphere, 1933–1941* (New Haven: 1967).

John Kenneth Galbraith, "Germany Was Badly Run," *Fortune*, 1945.

Essen M. Gale, "The Yangtze Patrol," *U.S. Naval Institute Proceedings*, 1955.

Józef Garlínski, *The Enigma War* (New York: 1979).

Lloyd C. Gardner, *Economic Aspects of New Deal Diplomacy* (Madison: 1964).

John A. Garraty, ed., *Quarrels That Have Shaped the Constitution* (New York: 1964).

Alexander Garth, *The Invisible China: The Overseas Chinese and the Politics of South East Asia* (New York: 1973).

Louis L. Gerson, *Woodrow Wilson and the Rebirth of Poland, 1914–1920* (New Haven: 1953).

Martin Gilbert, *Winston S. Churchill*, Vol. VI; *Finest Hour, 1939–1945* (London: 1953).

Betty Glad, *Key Pittman: The Tragedy of a Senate Insider* (New York: 1986).

Carl Glick and Hong Sheng-hwa, *Swords of Silence: Chinese Secret Societies—Past and Present* (New York: 1947).

Robert Justin Goldstein, *Political Repression in Modern America* (New York: 1978).

Robert Goldston, *The Road Between the Wars: 1918–1941* (New York: 1978).

Philip Goodhart, *Fifty Ships That Saved the World* (Garden City, New York: 1965).

Kent Roberts Greenfield, *American Strategy in World War II: A Reconsideration* (Baltimore: 1963).

Ross Gregory, *America, 1941: A Nation at the Crossroads* (New York: 1989).

Joseph C. Grew, *Turbulent Era: A Diplomatic Record of Forty Years, 1904–1945* (Boston: 1952).

Thomas E. Hachey, ed., *Confidential Dispatches: Analyses of America by the British Ambassador, 1939–1945* (Evanston: 1974).

Michael L. Hadley, *U-Boats Against Canada: German Submarines in Canadian Waters* (Montreal: 1985).

David Haglund, "George C. Marshall and the Question of Military Aid to England, May–June, 1940," *Journal of Contemporary History*, 1980.

———, *Latin America and the Transformation of U.S. Strategic Thought, 1936–1940* (Albuquerque: 1984).

Emily Han, *China to Me: A Partial Autobiography* (New York: 1945).

———, *The Soong Sisters* (Garden City, New York: 1942).

———, "Franklin D. Roosevelt and a Naval Quarantine of Japan," *Pacific Historical Review*, 1971.

Gerald K. Haines, "Under the Eagle's Wings: The Franklin Roosevelt Administration Forges an American Hemisphere," *Diplomatic History*, 1977.

John Maxwell Hamilton, *Edgar Snow: A Biography* (Bloomington, Indiana: 1988).

W. Averell Harriman and Elie Abel, *Special Envoy to Churchill and Stalin, 1941–1946* (New York: 1975).

Daniel F. Harrington, "A Careless Hope: American Air Power and Japan, 1941," *Pacific Historical Review*, 1979.

Ruth R. Harris, "The 'Magic' Leak of 1941 and Japanese-American Relations," *Pacific Historical Review*, 1981.

Richard A. Harrison, "A Neutralization Plan for the Pacific: Roosevelt and Anglo-American Cooperation, 1934–1937," *Pacific Historical Review*, 1988.

B. H. Liddell Hart, *History of the Second World War* (New York: 1970).

———, ed., *The Rommel Papers* (New York: 1953).

Thomas Havens, *Valley of Darkness: The Japanese People and World War Two* (New York: 1978).

Ron Heiferman, *Flying Tigers: Chennault in China* (New York: 1971).

Waldo Heinrichs, Jr., *American Ambassador: Joseph C. Grew and the Development of the United States Diplomatic Tradition* (New York: 1966).

———, *Threshold of War: Franklin D. Roosevelt & American Entry into World War II* (New York: 1988).

George C. Herring, Jr., Aid to Russia, 1941–1946; Strategy, Diplomacy, and the Origins of the Cold War (New York: 1973).

James H. Herzog, *Closing the Open Door: American-Japanese Diplomatic Negotiations, 1936–1941* (Annapolis: 1973).

———, "Influence of the United States Navy in the Embargo of Oil to Japan, 1940–1941," *Pacific Historical Review*, 1966.

Robert E. Herzstein, *Roosevelt and Hitler: Prelude to War* (New York: 1989).

Stanley E. Hilton, *Hitler's Secret War in South America, 1939–1945: German Military Espionage and Allied Counterespionage in Brazil* (Baton Rouge: 1981).

A. A. Hoehling, *The Week Before Pearl Harbor* (New York: 1963).

Peter C. Hoffer, "American Businessmen and the Japan Trade, 1931–1941: A Case Study of Attitude Formation," *Pacific Historical Review*, 1972.

Nancy Harvison Hooker, ed., *The Moffat Papers: Selections from the Diplomatic Journals of Jay Pierrepont Moffat, 1919–1943* (Cambridge, Massachusetts: 1956).

Cordell Hull, *The Memoirs of Cordell Hull*, 2 vols. (New York: 1948).

Julian G. Hurtsfield, *America and the French Nation, 1939–1945* (Chapel Hill: 1986).

Montgomery Hyde, *The Quiet Canadian: The Secret Service Story of Sir William Stephenson* (London: 1962).

Saburo Ienaga, *The Pacific War, 1931–1945* (New York: 1978).

Akira Iriye, *Across the Pacific: An Inner History of American-East Asian Relations* (New York: 1967).

———, *After Imperialism: The Search for a New Order in the Far East, 1921–1931* (Cambridge, Massachusetts: 1965).

———, *The Origins of the Second World War in Asia and the Pacific* (London: 1987).

———, *Pacific Estrangement, 1897–1911* (Cambridge, Massachusetts: 1972).

———, *Power and Culture: The Japanese-American War, 1941–1945* (Cambridge, Massachusetts: 1981).

David Irving, *Hitler's War* (London: 1977).

———, *The War Path: Hitler's Germany, 1933–1939* (New York: 1978).

Walter Issacson and Evan Thomas, *The Wise Men: Six Friends and the World They Made* (New York: 1986).

D. Clayton James, *The Years of MacArthur*, I, *1880–1941* (Boston: 1970).

Manfred Jonas, *Isolationism in America* (Ithaca: 1966).

Louis de Jong, *The German Fifth Column in the Second World War* (Chicago: 1973).

Matthew Josephson, *Empire of the Air: Juan Trippe and the Struggle for World Airways* (New York: 1944).

Thomas A. Julian, "Operation 'Frantic' and the Search for American-Soviet Military Collaboration, 1941–1944," Ph.D. diss., Syracuse University, 1968.

John Keegan, *Barbarossa: Invasion of Russia, 1941* (New York: 1970).

Ludovic Kennedy, *Pursuit: The Chase and Sinking of the Bismarck* (London: 1974).

Malcolm Kennedy, *A Short History of Japan* (New York: 1963).

Warren F. Kimball, ed., *Churchill and Roosevelt: The Complete Correspondence*, 3 vols. (Princeton: 1984).

———, "Lend-Lease: The Temptation of British Opulence, 1937–1942," *Political Science Quarterly*, 1971.

———, *The Most Unsordid Act* (Baltimore: 1969).

Betty Kirk, *Covering the Mexican Front: The Battle of Europe vs. America* (Norman: 1942).

William K. Klingaman, *1941* (New York: 1988).

Manny T. Koginos, *The Panay Incident: Prelude to War* (Lafayatte, Indiana: 1967).

Richard N. Kottman, *Reciprocity and the North Atlantic Triangle* (Ithaca: 1968).

William L. Langer and S. Everett Gleason, *The Challenge of Isolation, 1937–1940* (New York: 1952).

———, *The Undeclared War: 1940–1941* (New York: 1953).

Joseph P. Lash, *Roosevelt and Churchill, 1939–1941: The Partnership That Saved the West* (New York: 1976).

William D. Leahy, *I Was There* (New York: 1950).

Barry Leach, *German Strategy Against Russia, 1939–1941* (Oxford: 1973).

William M. Leary, Jr., *The Dragon's Wings: The China National Aviation Corporation and the Development of Commercial Aviation in China* (Athens, Georgia: 1976).

———, "Wings for China: The Jouett Mission, 1932–1935," *Pacific Historical Review*, 1969.

Bradford A. Lee, *Britain and the Sino-Japanese War, 1937–1939: A Study in the Dilemmas of British Decline* (Stanford: 1973).

Raymond E. Lee, *The London Journal of General Raymond E. Lee, 1940–1941* (Boston: 1971).

Michael Leigh, *Mobilizing Consent: Public Opinion and American Foreign Policy, 1937–1947* (Westport, Connecticut: 1976).

James R. Leutze, *Bargaining for Supremacy: Anglo-American Naval Collaboration, 1937–1941* (Chapel Hill: 1977).

———, *A Different Kind of Victory: A Biography of Admiral Thomas C. Hart* (Annapolis: 1981).

Issac Don Levine, *Mitchell: Pioneer of Air Power* (New York: 1972).

Ronald Lewin, *Ultra Goes to War* (New York: 1978).

Charles A. Lindbergh, *The Wartime Journals of Charles A. Lindbergh* (New York: 1975).

Richard R. Lingeman, *Don't You Know There's a War On? The American Home Front, 1941–1945* (New York: 1970).

Douglas Little, *Malevolent Neutrality* (Ithaca: 1985).

George H. Lobdell, Jr., "A Biography of Frank Knox," Ph.D. diss., University of Illinois, 1954.

Francis L. Loewenheim, Harold D. Langley, and Manfred Jonas, eds., *Roosevelt and Churchill: Their Secret Wartime Correspondence* (New York: 1975).

Walter Lord, *Day of Infamy* (New York: 1957).

———, *The Miracle of Dunkirk* (New York: 1982).

William Roger Louis, *British Strategy in the Far East, 1919–1939* (Oxford: 1971).

———, *Imperialism at Bay: The United States and the Decolonization of the British Empire, 1941–45* (London: 1977).

Peter Lowe, *Great Britain and the Origins of the Pacific War: A Study of British Policy in East Asia, 1937–1941* (London: 1977).

Mark M. Lowenthal, "Roosevelt and the Coming of the Second World War: The Search for United States Policy, 1937–42," *Journal of Contempory History*, 1981.

David J. Lu, *From the Marco Polo Bridge to Pearl Harbor; Japan's Entry into World War II* (Washington: 1961).

Robert James Maddox, *William E. Borah and American Foreign Policy* (Baton Rouge: 1969).

William Manchester, *American Caesar: Douglas MacArthur, 1880–1964* (Boston: 1978).

Arthur J. Marder, *Old Friends, New Enemies; The Royal Navy and the Imperial Japanese Navy: Strategic Illusions, 1936–1941* (Oxford: 1981)).

Frederick W. Marks, III, "The Origin of FDR's Promise to Support Britain Militarily in the Far East–A New Look," *Pacific Historical Review*, 1984.

———, *Wind over Sand: The Diplomacy of Franklin Roosevelt* (Athens, Georgia: 1988).

John W. Masland, "Missionary Influence upon American Far Eastern Policy," *Pacific Historical Review*, 1941.

Maurice Matloff and Edwin M. Snell, *Strategic Planning for Coalition Warfare, 1941–1942* (Washington: 1953).

Ernest R. May, ed., *Knowing One's Enemies: Intelligence Assessment Before the Two World Wars* (Princeton: 1984).

Kenneth G. McCarty, "Stanley K. Hornbeck and the Far East, 1931–1941," Ph.D. diss., Duke University, 1970.

Giles MacDonough, *A Good German: Adam von Trott zu Sol* (London: 1990).

W. David McIntyre, *The Rise and Fall of the Singapore Naval Base, 1919–1942* (London: 1979).

George McJimsey, *Harry Hopkins: Ally of the Poor and Defender of Democracy* (Cambridge, Massachusetts: 1987).

J. Lloyd Mecham, *A Survey of United States-Latin American Relations* (Boston: 1965).

W. N. Medlicott, *The Economic Blockade*, Vol. II (London: 1959).

Charles Messenger, *"Bomber" Harris and the Strategic Bombing Offensive, 1939–1945* (New York: 1984).

Philip Metcalfe, *1933*, (New York: 1988).

Milton E. Miles, *A Different Kind of War* (New York: 1967).

Marc Milner, *North Atlantic Rim: The Royal Canadian Navy and the Battle of the Convoys* (Annapolis: 1983).

Wolfgang J. Mommsen and Lothar Kettenacker, eds., *The Facist Challenge and the Policy of Appeasement* (London: 1983).

Ted Morgan, *FDR; A Biography* (New York: 1985).

Elting E. Morison, *Turmoil and Tradition: A Study in the Life and Times of Henry L. Stimson* (Boston: 1960).

Eric Morris, *Churchill's Private Armies: British Special Forces in Europe, 1939–1942* (London: 1986).

Louis Morton, "War Plan Orange: Evolution of a Strategy," *World Politics*, 1959.

William Fitch Morton, *Tanaka Giichi and Japan's China Policy* (Folkestone, Kent: 1980).

Leonard Mosley, *Hirohito; Emperor of Japan* (Englewood Cliffs, New Jersey: 1966).

———, *The Reich Marshal: A Biography of Hermann Goering* (New York: 1974).

John W. Mountcastle, "Trial by Fire: U.S. Incendiary Weapons, 1918–1945," Ph.D. diss., Duke University, 1979.

Rhoads Murphey, *Shanghai: Key to Modern China* (Cambridge, Massachusetts: 1953).

Robert Murphy, *Diplomat Among Warriors* (New York: 1964).

James Neidpath, *The Singapore Naval Base and the Defense of Britain's Eastern Empire, 1941* (Oxford: 1981).

William L. Neumann, *America Encounters Japan: From Perry to MacArthur* (Baltimore: 1963).

———, "Franklin D. Roosevelt and Japan, 1913–1933," *Pacific Historical Review*, 1953.

Harold Nicolson, *The War Years, 1939–1945*, Nigel Nicolson, ed. (New York: 1967).

Arnold A. Offner, "Appeasement Revisited: The United States, Great Britain, and Germany, 1933–1940," *Journal of American History*, 1977.

August E. Ogden, *The Dies Committee* (Washington: 1945).

Yoshutake Oka and Konoe Fumimaro, *A Political Biography* (Tokyo: 1983).

Shumpei Okamoto, *The Japanese Oligarchy and the Russo-Japanese War* (New York: 1970).

R. J. Overy, *The Air War, 1939–1945* (New York: 1981).

Thomas Parrish, *Roosevelt and Marshall; Partners in Politics and War: The Personal Story* (New York: 1989).

Robert Payne, *Chiang K'ai-shek* (New York: 1969).

Graham Peck, *Two Kinds of Time* (Boston: 1950).

Stephen E. Pelz, *Race to Pearl Harbor: The Failure of the Second London Naval Conference and the Onset of World War II* (Cambridge, Massachusetts: 1974).

Geoffrey Perrett, *Days of Sadness, Years of Triumph: The American People, 1939–1945* (Baltimore: 1973).

Hamilton Darby Perry, *The Panay Incident: Prelude to Pearl Harbor* (New York: 1969).

J. W. Pickersgill and D. W. Forster, *The Mackenzie King Record*, 3 vols. (Toronto: 1960–1970).

Forest C. Pogue, *George C. Marshall: Ordeal and Hope* (New York: 1966).

Edward P. Von Der Porten, *The German Navy in World War II* (New York: 1969).

John Deane Potter, *Yamamoto: The Man Who Menaced America* (New York: 1965).

Gordon W. Prange, *At Dawn We Slept: The Untold Story of Pearl Harbor* (New York: 1981).

———, *Target Tokyo: The Story of the Sorge Spy Ring* (New York: 1984).

Richard A. Preston, *The Defense of the Undefended Border* (Montreal: 1977).

Merlo J. Pusey, *Charles Evans Hughes*, 2 vols. (New York: 1951).

George H. Quester, *Deterrence Before Hiroshima* (New York: 1966).

John Bell Rae, *Climb to Greatness: The American Aircraft Industry, 1920–1960* (Cambridge, Massachusetts: 1968).

Armin Rappaport, *Henry L. Stimson and Japan* (Chicago: 1963).

Basil Rauch, *Roosevelt from Munich to Pearl Harbor: A Study in the Creation of a Foreign Policy* (New York: 1950).

Edwin O. Reischauer, *Japan: The Story of a Nation* (New York: 1970).

David Reynolds, *The Creation of the Anglo-American Alliance, 1937–1941* (London: 1981).

Benjamin P. Rhodes, "The British Royal Visit of 1939 and the 'Psychological Approach' to the United States," *Diplomatic History*, 1978.

Richard Rhodes, *The Making of the Atomic Bomb* (New York: 1986).

Amaury de Riencourt, *The American Empire* (New York: 1968).

Elliott Roosevelt, *As He Saw It* (New York: 1946).

John McCook Roots, *Chou: An Informal Biography* (New York: 1978).

Samuel I. Rosenmann, *Working with Roosevelt* (New York: 1952).

Leslie B. Rout, Jr., and John Bratzel, *The Shadow War: German Espionage and United States Counterespionage in Latin America During World War II* (Frederick: 1986).

Bruce M. Russett, *No Clear and Present Danger: A Skeptical View of the U.S. Entry into World War II* (New York: 1972).

"The Sack of Nanking," *Reader's Digest*, October, 1938.

F. M. Sallager, *The Road to Total War: Escalation in World War II* (Santa Monica: 1969).

Arthur M. Schlesinger, Jr., *The Coming of the New Deal* (Boston: 1958).

———, *The Politics of Upheaval* (Boston: 1960).

Paul W. Schroeder, *The Axis Alliance and Japanese-American Relations, 1941* (Ithaca: 1958).

Jordan A. Schwartz, *Liberal: Adolf A. Berle and the Vision of an American Era* (New York: 1987).

Munroe Scott, *McClure: The China Years* (Toronto: 1979).

Sterling Seagrave, *The Soong Dynasty* (New York: 1985).

James E. Sheridan, *Chinese Warlord: The Career of Feng Yu-hsiang* (Stanford: 1966).

Michael S. Sherry, *The Rise of American Air Power: The Creation of Armageddon* (New Haven: 1987).

Martin Sherwin, *A World Destroyed: The Atomic Bomb and the Grand Alliance* (New York: 1975).

Robert E. Sherwood, *Roosevelt and Hopkins: An Intimate History* (New York: 1948).

William L. Shirer, *Berlin Diary* (New York: 1941).

_____, *The Rise and Fall of the Third Reich* (New York: 1959).

Bernard Silberman and Harry Harootmian, eds., *Japan in Crisis* (Princeton: 1974).

Laurence H. Shoup and William Minter, *Imperial Brain Trust: The Council on Foreign Relations and United States Foreign Policy* (New York: 1977).

Robert Slater, *Guns Through Arcady: Burma and the Burma Road* (Sydney, Australia: 1943).

Geoffrey S. Smith, *To Save a Nation* (New York: 1973).

Janet Adam Smith, *John Buchan: A Biography* (London: 1975).

Edgar Snow, *The Battle for Asia* (New York: 1941).

_____, *Red Star Over China* (New York: 1944).

Ronald H. Spector, *Eagle Against the Sun* (New York: 1985).

_____, *United States Army in Vietnam* (Washington: 1983).

Jonathan Spence, *To Change China: Western Advisers in China, 1620–1960* (Boston: 1969).

A. M. Sperber, *Murrow: His Life and Times* (New York: 1986).

Nicholas John Spykman, *America's Strategy in World Politics: The United States and the Balance of Power* (New York: 1942).

Ronald Steel, *Pax Americana* (New York: 1970).

Richard W. Steele, "The Pulse of the People: Franklin D. Roosevelt and the Gauging of American Public Opinion," *Contemporary History,* 1976.

John J. Stepha, *Hawaii Under the Rising Sun: Japan's Plans for Conquest After Pearl Harbor* (Honolulu: 1984).

William Stevenson, *A Man Called Intrepid* (New York: 1976).

Edmund Stillman and William Pfaff, *The Politics of Hysteria: The Sources of Twentieth Century Conflict* (New York: 1964).

Henry L. Stimson and McGeorge Bundy, *On Active Service in Peace and War* (New York: 1947).

Richard Storry, *A History of Modern Japan* (Baltimore: 1960).

W. A. Swanberg, *Luce and His Empire* (New York: 1972).

Sandra C. Taylor, *Advocate of Understanding: Sidney Gulick and the Search for Peace with Japan* (Kent, Ohio: 1984).

_____, "Japan's Missionary to the Americans: Sidney L. Gulick and America's Interwar Relationship with the Japanese," *Diplomatic History,* 1980.

Telford Taylor, *Munich: The Price of Peace* (Garden City, New York: 1979).

Christopher Thorne, *Allies of a Kind: The United States, Britain, and the War Against Japan, 1941–1945* (New York: 1978).

Elliott Thorpe, *East Wind, Rain: The Intimate Account of an Intelligence Officer in the Pacific* (Boston: 1969).

H. J. Timperly, ed., *What War Means: The Japanese Terror in China; A Documentary Record* (London: 1938).

John Toland, *Adolf Hitler,* 2 vols. (Garden City, New York: 1976).

———, *The Rising Sun: The Decline and Fall of the Japanese Empire* (New York: 1970).

Kemp Tolley, *Cruise of the Lanikai: Incitement to War* (Annapolis: 1973).

Thomas F. Troy, *Donovan and the C.I.A.: History of the Establishment of the Central Intelligence Agency* (Washington: n.d.).

Barbara W. Tuchman, *Stilwell and the American Experience in China, 1911–1945* (New York: 1971).

Jonathan G. Utley, *Going to War with Japan, 1937–1941* (Knoxville: 1985).

———, "Upstairs, Downstairs at Foggy Bottom: Oil, Exports, and Japan, 1940–41," *Prologue*, 1976.

Martin Van Creveld, *Hitler's Strategy: The Balkan Clue, 1940–1941* (London: 1973).

Dan Van Der Vat, *The Atlantic Campaign: World War II's Great Struggle at Sea* (New York: 1988).

Paul A. Varg, *Missionaries, Chinese and Diplomats, 1890–1952* (Princeton: 1958).

John Chalmers Vinson, *The Parchment Peace: The United States and the Washington Conference, 1921–1922* (Athens, Georgia: 1955).

———, *Before the Trumpet: Young Franklin Roosevelt* (New York: 1985).

Geoffrey C. Ward, *A First Class Temperament: The Emergence of Franklin Roosevelt* (New York: 1989).

Donald Cameron Watt, *How War Came: The Immediate Origins of the Second World War, 1938–1939* (New York: 1989).

———, *Succeeding John Bull: America in Britain's Place, 1900–1975* (Cambridge, England: 1984).

Mark Seton Watson, *Chief of Staff: Pre-War Plans and Preparations* (Washington: 1950).

George Weller, *Bases Overseas: The American Trusteeship in Power* (New York: 1944).

Ralph E. Weber, *United States Diplomatic Codes and Ciphers* (Chicago: 1978).

Sumner Welles, *The Time for Decision* (New York: 1944).

Barton Whaley, *Codeword BARBAROSSA* (Cambridge, Massachusetts: 1973).

Burton K. Wheeler, *Yankee from the West* (New York: 1962).

Gerald E. Wheeler, "Isolated Japan: Anglo-American Diplomatic Cooperation, 1927–1936," *Pacific Historical Review*, 1967.

———, *Prelude to Pearl Harbor: The United States Navy and the Far East, 1921–1931* (Columbia, Missouri: 1963).

Keith Wheeler, *The Road to Victory*, 2 vols. (Hampton Roads, England: 1946).

John H. Wheeler-Bennett, *King George VI: His Life and Reign* (London: 1958).

Alan S. Wheelock, "False Dawn: The New York World's Fair and the Onset of World War II," unpublished paper, 1989.

Donald W. Shite, "World Power in American History," *Diplomatic History*, 1987.

Theodore H. White, *In Search of History: A Personal Adventure* (New York: 1978).

———, and Annalee Jacoby, *Thunder Out of China* (New York: 1946).

Thomas Wilds, "How Japan Fortified the Mandated Islands," *U.S. Naval Institute Proceedings*, 1955.

Peter Williams and David Wallace, *Unit 731: Japan's Secret Biological Warfare in World War II* (New York: 1989).

H. P. Willmott, *Empires in the Balance: Japanese and Allied Pacific Strategies to April, 1942* (Annapolis: 1982).

John E. Wiltz, *From Isolation to War* (New York: 1968).

———, *In Search of Peace* (Baton Rouge: 1963).

Allan M. Winkler, *The Politics of Propaganda: The Office of War Information, 1942–1945* (New Haven: 1978).

F. W. Winterbotham, *The Ultra Secret* (New York: 1974).

Dick Wilson, *When Tigers Fight: The Story of the Sino-Japanese War, 1937–1941* (New York: 1982).

———, *Zhou Enlai: A Biography* (New York: 1984).

Theodore A. Wilson, *The First Summit: Roosevelt and Churchill at Placentia Bay, 1941* (Boston: 1969).

Roberta Wohlstetter, *Pearl Harbor: Warning and Decision* (Stanford: 1962).

Robert K. Wolthuis, *United States Foreign Policy toward the Netherland Indies, 1937–1945* (Baltimore; 1968).

Tien-wei Wu, *The Sian Incident: A Pivotal Point in Modern Chinese History* (Ann Arbor: 1976).

Herbert O. Yardley, *The Chinese Black Chamber: An Adventure in Espionage* (Boston: 1983).

Arthur N. Young, *China and the Helping Hand* (Cambridge, Massachusetts: 1963).

ACKNOWLEDGMENTS

My many thanks for their patient, helpful, and critically constructive readings of the manuscript to Professors Paul Hooper, Alan Wheelock, Priscilla Roberts, James Roherty, and Irvine Anderson. Dr. Roherty was a bit shocked but, I think, convinced, and he certainly provided a useful overall challenge. Dr. Anderson sees middle-ranking bureaucrats as responsible for the finality of the 1941 oil embargo; I remain convinced that Roosevelt winked at their activities. But I also appreciate Dr. Anderson's challenge.

Three people pointed me toward critical materials. Richard Rhodes put me onto sources about Japan's pre-Pearl Harbor atomic bomb program. Sterling Seagrave, who went far out of his way to be helpful, was invaluable as a guide to the early China lobby activities. Kent Morrison, now a dean in Rhode Island, provided about one hundred pages of interesting photocopied documents.

A *Time For War* pertains to the hidden workings of America's government. In the course of my researches, nonetheless, I have been struck by the extraordinary openness of our system, or at least of our national archives, and by the dedication of archivists to conveying the truth. I am particularly appreciative of the help rendered by John Taylor of the National Archives, Susan Elter of the Franklin D. Roosevelt Library, and Marilyn Kann, until recently of the Hoover Institution in California. When, through some idiocy, I managed to lose a critical piece of evidence on America's impending air war upon Japan, Ms. Kann most graciously dug through the endless rows of boxes, arming me with a duplicate.

A former student, a Japanese who wishes to be unnamed, supplied a translation of General Tojo's postwar evaluation of what had led to Pearl Harbor. My editor, Paul Aron, has been nothing less than a writer's dream. My thanks to my late parents, Milton, for having instilled in me the love of our history, and Marian, for having instilled in me a love of our language; and to Ken and Polly Curfman for their longstanding support and faith. My wife, Judy, and my daughter, Polly, have been at the center of this, and all I have done.

INDEX